Women and
Experimental
Filmmaking

WOMEN AND EXPERIMENTAL FILMMAKING

Edited by
Jean Petrolle and
Virginia Wright Wexman

UNIVERSITY OF ILLINOIS PRESS
Urbana and Chicago

Library of Congress Cataloging-in-Publication Data
Women and experimental filmmaking / edited by
Jean Petrolle and Virginia Wright Wexman.
p.   cm.
Includes bibliographical references and index.
ISBN 0-252-03006-0 (cloth : alk. paper)
ISBN 0-252-07251-0 (pbk. : alk. paper)
1. Experimental films—History and criticism. 2. Women
motion picture producers and directors—Biography.
I. Petrolle, Jean. II. Wexman, Virginia Wright.
PN1995.9.E96W66   2005
791.43'3—dc22   2004029712

Contents

Acknowledgments

Our greatest debt, of course, is to the countless women around the world whose groundbreaking work continually challenges viewers and expands the boundaries of filmmaking. We are also indebted to Miriam Fuchs and Ellen Friedman, two literature scholars whose anthology *Breaking the Sequence: Women's Experimental Fiction* points out how frequently women's innovations in avant-garde form get overlooked and shows how much there is to be gained from highlighting women's contributions to experimental fiction. We hope that this volume does for film what their volume does for literature: reshape the history of the avant-garde to include women and direct interested persons to a wealth of neglected work that deserves further appreciation and research. We thank the contributors for their useful insights and careful work, as well as for their patience and collegiality. In addition, several skillful, energetic, and exacting people helped us round out the volume. Maggie Abreu, Shashona Chau, and Joanne Ruvoli Gruba compiled the filmography and distributor information that follows the essays, providing valuable resources for those who wish to engage in further viewing and/or research. Joanne assembled the bibliography and was particularly assiduous about tracking down distributor information. Eric Levy graciously provided assistance with library errands, untangling formatting snarls, and assorted other tasks. This project was made possible in part by a faculty development grant from Columbia College Chicago.

All of the following essays appear here for the first time, with three exceptions. Lucy Fischer's essay, "Passion, Politics, and Production in *The Tango Lesson*," was originally published as "'Dancing through the Minefield': Passion, Pedagogy, Politics, and Production in *The Tango Lesson*," in *Cinema Journal* 43:3 (2004): 42–58 (copyright © 2004 by the University of Texas Press; all rights reserved). An earlier version of Scott MacDonald's essay, "Avant-Gardens," appeared as a chapter in his book *The Garden in the Machine: A Field Guide to Independent Films about Place* (Berkeley: University of California Press, 2001), © 2001, The Regents of the University of California. A version of William Wees's essay, "Leslie Thornton, Su Friedrich, Abigail Child, and American Avant-Garde Film of the Eighties," was originally published as "Carrying On: Leslie Thornton, Su Friedrich, Abigail Child, and American Avant-Garde Film of the Eighties," in the *Canadian Journal of Film Studies* 10, no. 1 (2001): 70–95.

JEAN PETROLLE AND
VIRGINIA WRIGHT WEXMAN

Introduction:
Experimental Filmmaking
and Women's Subjectivity

The Los Angeles filmmaker Nina Menkes calls her cinema a form of sorcery, an aesthetic interaction with the world that rearranges perception and experience. Cinema is sorcery, Menkes contends, because it constructs and evokes reality while acting as a spell that tries to change reality. In Menkes's 1986 *Magdalena Viraga: Story of a Red Sea Crossing*, two women, one winged, sit together, contemplative, while the sound track chants variations of a "spell" borrowed from Gertrude Stein's *Ida:* "You can try you can just try never to be what he said never to be what he said never let me never let me never let me be what he said."

Like these characters, women who direct experimental films respond to a patriarchal context fraught with voices and images that describe the world from a masculinist perspective. Fred Camper's eschatological 1987 evaluation of the experimental film scene in his essay "The End of Avant-Garde Film" is accompanied by a nostalgia for the days of the New American Cinema when, in Camper's estimate, "giants"—who have since vanished from the avant-garde scene—walked the earth. Such dismissive pronouncements about the state of experimental film culture have frequently recurred in print and on the festival circuit despite the explosion in the 1980s and 1990s of new experimental work, much of it by women. Many critics tend to ignore or undervalue this work in part because women's experimental films frequently revise the very paradigms within which this cinema has traditionally been considered.

Women who create experimental cinema have not necessarily followed feminist agendas in their filmmaking practices; nor have many been comfortable with the idea of being categorized as feminist filmmakers. Yet these women have consistently inspired what has been termed "auteur desire" among ideologically oriented critics. Despite the poststructuralist turn away from the study of film authors, such critics have continued to examine the assumption of authorial agency by a historically marginalized group. This project is facilitated by the artisanal conventions of the experimental mode, which allow its women authors to place their own subjectivity at center stage in a manner not possible in mainstream productions, where commercial and collaborative considerations are omnipresent. One need not categorize female film artists as either originary geniuses or committed feminists in order to appreciate the cultural work they perform. They can be approached as social conduits with privileged access to oppositional discourses invisible to the mainstream. Alternately, they can be thought of as psychic scribes possessing a gendered consciousness that informs the nature of what they are capable of imagining. In the broadest sense, by the very act of making movies these women have positioned themselves as active agents, whatever political or aesthetic agenda they may represent. As such, they command the interest of feminist-minded critics. The present volume is one example of this desire for female authors.

In the realm of literature, Ellen G. Friedman and Miriam Fuchs have edited an anthology entitled *Breaking the Sequence: Women's Experimental Fiction*. Their stated aim in undertaking this project is "archaeological and compensatory," a necessary corrective and preventative for the astigmatisms of patriarchal histories" (xi). Friedman and Fuchs provide a theoretical rationale for the decision to generate "women's experimental fiction" as a category; this rationale, created for their anthology's history of experimental novelists, applies to the project at hand. In generating this category, one risks the appearance of separating gendered identity from its embeddedness with other variables like class, nationality, and sexuality. However, the benefits of the category, as Friedman and Fuchs argue, outweigh the dangers because of the visibility it confers on women who experiment with form. The two write, "Viewing these writers as a separate tradition is not isolationist; rather, it is a strategy in recovering them, in making them an object of discourse. Separation is a means of offering women writers visibility that they would not otherwise possess and enabling discussions that could not otherwise proceed" (41). Friedman and Fuchs go on to suggest that "the question of how the formal innovations characterizing experimental writing are pertinent to the whole women's tradition needs to be explored" (41). In constructing experimental films by women as a category, the present collection embraces both purposes: it heightens the visibility of women's contributions to traditions of formal innovation and explores how formal innovation enables women to enlarge discourses about women's subjectivity.

* * *

Most definitions of experimental filmmaking emphasize formal criteria to describe the kind of short works often shown at museums, universities, film festivals, filmmaker cooperatives, or specialty theaters. Such works typically feature nonlinear structures, nonnaturalistic performance styles, challenging subject matter, obtrusive camera work, and unconventional editing patterns. Though the literature frequently makes little or no distinction between the terms "experimental" and "avant-garde," avant-garde film may be thought of as a subcategory of experimental film, referring to short-format, usually nonnarrative films made and exhibited outside major channels of film production and distribution. "Experimental film" is a more spacious rubric. Women's experimental film practice often challenges masculinist avant-garde aesthetic dogmas by juxtaposing narrativity and non-narrativity, deploying narrative pleasure alongside narrative disruption, providing viewers with identification as well as critical distance, and so on. Adhering to such a definition allows this volume's sampling of women's formal innovation to encompass an array of non-mainstream film practices: the short-format films with formal preoccupations, traditionally termed "avant-garde," as well as feature-length, widely distributed works that use avant-garde strategies and hybrid forms that combine genres and mix filmic modes.

Lauren Rabinovitz's detailed discussion of the term "avant-garde" in *Points of Resistance: Women, Power, and Politics in the New York Avant-garde Cinema, 1943–71* cites additional limitations of the term. She reminds readers that "avant-garde" derives from military jargon and has been used by many artists, critics, and artistic movements since the mid-nineteenth century to celebrate artistic practices that anticipate dominant forms (14–15). Indeed, an avant-garde can be conceived *only* in terms of its relationship to other cultural products and practices; thus, what is considered avant-garde constantly shifts. Though the historicity implied in the concept of the avant-garde helps loosen the association between sheer formal novelty and experimentation, this same historicity makes the term "avant-garde" problematic because it casts history as a linear teleology that artworks anticipate: a succession of cultural orders rises and falls, heralded by prescient artist-heroes and masterworks. Since, as William Wees explains fully in chapter 1, one of the contributions of female filmmakers is the dismantling of a heroic narrative for the avant-garde, it seems appropriate to acknowledge the broader, more encompassing category—experimentalism—within which classical avant-garde film fits.

Some definitions of the classical avant-garde, often from Marxist and feminist perspectives, define the category according to its means of production, distribution, and exhibition, pointing out that avant-garde films are neither funded nor distributed through the entertainment industry. Such a generalization, however, overlooks the fact that a number of women, using avant-garde strategies in combination with other techniques, have gained access to industry-supported sources of funding and powerful distribution channels. Hybrid films like Jane Campion's *Sweetie*, Julie Dash's *Daughters of the Dust*, and Samira Makhmalbaf's *The Apple* have commanded large audiences and, relatively speaking, commercial success. More experimental than avant-garde, such films combine collage and linearity, aesthetic exploration and psychological drama, and/or documentary and fiction.

Responding to a cinema culture that in both classical Hollywood and avant-garde spheres has been dominated by male-authored depictions of women and male-centered accounts of cinema history, Laura Mulvey articulates a political purpose for formal experimentalism by women in her seminal essay, "Film, Feminism, and the Avant-Garde" (1978). Mulvey links form to content, identifying what she considers to be the fundamentals of a cinematic practice capable of re-presenting and recreating women's subjectivity:

> What recurs overall is a constant return to woman, not indeed as a visual image, but as a subject of inquiry, a content which cannot be considered within the aesthetic lines laid down by traditional cinematic practice. Pleasure and involvement are not the result of identification, narrative tension, or eroticised femininity, but arise from surprising and excessive use of the camera, unfamiliar framing of scenes and the human body, the demands made on the spectator to put together disparate elements. The story, the visual themes and the ideas are not in coherent conjunction with one another, and ask to be read in terms of developing relations between feminism and experimental film and psychoanalysis. ("Film, Feminism, and the Avant-Garde" 125)

The inextricability of form and content implied by Mulvey's vision of the purpose of experimental practice has sometimes been downplayed among avant-garde enthusiasts, but content must weigh heavily in any definition of experimental film. Thirty minutes of MTV may contain enough "surprising and excessive use of the camera" and "unfamiliar framing of scenes and the human body" to disorient even adventurous viewers. However, most MTV fare could hardly be described as revolutionary because it usually employs aesthetic novelty to reinforce culturally dominant thought-forms. Any definition of experimental film that understands it solely in terms of formal strategies misses this crucial distinction.

Experimental filmmaking by women undertakes to discover, among other things, formerly unknown principles at work in the lives and psyches of women. It further aims to explore these principles, test them, and improvise alternatives. One defining feature of an experimental film, therefore, is the spirit of discovery, inquiry, and innovation that animates such a project. Julie Dash's *Daughters of the Dust,* a feature-length, widely distributed production, employs illusionism, narrative, and linear plot to explore its themes; but it can be categorized as experimental because it draws on marginalized cultural traditions to examine the lives of several generations of women, and it combines heavily stylized language and acting with a visual style that both unsettles and delights.

Like their male colleagues, female directors may experiment with space, time, color, texture, structure, and other aesthetic or philosophical principles. They may pursue questions of epistemology, language, history, and all manner of phenomena that both implicate and transcend gender. In one sense, however, even the most formalistic experimental films by women can be viewed in political terms. Women engaged in such explorations make a feminist statement inasmuch as they occupy a different cultural space than that of their male counterparts. In the act of making movies, women remake cultural archetypes of their sex. Because they operate in the public realm, they strengthen the presence of a female subject who wields power in public space. By thus enlarging the public presence of women as cultural agents and re-presenting women's subjectivity, all experimental filmmaking by women can be seen as constituting a coherent cinematic tradition and a powerful sociopolitical force.

* * *

Despite the predominance of men in film-related professions, women filmmakers have from the earliest days of the medium shaped cinematic history. By some accounts, in 1896 Alice Guy-Blaché first used film as a storytelling medium instead of as a scientific curiosity or documentary tool. Lois Weber was among the first to employ cinema as agit-prop. The Russian director Esther Shub created the first compilation films and pioneered techniques later taken up by the cinema verité documentarians. The Italian moviemaker Elvira Notari's productions foreshadowed neorealism by experimenting with location photography and nonprofessional actors to chronicle the lives of the poor.

Women's contributions to the development of experimental film culture and technique have been especially noteworthy. As Jan-Christopher Horak's anthology, *Lovers of Cinema*, has shown, women were prominent in the amateur film movement in the United States during the 1920s and 1930s as directors, publicists, producers, editors, animators, and organizers. Mary Ellen Bute and Claire Parker, in particular, produced a number of extraordinary films over lengthy careers. Significantly, the amateur film movement inaugurated and celebrated the beginnings of a cinematic practice that posed an alternative to Hollywood's apparent monopoly on production and distribution. This concept of experimental film's role as the center of an alternative cinema culture persisted in the United States into the 1940s and 1950s and eventually became a defining feature of the New American Cinema of the 1960s. The amateur film movement valued the medium not only in terms of its potential for drama but also for its ability to render abstract form. In his book *Underground Film*, Parker Tyler singles out Bute as a significant progenitor of a formalist approach to cinema that first emerged in the twenties. "Mary Ellen Bute . . . was one of the purest [practitioners of the new cinema of abstraction]," Tyler writes, "a choreographer of light and color . . . obeying the patterns of classical music" (154).

Women outside of the United States pursued their own experiments. In 1923, a French journalist and political activist, Germaine Dulac, made one of the first feminist films, *The Smiling Madame Beudet* (*La souriante Madame Beudet*), connecting experimental formal strategies with explicit sociopolitical commentary in her depiction of the murderous fantasy life of a provincial matron. Dulac, a key figure in the surrealist and *cinéma pur* movements, also collaborated with Antonin Artaud in 1927 to make *The Seashell and the Clergyman* (*La coquille et le clergyman*), a monument of surrealist cinema. During the same period, the German experimental filmmaker Lotte Reiniger made a number of short animated productions as well as the first animated feature, *Prince Achmed*, ten years before Disney's 1937 *Snow White*. Reiniger's innovations in animation technique included the use of backlit paper cutouts to create silhouettes. She crafted extended abstract sequences with sliced wax and sand on glass. She also designed a camera that separated foreground from background, allowing an animator to exploit more fully the possibilities of multiple image planes.

Daringly original films like those of Dulac and Reiniger found their way to the United States and inspired a new generation of independent film-

makers in the 1940s. During this period Maya Deren became a vocal advocate and practitioner of a cinema that, in her words, would "relinquish the
narrative disciplines it has borrowed from literature and its timid imitation
of the causal logic of narrative plots" ("Cinematography" 72). Deren's film
Meshes of the Afternoon (1943), along with her theoretical writings, became
foundational texts in the emergent New York avant-garde of the forties and
fifties. In fact, several histories of the American avant-garde, including P. Adams Sitney's influential *Visionary Film,* begin with *Meshes.* Deren went on
to make numerous other films, all of which furthered her project of using
cinema to explore the psyche. She was fascinated with movement itself and
drew on her dance background to infuse her cinema with interdisciplinary
experiments with movement and space. Her productions emphasized formalism, abstraction, and the theme of subjectivity—attributes that became
central to the New American Cinema movement.

Like Deren's work, the films of another pioneering woman of the 1940s,
Marie Menken, dissolve disciplinary boundaries and veer toward abstraction.
Geography of the Body, a collaboration with Willard Maas (usually credited
to him alone), appeared in 1943, the same year as *Meshes of the Afternoon.*
Menken's solo effort, *Visual Variations on Noguchi,* came out two years later.
Geography of the Body anticipates the experimental cinema's attention to the
human form, a theme that later filmmakers like Stan Brakhage, Yoko Ono,
Andy Warhol, Carolee Schneemann, Storm de Hirsch, and Joyce Wieland
also explored. Menken is also credited with having invented the diary film,
which became a favored mode in New York avant-garde circles during the
sixties and seventies and was taken up by a subsequent generation of filmmakers. The diary film became so prevalent that Catherine Russell, writing
in 1999, devotes an entire chapter to the genre in *Experimental Ethnography:
The Work of Film in the Age of Video.*

Cinematic experimentation flourished in the 1960s, partly due to the avail-
ability of cheaper, more-portable equipment and film stock. Women during
this time helped create both audacious new work and enduring institutional
structures that enabled more female directors to make and exhibit experimental films. In 1962, Shirley Clarke cofounded the Film-Maker's Cooperative with Jonas Mekas. As an archive and distribution outlet for filmmakers,
scholars, and audiences operating outside the juggernaut of commercial
cinema, the Film-Maker's Cooperative remains an indispensable resource
to this day. In addition to her curatorial and administrative talents, Clarke
excelled as a filmmaker; she achieved recognition beyond the insular world
of the New York avant-garde by winning an Academy Award for her docu-

mentary *Robert Frost: A Lover's Quarrel with the World* (1963). Early in her career, she took up the tradition of multidisciplinary formal experimentation begun by Bute, Deren, and Menken, bringing a dancer-choreographer's sense of rhythm and juxtaposition to films like *Bridges-Go-Round* (1959) and *Skyscraper* (1959). As her career evolved, Clarke repeatedly ignited controversy with productions like *The Cool World* (1963) and *Portrait of Jason* (1967), which represented drug culture and street life with unprecedented frankness and unusual formal strategies. While she dissociated herself from any political movement, Clarke's films exemplify a growing tendency to connect formal experiment with sociopolitical commentary, a connection generally avoided by earlier experimental filmmakers and Clarke's male filmmaking colleagues.

Clarke helped launch another significant filmmaker, the Canadian Joyce Wieland. Wieland first raised critical controversy with sexually suggestive, abstract expressionist paintings. Later, she entered the New York avant-garde film community through the Film-Makers Showcases organized by Clarke and Mekas as an offshoot of the Film-Maker's Cooperative. The formalist film discourse that dominated the late 1960s caused critics of the day to underemphasize the sociopolitical dimensions of Wieland's early efforts, *Barbara's Blindness* (1965) and *Hand Tinting* (1967). However, her 1968 film *Rat Life and Diet in North America,* an animal parable about draft resisters, could not be so easily assimilated; it unambiguously departed from the New American Cinema's romantic formalism by adding an unmistakably political dimension to formal experimentation (see Rabinovitz, *Points of Resistance* 184–215).

Women filmmakers in postwar Europe also turned experimentalist strategies to political ends, often with a more rigorously theoretical edge than was typical of films produced in the United States. Women of the New German Cinema, which emerged in the politically charged environment of the 1960s, produced a rich tradition of formally innovative work. Ulrike Ottinger's stylized films, including *Ticket of No Return (Portrait of a Woman Drinker)* (1979), often combine fantasy with social critique, using exaggerated lighting and color as well as outlandish stories to explore women's relationships and female eroticism. Elfi Mikesch, whose career began in photography and cinematography, blends documentary and poetry in productions like *Life, Love and Celluloid* (1998), which portray the world from the perspectives of the least visible or vocal members of German society—a daydreaming teenager, two elderly women, women involved in fringe sexualities. The films of Helke Sander, whose speech at the 1968 Socialist Students' Association conference inaugurated the postwar German women's movement, focus on female self-image and women's roles. In France during the 1970s and 1980s, Marguerite Duras transmuted the aesthetic experimentalism of her novels into cinema with works such as *Nathalie Granger* (1973) and *India Song* (1975), which focus on female friendships and interior experience. And in England during the same period, filmmakers like Laura Mulvey and Sally Potter turned out rigorously theoretical feminist films such as *Riddles of the Sphinx* (1977) and *Thriller* (1979), respectively, using avant-garde techniques to explore and contest the gender politics of representation.

Meanwhile, in the United States, the New American Cinema movement's formalist orthodoxies had resulted in a largely male pantheon of cinematic innovators who denied any traffic between aesthetics and politics. Women changed this situation during the 1970s. Filmmakers like Michelle Citron, Laura Mulvey, and Yvonne Rainer, working in the complex context of the 1970s feminist film community, developed cinematic practices marked by theoretical sophistication and political engagement. B. Ruby Rich describes this evolutionary moment as one of productive tension. On one hand, women were successfully functioning in a largely male artistic arena; on the other hand, they were grappling with insights issuing from the women's movement. Rich writes,

> Women committed to the avant-garde were often unsympathetic to feminist concerns, having successfully acclimated to the individualism and elitism of the art world. Maintaining the *artiste* standard of strictly individualistic achievements, they are horrified by the prospect of collective movements and creations. . . . Many feminists, in turn, quickly copped an attitude of anti-avant-gardism based on notions of its experimental forms being intrinsically elitist, male-identified, and inaccessible to ordinary women, lacking in graduate school film education. (*Chick Flicks* 282)

As the seventies stretched into the eighties, however, women's cinematic practice demonstrated resoundingly that experimentalism, feminism, and other kinds of political engagements could successfully coexist, and a productive tradition of politically engaged experimental work emerged.

Yvonne Rainer's career as a director illustrates this trajectory. Feminist theorists of the seventies hailed Rainer works such as *Film about a Woman Who . . .* (1974) as exemplary feminist cinema; yet, ironically, Rainer herself rejected this categorization of her work and refused to align herself with feminist agendas. During the eighties and nineties, however, as understandings of experimentalism changed from a binary opposition between formal concern and political engagement to a both/and construction in which formal experimentation and politics work together, Rainer became increasingly comfortable with the situation of her work within feminist and other radical political discourses, especially that of queer theory. In the 1980s and 1990s other experimental directors, such as Barbara Hammer, Lizzie Borden, Rose Troche, and Cheryl Dunye, also began using formal radicalism to explore lesbian themes, extending the feminist agenda of the 1970s.

Prior to the eighties, the legacy of the civil rights movement had not yet resulted in significant numbers of women of color who were active in film production. As a result, cinematic experimentalism among women had largely been a white, middle-class project. More recently, though, inexpensive video formats have enabled increasingly diverse groups of women to gain access to filmmaking technology. The inclusion of video works in the present collection represents this growing dimension of women's filmmaking practice. Still, in Africa, South America, the Middle East, and other parts of the world where feminism lacks significant institutional support, access to production equipment and distribution mechanisms remains difficult. However, a few women from less industrialized parts of the globe have managed to produce work, sometimes by relocating to the United States or Europe, where they have invigorated film cultures with new political insights and unexpected formal innovations. In addition, filmmaking descendants of various diasporas continually expand the range of perspectives and richness of formal strategy available to experimental cinema, as they bring the aesthetic traditions and cultural histories of their ancestors to cinematic practice. The range of ethnicities, aesthetic traditions, and sociopolitical concerns represented by filmmakers like Frances Negrón-Muntaneer, Michelle Mohabeer, Ayoka Chenzira, Zeinabu Davis, Margaret Tait, Midi Onodera, Lizzie Borden, Ximena Cuevas, Shirin Neshat, and Julie Dash attests to the field's expanding richness and inclusiveness.

Besides helping to dissipate any perceived antagonism between the aesthetic and the political, women outside the United States have also helped to dissolve an artificial binary of narrative and nonnarrative cinema. The Belgian filmmaker Chantal Akerman's celebrated 1975 production *Jeanne Dielman, 23 Quai de Commerce, 1080 Bruxelles,* for example, tells a story about a murder, but Akerman is far more concerned with rendering the duration of everyday activities in its heroine's life: shopping for a button, making a meatloaf, doing the dishes. In a similarly eclectic spirit, the Cuban director Sara Gomez's *One Way or Another (De Cierta Maniera)* (1975) frequently interrupts its fictional narrative about the romance between Mario, a factory worker, and Yolanda, a schoolteacher, to accommodate nonnarrative elements such as Yolanda's direct addresses to the camera and documentary footage of housing construction for the poor in Havana. Such work invokes the allure of storytelling without sacrificing the dislocative strategies associated with experimental film.

In addition to reinventing narrative, women from around the world continue to reinvent documentary. The Iranian filmmaker Samira Makhmalbaf's first feature, *The Apple* (1998), a portrait of the reentry into public space of two preadolescent girls confined to home since birth, restages an actual series of events using as actors the people who lived the event before its filmic dramatization—a daring blend of traditional documentary observation and openly manipulated narrative craft. Similarly, in *Night Cries: A Rural Tragedy* (1989), Tracy Moffatt, an Australian Aboriginal filmmaker, blends Australia's history of forced adoption of mixed-race children with surrealistic dream imagery and generic pastiche to explore the effects of colonial rule on that country's native population. The Indian born filmmaker Pratibha Parmar also uses collage and other poetic elements in her documentary *Warrior Marks* (1993), which exposes and critiques the practice of female genital mutilation. Other women of diverse ethnic backgrounds, including Trinh T. Minh-ha, Lourdes Portillo, Helena Solberg, Angela Ricci Lucchi, Laura Kipnis, Laleen Jayamanne, Jill Godmilow, and Rea Tajiri, are similarly combining multiple modes of filmic and video discourses within documentary frameworks in order to examine wide-ranging sociopolitical issues from feminist perspectives.

Contemporary women in documentary filmmaking are also enlarging the capabilities of film and video technologies. For example, repetition, collage, surrealism, fragmentation, handheld camera, tight framing, first-person perspective, and digital effects make the humorous cine-poems of Ximena Cuevas into stunning visual adventures. Jeanne Finley's extreme close-ups, superimpositions, distorting lens, and hyperbrilliant lighting demonstrate that the filmmaker has as much interest in the possibilities of photography as in her thematic content. Elisabeth Subrin's *The Fancy,* an experimental biography of the photographer Francesca Woodman, has all the catalogic impulse and numerical fascinations of structural film, yet it expresses emotion and reverence through the use of slow pans that take in hundreds of objects and long takes that simulate still photography. Diane Nerwen's extensive sampling of found footage, combined with out-of-focus shots, quotations from classic films, and collagist structure allow her film *In the Blood* to concentrate as much attention on aesthetic issues as on contemporary Jewish attitudes toward Germany, its ostensible subject.

Today in the United States, distributors like Women Make Movies, Zeitgeist Films, Canyon Cinema, and the Video Data Bank have made experimental films by women more available than ever before. They are screened in an array of venues, including museums, college classrooms, and independent theaters. Some of these productions reject narrative entirely; others blend storytelling with fragmentation and collage. Some explore women's interiority and physicality; others treat politics, social interactions, and cultures; still others link the inner self and the body with the world in which women live.

* * *

This volume's closest cousins include Patricia Mellencamp's *Indiscretions: Avant-Garde Film, Video, and Feminism* (1990); Lauren Rabinovitz's *Points of Resistance: Women, Power, and Politics in the New York Avant-garde Cinema, 1943–71* (1991); Judith M. Redding and Victoria Brownworth's *Film Fatales: Independent Women Directors* (1997); B. Ruby Rich's *Chick Flicks: Theories and Memories of the Feminist Film Movement* (1998); and Alexandra Juhasz's *Women of Vision: Histories in Feminist Film and Video* (2001). Though all of these differ in format and focus from the present collection, they make excellent companions to the close readings offered here. Neither Mellencamp nor Redding and Brownworth discuss individual films in depth, Mellencamp because of her focus on theory and Redding and Brownworth because of their orientation toward a casual reader. Rich engagingly presents her readings of films within the context of a vivid memoir, colorfully evoking the flavor of feminist film culture in particular moments and places. Rabinovitz's *Points of Resistance* is admirably detailed in its discussion of films and their institutional contexts; it focuses exclusively on Maya Deren, Shirley Clarke, and Joyce Wieland. Juhasz's book of filmmaker interviews acknowledges a number of experimentalists also mentioned here. The present volume, which offers close readings of films, highlights a diverse group of filmmakers, draws from an array of methodologies, builds on these previous treatments of the topic, and contributes to an ongoing dialogue.

* * *

The films and filmmakers examined in the following chapters provide a snapshot or random cross-section rather than a comprehensive survey or detailed atlas. What motivates this collection is the consistency *across* a variety of genres, techniques, modes, and distribution channels—film, video, digital media, ethnography, animation, collage, narrative, feature, short, commercially distributed, privately exhibited—of the project of re-presenting women's subjectivity. The essays follow the thread of this feminist project across racial, economic, geographic, and temporal boundaries. The array of films and filmmakers discussed does not necessarily resemble those often found in courses about experimental cinema or women in film. Furthermore, the choices of films and filmmakers do not imply that the subjects of analysis constitute the best, the most influential, or the most important representatives of the tradition. Instead, we have assembled a portfolio of analyses that bring into sharper focus the array of thematic touchstones and formal approaches that have defined women's experimental filmmaking. The principles of selection operative in the following essays question the notion of canonicity itself. Rather than supplementing or remaking any canon, the pieces feature filmmakers whose practices exemplify a set of formal strategies and sociopolitical insights that any number of other films and filmmakers might exemplify equally well.

The following chapters encompass a wide array of methodological approaches and so reflect the diversity of research on women's experimental filmmaking. Nevertheless, taken together, they comprise a sustained analysis of the fruitful juncture of aesthetics and politics in both pioneer and contemporary experimental moviemaking by women. Each selection presents the films and filmmakers under consideration in terms of both formal strategies and sociopolitical relevance. The volume begins with an exploration of key issues and tensions of historiography and definition, then branches out into expositions of recurring thematic elements in women's filmic discourses. The eighth and ninth chapters extend the discussion of women's formal innovation in the experimental mode as it intersects with documentary and animation traditions. The final chapter offers summative echoes of thematic concerns touched upon throughout the volume and celebrates the spiritually affirmative and liberatory impulses in women's experimental practice. All of the essays provide glosses on works that some viewers find challenging or obscure. To further unify these diverse discussions, essays cross-reference one another where appropriate.

The essays by William Wees and Jerry White that begin the collection provide an essential foundation for the book by spotlighting institutional, definitional, and historiographic issues that animate both experimentalist practice and critical commentary about that practice. Their insights concerning gender and avant-garde tradition provide a backdrop against which analyses in subsequent essays can be viewed. Wees's essay, "No More Giants," discusses revised concepts of the creator-subject that have informed women's experimental moviemaking through the 1980s and 1990s and changed cultural understandings of film history. Women who made experimental films in the 1980s, Wees argues, reject the Romantic, Great-Man (or Great-Woman) theory of individual creation undergirding the New American Cinema movement and question the hierarchies and values embedded in such an understanding of the artist. By examining the work of Leslie Thornton, Su Friedrich, and Abigail Child, Wees identifies the hybrid forms these women invent and the paradigm shifts they mark, thereby providing a contemporary framework for considering how women's filmmaking remakes institutionalized ideas about film, filmmaking, and the nature of creativity.

The Romantic, Emersonian idea of the creator is not the only ideology of the New American Cinema to be unsettled by women's filmmaking. Feminist practice also questions the classical avant-garde's reification of particular aesthetic practices, as White's chapter, "Chantal Akerman's Revisionist Aesthetic," demonstrates. Akerman achieves her career-long focus on women's subjectivity through an array of aesthetic strategies. Her films alternate narrative with non-narrativity, blend genres, and maintain a productive tension between textual pleasure and critical distance. Examining a trio of films selected from early, middle, and later points of Akerman's oeuvre, White shows how the filmmaker juggles seemingly conflictual cinematic modes— the critical and the lyrical, romantic fantasy and arch deconstruction, high modernist formalism and subjective diary film—all to the purpose of dramatizing women's interiority. Using Akerman as an example, White argues that women's experimentalism transcends aesthetic dogmas associated with the avant-garde as it has been narrowly conceived.

In addition to subverting masculinist conventions in experimental film culture, women have played a role in redefining other avant-garde traditions, including the traditions of surrealism, allegory, autobiography, and modern dance. The essays by Maureen Turim, Jean Petrolle, Kathleen McHugh, Lucy Fischer, Patricia Levin, Gwendolyn Audrey Foster, and Amy Lawrence focus on examples of such interventions. Turim analyzes in her essay, "The Violence of Desire in Avant-Garde Films," how surrealist images by men have portrayed female bodies, violence, and desire. She goes on to show how the filmmakers Germaine Dulac, Abigail Child, Su Friedrich, and Yvonne Rainer, as well as the performance artist Marina Abramovic, respond to these depictions, which evoke the cultural role of victim frequently offered women. The artists Turim considers manipulate surrealist tradition by claiming the violence of creative, sexual energy as expressed in movement and montage to enunciate new cultural positions for women's bodies and desires, and for women's subjectivity.

In "Allegory, Politics, and the Avant-Garde," Petrolle discusses how Nina Menkes's film *The Bloody Child: An Interior of Violence* portrays women's subjectivity through surreal imagery and postmodern allegory. Allegory, Petrolle shows, enables the filmmaker to represent material that, because of its abstract and invisible qualities, resists representation. Allegorical gestures allow the film to render interior states of consciousness that precede, surround, and respond to physical acts of violence. Petrolle's discussion of Nina Menkes illuminates both the psychospiritual dimensions of violence and the operations of postmodern allegory.

McHugh examines women's appropriations of the traditions of autobiography in her essay, "History and Falsehood in Experimental Autobiographies." She argues that these filmmakers have re-engineered autobiography to extend the political reach of the avant-garde. These experimentalists, McHugh contends, drain the pathos from the personal, which has traditionally been designated women's place. Instead, they use their desires, situations, and histories to redirect self-expression from assertions about individual identity to questions about history, representation, and epistemology. All three artists blur any distinction between public and private, using their "selves" experimentally to connect interiority and emotion to political and social relations. Subsequent chapters by Fischer, Levin, Foster, Lawrence, and MacDonald address issues raised by women's cinematic autobiographies in related ways. Like McHugh, these scholars show how experimental films by women lift autobiography from its devalued status in masculinist epistemological paradigms and mine its potential for liberatory female subjectivity

Yet another motif emerges in essays by Turim, McHugh, Fischer, Levin, Foster, Lawrence, and MacDonald that focus on cinematic explorations of the body. Feminism has long grappled with paradoxical tensions in theoretical understandings of female physicality: To what extent can women's identities be defined in terms of their bodies? To what extent should identity be understood as malleable—a product of cultural milieu? Between biological determinism on one hand and social constructivism on the other, feminists run the risk of overloading or diminishing the body's importance. Rather than attempt to negotiate this impasse, the contributors gathered here address what Mary Ann Doane has referred to as "[the] complex relation between the body and psychic/signifying processes" ("Woman's Stake" [2000] 97). Not surprisingly, the body as source of pain or painful connectedness recurs frequently in women's experimental cinema, as Turim's, Levin's, and Lawrence's contributions emphasize. However, women's filmmaking traditions also portray the body as a source of freedom, presence, power, and pleasure. The contributions by Fischer, Foster, and MacDonald illustrate this more positive view.

As Lucy Fischer observes in "Passion, Politics, and Production in *The Tango Lesson*," women have also forged a tradition of interdisciplinary juncture between modern dance and film. The merger between dance and avant-garde moviemaking effected in the work of Maya Deren, Shirley Clarke, Yvonne Rainer, and Kathy Rose has heavily influenced uses of space and movement in experimental film. Patricia Levin's chapter on Rainer, "Yvonne Rainer's Avant-Garde Melodramas," complements Fischer's. Both chapters, echoing White's analysis of Akerman's more playfully exuberant strategies, explore uses of movement and melodrama in their respective subjects, showing how filmmakers have blended dance, romance, pleasure, and narrative with more typical avant-garde strategies.

A further expansion of the vocabulary of experimental cinema is effected in Gwendolyn Audrey Foster's chapter, "Experiments in Ethnography," and Amy Lawrence's chapter, "Two Sisters." These essays direct our attention to important subfields within women's experimental filmmaking: documentary, ethnography, and animation. Foster and Levin provide detailed discussions of filmmakers whose techniques and theoretical underpinnings exemplify these traditions of innovation by women.

Scott MacDonald's essay "Avant-Gardens" concludes the volume both because it brings together so many of the key motifs articulated in various earlier chapters—subjectivity, autobiography, daily life, body—and because it offers an appealing metaphor for understanding the cultural work that filmmaking women perform. Whereas the previous chapters, like much feminist discourse, generate a number of agonistic metaphors for the cultural work women perform through artistic production (such as resisting, subverting, opposing, contesting, appropriating, and protesting), MacDonald's essay offers an altogether peaceful, creative, and lyrical metaphor—the planting and tending of gardens. In experimental filmmaking by women, MacDonald suggests, the social and spatial commentaries developed through autobiography express the desire for a spiritual connection to something beyond the commercial, ephemeral, and topical. To illustrate this point, MacDonald has assembled a collection of women's cine-gardens: films in which women blend diary filmmaking and garden imagery to evoke visions of life-sustaining relationships with the earth, families, lovers, and the self. Discussing films by Marie Menken, Carolee Schneemann, Marjorie Keller, Anne Charlotte Robertson, and Rose Lowder, MacDonald traces a thematic tradition in which women's subjectivity becomes a lens revealing visionary possibilities for peaceful, nourishing relationships. These evocations of the garden, MacDonald suggests, constitute a strategy whereby women use film to enunciate conceptions of subjectivity informed by utopian hope. Through such cinematic visions, women not only revise and expand cultural possibilities for themselves, but provide leadership in what is perhaps the twenty-first century's most urgent quest: to reconcile ecological consciousness and spiritual need with industrial culture. Here again, the reconception of women's subjectivity that occurs as a result of their work in experimental film connects to larger sociopolitical projects, transforming not only the position of women but also the nature of the culture in which they exist.

1

Leslie Thornton,
Su Friedrich,
and Abigail Child

Although Leslie Thornton, Su Friedrich, and Abigail Child began making films in the 1970s, all three became major figures in the generation of American avant-garde filmmakers who came to prominence in the 1980s. Each has worked in video as well as film, and each integrates teaching into her professional life as a filmmaker. All three reside in New York.

Leslie Thornton is particularly important for her experiments in narrative forms and her recycling of archival footage. The result is a highly regarded but difficult-to-classify body of work that explores complex formal and subjective territories. She is best known for her seven-part epic serial, *Peggy and Fred in Hell* (1985–96), a singularly dark, meditative body of interrelated films and videos that contemplate issues of technology, ethics, and consciousness. It has been cited in "Year's Best" lists in the *Village Voice*, the *New York Times,* and *Cahiers du cinéma.* She began a second cycle of *Peggy and Fred* with *Chimp for Normal Short* (1999) and appears to have completed it with *Paradise Crushed* (2002). Included among the more than thirty other works she has produced to date are *Have a Nice Day Alone* (2001), *Another Worldy* (1999), *The Last Time I Saw Ron* (1994), *There Was an Unseen Cloud Moving* (1988), and *Adynata* (1983). She has received the Maya Deren Award and an Alpert Award in Media, as well as grants from the National Endowment for the Arts, the New York State Council on the Arts, the Jerome Foundation, Art Matters, and the New York Foundation for the Arts. She was included in the 1993 issue of *Cahiers du cinéma* devoted to "160 cinéastes d'aujourd'hui."

Among the institutions with her films in their collections are the New York Museum of Modern Art, the Centre Georges Pompidou, the Ecole Nationale Supérieure des Beaux-Arts (Paris), San Francisco State University, the University of California at Santa Cruz, the University of Michigan at Ann Arbor, and City University of New York. Since 1984 she has taught in the Department of Modern Culture and Media at Brown University.

Su Friedrich's work crosses several genre boundaries: documentary, autobiography, and experimental/avant-garde. Her works examine the forces that shape women's sense of themselves and their social/sexual relationships. She has produced and directed fifteen films and videos, including *The Head of a Pin* (2004), *The Odds of Recovery* (2002), *Hide and Seek* (1996), *Rules of the Road* (1993), *First Comes Love* (1991), *Sink or Swim* (1990), *Damned If You Don't* (1987), *The Ties That Bind* (1984), *Gently Down the Stream* (1981), and *Cool Hands, Warm Heart* (1979). Her films have won awards at the Athens International Film Festival, Outfest '97 in Los Angeles, the New York Gay and Lesbian Film Festival, the Melbourne Film Festival, the San Francisco Film Festival, and the Atlanta Film Festival. Retrospectives of her work have been presented at the Whitney Museum of American Art, the Rotterdam International Film Festival, the Stadtkino in Vienna, the Pacific Cinematheque in Vancouver, the National Film Theater in London, the New York Gay and Lesbian Film Festival, the Wellington Film Festival in New Zealand, and the Anthology Film Archives in New York. She has received, among other honors, a National Endowment for the Arts Fellowship, a Rockefeller Foundation Fellowship, a Guggenheim Foundation Fellowship, and multiple grants from the New York State Council on the Arts, the New York Foundation for the Arts, and the Jerome Foundation. Her work is in the collections of the Museum of Modern Art, the Art Institute of Chicago, the Royal Film Archive of Belgium, the Centre Georges Pompidou, the National Library of Australia, as well as many university libraries. She teaches at Princeton University.

Abigail Child is best known for her intricate, rhythmic editing of sound and image, which often derives from found footage. Formally rigorous, her work displays a wry, even dark, sense of humor combined with sharp-eyed critiques of cultural stereotypes and contemporary social mores. She also publishes poetry collections, among them *Scatter Matrix* (1996), *Mob* (1994), and *A Motive for Mayhem* (1989). Her recent film work includes *The Future Is Behind You* (2004); *The Milky Way*, a film-installation work (2003); *Where the Girls Are* (2002); *Dark Dark* (2001); and *Surface Noise* (2000). Her seven-part cycle *Is This What You Were Born For?* (1981–89) includes her most widely seen (and most controversial) film, *Mayhem* (1989), a mix of found and original footage that integrates the conventions of film noir with vignettes of goings-on in the East Village. Her films have won prizes at the Black Maria Film Festival, the Ann Arbor Film Festival, and the Images Festival in Toronto, and she has been awarded a number of prestigious fellowships and awards, including a John Simon Guggenheim Fellowship in Film, a Banff Centre for the Arts Residency Fellowship, and grants from the New York State Council on the Arts and Media, the New York Foundation for the Arts, the National Endowment for the Arts, and the Jerome Foundation. Major museums have acquired her films for their permanent collections: the New York Museum of Modern Art, the Centre Georges Pompidou, the Melbourne Museum (Australia), and the Art Institute of Chicago. She teaches at the School of the Museum of Fine Arts in Boston.

WILLIAM C. WEES

No More Giants

During the 1980s, North American experimental/avant-garde film underwent a paradigm shift that many supporters of the older generation of avant-garde filmmakers either failed to recognize or saw only as a falling off in quality, originality, and artistry. For example, in the *Village Voice* for June 16, 1987, J. Hoberman described the recent work of American avant-garde filmmakers as "increasingly sterile, derivative, and self-involved," and he later pronounced the avant-garde movement "moribund . . . the shadow of a shadow" (174). Similarly, Fred Camper announced "The End of Avant-Garde Film" in the spring 1987 issue of *Millennium Film Journal.* "The works of the newer generation," he complained, "for the most part lack the authentic power of the original, and often still-active, masters, and . . . the qualities that they do have instead often seem related to, but also only as diminished shadows of, the achievements of the original filmmakers" (109). And seemingly without irony, Camper headed the last section of his essay, "There were giants in the earth in those days.—Genesis 6:4" (122).

What Camper seemed unable to appreciate is that many of the avant-garde filmmakers who emerged in the eighties contested the whole notion of "giants." They rejected its Romantic, Emersonian, Great-Man Theory of individual creation as well as its perpetuation of a canon of great films and filmmakers, and they were well aware that, with the exception of Maya Deren, all the "giants" were men. Despite important work produced in the sixties and seventies by women avant-garde filmmakers like Marie Menken, Storm de Hirsch, Carolee Schneeman, Gunvor Nelson, Chick Strand, Joyce Wieland, and Barbara Hammer, there is a great deal of truth in Ruby

Rich's caustic comment on "the harshness of the avant-garde film world to-ward women and its condescension toward 'Maya,' as the boys liked to call her, now that she was gone and they safely held center stage for themselves" (*Chick Flicks* 50). Moreover, a potpourri of social, political, and cultural developments—from feminism and gay and lesbian politics to multiculturalism, poststructuralism, postmodernism, and a lifelong exposure to TV and a media-saturated "youth culture"—influenced younger filmmakers and channeled their interests and energies in new directions. It is hardly surprising, therefore, that they would introduce new subject matter and devise new, or revise earlier, formal strategies to suit the issues they wanted to explore.

What *is* surprising is that their accomplishments were not more readily recognized and appreciated by Hoberman, Camper, and others who had been committed to discovering, defending, and nurturing avant-garde film. Ironically, they *were* recognized in the form of fourteen programs of American avant-garde films from the eighties presented in Amsterdam and five other Dutch venues in the fall of 1990, and in a follow-up publication, *A Passage Illuminated: The American Avant-Garde Film, 1980–1990*, which included important discussions of the 1980s avant-garde by Paul Arthur, Tom Gunning, and Manohla Dargis.[1]

Another opportunity for recognition might have been offered by the International Experimental Film Congress that took place in Toronto in late May and early June 1989—the first event of its kind in more than ten years.[2] According to the congress organizers, Camper's essay and the debates it produced within the Toronto experimental film community were instrumental in bringing about the weeklong series of panels, talks, workshops, and numerous curated and open screenings. Although some filmmakers from the younger generation were represented in various programs, the overall planning of the congress seemed to favor the Camper/Hoberman view of the supposedly debilitated state of current avant-garde filmmaking. As one critic of the congress put it, "The desire to rescue, to celebrate and extend, the threatened virtue(s) of the old avant-garde peeped through the folds of nearly every program and every global decision informing the Congress" (Arthur, "No More Causes?" 23).

Two cases in point were screenings curated by Lauren Rabinovitz and Standish Lawder. Rabinovitz presented a program called "Women Film-makers and Past Avant-Gardes" (significantly, not *present* avant-gardes) in which there were no films made later than 1970, and Lawder's program of "Collage Films" included no film more recent than Bruce Conner's *Take the 5:10 to Dreamland* of 1977. The absence of recent work in Rabinovitz's and

Lawder's programs was particularly notable because two of the most important developments in North American avant-garde film during the eighties
were the increasing presence of important women filmmakers and the evolution of collage films into an incredibly rich and varied range of what had
come to be called, by the late eighties, found footage films.[3] Neither program
reflected these significant developments. To be fair, I should note that the
congress included a panel devoted to Abigail Child's 1987 film *Mayhem,* and
several curated programs were composed of films made during the eighties.
Nevertheless, taken as a whole, the congress seemed biased toward Camper's
and Hoberman's low opinion of new avant-garde work and reflected their
reverence for the achievements of past avant-gardes and their "giants."

Consequently, as preliminary information about the congress began to
circulate in the winter and spring of 1989, an anti-congress mood developed among younger American filmmakers, and shortly before the congress
opened, they issued an "Open Letter to the Experimental Film Congress."[4]
Declaring that "the time is long overdue to unwrite the Institutional Canon
of Masterworks of the Avant-Garde," they went on to complain that "the
overwhelming majority of [the congress's] announced participants consists
of representatives of the sixties Avant-Garde and its decaying power base."
The work to be featured at the congress, they said, was "chosen to minimize
linguistic, sexual, and cultural difference, typically to conform to the model
of the 'universal language of form' so dear to institutional esperantists." And,
they insisted, "The revolutionary frame of mind pervading activity in film in
the teens and twenties and again in the fifties and sixties—which seemed to
die in the seventies—continues to thrive, but only where it has shifted and
migrated according to changing historical conditions." The letter concluded,
"The Avant-Garde is dead; long live the avant-garde."

The uppercase "A" and "G" in "The Avant-Garde is dead" and lowercase
"a" and "g" in "long live the avant-garde" might be taken as a kind of typo-
graphic dismissal of the concept of avant-garde "giants," in favor of a more
democratic and egalitarian vision of an avant-garde that, in the language
of the open letter, "respect[s] the complexity of relations among the many
competing and overlapping histories which make up the activity within the
field." The letter was signed by seventy-six people, including the three filmmakers I will discuss here as representative of the new generation of American
avant-garde filmmakers: Leslie Thornton, Su Friedrich, and Abigail Child,
all of whom produced a substantial body of work during the eighties and
have continued working in both film and video up to the present.

Without downplaying their individual, unique accomplishments, I want to suggest three ways in which these filmmakers represent the paradigm shift I referred to at the outset of this essay—beginning, of course, with the fact that they are women, and their films offer points of view on issues like patriarchy, sexuality, and gender roles that are rare in the male-dominated "Institutional Canon of Masterworks of the Avant-Garde."

Secondly, their films engage in complex, dialectical relationships with the media and popular culture, which reflect postmodernist dissolutions of the traditional boundaries between high art and popular culture. This is particularly apparent in their use of found footage, though it should be noted that Friedrich makes less use of images and sounds appropriated from film and television than do Thornton and Child. In various ways all three find methods of, in Paul Arthur's words, "enmeshing the prerogatives of personal experience—memory, autobiography, direct observation of everyday life—with the constraints of a socially-shared past, recasting radical subjectivity as the interpenetration of public and private spaces" ("Lost and Found" 17).

Thirdly, they have reworked and made innovations in some of the principal forms and genres of traditional avant-garde film, notably, experimental narrative (in Thornton's *Peggy and Fred* cycle), autobiography (in Friedrich's *Sink or Swim*), and collage/montage (in Child's *Is This What You Were Born For?*). It would be a mistake, however, to reduce these works to a particular formal or generic category. Indeed, part of the strength of the films by Friedrich, Thornton, and Child (and a number of their contemporaries) is their resistance to categorization, especially of the kind P. Adams Sitney used in his extraordinarily influential *Visionary Film,* the third edition of which appeared in 2002. Moreover, their new or mixed or hybrid forms helped to subvert previous standards for measuring "giants" and opened the way for more flexible and heterodox measurements of value and relevance in avant-garde filmmaking.

Though different in many significant ways, *Peggy and Fred in Hell, Is This What You Were Born For?* and *Sink or Swim* have comparable overall structures. All three are large, open-form works that draw upon a variety of sources (original and "found") for their sounds and images, and all three are composed of distinct parts—separate films in *Peggy and Fred* and *Is This What You Were Born For?* and separate, clearly divided sections or chapters and a coda in *Sink or Swim.* Seen in their entirety, these works clearly reveal the unifying control of a single maker, but it is a unity incorporating diversity—diversity of sources, of cinematic styles, of voices, and modes of representation.

Su Friedrich could be speaking for all three filmmakers when she says, "To me the most fantastic part of constructing a film is taking many disparate elements and making some sense out of them, making them work together and inform each other" (MacDonald, *Critical Cinema 2* 305). Found footage, as I already noted, is one source of "disparate elements" for these filmmakers. Moreover, even their original footage (especially in *Sink or Swim* and *Peggy and Fred*) frequently has a removed, impersonal quality—"off-centered, disinterested," in the words of Catherine Russell—that makes it virtually indistinguishable from their found footage.[5] This tendency to play down the distinctiveness of their own footage can be seen as an implicit rejection of a high-modernist hierarchy of images, in which banal, work-a-day, mass media images are at the bottom and an artist's unique, personally expressive—yet, somehow, universally meaningful—images are at the top.

Friedrich's, Thornton's, and Child's films participate in, rather than rise above, media-saturated modern life, not passively nor in a shallow postmodernist spirit of pastiche or what Fredric Jameson calls "blank parody," but analytically, critically, and, sometimes appreciatively too. Abigail Child has put it this way:

> My generation of filmmakers, people born after World War II—we are TV kids. We were easily influenced by media and by how the media influence our world. . . . Now, what I think a lot of us are doing: we're using emotional images, images that mean something to us, powerful resonant images—not taking just anything, but being attentive to what images say and mean and how they can be read, actually approaching the flow of image-meaning, representation—and then rolling those representative images into structures that might share more formalist ideas. (qtd. in Wees 71)

The nature and consequences of these "formalist ideas" for all three filmmakers should become apparent as we take a closer look at *Peggy and Fred, Sink or Swim,* and *Is This What You Were Born For?* In these films we can find forms as subtle, complex, and meaningful as any employed by the earlier "giants" of avant-garde film.

Narrative as Free Fall

Leslie Thornton's film *Peggy and Fred in Hell: The Prologue* appeared in 1985; it was followed by *Peggy and Fred in Kansas* (video, 1987), *Peggy and Fred and Pete* (video, 1988), *[Dung Smoke Enters the Palace]* (film and video shown simultaneously, 1989), *Introduction to the So-Called Duck Factory* (video, 1993),

Whirling (film, 1996), and *The Problem So Far* (film and video shown simultaneously, 1996). The running time of what Thornton now calls *Peggy and Fred in Hell: The First Cycle* is eighty-seven minutes,[6] during which scenes with the children Peggy and Fred (Janis and Donald Reading) are juxtaposed with a wide variety of found footage, frequently accompanied by appropriated sound as well. Other than the fact that Peggy and Fred get somewhat older as the work progresses, there is little to suggest that a narrative is in progress. Indeed, as Catherine Russell observes, the children are "points of reference in an otherwise random, unordered series of images and events" (243). Nevertheless, narrative form preoccupied the filmmaker. "A fundamental objective of the *Peggy and Fred in Hell* project," Thornton has written, "is to challenge the limits of narrative form and push through to an uncharted, delicate space which we might call narrative, or we might not name" ("We Ground Things" 14). Whether we name it or not, that "uncharted, delicate space" requires examination if we are to appreciate the originality and richness of Thornton's work.

An interview with Thornton published in the Chicago-based magazine *Lightstruck* includes a drawing of a fat little girl falling head downwards through empty space. A friend, Thornton explains, made a series of drawings about "my relation to narrative." This particular one "he calls ... my 'theory of narrative' as a free fall. It's like that dream event," she continues, "that we all have, especially when we are children, of falling and falling. As you fall, you have an apprehension or understanding of everything in a way, but it moves very quickly past, while at the same time you do produce some understanding for yourself." Narrative as free fall implicitly repudiates what Thornton calls "2,400 years of beginnings, middles and ends," referring to Aristotle's *Poetics*, where, she says, "we find one of the earliest and most enduring formulations of narrative, a shape we still all privilege and practice." But she notes that in a university course on narrative, she gives the students "an exercise where they have to construct a narrative space around a kind of configuration that exists in Noh Drama—instead of Beginning, Middle, and End, they have to work with Introduction, Destruction, and Haste—they do it!" ("Leslie Thornton Interviewed" 9).

Her own search for alternative forms of "narrative space" is reflected in one of her descriptions of the *Peggy and Fred* cycle:

> Peggy and Fred are children. Every day they go out looking for a better place to live. In the evening they come home.
> They go out often.

> There are no other people in the world. Something has happened to them, but Peggy and Fred are unconcerned. Their problems are more immediate: how to make avocado dip, getting lost in their own house, receiving imaginary phone calls and death threats, deciding what things are for. They are adrift in the detritus of prior cultures, cast loose in a world of post-apocalyptic splendor.
>
> Peggy and Fred approach this flattened spectacle like one would any desert—they keep moving. ("We Ground Things" 13)

Despite the echoes of Samuel Beckett in this capsule scenario, the narrative space Thornton constructs for Peggy and Fred differs significantly from the wastelands and immobilized characters Beckett frequently used to chronicle the malaise of modernity and the twilight of modernism. Peggy and Fred "keep moving," in contrast to the resigned inertia typical of Beckett's characters ("VLADIMIR: Well? Shall we go? ESTRAGON: Yes, let's go. *They do not move.*" [61]), and unlike the spare, diminished worlds of Beckett's characters, Peggy and Fred's is chock-full of objects, images, sounds, and events that come from their own actions and immediate mise-en-scène and from Thornton's "found" images and sounds.

If "keep moving" describes the action of Thornton's protagonists, whose lives are governed by make-believe, improvisation, and bricolage (not unlike, in many ways, the film itself), it also applies to our reception of the work as we try to comprehend the content of, and relationships between, the episodes featuring Peggy and Fred and the appropriated images and sounds that occupy the rest of the narrative space. We too must keep moving, surrendering a fixed point of view to an openness to whatever comes next—as in a dream of falling when "you have an apprehension or understanding of everything in a way, but it moves very quickly past, while at the same time you do produce some understanding for yourself." Thornton's film not only forces us to give up the usual expectations about beginning-middle-end and causal links between narrative events, it also erases the line between the diegetic "fictional" world of Peggy and Fred and the nondiegetic "factual" world of the film's archival materials. For, although Peggy and Fred remain oblivious to it, the found footage is, as it were, part of their environment. An extension of their junk-cluttered rooms and the depopulated, anonymous exterior locations they occasionally explore, it represents "the detritus of prior cultures" and "a world of post-apocalyptic splendor" in which Peggy and Fred are "adrift" or, in more active terms, through which they (and we) "keep moving."

Peggy and Fred in Hell: Prologue introduces us to this interpenetration of diegetic and nondiegetic spaces composed, respectively, of "original" and "found" footage. Before Peggy or Fred makes an appearance, found footage from a film made by Bell Laboratories presents close-ups of vocal cords rhythmically vibrating in extreme slow motion. The disconcerting first impression produced by the image, as Thornton and others have noted, is of a vagina with pulsating and fluttering labia—a surreal metaphor that gives an erotic charge to a "scientific" penetration into the source of the human voice. It also alerts us to ambiguities and multiple meanings in many of the images to follow.

In this case, the original found footage was silent, and the sound track added by Thornton combines a segment of Handel's opera *Rinaldo* with the voice of Yma Sumac, once famous for its incredible range (supposedly seven octaves), and at one point there is near-perfect synchronization between Sumac's voice repeating "bom-ti-ti-bom" in a low register and the slow motion flapping of vocal cords. Shortly thereafter a very high note introduces the first shot of Peggy: a close-up of her head leaning into and drawing back out of the frame. But almost immediately the found footage returns with a step-printed shot of a man inserting a long thin light bulb into his open mouth, presumably to demonstrate how the vocal cords were lighted in order to be filmed.

An establishing shot of Peggy and Fred's room follows, beginning with a close-up of a light bulb and other debris on the floor, followed by a zoom back to reveal more debris and a partially obscured TV screen in the background. There is a cut back to the light bulb, then to another view of the room and the TV screen, which now contains images of a bullfight. At the same time, an appropriated sound track offers a discussion—with examples—of the "preferred pitch" for male and female voices. In both cases a lower pitch is "preferred." This unintentionally funny demonstration of cultural stereotypes shifts the Bell Lab's physiological representation of the voice toward sociological issues of gender construction. It also comments ironically on the aesthetics of Yma Sumac's performance of high ("female") and low ("male") pitches produced by the same set of vocal cords (though it would not be unreasonable to suspect that the two ends of her vocal range were extended artificially in the recording studio—a suspicion encouraged by Thornton's frequent modulation of "found" voices in subsequent sections of the *Peggy and Fred* cycle).

Peggy and Fred enter directly into this nexus of vocal cords, song, and voice as a site of culturally prescribed constructions and divisions of gender. When Fred appears for the first time he is energetically and unselfconsciously singing a mangled medley of songs ("took a luger and shot off her head. . . . bang-ba-bang-bang. . . . Oh Mr. Noah, oh Mr. Noah. . . . They all went down to Amsterdam, Amster, Amster, dam, dam, dam," etc.), all the while stuffing puffed cheese sticks into his mouth. In contrast to Fred's boisterous, self-confident performance, Peggy's is restrained, self-absorbed, and oddly affectless as she sings Michael Jackson's "Billy Jean." In addition to the incongruity of a young girl representing a boy singing about a girl who gave birth to his child, the scene is striking for its implicit summary of the issues of gender, socialization, self-fashioning, and self-expression introduced through the combination of the found and original material dealing with the human voice and the range of sounds it can produce.

While the voice plays an important role, formally and thematically, in the rest of the work, I use it here simply to illustrate the kinds of readings Thornton's open, free-fall narrative sets into play. As the work proceeds, found footage continues to introduce and expand upon references to cultural and historical forces that have shaped the (post)modern world, most notably: mass media, technology, and war. Meanwhile, the two children provide a reference point, a dual subjectivity, through which those cultural and historical forces are given an immediate, human context. While we can appreciate and identify with them because of the strong impression they make as unique individuals who are ingeniously coping with unpromising and unpredictable circumstances, they also serve as, in Thornton's words, "ciphers for everything else that is going on in the film. In a way they are the center of the work, but only in the sense that everything passes through them, or surrounds them, or contextualizes them. They are markers. Subjects" ("Leslie Thornton Interviewed" 9).

If voice provides a basis for one kind of contextualization, another is flight. "Hey, look at this picture!" Peggy calls out to Fred in *Introduction to the So-Called Duck Factory*. She has just noticed a huge photograph of the surface of the moon at one end of their crowded, debris-filled room. Earlier, in *[Dung Smoke Enters the Palace]*, similar NASA images of the moon are juxtaposed with old Edison films of a foundry and a turbine plant. The broken machinery and other debris of Peggy and Fred's world are like remnants of the machines of early twentieth-century, labor-intensive, heavy industry preserved in the Edison films, which are now obsolete due to the ascendancy of "clean," high-tech industries epitomized by the space program and represented in the NASA footage—though now even the NASA footage looks dated. It is already archival and, in that sense, on a par with the much older Edison films. In *Peggy and Fred in Kansas*, Fred evokes the space program when he puts a broken glass globe from a lamp on his head. It becomes his space helmet as he hunches down in a chair, goes through a contorted "count-down," and "blasts off," making rocket sounds as he steers his imaginary ship like a fighter pilot or racing car driver. Then, after a few intervening shots, he suddenly brings the whole game back to earth by grabbing an alarm clock and gasping, "Oh God, I'm going to be late for work! Oh no, I have to get the milk!"

A reminder of an earlier, heroic age of flight appears in *Peggy and Fred in Kansas* when Fred, pretending to be a talk show host, interviews Peggy, who is supposed to be Amelia Earhart. "All clap your hands for Amelia Earhart," Fred urges at the end and then adds, for no apparent reason, "And folks, don't, don't, don't forget Jack Nicholson," after which he launches into a frenzied dance while chanting, "Get down, baby. C'mon, ya gotta get down, baby!" It's not clear if either Fred or Peggy has any clear notion of who Amelia Earhart is, or was. It's enough that she is someone who might be interviewed and therefore is a celebrity, like Jack Nicholson. Four films later, at the beginning of *Whirling*, the real Amelia Earhart appears in a newsreel interview. Standing by her plane in her pilot's gear, the wind blowing her hair, she speaks loudly and clearly for the sake of the microphone. She compares flying over the Atlantic with flying over the Pacific and concludes with a smile, "Of course on both flights, I was very glad to see land." Black leader immediately follows, and "tail," written on the film, flashes past, an ironic reminder, perhaps, that Earhart's final flight did not achieve such satisfactory closure.

Narrative as free fall has no closure either. On the other hand, due to Thornton's careful balancing of serendipity and conscious artistic control, neither is it formless. As I have tried to indicate with a few examples of parallels, intersections, and cross-references that emerge as the cycle of films progresses, narrative as free fall makes connections—and makes sense—tangentially, at a distance, in passing. It integrates the past with an ongoing present and remains open to the future. At one point in *Introduction to the So-Called Duck Factory* Peggy asks Fred what he is eating.

> I dunno, just found it in the refrigerator.
> What refrigerator?
> Over there [he points off-screen].
> I don't see no refrigerator.
> You will.

Third-Person Autobiography

Su Friedrich's forty-eight-minute film *Sink or Swim* (1990) does not announce itself as autobiography, and in fact Friedrich has said, "Some people have told me that they weren't even aware it was autobiographical, which I like" (MacDonald, *Critical Cinema 2* 309). The film's most obvious deviation from the usual autobiographical mode is its third-person, voice-over narration spoken by a young girl who recounts, in chronological order, episodes in the life of an unnamed woman to whom she refers as "the girl," "she," and later, "the woman."[7] Friedrich explains,

> I was using stories from my own life and began by writing them in the first person, but I got tired of that very quickly. I sounded too self-indulgent. Writing them over in the third person was quite liberating. The distance I got from speaking of "a girl" and "her father" gave me more courage, allowed me to say things I wouldn't dare say in the first person, and I think it also lets viewers identify more with the material, because they don't have to be constantly thinking of me while listening to the stories. (MacDonald, *Critical Cinema 2* 308)

No doubt these are valid reasons for adopting the third person in order to tell the story of her deeply ambivalent relationship with her father, but Friedrich's decision has broader implications, which relate not only to the form of the work and how it is received, but also to the very notion of a unique, unified subject "I" and the possibility of representing it on film.

By switching from first to third person, Friedrich removed her work from the orbit of autobiographical films by American avant-garde "giants," such as Jerome Hill's *Film Portrait* (1970); Bruce Baillie's *Quick Billy* (1970); James Broughton's *Testament* (1974); Stan Brakhage's *Sincerity* and *Duplicity* series (1973–80 and 1978–80, respectively); and Jonas Mekas's *Walden* (1964–69), *Lost, Lost, Lost* (1949–75), and *He Stands in a Desert Counting the Seconds of His Life* (1969–85). Not only do these filmmakers represent themselves in their autobiographical work, but they draw upon an aesthetics of "personal expression" that equates the form and style of a work with a filmmaker's unique perceptions, feelings, and life experiences. Every aspect of their films is intended to express a first-person point of view. Friedrich's third-person point of view, on the other hand, distances the filmmaker from her film, allows viewers a greater range of readings ("they don't have to be constantly thinking of me while listening to the stories"), and encourages a view of the autobiographical "self" as a social subject and, in cinematic terms, as an *effect* of the film's form and content rather than its *cause.*

The film's narration puts the filmmaker's personal experience in third-person terms; but its most innovative formal device imposes strict, arbitrary constraints on "personal expression" and, at the same time, emphasizes the social basis of individual identity, or in poststructuralist terms, the construction of the individual as subject through language, as a *locus* of discourses. The form of the film is based on the minimal units of our symbol system for written language—the letters of the alphabet. It is composed of twenty-seven short sections (the letter "m" is accorded two sections) with their titles in reverse alphabetical order (from "Zygote" to "Athena/Atalanta/Aphrodite"), followed by a coda that wittily repeats the alphabet in the form of a children's song while ironically—timidly yet defiantly—introducing the first-person singular to end the film.

Although Friedrich has linked her use of the alphabet to "the fact of [her] father's being a linguist" (MacDonald, *Critical Cinema 2* 308), it has much broader ramifications, beginning, as I have suggested, by determining the number of parts the film could have and limiting the choice of words that could serve as titles for each part. This produces a strict and predictable pattern that has some affinities with avant-garde "structural films" of the late sixties and the seventies. Friedrich has acknowledged, "I feel somewhat akin to the structural filmmakers, since I do like to play with the frame, the surface, the rhythm, with layering and repetition and text, and all the other filmic elements that are precluded when one is trying to do something more purely narrative or documentary." But at the same time she characterizes the structural filmmakers as "avoiding the use of personal, revealing subject matter," and as being "more concerned with how film affects one's perception of time and space than with how it can present a narrative" (MacDonald, *Critical Cinema 2* 308).

Nor have structural filmmakers shown the kind of interest in exploring the formation of the social subject that one finds in *Sink or Swim.* Moreover, the alphabet in Friedrich's film is not only a formal structuring device and a means of alluding to the construction of self through the socially shared medium of language; it also alludes to one of the earliest experiences (along with learning to count) of formal, systematic learning. Memorizing the "A-B-Cs" is a significant step in "growing up." It marks the beginning of the transition from the immediacy of oral learning and verbal expression to a more indirect, regimented, and fixed form of communication: the printed word.

While this is a universal experience among literate people, it applies specifically to Friedrich's film, in which books and writing figure significantly in the girl's development and her relationship with her father. There are references to articles and books published by her father, a linguist and anthropologist, including two articles on kinship systems written during the year of her parents' divorce. Years later, the girl—now a woman—looks up the articles "in the hopes of learning something about [her father's] approach to family life. . . . For an hour she tried to read through the first one, but couldn't understand a word he'd written." But she eagerly reads his book on Aphrodite and Demeter, in which he speculates on the possibility of there being "an earlier goddess who embodied the qualities of both Aphrodite and Demeter, and argues for the need to reintegrate those two states of being. The book," the narrator adds, "is dedicated to his third wife."

The girl's own book learning is encouraged by her father, who gives her a book of stories drawn from Greek mythology for her seventh birthday. "She would sit in the closet and read the stories long after being sent to bed." One night she recounts the story of Atalanta to her father, but he falls asleep before she reaches the end (Atalanta's marriage to Hippomenes and their subsequent transformation into lions by Aphrodite). Her own writing includes entries in a diary that "she carefully hid under her bed." Nevertheless, she discovers that an entry on her parents' impending divorce has been erased: "Her mother was the only possible suspect." There is also a letter to her father written after she is a grown woman. Typed out on screen, it recalls her mother's unhappiness after the divorce and refers to a recording of Schubert's "Gretchen at the Spinning Wheel," which her mother would play over and over again (it is heard on the sound track of an earlier section of the film). The "tragic lyrics" and "ecstatic melody," as she calls them, perfectly express, she concludes, "the conflict between memory and the present." Then she adds a wistful postscript: "I wish that I could mail you this letter." In many different ways, then, written language and its various modes of presentation embody the ironies, ambiguities, thwarted communication, and occasional revelations that are central to the film's account of suffering and surviving the unequal, shifting balance of power in family relationships.

If the alphabet is the foundation for learning to read and write, it also offers a simple, familiar system for organizing information. Friedrich uses it to impose order and organization on the welter of conflicts, anxieties, traumas, desires, and discoveries in her life by alphabetizing them under headings like "Realism," "Quicksand," "Pedagogy," "Oblivion," "Nature," "Memory." However, the relationship between the title of each section and the accompanying images and narration is, more often than not, indirect, metaphoric, or symbolic; adding to the complexity and richness of these relationships are many cross-references between different sections. This is still another way Friedrich breaks down the usual first-person, one-to-one relationship between an autobiographical subject and the form and content of an autobiographical film. The "I" is dispersed among cultural references, recollected personal experiences, and the open, multilayered structure of the work itself.

One example has already been mentioned: Schubert's "Gretchen at the Spinning Wheel" played on the sound track of "Kinship," while the young woman's description of the song appears in a letter to her father typed out in "Ghosts." Kinship, meanwhile, is dealt with explicitly in "Discovery," where the father's articles on kinship systems are described as unreadable, and the imagery is an animated chart of the father's three marriages and the offspring they produced. In a sly critique of patriarchy and the nuclear family, Friedrich labels the chart "The American Kinship System ca. 1950–1989." In "Homework," the narrator's description of the girl coming home after school to watch TV is accompanied by vintage footage (without the original sound tracks) from the opening sequences of *Make Room for Daddy*, *The Donna Reed Show*, and *Father Knows Best*—all family shows with well-behaved, cleancut kids and handsome, smiling parents. The section concludes with a scene from *Father Knows Best* in which Robert Young consoles an unhappy little girl, who responds with a smile and big hug—a bittersweet contrast to the episodes of conflict and neglect the girl in Friedrich's film experiences with her own father.

Another idealized relationship of father and daughter is evoked in the film's opening section, "Zygote." While microscopic images from a science film show the union of ovum and sperm and the beginning of mitosis (thus equating the beginning of this autobiography with the biological beginning of "life" itself), the film's young narrator tells about how Athena "sprang from [Zeus's] head fully grown and dressed for battle. She became chief of the three virgin goddesses and was known as a fierce and ruthless warrior. Because she was his favorite child, Zeus entrusted her to carry his shield, which was awful to behold, and his weapon, the deadly thunderbolt." This juxtaposition of ordinary human procreation (announced in the section's title and illustrated by the found footage) with the miraculous, asexual creation of Athena (a story that not only eliminates the mother but glorifies the father and fulfills a daughter's desire to monopolize the father's attention and love—to be his "favorite") introduces the film's main theme: the conflict between the girl's unrealistic expectations and the realities of actual family relationships, exacerbated by divorce and the father's departure.

The opening section also introduces a subtheme concerned with issues of sexuality and gender, beginning with its characterization of Athena as a virgin and a "fierce and ruthless warrior." The girl's diary, described in "Journalism," includes entries about "fighting with boys," and in "Pedagogy" we are told, "The girl loved to play games and also loved to win. It gave her a special thrill whenever she beat a boy in a game or a wrestling match." (However, when the girl beats her father in a game of chess, "the victory tasted sweet until she realized that the price had been the loss of her favorite partner. From that day on, he never played her again.") In "Temptation," the girl tells her father the story of Atalanta, "a great athlete and hunter" who "vowed never to marry, and would race any man who hoped to win her hand." She always won until, with the help of Aphrodite, Hippomenes tricks her into losing the race. The visual accompaniment to the story is footage of oiled, muscular bodies of female bodybuilders: contemporary Atalantas, perhaps, but also "temptations" for women desiring other women—a reading that is supported by the inclusion, in "Kinship," of murky images of naked women in a sauna and shower room, including one of two women embracing in the shower. In "Competition," the section describing the father's book on Aphrodite and Demeter, there are erotic drawings of Asian women making love—intercut with similar drawings of heterosexual couples and paintings of the Madonna and Child. And in the young girl's imaginary world described in "Virgin," "her tree house was a harem filled with beautiful women wrapped in silk and covered with jewels."

The film's accumulated images and allusions leave little doubt about the girl/woman's sexual orientation, but unlike some of Friedrich's other films, such as *Gently Down the Stream* (1981), *Damned If You Don't* (1987), and *Hide and Seek* (1996), *Sink or Swim* does not present lesbian desire as a major theme. It is implied to be an important factor in the daughter's sense of herself and her social relationships, and it provides a means of escape from the nuclear family and its patriarchal power structure, but it is secondary to the film's exploration of the ambivalent and sometime abusive father-daughter relationship—and the daughter's ability to survive it.

Survival is implied by the film's title. Rather than sink under the weight of that relationship, the daughter learns to swim, to become independent and self-reliant. The title is given literal meaning when the father teaches her to swim. He takes her to a swimming pool, we are told in "Realism," and after explaining "the principles of kicking and breathing," he tosses her in. "She panicked and thrashed around for awhile, but finally managed to keep her head above water. From that day on, she was a devoted swimmer." The swimming motif recurs several times, most poignantly in the story of the father's sister, who drowned when they were still children, but its full metaphorical significance only emerges in "Athena/Atalanta/Aphrodite." At the lake where she had spent her summers as a girl, the daughter decides to swim all the way to the opposite shore as her father had often done, but at the halfway point she begins to debate with herself: "[H]e loves me in spite of this . . . he loves me not . . . I have to do this . . . I'll never make it . . . I'm halfway there . . . I want to rest." If she drowns, she wonders, will her father realize she was swimming across the lake "for his sake"? Then she remembers how long and fruitlessly her mother tried to hold on to her father, and after resting, she turns around and swims back to shore. Her decision *not* to prove herself by her father's standards breaks his hold on her sense of her own self-worth.

Although this makes a suitable conclusion for an autobiography, the film continues with a coda that not only reopens the question the previous section seemed to have answered, but gives the final word to the filmmaker—in the first person. In home-movie footage, a long-legged girl in a bathing suit (Friedrich at approximately age twelve) smiles and waves at the camera. The image is superimposed on itself and then superimposed again and again, until there are six layers of images, at which point the superimpositions gradually disappear, and the film ends with the original single image of the smiling, waving girl. At the same time, a mature woman's voice (Friedrich's) sings the traditional children's "Alphabet Song," which is rerecorded and superimposed to create a canon or round that duplicates in sound the increasing and decreasing layers of images, until the final, single image is accompanied by the single voice singing, for one last time, the final lines of the song: "Now I've said my A-B-Cs / Tell me what you think of me." It is a brilliant recapitulation of the alphabetical organization of the film (while reestablishing the conventional A-to-Z order of the alphabet).

At the same time, it alludes to the multiple selves that make up a single individual, and given what we have learned about the girl's life, it prompts a skeptical reading of this typical home-movie image of happy childhood. Moreover, it challenges the basic premise of all autobiographical films by implicitly asking, can any image truly represent who someone is or what she feels? Isn't anyone, including the filmmaker, always a third-person character in film? The sound track complicates the issue further. At one level it suggests a reversion to a child's desire for parental approval: "What do you think of me?" But at another level, where first and third person meet, the question comes directly from the filmmaker and is addressed to us, the film's viewers. Now that she has recited her A-B-Cs in the form of a thematically complex and formally intricate film, what do *we* think of *her?* Closing with that question perfectly suits the film's problematic relationship of autobiographical subject, third-person narrative, and indeterminate audience reception.

"Think Is Cut"

Abigail Child's *Is This What Your Were Born For?* includes seven short films running for a total of seventy minutes.[8] The title comes from one of Goya's etchings in his famous series *The Disasters of War,* "Para eso habeis nacido," which is commonly translated as "Is This What You Were Born For?"; it has also been translated more literally as "For This Were You Born." In the etching, several corpses lie together on the ground, a man stands over them vomiting, and a dark cloud of smoke looms in the background. Nothing this grim appears in Child's films, but by appropriating Goya's title, Child prompts us to recognize that some of the outrage and the sardonic view of the human condition graphically expressed (in both senses of the term) in Goya's work also inform her cooler, hipper critique of contemporary mores.

Unlike *Peggy and Fred in Hell,* the cycle's films are not arranged in strictly chronological order, and unlike *Sink or Swim* and *Peggy and Fred in Hell,* there are no central characters or overall narrative devices (however loosely construed) to hold the work together as a whole. In fact, Child has called *Is This What Your Were Born For?* a work of "detachable parts, each of which can be viewed by itself for its own qualities. The films don't form a single line, or even an expanding line," she says, "but rather map a series of concerns in relation to mind, to how one processes material, how it gets investigated, how it gets cut apart, how something else (inevitably) comes up" (*Retrospective* n.p.). While this critical and creative practice has significant ties to dadaist and surrealist collage, as Maureen Turim shows in her contribution to this volume, the resulting films are thoroughly, even aggressively, contemporary in form as well as thematic concerns.

Prefaces (1981), composed principally of found footage from many different sources and edited at a very fast tempo, or what Child has called "bebop rhythms," introduces the series. "It becomes," Child says, "a kind of preconscious of the films to follow, whose scope and image banks are more narrowly defined" (*Retrospective* n.p.). *Mutiny* (1983) presents a kind of collective portrait of modern, urban women with a variety of footage (most of it original rather than found) cut to a fast tempo that gives the film as a whole the intense energy depicted in some of the individual shots (e.g., an acrobatic dancer, two women stomping on a trampoline, a woman rapidly bowing a violin with a toothbrush). With some nice comic touches, the film playfully, exuberantly, celebrates women's diversity, individuality, independence, and inventiveness. *Both* (1988), a short, silent, black-and-white study of two nude women, temporarily slows the pace and reduces the intensity of the previous films' montage.

But the intensity and staccato pacing return in *Perils* (1986), where Child uses actors to stage scenes and adopt poses reminiscent of silent-film melodramas and cliff-hangers (the title recalls *The Perils of Pauline*). Black-andwhite film stock, jump cuts, and occasional undercranking (to make movements appear unnaturally quick and jerky) add further references to old, silent films, but the film retains, at a somewhat slower pace, the editing rhythms of *Prefaces* and *Mutiny*. The tempo picks up in *Covert Action* (1984), and in place of the overwrought gestures and melodramatic situations staged for the camera in *Perils,* Child works with real-life situations also staged for the camera, but in this case it is the home-movie camera. With her quick and compelling editing rhythms and sharp eye for revealing details, Child deconstructs home-movie footage of couples on holiday (two men with, it appears, different women on each occasion). By breaking apart and reconstructing shots of the couples kissing, horsing around, or just posing for the camera, Child cracks the veneer of the original home movies' holiday "good times" and exposes the barely repressed aggressiveness and self-satisfaction of the men in their relationship with the women and the women's compliance with the men's expectations. Although there are occasional hints of resistance on the women's part, the only empowering moments for the women appear to be when they are enjoying each other's company, including a frolic in a field with two women playing leap frog. But even then, they are aware of the camera, which, no doubt, is in the hands of one of the men.

Mayhem (1987) is the longest (at twenty minutes) and most ambitious film in the series, and it pursues, more elaborately and aggressively, the gender issues raised in *Covert Action* and *Perils*. While shades of melodrama persist (particularly in scenes of two men dressed like Parisian *apaches* stalking a fearful woman), *Mayhem*'s more specific cinematic reference is to film noir, in part through found footage, but principally through Child's cinematography (threatening shadows, dark corners, ominous spaces) and staging of noirish moments of shock, fear, and (imagined or implied) violence against women. But rather than concocting a pastiche of Hollywood conventions, Child deconstructs them through imitation and by depriving them of narrative continuity and Hollywood's high production values.

At the same time, Hollywood's adherence to heterosexual standards of sexuality and gender roles undergoes a radical revision. The film, as Liz Kotz has put it, "embraces sexuality and the relationality of sexual identities" and offers "a multiplicity of gazes and forms of desire" ("Complicity" 115). In images that are more documentary than film noir, men and women pose provocatively, touch, kiss, engage in mild forms of S&M, and join in tableaux of hetero-bi-homo sex play (reminiscent, at times, of the somnolent orgy in Jack Smith's *Flaming Creatures* [1963]). Child intercuts these images with her own film noir and melodramatic images, as well as passages of found footage, and she brings the film to a conclusion with old, faded pornographic footage of two women enjoying sex together (briefly joined by a man). Accompanied by lively Latin music, a looped shot of one woman mounting the other from behind (echoing the leap-frogging women of *Covert Action*) brings the film to a sprightly, comic conclusion. Throughout, Child combines intricate visual montage with an equally intricate collage of sound effects, fragments of dialogue, musical phrases, and moments of pregnant silence. While maintaining the formal ingenuity of the earlier films, Child raises the level of critique and provocation as she weaves together images of anxiety, fear, and threatened violence (with men the aggressors and women the victims) and images of desire, pleasure, and gratification (participated in equally by men and women).

Mercy (1989) completes the cycle by returning to the style of the first film of the series, *Prefaces*. With a witty, paratactic montage of original and found footage drawn from a wide diversity of sources, Child develops a cluster of associations among images of science, technology, heavy machinery, metallic surfaces, muscular males, and the military ("How does it feel to see your son become a man?" intones a male voice in a recruitment ad, as a young man in uniform runs across a parade ground to embrace his mother). Some images suggest that women too are caught in these forces of domination, control, and regimentation: switchboard operators at work; drum majorettes in short-skirted uniforms marching in tight formation; a woman inside a huge MRI apparatus that is turning her like meat on a spit; a woman rolling the length of a shiny board-room table—and off the end; a woman gyrating on the sidewalk in front of a pile of dirt while the jaws of a backhoe hover nearby.

The film ends, however, with an alternative to the domination of machinery, rigidity, and social control. In a time-lapse shot, a dark rhizome sends out many tiny white rootlets, each slightly different in shape, size, and rhythm of its movement, but together they form an organic pattern of growth spreading in all directions (and offer a striking contrast to the final image of *Covert Action* in which a tree chained to the back of a tractor is violently pulled out of the ground). On the sound track a male voice barks, "Nein!" A soft female voice responds, "Yes, yes." Another "nein" follows, but it is said more quickly and with less assurance and is answered by a strong female voice swooping down two or three octaves singing, "Ahhh-ooooooah," ending in a series of nonsense syllables—or pure sound poetry. The screen goes dark, and in the darkness there is a soft rapid tapping and a final distinct "tap." Thus the film—and the series—concludes with rhizomic growth and a female affirmation countering male negation—a suitable metaphor for the way Child's films send out many suggestions rather than asserting a single position. Their montage sequences generate meanings through clusters of associations that are always growing in complexity rather than following a straight, strictly logical argument to a foreordained conclusion.

A brief passage in *Mercy* offers one among many examples of the formal and thematic complexity of the sound-image collage or "vertical montage" that is characteristic of Child's films. It begins with a man in his undershirt breathing through a tube attached to some sort of measuring device. A male voice announces, "It's colorless, it's odorless," and continues, "and if you could drink it, it would be tasteless!" over a brief shot of a dark shadow advancing along a railroad track (accompanied by a rattling sound and strong bow strokes on a cello), an equally brief and ambiguous image of water or steam streaming behind rocks or a metal structure, and a longer shot of a man's bare arm bending at the elbow and flexing its muscles synchronized with the sound of a creaking door or floorboard. A cacophonous mix of sounds dominated by a pulsing rhythm on the cello coincides with the arm unbending, followed by a dissolve to a schematic drawing of an arm's muscles and tendons. The sound continues over a very brief shot of two large disks or wheels turning on what may be a ship's deck, followed by an even briefer shot of a mechanical hammer striking red-hot metal. A strong, firm note from the cello is synchronized with a cut from the fiery blow of the hammer to an aerial view of a line of simultaneous explosions along the edge of a quarry. In addition to the man-machine, arm-hammer associations, Child's editing creates an action-reaction effect: the impact of the hammer "detonates" the explosions; its downward thrust "produces" an upward burst of dust and debris and at the same time releases the mounting tension generated by the tempo of the montage and by energetic movements within the shots. Taken together the shots and accompanying sounds of this brief sequence produce an image embodying one of the film's major themes: the domination of nature and human beings by science and technology.[9]

Child's ingenuity in reworking sounds and images is the most distinctive quality of her work. Her editing is, in and of itself, an investigation of "how one processes [audio-visual] material," as Child put it in the statement quoted earlier. Like the great theorist (and practitioner) of montage, Sergei Eisenstein, she brings social-psychological and ideological considerations to bear on her practice of montage, as well as exploiting its potential for creating thematic coherence among extremely diverse images and sounds, while binding them together in rigorously structured graphic and rhythmic relationships. A virtuoso of montage, Child combines a formalist's skill at creating unexpected and illuminating juxtapositions with a deconstructionist's determination to prevent a purely aesthetic appreciation or easy, unthinking consumption of media-generated images and sounds—including her own: "My goal," says an intertitle in *Covert Action*, "is to disarm my movie."

The same might be said of Friedrich's and Thornton's films. But to "disarm" a movie is not to discard aesthetic considerations or deprive audiences of the pleasure offered by skillfully made, formally complex works of art. Rather, it means finding ways of assuring that the art of the work furthers, rather than forestalls, insights into *how,* as well as *what,* the work communicates. Perhaps Leslie Thornton says it best: "I think if it's important right now in this world to have a critical perspective as a cultural producer, it's just as important to pursue forms of address that we call aesthetics. You can't just cut one off and say it's, you know, questionable, bourgeois, corrupt, or whatever. It all goes together, and the work that's going to last is art. Art's going to be there" (Wees 99). While earlier avant-garde "giants" would fully concur with the last part of Thornton's statement, it is the coupling of aesthetic concerns with "a critical perspective as a cultural producer" that makes the films of Thornton, Friedrich, and Child exemplars of the best avant-garde work of the eighties—and after.

NOTES

1. See Arthur, "Lost and Found," and in the same volume, Tom Gunning, "New Horizons: Journeys, Documents, Myths and Counter Myths," 35–49, and Manohla Dargis, "Beyond Brakhage: Avant-Garde Film and Feminism," 55–69. See also Tom Gunning, "Towards a Minor Cinema: Fonoroff, Herwitz, Ahwesh, Lapore, Klahr and Solomon," *Mo-*

tion Picture 3.1–2 (1989–90): 2–5; Steve Anker, "Testament to an Orphaned Art," *Blimp* 20 (1992): 26–31; and Mellencamp, "An Empirical Avant-Garde."

2. A more extensive discussion of the Toronto Congress, accompanied by relevant documents, appears in William C. Wees, "'Let's Set the Record Straight': The International Experimental Film Congress, Toronto 1989," *Canadian Journal of Film Studies/Revue canadienne d'études cinématographiques* 9.1 (2000): 101–16.

3. These two developments are highlighted in Scott MacDonald's "Experimental Cinema in the 1980s," in *A New Pot of Gold: Hollywood under the Electronic Rainbow*, ed. Stephen Price (New York: Scribners, 2000), 390–444, which is volume 10 of *The History of American Cinema*. MacDonald calls the eighties "a remarkable decade for women filmmakers" and notes, "If a new sensually aware, cinematically refined feminism was the most discussed ideological trend of the 1980s, what has come to be called *recycled cinema* (*found footage film* remains a popular term for it) was the most visible formal tendency of the decade" (408). P. Adams Sitney makes the same points about feminism and found footage films at the beginning of the chapter entitled "The End of the 20th Century," in his *Visionary Film: The American Avant-Garde, 1943–2000*, 3rd ed., rev. (Oxford: Oxford University Press, 2002), 410.

4. The open letter was distributed in Toronto just days before the congress began and published in the *Independent Film and Video Monthly* 12.8 (1989): 24, and in the newsletter of the Chicago Experimental Film Coalition, *Workprint* 6.3 (1989): 17.

5. Russell is referring specifically to the conflation of original and found footage in *Peggy and Fred in Hell:* "Thornton's combination of archival imagery with original footage tends to blur the edges between the two orders of representation, mainly because she has shot the scenes with the children in an off-centered, disinterested way, evoking the sense that is often created by found footage, of a lack of purpose" (244).

6. The first installment of *Peggy and Fred in Hell: The Second Cycle*, entitled *Chimp for Normal Short*, appeared in 1999. Other films in the second cycle are *Bedtime* (2000–2002), *Have a Nice Day Alone* (2001), *The Splendor* (2001), and *Paradise Crushed* (2002).

7. The complete text of the film appears in MacDonald, *Screen Writings*, 241–56.

8. Abigail Child's remark "Think is cut" is quoted in Monica Raymond, "The Pastoral in Abigail Child's *Convert Action* and *Mayhem*," *Cinematograph* 3 (1988): 61. At one state of its evolution, Child's series included another short, silent, black-and-white film of a beating heart, which was called *Both 1,* and the current *Both* was called *Both 2.* Moreover, Child writes that in recent screenings of *Is This What You Were Born For?* "I have been showing the work in other orders and in combination with other of my films" (letter to the author, August 30, 1999).

9. The description of this sequence, somewhat modified here, previously appeared in Wees, 17–18.

2

Chantal Akerman

Chantal Akerman, born in Brussels and now based in Paris, has been making films since 1968. She made several short films in the late 1960s and early 1970s before finishing her first feature-length film, *Hotel Monterey,* in 1972. Her next feature film, *Je tu il elle* (1974), is a brooding, minimalist, visually drab meditation on late-adolescent sexuality. Akerman emerged into wide international attention in 1974 with her epic yet minimalist work *Jeanne Dielman, 23 Quai de Commerce, 1080 Bruxelles,* which depicts the daily routine of a Belgian widow trying to raise a son and working as a prostitute on the side. In overwhelming detail, the more than three-hour film evokes the maddening, mind-numbing routine of Dielman's daily life. The film made Akerman an important force in a nascent feminist avant-garde cinema. Akerman made her next film, *News from Home* (1976), while she was living in New York. Pairing images of New York with a voiceover reading letters from Akerman's mother in Belgium, the film features the hallmarks of the 1970s New York avant-garde—elements of structuralist filmmaking, city symphony films, and competing, rather than complementary, image and sound.

During the eighties and nineties, Akerman became an important force in European cinema as it redefined narrative form. She began exploring longing and exile, evident in the melancholy *Les rendez-vous d'Anna* (1978); repetition and lyricism, most evident in *Toute une nuit* (1982); self-reflexivity, as in *Les années 80* (1983) and the Akerman film it deconstructs, *Golden Eighties* (1985); and wandering, voluptuous narrative, as appears in *Nuit et jour* (1991) and *A Couch in New York* (1996). Akerman has also undertaken documentary, producing a trilogy of travel films: *D'est* (1993), about post-

Communist Eastern Europe; *Sud* (1999), about racism in Texas; and *De l'autre côté* (2002), about migrant Mexican workers on the Arizona-Mexico border.

The Venice Film Festival gave Akerman a retrospective in 1975, when the director was twenty-five years old; her work has been widely exhibited and celebrated since. In 1995, she staged a multimedia installation version of *D'est* at the Walker Art Center in Minneapolis; the installation then traveled to San Francisco, Paris, Brussels, Valencia, and Wolfsburg, Germany. In 1997–98, Akerman served as visiting professor at Harvard, and she held a similar appointment in 2004 at the European Graduate School in Saas-Fee, Switzerland. J. Hoberman has written that Akerman "is arguably the most important European filmmaker of her generation" (148).

JERRY WHITE

Chantal Akerman's Revisionist Aesthetic

Divisions of period and aesthetic style tend to reveal more about the critic making the distinctions than about the work itself. The films of Chantal Akerman provide a delicious example of the pitfalls of critical simplification. Three of her films, *News from Home* (1976), *Les années 80* (1983), and *A Couch in New York* (1996), provide a fascinating case study in the ways that Akerman works with similarly radical aesthetic and political assumptions even though the films themselves look completely different on the surface. Indeed, part of the reason these three films work so well as case studies is because they could easily embody three distinct stages of Akerman's work: avant-garde/structuralist, counter-cinema/deconstructionist, and conventional art film.[1] This easy division breaks down, however, when one considers the way that each film centralizes a subjective voice, makes it clear in each frame that this subjectivity is female, and maintains an uneasy—and very Barthesian—tension between textual pleasure and critical distance. What has made Chantal Akerman such an important part of world cinema has been her ability to raise, across a wide variety of forms, common questions that touch the core of both cinematic aesthetics and feminist political practice. The flexibility she has exhibited over the years should confirm her status not as a progressively more compromised filmmaker, but as an artist committed enough to ask questions in different idioms, instead of piously relying on one (supposedly) politically or aesthetically purified form, as so many members of both the political and romantic avant-gardes have.

This essay shows how Akerman's work exposes the inadequacies in traditional understandings of "the avant-garde." While P. Adams Sitney's book

Visionary Film is, at least in the United States, the most widely read and cited text on the avant-garde, a goodly number of positions on the movement, often in explicit opposition to Sitney's, have sprung up since his tome was first published in 1974. These counter-histories, although they adjusted the official version of film history, never really moved beyond binaries. Though some post-Sitney essays speak to Akerman's condition, they miss some of the more subtle (and arguably the most important) aspects of her films—aesthetic eccentricities that draw on a wide number of traditions, refusing any kind of either/or assessment. William Wees writes about this problem in his essay in this volume; for several decades now, it has been very difficult for the community of critics interested in avant-garde cinema to move beyond foundational canons and aesthetic expectations. Wees focuses on the Americans Leslie Thornton, Abigail Child, and Su Friedrich, but the historiographic problems posed by their political, non-Romantic but still formally experimental work are relevant to Akerman's cinema as well.

The tendency to carve avant-garde film into two parts has been visible in most revisionist criticism of the movement, and while the revisionist impulse is a laudable one given the relative exclusiveness of Sitney's influential scholarship, it has not really addressed the challenging and ambiguous aesthetic embodied by Akerman. Peter Wollen's essay "The Two Avant-Gardes" is among the earliest and most well known of these salvos, and the article's sense of binaries leaves no room for Akerman and her combination of emotion and distance. He opens his article by describing the sides, writing that "[t]he first can be identified loosely with the [British] Co-op movement. The second would include filmmakers such as Godard, Straub-Huillet, Hanoun, Jansco. . . . There are other filmmakers too who do not fit neatly into either camp, and films which fall somewhere in between or simply somewhere else . . . but in general the distinction holds" (92). Akerman, in this schema, would seem to fall closer to the second avant-garde, a classification toward which the deconstructive *Les années 80* would especially seem to point. However, her work is far more based in traditional notions of narrative pleasure, even in her most formally rigorous moments, than the other members of this camp. Patricia Mellencamp, like Wollen, constructs a binary when she writes of the change in avant-garde filmmaking between the 1960s (which she dubs "the romantic avant-garde") and the 1980s and 90s (which she dubs "the empirical avant-garde"). Assessing the same difficulty Wees writes about, Mellencamp writes, "Logics of purity and origin excluded these [more contemporary] artists, or were used violently against them" ("Empirical Avant-Garde" 175). Mellencamp also observes that "[w]hile the empirical avant-gardists speak to history, it is with the wary skepticism of those whose stories have been eradicated or forgotten" ("Empirical Avant-Garde" 175). Mellencamp's is a more historically informed version of experimental filmmaking than Wollen's, and she speaks with the same wary skepticism of empiricists; but her formulation still cannot account for the logic of purity, combined with sociopolitical savvy, that defines Akerman's aesthetic (even in *A Couch in New York* and, in different ways, in *News from Home* and *Les années 80*). Akerman's films, as these three examples show clearly, are as political and accessible as contemporary avant-garde work by filmmakers like Tracey Moffat or Laleen Jayamanne, whom Mellencamp discusses; they are also as formally rigorous as any of the work from the New American Cinema or the European Counter-Cinema tradition.

Ivone Margulies has done more than probably any film scholar to complicate Akerman's place in the avant-garde by challenging the simplification that Akerman is either explicitly "feminist" or "modernist." Indeed, Margulies's *Nothing Happens: Chantal Akerman's Hyperrealist Everyday* helps complicate the term "experimental film," and I share Margulies's conviction that no one set of formal criteria can adequately define what is "experimental" and what is not. Margulies elaborates this point of view in relation to Akerman when she writes, "First, no formal strategy can be essentially feminist, anti-illusionist or political. Second, the retreat from those classifications doesn't necessarily help us understand Akerman's formal and political integrity. . . . given the hyperbolic quality of Akerman's referentiality, her work doesn't need to be defended from being co-opted by realism. On the contrary, the alienating force of the work's hyperrealism is enough to place it alongside other progressive currents of realist cinema" (7). I proceed from these assumptions as well: it is inadequate to say simply that Akerman's formal choices are inherently political, *and* it is crucial to recognize that Akerman's oeuvre bears a remarkable political (feminist) and aesthetic (realist) coherence, even though her work exhibits a wide variety of specific political and formal interests.

Paul Willemen also carves up the world of experimental film in a binary formulation Margulies opposes. However, because his distinction between "avant-garde" and "modernism" is couched in such broad terms, it is useful in understanding Akerman's overall project. Differentiating between the two terms, Willemen writes,

> The very concept of an avant-garde, of a vanguard, implies a set of historical relations. Introduced as a phrase borrowed from military terminology by

the French utopian socialists, the term implies such questions as: the vanguard of what, going where and to what purpose? In contrast, the notion of modernism reduces artistic practice to a set of formal characteristics, a set of procedures frozen into a specific generic practice and suggesting that modernism is a period style, as was impressionism or expressionism, or any other historically circumscribed style. (143)

Given this terminological framework, it is clear that Akerman's films, especially the three under discussion here, are part of a tradition of avant-gardism, as opposed to modernism. To say they follow no common formal procedures or generic practice is an understatement. Instead, Akerman's practice occupies the "front-guard" position that Willemen's schema underscores: it is a vanguard of European cinema, always searching for ways to stretch and revise generic assumptions, including assumptions about the avant-garde and what formal strategies properly belong to an avant-garde practice. What none of the binary approaches to defining avant-garde film offers is a structure for explaining more eloquently and clearly how Akerman continually invents and reinvents experimental strategies for exploring what it means to be a woman in the age in which the films are made. While a certain amount of reference to the formal traditions in which she participates helps illuminate Akerman's work, it is equally helpful to notice how she revises and departs from these traditions.

News from Home (1976)

Although it seems to be one of Akerman's clearest works of structuralist filmmaking, News from Home is most significant in the ways it departs from that movement's basic assumptions. These departures make the film a central part of Akerman's oeuvre. To understand it simply as an early work influenced by the filmmakers of the New American Cinema is a radical misreading. This is not to discount outright the influence of these filmmakers on Akerman's work: she was living in New York when the film was made and the traces of American structuralist filmmakers of the 1970s are not difficult to see. However, for Akerman, what becomes most important in this relationship are the Barthesian ruptures in its consistency, which I identify and interpret in the following discussion. News from Home eventually takes on an abstract and consequently emotionally raw quality, which is very much *not* what structuralist filmmaking is supposed to do, and in this way it both bears the mark of the profound melancholia of earlier Akerman films like *Je tu il elle* (1974) and foreshadows the almost sentimental emotional appeal of *A Couch in New York*.

"Structural filmmaking" is hardly a unified aesthetic; nonetheless, several attempts have been made to define it that are germane to Akerman's film.[2] Sitney provides a concise description of the genre, writing, "The structural film insists on its shape, and what content it has is minimal, and subsidiary to the outline. Four characteristics of the structural film are its fixed camera position (fixed frame from the viewer's perspective), the flicker effect, loop printing, and rephotography off the screen. Very seldom will one find all four characteristics in a single film, and there are structural films which modify these usual elements" (*Visionary Film* 370). Sitney has perhaps too strenuously attempted to codify and valorize structuralist film, as numerous writers after him have observed. He does, however, help us understand what is central to a structuralist aesthetic: the filmmaker's calling attention to the cinematic material itself (which is why the aesthetic is sometimes called "Materialist Film") and subsuming whatever referential function the images might have in order to elicit consideration of some basic material aspects of the filmmaking process.

News from Home exhibits many of the traits of structuralist cinema. It is in some sense a diary film, although it has a minimalist visual design. The sound track consists of Akerman's voice reading her mother's letters from Belgium in a flat, monotone voice, accompanied by the sounds of New York, which sometimes drown out Akerman's voice entirely; the letter reading by the filmmaker gives the film its diarist dimensions. Visually, *News from Home* consists almost entirely of grainy, static shots—some composed, some quite awkward, but all of them very long takes—of New York City. All of the images, though, picture decidedly quotidian subject matter: a woman sitting on a street corner, the inside of a subway, highly composed images of alleyways, Tenth Avenue shot from inside of a car, and so on. The film's last image is shot from the back of a ferry pulling away from Manhattan. Toward the end of the film Akerman begins to move the camera, adding some zooms and pans to her vocabulary, but the static, artificial quality of the film remains largely unchanged by this variation. Dana Polan, however, reads this development as extremely significant, writing that "the movement is an ambiguous one: a smooth, geometric, 360-degree pan that ends up where it started from. Ackerman's [*sic*] camera seems caught between the liberatory gesture of altering the empirical through cinematic means and the final realization that this engagement on the level of technique changes nothing about the empirical reality" (71). This movement does not undercut Akerman's essentially structuralist aesthetic; what Polan identifies here evinces a frustration with representation that recurs in structuralist filmmaking practice. The disparity between the visual and sound tracks emphasize the abstract—as opposed to referential—quality of the images. Although Akerman's voice mingles with the sounds of the city (subway doors closing, people chatting), her words never synchronize with the images. The referential dimensions of Akerman's visual and auditory imagining of New York and Belgium remain secondary. Forming the referential center of the film instead are cinematic mechanics: the duration of the takes, the presence or absence of sound, the stasis or motion of the camera.

These materialist explorations, however, serve not only as meditations on cinema, but also as evocations of a deepening melancholy—an emotion that occupies the core of Akerman's oeuvre. Margulies offers useful insights into how the film's sound/image disjuncture conveys alienation and depression. Margulies writes, "Random waving of attention through words (letters), referential sound, and images—a common tactic in structuralist minimalist film—bolsters Akerman's subversion of a fixed locus for the 'I.' The alienation between image and sound parallels the disjunction between the mother's space of letter writing and Akerman's space of performance—between the foreign reality and New York" (152). In manipulating the plastic elements of the medium to evoke this alienation, News from Home is structuralist. The act of *evocation,* however, distinguishes it from a good deal of structuralist film practice. Ultimately, News from Home is not about the filmmaking process itself but attends to something external—a mother's and daughter's distance from each other. Peter Gidal's rather dogmatic assertion that in structuralist filmmaking "the attempt to decipher the structure and anticipate/recorrect it, to clarify and analyze the production-process of the specific image at any specific moment, are the root concern of Structuralist/Materialist film" (1) does not hold true in News from Home. What sits at the *root* of the film overall is a longing for home, for familial comfort. The film also extends Akerman's ongoing concern with wandering and displacement (visible most clearly in Je tu il elle, Les rendez-vous d'Anna [1978], D'est [1993], and, of course, A Couch in New York). These thematic preoccupations find expression through a structuralist aesthetic, but the film, in showcasing theme, makes a fairly radical break with structuralism's hermetic focus on the medium itself. While looking like fairly cold structuralism, News from Home is more emotionally expressive than its construction suggests. Michael Tarantino acknowledges Akerman's unity of form and content when he notes that *News from Home,* "not despite but because of its stripped-down images and the deadpan reading of the text, manages to deliver an emotional impact that is not usually associated with such minimal means. Here is a key to understanding Akerman's work: the ability to combine the close and distant view through a rigorously controlled mise-en-scène" (52). In mise-en-scène, *News from Home* differs considerably from, say, *A Couch in New York* but the dialectic of form and content—formal control and ennui—proves central to both films.

Further, *News from Home,* despite its alienating and distanced aesthetic, displays a deeply subjective voice. Placing the film in the context of 1970s avant-garde, Janet Bergstrom notes, "As in Rainer's *Film about a Woman Who* . . . and much of Duras's work, autobiographical reference serves a complex function, one which draws on a woman's lived experience while at the same time complicating the question 'who speaks' by dispersing the origin of the enunciation across many positions; the filmmaker, like the filmic system and its characters, is shaped by conflicting desires" (Bergstrom and Penley 127).

As Bergstrom's remark indicates, Akerman's autobiographical gestures serve the purpose of both theoretical speculation and personal self-reflection; and the tension between these purposes gets mirrored in the formal disruptions of *News from Home.* The film's autobiographical character, although central, is seriously complicated by its fragmented forms. "Who Speaks?" has become something of an obsession for Foucault-influenced critics (including Bergstrom), but Akerman's handling of the problem lands the film not in the realm of the decentered subject so sought after by poststructuralists (of the critical-theory variety, that is), but rather in the vicinity of the diary film. Though 1970s feminists criticized this avant-garde mode for its self-indulgence and Romantic tradition, Akerman manages to redeem the form without abandoning it. She does this by drawing attention to the artificial and mediated quality of her personal crises, as opposed to seeing the camera as an extension of her eye or a window into her soul, à la Brakhage. It is clear that Akerman is the one who "speaks" in this film, but she also displays skepticism about narrative authority—a skepticism that will later be used in a more explicitly political way—that is plain to see (and hear) in every frame of *News from Home.*

Her skepticism, even in this cool, almost dreamlike state, still draws attention to Akerman's feminist concern with a specifically female subjectivity. Angela McRobbie has written eloquently about Akerman's abiding concern with feminine qualities of interior experience. McRobbie writes that "[t]he threat of uncertainty and ambivalence that winds its way through all of [Ak-

erman's] work, together with a kind of daydreaming, introspective femininity occasionally bursting into passion or violence, are what characterize her
vision of what it is to be a woman" (29). This pattern of stillness erupting
into explosive energy also characterizes Akerman's formal modus operandi.
While the closing image of *News from Home*—the long take of Manhattan
from a ferry—could not literally be described as violent, in light of the stasis
(or, to elaborate the parallel, the ambivalence, introspection, and daydreaming) of the rest of the film, the comparatively kinetic quality of the image
makes it feel passionate and almost climactic. Overall, the structure of the
film, with its material manipulations, moves between conflicted alienation
and forward movement in a way that enacts through form Akerman's feminist concerns about female subjectivity.

The film also echoes some of structuralist filmmaking's debt to modernist aesthetic practices, but again, Akerman also revises the formal traditions
in which she participates. Modernism, in Astradur Eysteinsson's estimation,
deploys radical formal strategies to enact its preoccupation with subjectivity
while avoiding any pretense of being "objective" in its portrayal of subjectivity. In modernism, Eysteinsson suggests, "[w]hile subjective experience
is to be mediated through objectification . . . this objectification, in order to
express the negativity of the experience, must be constructed in a radically
'subjective' manner—it must not take on the shape of a 'rationalized' objective representation to which as social beings we are accustomed" (43). As
with her reworking of diary filmmaking, Akerman both participates in and
revises modernist form. The filmmaker certainly avoids any "'rationalized'
objective representation" that might reduce and contain subjectivity; and
the alienation *News from Home* evokes is no doubt linked to what Eysteinsson identifies as our expectations as social beings. However, while remaining resolutely subjective, as any good modernist should, Akerman ultimately
balances her explorations of interiority with awareness of external pressures
shaping interior experience. High modernism almost fetishizes the interior;
Akerman does not. Affirming the centrality of interiority to modernism,
Douwe Fokkema and Elrud Ibsch have observed that "[a]t the center of the
modernist semantic universe is the individual consciousness, which tries to
make itself immune from external influences in order to observe the world
from an independent position" (43). Akerman's work departs from a modernist sensibility in that it claims no immunity from external influences.
Discovering external influences—like the operations of a male-dominated
world—on female subjectivity is part of Akerman's ongoing project, and such
discoveries certainly display themselves in *News from Home*. Structuralist

classics like Michael Snow's *Wavelength* or Paul Sharits's *T.O.U.C.H.I.N.G* are unambiguous examples of the interiority that Fokkema and Ibsch identify. Akerman, a much more conflicted filmmaker, has some modernist tendencies, but she ultimately connects the interiority she portrays to the social landscapes surrounding and shaping individuals.

The impossibility of classifying her cinema according to any simple binary, whether it be structuralist/nonstructuralist or avant-garde/modernist, also extends to her uses of alienation effects, which can both discomfit and entertain the viewer. Rejecting any binary between critical thinking and entertainment, alienation effects and amusement, Brecht remarks in connection with "epic theater" that "there is felt to be a very sharp distinction between learning and amusing oneself. The first may be useful, but only the second is pleasant. So we have to defend the epic theater against the suspicion that it is a highly disagreeable, humorless, indeed strenuous affair" (72).

News from Home redeems the structuralist film from its reputation as highly disagreeable, humorless, and strenuous (criticisms familiar to anyone knowledgeable about the genre) and instead combines emotional, critical, and political registers. The film calls attention to the artificial nature of filmmaking in Brechtian fashion. (Margulies notes that the letters on the sound track are read "much in the way one hears scripts read mechanically at rehearsals [an alienation technique suggested by Brecht]" (153). However, it engages the viewer emotionally *and* critically in subjects relating to the world outside the frame, like the alienating effect of large cities, the oppressive loneliness that many women face, and the challenges of asserting a female subjectivity in a male-dominated world. *News from Home* is arguably the most truly Brechtian of the films under discussion here, precisely because of the way that its aesthetic garment opens up but does not fully break down.

Like all of Akerman's work, *News from Home* also tackles a version of a theme Barthes considers central to Brecht's practice: "how to be good in a bad world [*comment être bon dans une société mauvaise*]" (*Essais critiques* 88). Barthes's formulation may reduce Brecht's complex politics a bit, but it recognizes a moral core to his work that many fail to acknowledge; Akerman's work also revolves around a compelling moral vision. *News from Home* is not so much about being good in a bad world but about trying to find voice and connection under circumstances that encourage silence and alienation. Just as Brecht rebels against (but does not abandon) a modernism he saw as increasingly apolitical, Akerman moves structuralist filmmaking away from a cold, elitist, sociopolitically disengaged formalism.

News from Home, then, proves deeply ambiguous, embodying and rejecting a number of formal and political identities. This strategy of exploiting fissures in reasonably well established norms displays a kind of Barthesian playfulness that has served Akerman well throughout her career. Early in *Le plaisir du texte,* Barthes seeks to define "plaisir/jouissance," which he understands as follows: "terminologically, it still sways. I stumble, I get tangled up. In every way, there is always a margin of indecision; the distinction won't be the source of clear classifications, the paradigm will creak, the sense will be precarious, revocable, reversible, the discourse will be incomplete" (10).[3]

It is precisely such a resistance to clear classification (neither diary nor structuralist nor modernist, exactly) that creates the political and emotional impact of *News from Home.* To see this ambiguity in the light of Barthesian textual pleasure or Brechtian practice is to understand this film as something very different from the mechanical tinkering that defines a good portion of (mostly male) structuralist filmmaking of the 1970s. In the place where the structuralist paradigm, so carefully laid out by Sitney and Gidal, creaks, a great deal of emotional impact and political exposition is to be found. This slow, subtle breaking of even the most esoteric of conventions has always been central to Akerman's project, and as in *Les années 80* and *A Couch in New York,* this project can often entail finding the radical potential in what appear to be the most apolitical of aesthetic strategies.

Les années 80 (1983)

If *News from Home* can be seen as Akerman's revision of modernism, then *Les années 80* is her revision of postmodernism. The film, ostensibly a deconstruction of Akerman's musical comedy *Golden Eighties* (also known as *Window Shopping,* 1985) and the ways *Golden Eighties* lays bare the mechanics of film narrative production (in this case, musical narrative), echoes that loss of faith in narrative associated with postmodernism (see the critique of *meta-récits* in Jean-François Lyotard's manifesto *La condition postmoderne,* for instance). Simultaneously, though, Akerman rejects postmodern antinarrativity and offers plenty of space in her deconstructed universe for narrative identification and pleasure, as well as emotional and political impact. *Les années 80,* then, proves more complex and ambiguous than its aesthetic might immediately suggest, and it contributes to Akerman's ongoing revisions of broadly (and sometimes not so broadly) distributed and consumed genres.

Les années 80 divides into two parts, marked by title cards. Part one contains mostly shots of actors rehearsing, reading, rerecording, getting direction from off-screen, and generally preparing for the production of what seems to be a musical melodrama. Part two features a more straightforward set of production numbers—numbers that the performers in part one had been preparing. Indeed, the film explores the *work* of a musical: its fragmented, sometimes slightly incoherent, series of images highlights the bits and pieces of artistic creation that classical narrative strives to hide. In the film's second part, though, Akerman makes whole that which she had dismantled in part one. In considering *Les années 80,* Lucy Fischer sees the two parts as linked through their attention to the mutual dependence of melodrama and musical, arguing that part one privileges melodramatic forms whereas part two privileges musical forms. Fischer writes that "what Akerman addresses is the paradigm of melodrama—the narrative 'hook' on which the musical form is frequently hung" ("Shall We Dance?" 10). Interestingly, the filmmaker's uses of melodrama and musical manage in both parts of the film to offer viewers considerable narrative pleasure; whether deconstructing or contriving the essential elements of either genre, Akerman's film makes narrative pleasure a primary value. This two-part structure, therefore, proves less dualistic than its surface may seem. In fact, Akerman makes clear in laying out the film this way that deconstructed images and illusionist narrative can have similar effects on viewers. In the same way that Brecht defends "against the suspicion that it [the critical aesthetic] is a highly disagreeable, humorless, indeed strenuous affair," Akerman's usage of two radically different techniques to treat similar content (it's the same musical, after all) defends against the notion that narrative pleasure arises only from illusionism. Even more than *News from Home, Les années 80* offers alternative forms of narrative pleasure.

This search for an alternative narrative pleasure, always central in Akerman's work, becomes the animating principle of *Les années 80.* The film opens with a black screen and Akerman in voice-over, giving instructions. Fischer writes of this strategy that "the very nature of the initial shot (its total refusal of visual sensation) also suggests that in *The Eighties* the notion of theatrical spectacle will be refused" ("Shall We Dance?" 10). While Fischer correctly observes that this odd opening prepares the viewer for the film's self-reflexivity and defeats any expectation of classical, "invisible" forms, her assessment suggests a cooler film than that which actually unfolds. In fact, spectacle *is* on display here, although not the spectacle that would be expected of a conventional musical. Later on in her essay, Fischer remarks on similarities between the spectacle of self-reflexivity and the spectacle of melodrama. Describing a rehearsal scene, Fischer writes, "What is important about the sequence, however, is its focus on bodily and gestural language, *the same kind of physical discourse that has been coached in the melodra-matic scenes,* here executed by both the singer and the conductor" ("Shall We Dance?" 13, emphasis mine). The discourse between these two kinds of scenes is quite similar. Akerman's cinematography—in particular her use of close-ups and abstract, lyrical emphasis on movement that does not ad-vance a narrative—resembles the visual operations of melodrama and the musical. Of course, given the documentary rather than illusionist quality of the image, such strategies also depart from melodramatic/musical form, but Akerman steadfastly ignores distinctions between edification and entertain-ment throughout the film, illustrating what Brecht means when he writes that "all that can be said is that the contrast between learning and amusing oneself is not laid down by divine rule" (72). The aesthetic of *Les années 80,* following a Brechtian interest in anti-illusionism without righteousness, is very fluid and suggests no rules to help Akerman's viewer distinguish be-tween documentary and fiction, deconstruction and melodrama.

This absence of a "divine rule" encourages a playfulness and provision-ality that Lyotard associates with the dissolution of grand knowledge nar-ratives—*meta-récits.* He writes that "in society and contemporary culture, post-industrial society, postmodern culture, the question of legitimization of knowledge poses itself in other ways. The great narrative has lost its cred-ibility," and in its place is now "speculative narrative, emancipatory narra-tive" (63).[4] The problem of verifying knowledge for Lyotard, then, entails both parts crisis and opportunity. Akerman's style in *Les années 80* also en-genders interpretive crisis and opportunity: it problematizes knowledge for the viewer, making it difficult to settle comfortably into critical language and categories for understanding the film. But this critical discomfiture gives rise to play. Akerman dissolves categories of *différence* central to domi-nant theories of film—documentary/fiction, rigor/lyricism, nonlinear/lin-ear movement—and engages instead in free play with multiple modalities and strategies that elaborate common themes. This sense of "play" is cen-tral for *Les années 80,* which is as jubilant as *News from Home* is mournful and alienated, delighting in the visceral giddiness of music and dance. This giddiness or playfulness fits Lyotard's characterization of postmodernism, especially considering the theorist's insight that "narrative form, in contrast to the developed forms of knowledge discourse, will allow for a plurality of language games" (39).[5] Playful language games (as opposed to stable, inar-guable meaning) define postmodern discourse for Lyotard; playfulness also defines the way Akerman facilitates pleasure for her viewers. She allows her viewers to understand the images in a less structured, more abstract and more gamelike fashion than would be demanded by an intellectualized process of interpretation or deconstruction.

To understand *Les années 80* strictly as postmodernist game playing would be to miss the complexity of the film's dialogue with postmodernism. Postmodernism in general—and certainly this includes Lyotard's work—has a way of dulling the political possibilities of art through its reduction of every text to questions of language, unrelated to anything beyond its own form. While the metaphor of "language games" certainly helps describe *Les années 80*, these games are not played for the sake of game playing: Akerman marshals her playfulness to the task of evoking the fragmented subjectivity available to women within a patriarchal society. J. Hoberman acknowledges the film's feminist dimensions when he remarks that "it takes no great powers of imagination to see *Les années 80* as a movie about how women learn to *play* their roles—as lovers, workers, 'women,' and movie directors. . . . No less than *Jeanne Dielman* [1975], *Les années 80* is a film about the female condition" (149). The political imperative so important to Akerman's work remains undiminished in *Les années 80*, although the film's political perspectives, like political perspectives in *News from Home*, circulate within seemingly esoteric and potentially apolitical forms.

Whether *Les années 80* constitutes a critique of postmodernism is debatable, but it certainly explores and revises how a film takes viewers from a passive/consumption to an active/critical position. The film rebels less against postmodernism itself than against an essentially Godardian version of counter-cinema. Godard's more aggressively avant-garde work, such as the similarly deconstructive *Scénario du film Passion* (1982), is more or less contemporary with *Les années 80*, although Godard's film, more jagged and dense in organization, offers less room for identification and narrative pleasure than Akerman's work. Akerman's film, although less aggressively alienating or "Brechtian" than much of what Godard was doing at the time, balances critique and pleasure more successfully than anything her Parisian colleague had made. Unconcerned with ideological purity, Akerman was free to recruit a variety of strategies, modalities, and forms to her project of representing female subjectivity in film.

Searches for ideological purity, and the limitations such searches impose, have always haunted counter-cinema. So doggedly have they done this, in fact, that some theorists of the counter-cinema project have actively discouraged too great a divide between counter-cinema and its alleged opposite, dominant cinema. Annette Kuhn actually emphasizes the inseparability—rather than antagonism—of the two: "If deconstructive cinema thus defines itself in relation to dominant cinema, it is not a static entity, because its character at any moment is always shaped, in an inverse manner, by dominant cinema. Deconstructive cinema is always, so to speak, casting a sideways look at dominant cinema" ("Textual Politics" 254).

Kuhn's articulation of the relationship between avant-garde and conventional forms offers an important insight into Akerman's film, given that *Les années 80* literally deconstructs the conventional musical. The sideways look Akerman casts toward this genre—in the second section, in the first section's focus on interaction between actors back stage, in lyrical shots of singers, musicians, and conductors—simultaneously deconstructs and celebrates the musical by acknowledging its dominant conventions while heightening its lyricism. Hoberman calls the film "raw but sensuous" (148) and this combination sums up an essential paradox of Akerman's deconstructive cinema. Akerman understands that formally adventurous filmmaking need not exist in a vacuum; *Les années 80,* in characteristic fashion, connects avant-garde filmmaking to the dominant cinema that surrounds everyone. Fischer appreciates this paradoxical dimension of Akerman's project as well, noting that Akerman's film is "re-writing the patriarchal Hollywood musical in terms of a feminist cinematic vocabulary" ("Shall We Dance?" 16). Akerman's interactiveness with cinematic conventionality is quite different from the narrative tinkering of Godard, which always seems about to career off into complete incomprehensibility. It is also different from the feminist practice on display in films like Laura Mulvey and Peter Wollen's *Riddles of the Sphinx,* which, though deconstructive in aim, exhibits less interest, flexibility, and confidence in its ability to draw upon Hollywood conventions to add impact to its political message. Akerman rejects purist posturing in favor of a nuanced and interactive, but no less political, strategy of paradox.

The film's fragmentary nature contributes to its political resonance, and Barthes's insights on continuity and literature are especially relevant here. There is little continuity between sequences in *Les années 80,* and the film's diverse visuals reinforce its fragmented quality. Mixing video and 35 mm, handheld and stationary camera work, Akerman's cinematography accentuates disjuncture. The film's supreme example of fragmentation inheres, of course, in its structural division into two pieces, each of which reworks *the same material* using different stratagems. Fragmentation or discontinuity constitutes, for Barthes, an emblem of a text's triumph over the staid and complacent, and Akerman's use of discontinuity supports the theorist's contentions. Barthes writes that discontinuity is the fundamental law of all communication. . . . The aesthetic problem is simply to know how to mobilize this fatal discontinuity, how to give it a breath, a time, and a history. Classical rhetoric has responded, majestically over the centuries, in edifying an aesthetic of *variation* . . . but there is another rhetoric possible, that of *translation:* modern, no doubt, since one only finds it in some works of the avant-garde, and sometimes, far away, in some ancient texts, according to the hypothesis of Claude Lévi-Strauss (*Essais critiques* 185).[6]

A rhetoric of *translation,* or *explanation*—viewed as the motivation and purpose for discontinuity—bridges both myth and experimental texts (Barthes was writing about the novel *Mobil* by Michel Butor); acts of translation populate the landscape of *Les années 80.* The film uses discontinuity to evoke the filmmaker's historical and cultural moment, explaining (or "translating") social and political concepts, building community, and providing narrative pleasure. Such strategies share a social space with mythology (*pace* Lévi-Strauss), but they also echo Willemen's assessment of the role of an avant-garde. Willemen writes that in contrast to modernism, the avant-garde exhibits "a politics of negation and transformation, aligned with a process of change in a socialist direction, that is to say, a transformation instead of a modernization" (146). This transformation of the musical form into something that both provides pleasure and demands critical distance, that is both abstract and deeply rooted in its historical moment, is experimental in the most radical sense and fragmented in the most progressive, Barthesian sense.

The film, then, can be approached not by trying to understand what it unambiguously *is* but by noting all the things it isn't; it is never fully one genre or another. Its primary energy emerges, as Barthes argues, in its slippages—the places where it strays suddenly from its appropriated generic norms. In evoking how he experiences textual pleasure, Barthes writes, "isn't the most erotic place on a body *where the garment gapes?* In perversion (which is the morality of textual pleasure) there are no 'erogenous zones.'. . . it is intermittence, just as psychoanalysis says, that is erotic; that place where the skin sparkles between two pieces of clothing (the pants and the sweater), between two sides (the half-open skirt, the glove and the sleeve)" (*Le plaisir du texte* 17).[7]

This schema of textual pleasure (or, for Barthes, textual erotics), based on ruptures rather than unity, helps explain why *Les années 80* is so enjoyable, as well as politically and formally radical. With its fragmented, intermittent quality, Akerman's film offers pleasure through its gaps—its digressions from orthodoxy. Akerman uses various generic forms intermittently and selectively, avoiding some sort of aesthetic totality while making the most of multifarious aesthetic strategies. Understanding the film in these terms, like understanding *News from Home* in terms of how it is *not* structuralist, helps bring *Les années 80* into harmony with Akerman's oeuvre as a whole and with the difficult, sometimes paradoxical, project of an experimental feminist counter-cinema.

A Couch in New York (1996)

Although it could be argued that *A Couch in New York* is a thoroughly crowd-pleasing, mainstream film, it contains surprisingly stark moments of re-flexivity and experimentation, making it one of Akerman's most deceptive films. The presence of stars like William Hurt and Juliette Binoche made the film more distributable than any other Akerman production, but by inject-ing avant-garde strategies into the narrative, Akerman also renders the film quite unlike a conventional love story. Akerman's trademark long takes and flattened dialogue are present, as are her distancing effects, which, though exerting less pressure on the narrative than felt in, say, *News from Home*, still represent a meaningful, if not total, rupture of classical closure. This is a kinder, gentler Akerman to be sure, but *A Couch in New York* nevertheless balances distance against pleasure and therefore has more in common with her more "rigorous" films than might be at first apparent.

A Couch in New York tells the story of a young Parisian woman (Juliette Binoche) who longs for New York and a high-powered New York psychologist (William Hurt) who wants to escape to France. They arrange an apartment exchange, and he arrives only to find that her lifestyle is a bit too bohemian for him, while she essentially takes over his life, including his psychology practice, during her residence in New York. When he returns and discovers what has happened, he poses as a patient, slowly trying to re-infiltrate his own life. Predictably and lyrically, they fall in love against the backdrop of summer and autumnal New York.

The film's strikingly slow pace, however, belies the conventionality of its plot. Akerman unfolds the film slowly, emphasizing long takes over a classi-cal editing style. This strategy recalls the stately tableaux of *News from Home*, although *A Couch in New York* is full of camera movement, a piece of cinematic vocabulary that occurs late and with a much more specific purpose in her earlier, more structuralist film. Long takes are, of course, favored in the theoretical position mapped out by André Bazin, whose writings offer insight into Akerman's film. Just as *News from Home* revises structuralism/ modernism and *Les années 80* revises deconstructionism/postmodernism, *A Couch in New York* revises Hollywood/classicism, although it does so *through* Akerman's more explicitly avant-garde work. David Bordwell's maxim that "[t]he historical and aesthetic importance of the classical Hollywood cinema lies in the fact that to go beyond it we must go through it" (Bordwell, Staiger, and Thompson 385) explains why an avant-garde filmmaker would evince interest in Hollywood forms. The constant presence of narrative pleasure, a primary Hollywood aesthetic value, demonstrates how Akerman moves continually through and beyond classical cinema in her pursuit of alternative forms of pleasure and expression. *A Couch in New York* shows just how indebted Akerman's practice has been to Hollywood, but it also shows the radical potential that classical form can contain without being ruptured outright.

Focusing on Bazin's relevance to Akerman may seem perverse according to the norms of contemporary film theory, but the ethic of openness that his writings on cinema convey (an ethic that has been largely ignored in favor of an obsession with his "realist" simplifications) aligns with Akerman's aesthetic flexibility and political concerns. Bazin can be helpful in understanding the manifestation of those concerns in *A Couch in New York*. The ruptures in illusionist closure that Bazin attributes to the deep-focus/long-take style in Italian neorealism make it possible to apprehend why *A Couch in New York* remains, despite its Hollywood appearance, a hallmark Chantal Akerman film. While quite reasonably rejecting some of Bazin's more dogmatic realist formulations, Margulies writes that "when I first came to write about *Jeanne Dielman,* it struck me that André Bazin's description of Italian neorealism . . . could be applied almost word for word to Akerman's film" (8). The same can be said of the very different *A Couch in New York*.

Akerman's *A Couch in New York,* which has an ambiguous relationship with realism, seems to have absorbed and adjusted Bazin's position favoring long takes and composition over either Soviet or Hollywood montage. When we remind ourselves of Bazin's three claims for the effects of long take/depth of focus and recall the slow pace and carefully composed mise-en-scène of Akerman's film, we can see how the plot conventions of *A Couch in New York* coexist with an ambiguity, discontinuity, and alienation effect born of the film's cinematographic style. Bazin's trio of assertions about neorealist strategy conveys an ethic that resonates readily with the avant-garde sensibilities we have come to associate with Akerman. Bazin claims,

1. that depth of focus places the spectator in a rapport with the image that is closer to the one he has with reality. It is therefore right to say . . . its structure is more realist;
2. that as a consequence this implies a more active mental attitude and even a positive contribution on the part of the spectator to the mise-en-scène . . . ;
3. from the last two propositions, which are in the realm of psychology, there ensues a third that one can qualify as metaphysical. In analyzing reality, montage [as opposed to long takes] supposes, by its very nature, the unity of the dramatic environment. Certainly another course is possible, but then that would be another film. In summary, montage is by its very nature opposed to the expression of ambiguity. (143–44)[8]

Considering the relationship Bazin posits between the long take and spectator activity, as well as semiotic ambiguity, or conversely, the relationship between montage and spectator passivity on the one hand and manipulation and semiotic contrivance on the other, it becomes possible to see how the cinematography in A Couch in New York works against closure, stability, and viewer passivity. Akerman thus retains space for the subjectivity of the spectator even as she co-opts classical Hollywood forms.

All of Akerman's work reinvents classical style to accommodate the subjectivity of the spectator, opposing stylistically the more manipulative and closed-off effects of montage in either its Hollywood or Soviet forms. While the mise-en-scène in A Couch in New York is nowhere near as densely baroque as the films Bazin has in mind (for example, The Magnificent Ambersons), it does display a pronounced rejection of classical Hollywood visual manipulation, which relies on editing to control viewer attention. Most of the images inside the apartments that the film centers around—one cramped and cluttered in Paris, one spacious and posh in New York—are shot with a roaming camera, with shot–reverse shot coming into play only in occasional, dialogue-heavy sequences. Images of Henry (Hurt) walking through Brooklyn and Béatrice (Binoche) walking through Central Park are rendered in single shots. The camera is mobile, with people coming in and out of the frame but with their respective urban landscapes *always* an important part of the composition. These are elaborate, open images, quite close to the studious framing of *News from Home* or even *Jeanne Dielman*. Bazin and Akerman clearly find such elements of film form radical. Even though one gets dismissed as a naïve Hollywood apologist and the other categorized as a radical anti-illusionist, they share a similarly avant-garde sensibility in searching for new understandings of forms that respect specific historical moments—Bazin in his defense of 1950s Hollywood and Akerman in her revision of 1980s and 90s romantic comedy.

Like his ideas about deep-focus/long-take cinematography, Bazin's ideas about neorealist acting also apply to *A Couch in New York*. Bazin sees actors in a neorealist aesthetic as more *and* less than mere signifiers of physical reality. Writing about neorealism's rejection of professional actors, he says that "[the actor's] ignorance of the theatrical technique is less a positively necessary condition than a guarantee against the expressionism of 'acting.' For de Sica, Bruno was a silhouette, a face, a way of walking" (77).[9] Although they are certainly not the nonprofessionals of neorealism, Akerman uses her actors in a similarly abstract way. Like de Sica's Bruno, Béatrice and Henry are not characters as much as they are bodies to put in the wrong apartments or voices to build abstract, soothing sequences around. The performances of Hurt and Binoche are relatively flat: they often deliver dialogue in deadpan, emotionless tones. This cool approach, fundamental to Akerman's repertoire, stands out curiously in a "romantic comedy" and so draws attention to the constructed nature of the narrative, rupturing a measure of its illusionist/realist unity. These performances represent a significant departure from the classical demand for verisimilitude, and Bazin certainly would have recognized the awkward, open, narrative form on display in *A Couch in New York*.

Beyond Bazin, another point of contact between Akerman's earlier work and *A Couch in New York* is the way that the film deals with musicality. The film's lack of background music further unsettles its classical form. While not completely absent, music is much less pronounced in *A Couch in New York* than in most Hollywood films. This relative quiet makes the film feel not quite right, more austere than the average romantic comedy. Yet Akerman infuses the film with musicality using alternative aesthetic means. Réal La Rochelle has pointed out that throughout Akerman's career, the director's corpus of films is "among the most solid of the rare, modern *postmusical*" and writes that the film's sound track, which includes slow conversations on the sofa, the sound of water dripping, and constant phone calls, gives the film a "spirit of musicalization" (50).[10] This spirit, as La Rochelle points out, can easily be traced to *Les années 80* but can also be seen in the abstract, plastic aesthetics of *News from Home*. Even when Akerman is most conventional, therefore, she creates opportunities, as in the film's unconventional sound track, that expand and complicate classical form.

A Couch in New York, then, while the least explicitly political film under discussion here (for none of these formal eccentricities should be understood as having *inherent* political value), contains a revisionist, passionate spirit that is very much in line with Akerman's other work. Her goal here is essentially the converse of her goal in *News from Home* and *Les années 80*. In those films, she located the pleasurable in the rigorous and open ended; in *A Couch in New York*, she locates the rigorous in what has in the past been used purely to provide easy, exploitative pleasure.

Conclusion

These three films, in sheer breadth of formal difference, offer potent evidence for the claim that Chantal Akerman may be the most versatile, innovative, and consistent European filmmaker of the postwar generation. Akerman's versatility is without peer, but equally unprecedented is her ability to balance critical distance with identification, and political possibility with narrative pleasure. Always open ended, her political engagement with the presentation and re-presentation of feminine subjectivity avoids pedagogy or propaganda. She toys with her viewers, invoking recognized forms only to radically revise them. In such textual deceptions, however, subversion and pleasure meet. Barthes, from whom contemporary theory has received crucial insights into textual pleasure, writes that the value of modern texts "comes from their duplicity. It's necessary to always hear in them two sides. The subversive side can appear privileged because it is the side of violence; but it's not violence that upsets pleasure; destruction doesn't interest it; what it wants is the place of a loss, it's the flaw, the cut, the deflation, the fading that takes hold of the subject at the heart of *jouissance*" (*Le plaisir du texte* 14).[11] Akerman's aesthetic is never one of destruction but of longing, of a gentle curiosity that makes the viewer wonder what exactly is missing and why. She is valuable especially because she illustrates the reductiveness and ultimate futility of terms like "avant-garde," "experimental," "classical," or "antibourgeois camera style." Her concerns cannot be contained by the boundaries of these pigeonholes. William Cadbury takes Bazin to task for drawing his "cleavage plane" between silent and sound cinema, montage and deep focus. Cadbury suggests that for any plane of division, the "division is not between good and bad or cinematic and uncinematic, but rather between rhetorical points that can be made in a number of ways and that cannot be attached simply to devices or styles" (Cadbury and Pogue 47). Akerman's cinematic practice has been a potent realization of this flexibility and multivocality Cadbury espouses. Akerman's versatility—her ability to facilitate an active, Barthesian textual pleasure across a wide range of historical and generic forms—makes her avant-garde in the truest sense.

NOTES

1. My primary concern in this essay will be with the presence of lyricism in Akerman's films, and there are certainly better examples of this than the three that I will deal with here. *Toute une nuit* comes to mind immediately for its images of dancing and desire (the film in many ways recalls the Godard of *Band à part*), and *Jeanne Dielman 1080 Quai de Commerce Bruxelles* is an equally good example, given its constant tension between lyricism and boredom. I choose not to deal with these films (and others in the Akerman corpus like them) because they more clearly invite *both* distance and pleasure than *News from Home, Les années 80,* and *A Couch in New York. Toute une nuite* seems hard to pigeonhole, while *A Couch in New York* and *Les années 80* seem easy. My task here is to show that despite outward appearances that sometimes seem clearly to dictate otherwise, Akerman is always paradoxical; she is never easy to classify.

2. The term "structural film," which was coined by the very unstructuralist (indeed, very humanist) Sitney, should not be confused with structuralist criticism, even though the insights of Roland Barthes are liberally sprinkled throughout this essay. While there is arguably a relation between the two concepts, such an argument is far beyond the scope of this essay and not entirely relevant to an understanding of Akerman's aesthetic concerns.

3. "Plaisir/Jouissance: terminologiquement, cela vacille encore, j'achoppe, j'embrouille. De toute manière, il y aura toujours une marge d'indécision; la distinction ne sera pas source de classements sûrs, le paradigme grincera, le sens sera précaire, révocable, réversible, le discours sera incomplet." Translation mine, as are all that follow.

4. "Dans la société et la culture contemporaine, société post-industrielle, culture postmoderne, la question de le légitimation du savoir se pose en d'autres termes. Le grand récit a perdu sa crédibilité, quel que soit le monde d'unification qui lui est assigné: récit spéculatif, récit de l'émancipation."

5. "La forme narratif, à la différence des formes développées du discours de savoir, admet en elle une pluralité de jeux de langage."

6. "Le discontinu est le statut fondamental de toute communication. . . . Le problème esthétique est simplement de savoir comment mobiliser ce discontinu fatal, comment lui donner un souffle, un temps, une histoire. La rhétorique classique a donné sa réponse, magistrale pendent des siècles, en édifiant une esthétique de la *variation* . . . mais il y a une autre rhétorique possible, celle de la *translation:* moderne, sans doute, puisqu'on ne

la trouve que dans quelques œuvres d'avant-garde; et cependant, ailleurs, combien an-
cienne: toute récit mythique, selon l'hypothèse de Claude Lévi-Strauss."

7. "L'endroit le plus érotique d'un corps n'est-il pas *là où le vêtement bâille?* Dans le
perversion (qui est le régime du plaisir textuel) il n'y a pas de 'zones érogènes.' . . . c'est
l'intermittence, comme l'a bien dit la psychanalyse, qui est érotique: celle de la peau qui
scintille entre deux pièces (le pantalon et le tricot), entre deux bords (la chemise entrou-
verte, le gante et la manche)."

8. "1. que la profondeur de champ place la spectateur dans un rapport avec l'image plus
proche de celui qu il entretient avec la réalité. Il est donc juste de dire, qu indépendam-
ment du contenu même de l'image, sa structure est plus réaliste; 2. qu'elle implique par
conséquent une attitude mentale plus active et même une contribution positive du spectateur à la mise-en-scène . . . ; 3. des deux propositions précédents, d'ordre psychologique,
en découle une troisième qu'on peut qualifier de méta-physique. En analysant la réalité,
le montage supposait, par sa nature même, l'unité de sens de l'événement dramatique.
Sans doute un autre cheminement analytique était possible, mais alors c'eut été un autre film. En somme, le montage s'oppose essentiellement et par nature à l'expression de
d'ambiguïté."

9. "Son ignorance de la technique théâtrale étant moins une condition positivement
nécessaire qu'une garantie contre l'expressionisme du, 'jeu.' Pour de Sica, Bruno était
une silhouette, une visage, une démarche."

10. "La cinéaste belge a construit un opus filmique parmi les plus solides du rare *postmusical* moderne. . . . Pour ponctuer ces drôles de jeux de l'amour en hasard, Chantal
Akerman se sert autant de bruits musicales (marteaux des ouvriers sur les toits de Paris,
sifflement des fuites d'eau, gratouillements incessants des répondeurs téléphoniques). . . .
Et puis, quoi de plus sublime, dans cet esprit de musicalisation, que ces dialogues feutrés
autour du divan."

11. "De là, peut-être, un moyen d'évaluer les œuvres de la modernité: leur valeur vi-
endrait de leur duplicité. Il faut entendre par là qu'elles ont toujours deux bords. Le bord
subversif peut paraître privilégie parce qu'il est celui de la violence qui impressionne le
plaisir; la destruction ne intéresse'intéresse pas; ce qu'il veut, c'est le lieu d'une perte, c'est
la faille, la coupure, la déflation, le *fading* qui sassait le sujet au cœur de la jouissance."

3

Germaine Dulac, Maya Deren, Yvonne Rainer, and Marina Abramovic

Germaine Dulac was born in Amiens, France, in 1882. Raised in Paris, she studied art and music, but she moved into journalism and political activism when, as a young radical feminist, she became editor of *La française,* the premier newspaper of the French suffragist movement. She also served as the film and theater critic for the newspaper and became keenly interested in film. In 1915, she and her husband, the engineer/novelist Marie-Louis Albert-Dulac, formed a production company and began making films. She thus became the second female film director in France, following Alice Guy-Blaché. Her films *La fête espagnole* (1919) and *La souriante Madame Beudet* (1923) established her as a leader in the French impressionist cinema. The latter film, a drama about an unhappy housewife, is often considered the first feminist film. In the later twenties, Dulac's film *La coquille et le clergyman* (1927), a collaboration with Antonin Artaud, established her as a leading figure in the French surrealist film movement. She also began producing influential theoretical writings about film. Her directorial career did not survive the transition to sound, and from 1930 onward she worked in newsreel production. Dulac died in 1942.

Maya Deren, who has become a legendary figure in the world of experimental film, is considered a founding force in the emergence of the avant-garde film movement in New York, beginning in the forties, extending into the following decades, and, according to some estimates, reaching a peak of vibrancy throughout the sixties. Her 1943 film *Meshes of the Afternoon* is considered a seminal work in this tradition and has served as inspiration and model to subsequent generations of experimental filmmakers. Born in Russia in 1917, Maya Deren immigrated to the United States, received her education in Geneva, Switzerland, and at Syracuse University and New York University, and began her career in dance, writing, and filmmaking by accompanying the dancer-choreographer Katherine Dunham on a national tour in the early forties to write a book about dance. In 1942, she met and married the Czech filmmaker Alexander Hammid, who helped her start making films and with whom she relocated to New York, where she became an important figure in avant-garde artistic circles, hosting gatherings of artists, making films, and lecturing and writing about film. She also developed a strong interest in Haitian *vodun*—or voodoo—practices, traveling to Haiti often and eventually publishing what was to become a seminal anthropological study of Haitian *vodun* culture. Mara Deren died at age forty-four after a series of brain hemorrhages.

For biographical information about Yvonne Rainer, see chapter 7 of the present volume.

Among the most prolific, accomplished, challenging, and disturbing of performance artists, Marina Abramovic has also become a key figure in the intersection of performance art, installation work, and video aesthetics. Her work also has significant implications for feminist and psychoanalytic theories, raising new dimensions in ongoing inquiries into the dynamics of the gaze, the body, and the psyche as related to textuality and reception. Abramovic's performance art is well documented and has reached far beyond those who actually have attended her performances at galleries and museums throughout the world. She has produced impressive retrospective volumes and catalogs of individual performances, as well as a number of documentary photographs and videotapes of these events. The most comprehensive of these is the handsome *Marina Abramovic: Artist Body*, a volume that not only traces her performance art, offering descriptions and photo documentation for each performed piece, but includes interviews and essays on her work. Her career divides into three stages: her solo performances from 1969–76 in Yugoslavia; performances with the Dutch performance artist Ulay (1976–88); and her return to solo performances after the breakup of that partnership (1988–98).

MAUREEN TURIM

The Violence of Desire
in Avant-Garde Films

The avant-garde bears witness to the violence of desire. Of course,
one might immediately interject a question: why cite just the avant-garde?
Every western, every film noir, every action film, and every chase scene also
bears witness to the violence of desire. When I speak of an avant-garde bearing witness to desire's violence, I take as the starting point the historical avant-
gardes of dada and surrealism. Something in the way surrealism imaged the
violence mysteriously underlying desire discloses more than we see at first
in the ordered narratives of various genres of realism; retrospectively we see
realism's violence through the frame surrealism offers. A surrealist eye helps
us take another look at the incestuous shoot-outs and triangular confrontations of our realist genres, allowing us to see the schema of their exaggerated
violent structures. For the surrealist eye sees even as it is cut, sees the cut, sees
the violence of the cut, and sees the desire to see in all its violence.

Much of our more recent filmic avant-garde owes its heritage to dada
and surrealism. Certainly central to this heritage is the cut that appears as
emblem in *Un chien Andalou;* the action of a man taking a razor to a woman's eye as a moon slices a cloud joins with the mode of cutting in this film,
and in so doing, performs a surrealist visual poetics: the filmic cut in this
metaphoric construction is as painful as the lesion of a woman's eyeball on
a balcony under the moon. There where romance should be, violence takes
its place. Cutting, moon, shadows, male razor, female as passive object of
the violence: the artist, violently clever in his cutting, establishes a pattern
of gender and of creativity that looms large over the women who might
try to cut in on this avant-garde dance. Later in the film the woman plays a

slightly more active role in exchanges of desire, and androgyny is assigned a role in defining gender.

Still, this key sequence poses the question whether cutting as progenitor of an avant-garde vision is forcibly linked to a male perspective, a certain male ethos to the historical avant-garde. Are women primarily the object of a violent male power play? Consider the scene enacted in the fourth book of Max Ernst's *La semaine de bonté:* the male artist, at best taken self-consciously, depicts through collage the sadistic bird-male impaling on his knife the exposed sole of a naked woman's foot as she floats helplessly and seductively (141). Certainly this image releases violence in the very drawing rooms that should promise bourgeois calm. The representation of the unsettling violent desires seems to need to aim its aggression toward woman, cutting the foot that it might kiss. Each of Ernst's images and each of the books that comprise *La semaine de bonté* is complicated; women throughout Book 2, for example, are associated with dragons and a certain demonic power. Yet some of the most powerful images of the surrealist canon depend on gendered roles that associate men with power and, in a corollary, male fear of women.

The search for alternatives might be addressed in part by recent research examining women in those movements, recovering their oeuvres and their biographies and establishing a comparative analysis of their aims, their desires in art making. Leonor Fini's illustrations for a 1944 edition of De Sade's *Juliette* are in Whitney Chadwick's view "the frank expression of women's sexual power and dominance. Wielding the whip, women become in these drawings an active, bestial presence. The lust that transforms their faces into masks of depravity is manifested in a nervous, charged line that flickers across the page like the tip of a lash" (110). When the "expression of women's sexual power and dominance" also carries connotations of the "bestial" and "depravity," does it color the interpretation of women with the power to cut? Is the whip that cuts in Fini's illustration the appropriation of a male fantasy or the reiteration of male fears? We have in Fini an artist who appropriates the "Sadeian woman," a controversial representation, but one available, as Angela Carter has shown (1978), to feminist interpretations. Is Fini's work etching out a cutting response to the way male artists and writers view female power? Is it using the character de Sade offers as a means of projecting her own fantasies of being able to lash out powerfully with her sexuality? Fini in a 1982 interview could be quite clear theoretically about her argument with male privilege in surrealism: "I was hostile at first because of Breton's Puritanism; also because of the paradoxical misappreciation for the autonomy of woman—characteristic of this movement which pretended to

liberate men" (qtd. in Chadwick 111). Obviously, women artists find themselves struggling to figure out how their own fantasies locate them within the
doctrine of surrealism, where the release of violence and sexuality by male
colleagues seems to precondition if not preclude any parallel outpouring
on their part. Valentine Hugo's *Dream of 21 December 1929* features slender,
somewhat disembodied, batlike claws piercing a woman's cheeks and one
eye; this portrait hovers over a reflecting pool in which a woman seems to
be drowning. Hugo's art imagines surrealistic violence aimed at women,
while the double imaging of woman as portrait and drowning body asks us
to focus on the sacrificial effects of such violence rather than just its force.

Stepping outside surrealism proper to an artist now often assimilated to
that movement, let us consider how Frida Kahlo created compelling images in
which cutting figures as violence to her body. Notably *The Two Fridas* (1939)
shows one of the self-portrait figures holding an operating clamp that binds
the severed, bleeding end of an exposed artery emanating from the open, interconnected hearts of herself and the other self-portrait. This clamp has the
appearance of a pair of scissors, a visual double-entendre linking suturing to
cutting, an issue we will examine shortly. Kahlo's *The Broken Column* (1944)
again portrays the cut of an operation, this time opening the torso to the
spinal column of the self-portrait to reveal a broken Doric column. This cut
is "closed" by a binding apparatus, while sharp nails pierce points of Kahlo's
body and face in a manner that recalls African fetish figures. Biographical
connections allow us to interpret elements in Kahlo's imagery as illustrating her divided identities (Mexican peasant heritage and international Bohemian artist) and her health problem, scoliosis. Biographical explanations,
however, underemphasize the fascination with violence inflicted upon one's
own body, which connects these images. The cut body yields new connections to the mind, to imagination, and to desire. The organic body becomes
a symbolic body, one whose dissection or reduplication through a surgical
binding of difference reveals thoughts and social meanings.

From these examples, we can see that female surrealist artists appropriated violence as auxiliary to and emblematic of their own power. Yet, often
they were unable or unwilling to do so by simply assuming an active role as
cutter. They portray women as she who is cut.

Perhaps the surrealist women enter so early into the historical parries of
gender role transformation that their own fencing must take the form of
violence directed symbolically at representations of their own bodies. Their
strength of expression manifests the cut and its violence, but these women's
stabs at violent expression gain an edge offered by the artists' own suffering,

and even suggest masochism. This desire for pain, or at least the acknowl-edgment of pain as an inevitable route to pleasure, seems self-conscious. Chadwick suggests that this self-inflicted violence is perhaps a necessary correlative of historical circumstances, but one could easily challenge the inevitability inherent in this hypothesis by looking to women artists in other movements and media whose expression adopts a different attitude toward violence. I take this question as a spur to examine how avant-garde films made by women use motifs of violence and cutting.

Consider the depiction of violence and women's desires in a work that anticipates surrealism, one that is relatively contemporaneous with Dada-ism, Germaine Dulac's *La souriante Madame Beudet* (The Smiling Madame Beudet, 1923). As has often been remarked, this film borrows narrative ele-ments from Gustave Flaubert's *Madame Bovary* (1857), as both tell the story of a young wife in the provinces who, bored with and alienated by her bour-geois husband, seeks refuge in solitary reading. The film uses these narrative similarities to highlight its visual strategies of narration, carefully building images into a description of the everyday life of its heroine. It pays great vi-sual attention to subjectivity, creating in montage a character portrait sensi-tive to the inner life of a woman with aspirations to high culture belittled by her crude-mannered husband. Unlike Flaubert's heroine, Madame Beudet chooses neither affairs nor suicide; instead she becomes obsessed with a vio-lent fantasy of murdering her husband by putting a bullet into the normally unloaded revolver he uses as part of a running joke in which he pretends to commit suicide. Dulac focuses on Madame Beudet's subjective memories of her husband's behavior. Images rendering his boorish games and belittling, offensive displays penetrate her solitude. The evolution of her reaction into a violent revenge fantasy relieves her boredom and passivity. Her dream of life beyond the provincial blocked, she develops an elaborate and violent inner life. As a female protagonist who entertains a desire that translates as violence, Madame Beudet possesses a sensitivity that seems to motivate the associative and freely impressionistic cutting of the film. Still, her desire to murder remains unrealized; first she reacts in terror when her husband reiterates his joke suicide ritual with the gun she has loaded, and then her husband fires the gun at her instead of himself, acting out his antagonism to her as yet another joke. When he misses her but shatters a vase on the mantel behind her, he assumes that she loaded the gun while contemplating her own suicide. His mistaken assumption leads him to comfort her and pledge that he couldn't live without her. Dulac ends the film with the reinstatement of the couple and the perpetuation of calm (and boredom) in this provincial marriage, iterated by a shot of the provincial street devoid of activity. It is useful to compare Dulac's montage of subjective violence to the powerful montage of actualized violent desires in Dimitri Kirsanov's *Menilmontant* (1924–25).

Menilmontant constitutes a forceful avant-garde recutting of the melodrama. Cuts are central. Violence is visceral. Montage offers a means of representing the interiority of the female protagonists, as we see psyches slashed by the blows of antagonistic and cruel worlds responding to that psychic hurt with violent desires. In a final revenge murder, Kirsanov links through montage a woman's shoe thrust forward and a knife she thrusts. The film thus not only connects violence to the feminine, but does so in a particular context in which women found themselves in Paris in the 1920s. Displaced from the countryside, alone in the city, drawn into its factories and placed in a context of unstable flirtations, the young female worker seems to be challenged by modernity itself. The displacement of revenge here is in many ways comparable to the renunciation of revenge in Dulac's *The Smiling Madame Beudet*. Motivations for violence are presented sympathetically, while the sisters in Kirsanov's film and the wife in Dulac's are removed from the ethical consequences of their murderous desires.

The fantasy structure of the editing plays a similar role in Maya Deren's *Meshes of the Afternoon* (1946). This most famous of avant-garde films abounds in violent imagery. Knives, the shattered mirror face, and the mermaid suicide provide direct representation of violent fantasies, and the power of Deren's editing is connected to the violence of her desires. Consider the context of this violent fantasy.

Deren's images of violence are within what I have described elsewhere as a fantasy riddled with parapraxis. Parapraxis, the psychoanalytic term for the traces of failed actions, governs numerous events in the film: a key falls down the front stairs of the house, beyond the reach of a hand; a phone is found off the hook; a record player is turning relentlessly beyond the borders of its inscribed musical information; a knife falls from where it is precariously poised on a loaf of bread. The "failed action" fails because of an unexpressed desire or conflict. Yet if we trace the knife imagery we see that after it falls seemingly by its own animation from the bread, it returns to unite the multiplied self of the female protagonist (played by Deren herself) in a ritual form of trial by fire. Each manifestation of the self is presented in succession with a key resting on her outstretched hand, and that key, for the first three bearers, flips its position to rest on the table, retaining its form as a key. In the hand of the fourth self, however, the key turns into the knife now resting on a darkened palm. This knife is then carried by the female protagonist across jump cuts that link disparate landscapes, its sharp edge held ominously pointed down while the hand remains poised to stab at something. The stab is later actualized when the woman mounts the stairs of her bungalow (in a series of cuts that displace action and its temporality, rendering it syncopated and open to inversions) following the man, who has entered the house and has awakened her sleeping self on the chair. Once she lies down on the bed, he first caresses her with his hand and then is shown, in the shot/reverse editing, looking at her. His face transforms into that of the mirror-faced figure, which previously had loomed just beyond her reach when she climbed the pathway to the house. Her knife shatters this mirror face. This cedes to a filmic cut that shows the shards of the mirror landing at the edge of the sea. The shards are then linked through a cut to an image of a beached mermaid, which takes the form of the protagonist once again shown seated in the living room armchair draped with seaweed, seemingly dead. If earlier, a kiss from the man cuts to the woman's revival, in an ironic reversal of her earlier stabbing at (as opposed to kissing) his face, finally, the accrual of violent desires seems to foreclose the fairy tale reawakening. Deren's violence and embrace of the unexpected in fantasy are elements that link her work to surrealism, and like that movement, she famously argues against psychoanalytic decipherment. What seems to bother her is a one-to-one matching of interpretation with images that can account neither for transformative energies nor structure. Instead, as in surrealism, Deren creatively mobilizes elements of the dream to unleash the power of the unconscious, illustrating its violence through filmic cutting.

Deren takes a different perspective on violence and cutting in *Meditations on Violence* (1948). Here she explores a dialectic between interior and exterior forms of response to aggression characterized respectively by wutang and shaolin Chinese martial arts. The wutang opening uses a fluid camera with few cuts to follow the flow of meditative movements of breath and body. The aim of wutang becomes to absorb and counteract the other's violence through a refocusing of that energy. With its emphasis on interiorization aimed at turning aggression around against itself, wutang is an active defense, one that elegantly pushes through a multiplanar space with the force of continual motion, folding and unfolding from a balanced center. A flute accompanies these arabesque-like gestures of restructuring balance and position in an endless chain of gestures. The movement toward shaolin then is gradually introduced by shifts in background; from a soft white surface reflecting gentle twin gray shadows of the movements, the background changes to a corner space where walls of sharply contrasting black and white meet a triangular floor. At the same time the music becomes percussive and the montage becomes more abrupt. At the center of the film, the shaolin reaches its full aggressive energy as the cutting becomes more rapid, fragmenting the figure's movements rather than following their flow. His thrusts into space take various directions but most forcefully toward the camera. A section of sword shaolin augments the aggression as the performer, in costume, now wields a large, curved sword. His actions are set against an exterior stonewall overlooking a vast countryside.

From this most aggressive point, the film works back toward wutang. The motion is reversed. Deren's own diagrams of the film (*Anagram* 21–22) emulate a swordlike shape to chronicle the parabolic structure of the film's flow and return. Each of the three diagrams she prepared marks out changes in performance, music, and camerawork. Her writing traces how this structure describes a meditative process in itself. The viewer moves toward the attraction of violent action, marked at its pinnacle by silence, and then lets it flow past; thus the first half of the film echoes itself in reversal. This mimics the "letting go" or out-breath of meditation, the release. There is of course a feminine and masculine polarity that can be read into the film's structuring oppositions. The wutang, with its naked torso and undulating movements that evoke a feminine grace, contrasts with the shaolin warrior costume and sword that evoke a traditionally more masculine sphere. Yet there is gender fluidity in both forms. This film offers another variant of how women cut films to work through violence; it demonstrates a woman filmmaker's willingness to embrace Eastern traditions that explore the interiorization and remobilization of violence for a dynamic defense. Yet even here the film recognizes the place of violence and exteriorized aggression as a place one may need to reach. What Deren's structure suggests is that such extreme violence should not be sustained or fetishized. Rather the flow beyond its assertion and the return from its extension become crucial to its occasional deployment. Knowing how to move beyond and recover from its attraction and force reestablishes stability and equilibrium. For Deren the attraction to surrealism and to violence is mitigated by her knowledge of the healing rituals of non-Western cultures. *Meditations on Violence* responds to the expression of violent desires in *Meshes of the Afternoon* by suggesting that meditation may help us master expression, to create new and different forms.

Another one of surrealism's heirs (though not an heir to surrealism alone), Abigail Child creates images that evoke avant-garde films of the 1920s, as well as the desires that violently lace Deren's *Meshes*. Her film *Mayhem* (1987) and her prose poem "A Motive for Mayhem" cut deeply and powerfully into the issues surrounding the representation of women. The cuts that her cinema brings to imagery and sound pose sharply drawn questions. The very title *Mayhem* historically meant mutilation of the body, though the more common "wreaking havoc" or "creating disorder" still retains the notion of a violent dispersal. *Mayhem* strews the shards of a broken order into a new configuration. Certainly Child's cutting strives to maximize our appreciation of disorderly conduct, giving us playful gestures in odd retakes on film history intercut with found footage. She emphasizes the display of the female body and the edge of danger that seems to emanate from or be assigned to such display.

Mayhem divides into sections of montage intervals, which can be illuminated by theories of the intervallic structure as a paradigmatic relationship between elements as defined by the writings and exemplified in the work of Sergei Eisenstein and Dziga Vertov. Annette Michelson discusses the differences between the two theorist filmmakers' use of the term "interval," associating Eisenstein with a musical impetus influenced by Scriabin, and Vertov with a mathematical impetus influenced by calculus and relativity. Both derivations emphasize an abstract patterning of visual elements. These elements interweave as visual motifs and correlations between movements. Intervallic structuring highlights elements other than dominant action and logical sequence of movement and event. Space and event are restructured in time, subject to forces of repetition and variation. These montage intervals can roughly approximate narrative developments, such as the procession sequence in Eisenstein's *The Old and the New,* or they can cut into an action, such as the athletic sequences in Vertov's *Man with a Movie Camera,* rendering a dive as the temporally reorganized total of its movements no longer presented in measured, linear sequence.

Mayhem seems roughly to approximate narrative developments in its intervallic structure, but it conveys them through a paradigmatic choice of elements that disperses the narrative event into restructured, virtual fragments. In part this is accomplished through the film's mixture of stylistic references: shots referring to Hollywood films of the teens are cut with shots evoking the avant-garde of the twenties on one hand, and traces of forties noir on the other. Diverse elements of film history are replayed through scenes set in Soho and the Lower East Side in New York, then cut as intervals roughly corresponding to narrative categories. These types of narrative sequences remain overtonal here, rather than forming a dominant. Action supplies a ground against which coloristic elements are articulated, such as the graphic matching of glances or a particular element of composition. We can segment the film into the five categories of action that provide the ground for the film's montage:

1. Interrogation—men gazing, linked to polka-dot-wearing, venetian-blind-shadowed woman;
2. Escape/chase/street scenes—some images are quite reminiscent of street chases in *Menilmontant* and *Meshes of the Afternoon;*
3. Stairway/interior scenes;
4. Seduction, sexual couplings, and bondage scenes;
5. Negative images of a nightclub, individuals in formal dress, and dancing.

The seduction, sexual couplings, and bondage scenes can be further delineated into three separate series of images:

1. Telephoning woman—reiteration of an image in which a woman places a phone between her spread legs to make a call, with each repetition beginning and ending at slightly different points in the action and including different angles on the action;
2. Woman sprawled on bed;
3. Sexual couplings—including threesomes and then a lesbian seduction in Japanese costume that seems to be drawn from a porno film, cut with jocular images of a cat burglar voyeur.

Throughout these visually delineated sequences organized on narrative themes, an active, independent sound montage further cuts into the images. A combination of "improvised" sound and sampling from different musical traditions, the sound track variously underscores and highlights, mocks or interrupts. In all these functions the sound augments the violence of desire the film expresses. Edgy, sharp, ironic, the sound urges us into the dance of bodies, no matter how bound they are to the fetishes of a tradition of representation. If ropes tie flesh, how does that differ from the stretched cord of a telephone dancing between the long legs of a troubled woman? The film draws its fetishes comparatively, cutting them together to ask why these images draw us in despite their displacement. Spunky and energized, the film uses violence to fuel its rhythms. The humor found in each element—in the recombined found footage, in the staged footage, in the cuts—allows us to be aware that the onslaught of imagery, its pace and density, forms part of the furious fun. Such effects of montage are never more evident than when Latin rhythms underscore sexual activities; the deliberate excess of such emphatic musical commentary adds a humorous irony. Verbal articulations, left fragmentary and detached from any source in the action, often correspond to gestures in ironic ways. A voice poses such questions as "Why do you ask?" which floats over the interrogation scene, and "Do you want me to be more violent?" which comes in the midst of the seduction and bondage images. A scream of terror marks a rhythmic climax, without the simple logic of causality that one associates with the scream on a sound track. Denaturalized from any incipient cause, the scream that heralds an unseen mayhem here is generalized, hovering over the cuts this film makes in narrative consequence.

Stripes and dots that adorn the clothing of various characters form graphic oppositions and matches. Through these graphic flourishes the film develops a style that borrows from both European avant-garde films of the twenties and film noir. They are part of an overall compositional style that unifies the fragmentary footage and integrates found footage with newly acted footage, in much the same way that Child's earlier film *Perils* (1986) blended the aesthetics of American silent film into her restagings. Toward the end of *Mayhem*, we suspect that the genesis of this film may in fact lie in the found footage of pornography. The Japanese-styled lesbian encounter seems to be crosscut with a cat burglar sequence from another film. Yet once the cat burglar voyeur enters the scene of the lesbians, what crosscutting made seem a collage effect was actually a narrative development. The pornographic vignette ends in a joke as the burglar intervenes, becoming the male sex partner to the women. Breaking the contact between the women, the burglar seems to seal heterosexuality securely in place, but as film, *Mayhem* has already thoroughly undercut any such resolution. The women chasing, telephoning, stretching out on a bed, or engaging in sex become, like the dots and stripes, compositional elements that connect across the cuts, transforming the found footage into a collage representation of women's energetic movement across the history of film.

One is reminded here of the "portraits, dancers, and coquettes" that Maud Lavin analyzes in *Cut with the Kitchen Knife: The Weimar Photomontages of Hannah Höch.* In particular, Höch's *Deutches Mädchen* (1930) displays the mismatched features of the German woman, her eyes too small and of different sizes, while hair borrowed from a black-and-white portrait of a Geisha slips down toward her nose across her forehead. Lavin takes the title of her study of Höch from another of Höch's photomontages, *Cut with the Kitchen Knife,* which also speaks to issues of female artistic violence in their social context. The full title of the work is *Schnitt mit dem Kuchenmesser Dada durch die letzte weimarer Birbauchkulturepoche Deutschlandes* (Cut with the

Kitchen Knife Dada through the Last Weimar Beer Belly Cultural Epoque of Germany), giving the full measure of how cuts work as social protest. Of the photomontage's positioning of women Lavin says:

> The centrifugal composition rotates around a cut-out photograph of the body of the popular dancer "Niddy" Impekoven. Headless, she pirouettes below the tilted head of Käthe Kollwitz that has been pierced by a spear. In the Dada world section of the montage, three other female faces appear: Niddy Impekoven again (bathing John Heartfield), the dancer Pola Negri, and Hannah Höch herself. Höch's face appears in the lower right corner, in what is commonly the signature area, abutting a map of Europe showing the progress of Women's enfranchisement. The bodies of female athletes and dancers punctuate this section; for example, the heads of George Grosz and Wilheim Herzfelde are attached to a ballerina's body. By their professions, movements and locations in the montage, the women represented are strongly and positively associated with Dada and the new. (22)

Höch cuts images of culture with a kitchen knife to rearrange them as statements on the role of women within a politically contestatory art movement. She thus forcefully projects the violence of her reaction to disenfranchisement and the strength of her conviction in the necessity of change. Although all collage inevitably evinces associations with cutting, Höch's direct verbal reference in her phrase "cut with a kitchen knife," as well as her play with decapitations and rearrangements of heads with different bodies, provides powerful metaphoric associations with cutting. Use of such metaphors are vital to understanding the energy of many avant-garde works by women.

Höch's exemplary collage praxes can help expand interpretations of another of Child's films, *Covert Action*. The film's images are taken primarily from home movie footage that one eventually understands as the chronicles two men made of their amorous encounters with various women at a vacation house. Mainly the personages are seen cavorting in the backyard, but there are also a number of close-ups, many of them shots of kisses. Child fragments the shots to an extreme—some are only a few frames long—then systematically repeats, varies, and interweaves them, matching or contrasting the motion or graphic dominants involved. As in *Mayhem*, the frenzied pace is augmented by an autonomous and equally rapid sound track montage of musical clips, conversational fragments, random phrases, and periodic announcements.

Once an image fragment is introduced, it is submitted to variations such as a flipping of the frame from left to right, which inverts the graphic elements of the image. Thus a close-up of a woman turning left will be followed by the same shot with the direction of the movement inverted, in a manner that recalls the interval montage of Fernand Léger's *Ballet mécanique*. However, unlike the topically or spatially oriented series in *Ballet mécanique*, devoted to object types or actions, each series here is even more pronouncedly determined by kinetic or graphic patterns. In *Covert Action*, shots migrate into new montage contexts, becoming a part of many different heterogeneously ordered series.

Over the course of a screening, one begins to recognize the shots through their repetitions. One begins to know the image of a woman in the cloche and distinguish it from the woman in the fedora, or the one in the bandana from the young girl in the Eskimo jacket. The images gradually accrue, acquiring referential weight, and we can reconstruct the individual women or the events of each visit. Thus a walk by a stream, acrobatics on a lawn, a game of leap-frog, drinks by the beehive, or an embrace on a wicker chair become events through the sum of their fragmented parts, dispersed throughout the body of the film. Women's faces and their bodies dominate the imagery, creating a swirl of sensuality, of performance for the camera, alternately self-aware or captured in unsuspecting innocence. This ambiguity of the means through which these images were taken (complicity or naïve abandon) adds to the violence built by graphic contrasts and fast pace. The sounds, especially the screams and screeches, accentuate this violence. Intertitles such as "He had to be eliminated" / "She had to be bitten" comment upon this violence, as do even more metacritical titles, "Ending with a rupture of the hypnosis," and "My goal is to disarm my movie."

Found footage of a different sort also circulates through the film, including fragments of documentary footage such as a hula dance, a waterfall, a tree being uprooted, Chinese junks in a harbor, a masquerade ball, and a bathing suit competition. Reminiscent of the documentary views produced by early cinema, such as the Lumière brothers' films, even this is presented metacritically through the inclusion of an image cabinet displayed as an attraction on a sidewalk by a Chinese showman. A tracking shot allows us to appreciate this popular entertainment as a form of paracinematic sculpture. Similarly, a whirling merry-go-round forms a visual metaphor for the montage of this film.

Like Höch, Child places her fragmented women in the context of machinery and the social circulation of signs, deriving an energy from them even as she places them as ciphers within a kinetic puzzle. Yet the social references here are far more attenuated than in Höch, though Child's later *Mercy* (1989), which takes its found footage primarily from the consumerist world of the fifties in conjunction with images of science and technology, more closely resembles Höch's concern with a larger economic context. *Covert Action* is composed of frenetic gestures, repeated for our scrutiny. Its repetition and deconstruction reveals the gestural, without fixing a commentary on what it shows of gestures. Spying is ambiguously inscribed in its title. Are we, as spectators, spies, or are we analysts of the otherwise hidden elements of the social *geste?* What do we feel about these women as elements of a double spectacle, both the one constituted by the home movie and the one reconstituted by the deconstructive montage of this film? Seeing Child's work in relationship to earlier dada and surrealist works by women helps illuminate a dynamic in which the voyeurism and brutality of past representations may be turned around by women artists. This inversion and appropriation may combine with the release of the artist's own fantasies and allow those fantasies to surface.

Such art images can be linked to what has been called the "graphic nonverbal message of cutting," where the cutting in question is not that of film, but directly of the flesh: self-mutilation (Egan). Recently, medical researchers have explored this psychological syndrome independently of the rubric of female masochism to which it earlier was subsumed (Hewitt; Levenkron; Strong). Investigation of self-mutilation often complements and overlaps research on eating disorders. Both syndromes, current research suggests, start with an effect on the body. Sometimes researchers fail to see these effects as symptoms of a larger psychoanalytical configuration. The body is material and concrete; research in social science and cultural studies explores the body as its access to the psyche in a manner parallel to the activities of cutters, anorexics, and bulimics themselves. Still, the cuts on a suffering body evoke testimony from the cutters in numerous studies of the syndromes. I wish to look at how the "graphic non-verbal message of cutting," explained by a cutter's verbal testimony, might be useful to analysis of artworks that associate the cut with power and sexuality.

The testimony of two women cutters resonates:

> I had so much anxiety, I couldn't concentrate on anything until I somehow let that out, and not being able to let it out in words, I took the razor and started cutting my leg and I got excited about seeing my blood. It felt good to see the blood coming out, like that was my other pain leaving, too. It felt right and it felt good for me to let it out that way. (Egan 21)

I can look at different scars and think, yeah, I know when that happened, so it tells a story. I'm afraid of them fading. (Egan 24)

The second cutter speaks to the narrative function of cutting, lauding its symbolic function in creating a personal memoir of her anguished history. If the reference here to a clinical disorder might seem too strained a connection to creative art, collage, and filmmaking, we can see a more direct connection between this cutting and the masochism of performance art. Unlike film, which provides representational distance and the filmic object to cut, performance art takes as its object the body of the performer and the relationship of that body to the audience. There is a pronounced connection between pathological cutting and the masochistic rituals of performance art in the works of Marina Abramovic, which as we shall see have their own choreography for the camera. The acts of ritual violence and self-sacrifice, coupled with a studied performance of eating as ritual, figure prominently in Abramovic's 1975 two-hour performance *Thomas Lips* for the Krinzinger Gallery, Innsbruck. Here is the artist's description: "I slowly eat 1 kilo of honey with a silver spoon. I slowly drink 1 liter of red wine out of a crystal glass. I break the glass with my right hand. I cut a five-pointed star on my stomach with a razor blade. I violently whip myself until I no longer feel any pain. I lay down on a cross made of ice blocks. The heat of a suspended heater pointed at my stomach causes the cut star to bleed. The rest of my body begins to freeze. I remain on the ice cross for 30 minutes until the public interrupts the piece by removing the ice blocks from underneath me" (Abramovic et al. 98). Collaging obsessive eating and self-flagellation with self-mutilation, *Thomas Lips* sets up a comparison among these acts. Abramovic's female body gives particular inflection to the food obsessions and masochistic aspects of these works. We might choose one of two explanations for the accumulation across these works of torturous acts in which the self subjects its body to pain. One explanation lies in shamanistic ritual and transcendence of the body, derived from religious practices.

Another explanation lies in a historically based psychoanalytic theory: subjects perform such rituals to act out unconscious desires that they can't express otherwise. Abramovic's performances are conscious designs, but their unconscious motivations and their meanings when interpreted psychoanalytically often receive less attention than they might were it not for the philosophical and religious explanations that dominate the artist's discourse and from which the critical response takes its cue. Yet these performances alternate between the desire to control (note the minimalist precision in her scripts for the performances) and the desire to submit (once committed to the script, she endures the fate that she has planned). Pain here is clearly eroticized, presented in its discrete penetrations on a nude body. The star covers the region of the womb, substituting itself for caesarean surgery. The woman mutilates the expanse of flesh between breasts and vagina—that flesh most connected to breath, birth, life.

Here we might consider how masochism is often misconstrued as direct pleasure from pain, rather than as a complex desire for pain. Although Abramovic's performances differ from the pornographic staging of masochism for immediate sexual gratification, they place before an audience the accomplishment of pain as something staged for interpretation and appreciation. Her performances with her collaborator Ulay trace the heterosexual union through displaced acts in which bodies remain detached, often separated in space, even as they strike out at one another or until they collide. Despite the tension of violence, given the couple through which desire may be displaced, the performances are less violent and less about pain than are Abramovic's solo works before or after collaboration with Ulay. Yet the tension is often graphic, as in *Rest Energy* (1979), in which each artist holds on to a bow with an arrow pointed at Abramovic's heart for four minutes and ten seconds, as microphones amplify their heartbeats. In her more recent video installations, *Luminosity, Insomnia,* and *Dissolution,* all from a 1997 work entitled *Spirit House,* Abramovic frames three quite distinct performances that she choreographs for the camera. In each, a single activity is held in view, so that we might witness it as ritual. Disturbing images projected as a nexus of performance art and video installation art, Marina Abramovic's three "stations" (as she calls these works) offer a perspective on eroticism, pain, and self-inflicted violence. The artist's body, often central in Abramovic's work, becomes a site for scrutinizing what we might call "a limit," while the artist reconceives her relationship to us, her witnesses.

In *Luminosity* the artist, nude, balances painfully on a bicycle seat attached to a pedestal apparatus. The image is bathed in a changing light and framed centrally in a deliberately minimalist aesthetic. The play with light on the body connects this work to *Insomnia,* in which the artist dances solo, a slow, introspective tango (popular historically in Europe), here in a Tunisian tango rendition; she is dressed in the black lace dress and heels traditionally associated with the Latin dance. Finally in *Dissolution,* the artist, framed with her bare back to the camera, whips herself repeatedly; only in this piece does the camera move, to explore the flesh after the flogging. These are powerful images, potentially frightening images. Abramovic performs and records rituals that beg us to question our witnessing.

Why do we watch? What gaze are these images meant to evoke or to discomfit? What is the aesthetic of composition, display, duration, and transformation implied in these works as installations? We begin to answer these questions by seeing these works as coupling the spectator solicitation and the manipulation of duration characteristic of performance art, while annexing to this the aesthetics of representational form that installation work affords. Abramovic brings to these art forms a social, historical context in which her biography and her engagement with history speak through the acts presented. Her desire to build on her corpus of works and on their relationship to other performance art is another key to understanding these "stations." Her works evoke psychoanalytical and anthropological elements; as shaman, she mediates through ritual a community's violence, sexuality, and willingness to endure. Abramovic's works explore the body in pain and the body as a source of pleasure, the body tested, the limit approached. If we can support their intensity, it is to learn how much they have, despite their deceptive simplicity, to tell us about the history of art.

Performance art tends to provoke controversy and uneasiness as the artist's body becomes her element of signification, emotional expression, and confrontation. True performance art is live, staged with an audience, and perhaps documented. Marina Abramovic built her early career on just such performance events. One that resonates with the work discussed here, especially in its division into two parts and its witnessing through video recording, is a performance for nude body and ventilator fan entitled *Rhythm 4*, a forty-five-minute work for the Galleria Diagramma in Milan (1974). Abramovic describes the performance in space A: "I slowly approach the air blower, taking air in as much as possible. Just above the opening of the blower I lose consciousness because of the extreme pressure. But this does not interrupt the performance. After falling over sideways the blower continues to change and move my face." Space B is the space of witnessing: "The video camera is only focused on my face without showing the blower. The public looking at the monitor has the impression of my being under water. The moment I lose consciousness the performance lasts 3 more minutes, during which the public is unaware of my state. In the performance I succeed in using my body in and out of consciousness without any interruption" (Abramovic et al. 76). Separation of the performance from its viewing through a framed representation creates a mystery: the unconsciousness of the performer is seen yet unrecognized. Both aspects of the performance are, however, documented in photographs, as is the tradition in much performance art, which, along with descriptions, becomes a third way of experiencing the art event.

Ironically, Abramovic cuts and enacts violence on her body while the image offered as installation proceeds in continuity, without cutting. Yet even without editing cuts, collage occurs. Actions are collaged as subsets of performances or they become separate installations meant to be viewed one in the shadow memory of the other. In many works the artist submits her body to violence, willfully enregistering her power to sustain her self through this submission and playing out a complex relationship to her audience.

In considering films that themselves stage elements of performance art, we might see in the works of Yvonne Rainer a response to the sorts of displays of violence that inform the work of Abramovic. In MURDER and murder surgical cutting, the removal of breast tissue as part of a cancer treatment, is revealed when the narrator, the ringmaster figure of the filmmaker herself, faces the camera to expose flesh and scar. Here the body has been cut, and the direct frontal view holds out a performance that through its presentation of and demand for acceptance understands this act not in its violence but in its healing.

This scene resonates with a scene in Rainer's *Film about a Woman Who . . . .* The capitalization in the title MURDER and murder, of course, suggests levels of rage and violence, differences in degrees of misfortune on one hand (as in the figurative slang, "it was murder to experience X") and crime on the other hand (justified homicide, mercy killing, manslaughter, third to first degree). Comedians murder an audience, and our filmmaker has several compassionate jokes up her sleeve in this latest collage of vignettes and images expressing lesbian love as fruition, and aging as an accumulation of strength, irony, and a critical eye, tools for survival. Yet one might take murder as an intertextual reference to a scene in Rainer's *Film about a Woman Who . . .* in which a woman named R is described as having come to understand murderous desires. The prelude to this development begins with a close-up of R's lover, D, looking at the camera as he says, "Because she has younger-looking breasts than you . . . because she has younger-looking breasts than you." A medium long shot follows of R dressing in slow motion with D's voice-over, "I'll leave. I don't want you to go down there alone at this time of night." Then Y's voice: "Propelled by an avalanche of rage, her limbs catapulted her body into her clothing. She hardly knew what she was doing, and when her voice came out, it surprised her." R is seen in close-up as she says, "You're not moving fast enough." Y's voice continues her narration: "He lost no further time and bolted out the door. Then she became aware of her heartbeat. When it had settled down she thought that she had never been that angry in her whole life. She thought she knew how someone could murder."

This short segment of a domestic squabble is defamiliarized by cutting to the minimal heart of the dialogue, paring down the action, and supplying, through the novelistic narrator's voice, the interiority film normally demonstrates through externalized action or dialogue. Women's anger and suppressed violence leads to an escalating tension of which the scene in its totality is the emblem. The repeated "because she has younger-looking breasts than you" is the *unsaid,* put in the voice of the male tormentor, a weapon he might unconsciously wield. Having him voice what would have remained unsaid turns this enunciation into the mark of his shallowness. The unlikely enunciation becomes an author's weapon against her character.

Using the scene from the earlier Rainer film to underscore the resonance of the scar-baring scene in MURDER *and murder,* the wounds of the past, associated with an unfeeling heterosexuality, are healed in a lesbian present. Body parts are seen differently, adjusted to the measure of the history they have lived, indeed bearing in their form or their absence a story more important than youthful perfection. Piecing together scenes in montage becomes a way to narrate this history. If healing collages of stories fill the gap that the image of surgery opens, if history sutures the body, allowing compensation for its deficits, we might see another strategy of cutting appearing in the art of women. Here the inspiration is healing the cuts of the past, finding ways to acknowledge a power that comes not so much from lashing back as piecing together. Let me emphasize that I am not privileging films of healing over films that express raw cuts or lash out; rather I see all these symbolic acts of filmic cutting as elements of a process. We need to beware as well that one can assume the role of self-healer preemptively, or as merely the extension of self-mutilation, as in this assessment of one of the bodily cutters whose syndrome included masking her cutting activities: "She had a successful career as a sales executive at a medical-supply company, whose wares she frequently used to suture and bandage her self-inflicted wounds" (Egan 24).

Two films by Su Friedrich exemplify how the suturing of wounds may necessitate their reopening. Friedrich's film *Sink or Swim* looks at the wounds caused by her father, while *The Ties that Bind* examines her mother's life not only for the wounds her father initiated, but for other wounds as well. Love and identification with father and mother permeate the films, yet Friedrich struggles with her anger and pain toward each parent. Her montage of voice and image seeks to explore the cutting moments of abandonment that left wounds.

Given this subject, the films' cutting of footage is all the more striking, for Friedrich brings to each enunciation a specific visual association as she establishes the formal rhythms of an artwork. *Sink or Swim* divides into short segments, each given an abstract label: Zygote, YChromosome, XChromosome, Witness, Virginity, Utopia, Temptation, Seduction, Realism, Quicksand, Pedagogy, Oblivion, Nature, Memory, Loss, Kinship, Journalism, Insanity, Homework, Ghosts, Flesh, Envy, Discovery, Competition, Bigamy, and finally, a section titled after a mythological triumvirate: Athena, Atalanta, Aphrodite. In this charged list some terms are more directly related to the voiced narrative than others, just as some of the images selected are more associated with certain passages than others.

The junctures formed by these loose but provocative associations underscore the construction of the oral history along associative lines. The father's poetry, both his actual verse and his anthropological investigations, resonate with revelations of his unconscious, which the daughter reads by associating them with suggestive images and abstract labels. The daughter types out her reminiscences, striking them on a mechanical typewriter first seen in close-up as a negative image in the "Ghost" section. Here she types a letter to "Dad," describing her mother's ritualistic listening to the Schubert lied "Gretchen at the Spinning Wheel." The typewriter returns in the "Bigamy" section, this time in positive as the daughter writes the very reminiscences we hear voiced, describing the young narrator watching her father with her younger half-sister from his second marriage, realizing that this young girl was the same age as she had been when her father left. Violence emanates from the loose associations that bind these images and words. "Temptation" defines a segment in which the narrator remembers reading the story of Atalanta to her father: a daughter whose pact with her father had allowed her to avoid marriage by outracing her suitors, until she loses to a suitor who throws golden apples in her path to distract her. Atalanta succumbs to temptation, as does Eve, drawn to an apple. The snake that offers Eve's apple in the daughter's diaries finds displaced figuration in the water-moccasin motif; the daughter tells of fearing water moccasins in a northeastern lake after hearing of their danger from her father, even when she learns from her mother that they don't inhabit this region. Later, she tells how her father barely missed encountering water moccasins when he nearly went swimming in an infested lake in the Midwest.

Such narrative displacements are typical of the film's structure, introducing fragments of imagery or concepts that reemerge later, unexpectedly. These displacements follow a dream logic, as does the film's sexual undercurrents, its swiftly flowing sweep of desire and fear. The pose-downs of female body builders accompanies the daughter's telling us she was caught in the closet reading her Greek mythology book late into the night. As the closet is a refuge for reading the Atalanta story, the story of a young girl hoping to prove herself "good as a man," the muscled goddesses whose bodies statuesquely fill the image track seem to enforce this pun. They charge the challenge of the virgin with a lesbian resistance to heterosexuality. Yet in the next section, "Seduction," a lion tamer subdues his cats as the Atalanta story continues to relate her deep romantic attachment to the victorious suitor, which enrages Aphrodite, forgotten by the newlyweds, who turns them into lions for failing their duty to her. If stories are cut from the context of purely illustrative images, to be joined with displaced associations, the film also weaves the threads back together, asking us to link the meanings across diverse signifying material.

Friedrich is as concerned with this weaving and binding, this bringing back together, this suturing of the gaps and the wounds as she is with exposing the violence of the cuts to the psyche. Thus *The Ties that Bind* cuts both to and through her mother's voice-over reminiscences of childhood and adolescence in Nazi Germany, as well as her narrative of divorce and single motherhood, asking questions represented on the sound track by etched, jagged writing scratched into the film emulsion. If cutting ties might be a reaction to a too-close bonding enforced by the mother, recognition of the bind may also constitute an acceptance of the tie. This interview film then uses its film images and cutting as visual counterpoints to the tension between cutting ties and enforcing them, between potential rejections or renewed attraction to the mother's stories. Again the female body—the mother, swimming and sitting—figures in the image, providing a space through which to listen. If so many of the women artists and filmmakers I have discussed here metaphorically cut their bodies, or show the cuts on women's flesh, or lash out to cut, this attention to the violence of the cut is never without the request for healing suture. Friedrich's films pose the need for such healing, even as the last image in *Sink or Swim* offers an image of a young girl in long shot, waving good-bye, ambiguously; she might be abandoned, or she might be taking charge of her departure.

Women's art clearly grows richer by its willingness to represent violence rather than avoid it. Women bring the avant-garde's preoccupations with violence the unique metaphors of their bodies. They write on their filmic, performative, or tableau bodies by cutting through to a specific anger and a corollary need to heal.

4

Nina Menkes

Since her first film (*The Great Sadness of Zohara*, 1983) as a UCLA student, Nina Menkes, in collaboration with her sister, Tinka Menkes, has been making challenging independent films that have attracted international acclaim on film festival circuits and in theaters. Her first feature-length film, *Magdalena Viraga* (1986), won the Los Angeles Film Critics Association Award for best independent film of the year and was later featured in the Whitney Museum of Art's Biennial. Her next feature, *Queen of Diamonds*, premiered at Sundance in 1991 and won wide international critical acclaim. *The Bloody Child* (1996), which also debuted at Sundance, garnered even more praise, receiving glowing attention from *Variety, Film Threat, Artforum, Cahiers du cinéma, Filmmaker Magazine, American Cinematographer,* the *Los Angeles Times,* and the *Chicago Tribune.* Menkes's films have been shown in numerous international film festivals including Toronto, the Viennale, Rotterdam, Locarno, and London, as well as at the Cinémathèque Française, the British Film Institute, the Beijing Film Academy, the Walker Art Center, the American Museum of the Moving Image, the Carnegie Museum of Art, the Whitney Museum of Art, and the Museum of Modern Art in New York City. The Los Angeles Film Forum and Berlin's Arsenal Theater have already held Menkes retrospectives.

Menkes, who prides herself on being "the only woman alive who produces, directs, and shoots her own 35 mm features" (*Bloody Child* press kit) maintains creative control over her work by funding it through such sources as a Guggenheim Fellowship, National Endowment for the Arts grants, an Annenberg Foundation grant, an AFI Independent Filmmaker Award, and a Fulbright. She travels extensively in the Middle East and Africa, shooting on location and gathering footage for later use. Working closely with her sister, Tinka, who acts in all her films, Nina Menkes uses filmmaking as a political and spiritual practice—a direct intervention into discourses and events she considers socially destructive. By choosing production strategies that allow her to maintain complete creative control, Menkes has developed into an auteur for whom filmmaking remains as intensely personal as it is political.

JEAN PETROLLE

Allegory, Politics,
and the Avant-Garde

Allegory seems regularly to surface in
critical or polemical atmospheres, when
for political or metaphysical reasons there
is something that cannot be said.

—Joel Fineman

Marxist cultural theorists have long recognized conjunctions between the aesthetic and the political and have hotly debated the relative
revolutionary efficacies of particular aesthetic modalities. Since at least the
expressionism-realism debates of the interwar years, Marxists have argued
for and against the power of avant-garde aesthetic practice to mobilize revolutionary impulse. Of course, feminist film theorists, inspired and provoked
largely by Laura Mulvey, enlarged debates over realism in the late sixties and
early seventies, recognizing the interconnections between mainstream narrative cinema and patriarchal ideologies and wondering whether feminist
re-envisionings of culture and cinema might find appropriate expression
only in avant-garde forms. Nina Menkes's *The Bloody Child: An Interior of
Violence,* an exploration of the nonphysical dimensions of violence, deploys
the alienating, revisionist aesthetic strategies advocated by those Marxists and
feminists convinced that an ideological "taint" haunts traditional narrative.
In particular, *Bloody Child* uses what Mary Beth Tierney-Tello calls "allegorical gestures" (11) to explore social relations and spiritual insights so subtle
and intricate as to defy direct exposition and to challenge the photographic
propensities of film, which, though well suited to exploring visible phenomena, necessarily falter before the task of picturing the invisible. Menkes's

use of allegory stretches the medium around and over the representation of the complex and invisible dynamics preceding, surrounding, and following physical acts of violence. In this re-presentation of violence, the physical and psychospiritual become a continuum instead of a dichotomy; understanding violence to the body involves understanding a psychospiritual violence of which damage to bodies constitutes only the most visible aspect.

Before undertaking an examination of the film and its allegorical content, it is necessary to understand how postmodern allegory works. Twentieth-century literature and film moved far from the one-to-one correspondences of didactic medieval allegories like *Pilgrim's Progress* and *Le roman de la rose*. In her discussion of allegorical procedures in Latin American women's writing, Tierney-Tello invokes etymology to arrive at a more flexible understanding of allegory, pointing out that "the very etymology of allegory alludes to its *modus operandi:* from *allos* (other) and *agorein* (to speak publicly), allegory tells one story to refer to another" (16). Usually, "one concrete story is told to refer to other, less representable or more abstract ideas" (16). To produce an allegorical reading of *Bloody Child,* therefore, is to ask, To what untold story does the story of the wife murder refer? What "less representable or more abstract ideas" inhabit the story of this murder?

It is also necessary to understand what features mark the film as allegorical and how these allegorical features enable the film to tell a "less representable . . . more abstract" story about violence. Again, recent theories of allegory help clarify these matters. Though a review of the theoretical literature about allegory reveals considerable disagreement about how allegory should be defined, theorists repeatedly discuss a constellation of figures considered constitutive of allegory. An essentially non-naturalistic, nonillusionistic form, allegory often includes dream-vision, episodic structure, battle or progress, intertextuality, personification, and spiritual/religious gnosis. *Bloody Child,* with its dreamlike images, radical fragmentation, dense intertextuality, iconic characters, and numinous imagery, invites allegorical reading. In fact, the film's most prominent hallmark of allegory inheres in the way it demands to be read. Gay Clifford writes in *The Transformations of Allegory* that the most fundamental characteristic of allegory is what it demands of the reader. In a nonallegorical text, Clifford suggests, readers read on to find out what happens; in an allegorical text, readers read on to find out what it means (3). One can *read* almost any text allegorically in the sense that one can probe a text for multiple levels of meaning. Surface levels of narrative can be absorbed unreflectingly or plumbed for "deeper" meanings. Such hermeneutic activity is not optional, however, with allegorical *texts:* allegory just doesn't make sense without interpretation. The interpretive challenges *Bloody Child* poses, in combination with the textual features mentioned above, make it sensible to read the film as allegory.

Bloody Child, based on a real incident in which a Gulf War veteran murdered his wife, departs drastically from cinematic conventions of portraying violence, war, and the military. Using fragmentation, repetition, accretion, and surrealism, *The Bloody Child* disrupts chronology and problematizes identification, while constructing an allegory of the psychospiritual devastation wrought by contemporary American military-industrial culture on individuals of both sexes, other countries, and nature itself. The film avoids replicating the act of violence by refusing to show it, evoking instead the wholly unsensational, dreary, and banal psychic deterioration left in its wake. In particular, *Bloody Child* illustrates the connections between individual acts of violence and acts of war, imperialism, and environmental irresponsibility. Further, the film's radical aesthetics require the spectator's participation; its convoluted narrative structure and puzzling, surreal juxtapositions necessitate an active, ongoing interpretive process. The film's editing, which declines to determine relations among its images authoritatively, foregrounds the spectator's own processes of inference and the undeniably subjective dimensions of meaning production. Given the obvious sociopolitical *engagement* of such dislocations, Menkes's film *The Bloody Child* demonstrates that a sociopolitically radical vision not only *coexists* with radical aesthetic strategies but *requires* them.

The murder story on which the film was based appeared in the back pages of the *Los Angeles Times:* two military police on routine patrol discovered a young U.S. marine, recently back from the Gulf War, digging a hole in the Mojave Desert. The young man's car, parked nearby, contained the bloody body of his wife; he was arrested on suspicion of murder (Menkes, *Bloody Child* press kit 4). The incident raises by-now familiar suspicions about the connections between military violence and violence outside the military: by using war to solve international disputes, American culture implicitly accepts that killing constitutes a viable response to conflict. Further, the propaganda necessary to sell the idea of war and popularize the military also involves constructing a masculinity defined by aggression; homosocial bonding; and the suppression of vulnerability, tender emotion, and psychospiritual need. It is this abstract story—the story of violence begetting violence and stunted masculinity—that the concrete story of the murdered wife tells and that requires the indirectness and ambiguity of allegory.

The filmmaker herself speaks explicitly in press materials about this abstract story told in *Bloody Child,* though she would undoubtedly be the last to push viewers toward some programmatic reading of the film:

> *The Bloody Child* was inspired, on one level, by an R & R visit I took to Palm Springs, California, during the Gulf War. I was sitting in a hotel jacuzzi, alongside a number of young marines. They had been sent there to recuperate from combat duty in Saudi Arabia. While drinking beer, they were discussing incidents of friendly fire . . . on purpose. The footage in *Bloody Child* that I shot in Arab Africa is meant to suggest not only the Gulf conflict, but the American military's ubiquitous violent relationship to the Third World in general, of which the recent resumption of hostilities in the Gulf is yet one more example. (*Bloody Child* press kit 4)

Menkes's creative processes represent a quite literal determination to involve herself, via filmmaking, with the aftermath of the Gulf War and with the American military. In addition to hiring a recently discharged marine with no experience in film as her assistant director, Menkes recruited active marines—Gulf War veterans—to write their own lines and act in the film (*Bloody Child* press kit 3). These choices yield the effective cinema verité elements of *Bloody Child,* in which the quotidian violences of military life (emotional repression, demeaning hierarchies, inhospitable tones of address) figure prominently. The film's indirect strategies of exposition—collage, repetition, juxtaposition, surrealism—aim to probe the story behind the story of military and imperialist violence; this story, which remains rooted in social exchange, individual psyche, and spiritual suffering, is elusive in its abstractness and cannot be told using the direct strategies of conventional narrative.

Were the film to tell this story conventionally, it would risk reducing the social and spiritual complexities Menkes means to capture and reinforcing structures of viewing and signification that help sustain the very ideologies it critiques. Specifically, by using allegory and other dislocative, nonillusionistic stylistic strategies, *Bloody Child* manages to present an act of violence against a woman without permitting voyeurism or sensationalism—tendencies of realist depictions of violence against women that unwittingly replicate the abject subject position of the woman-as-victim. The same strategies enable the film to alienate viewers in a Brechtian sense, eliciting a critical consciousness that, instead of lapsing comfortably into identification with any of the characters, must work strenuously to forge connections out of the images and sounds represented: the repeated scenes of arrest, images of the slain woman, fragments of the arresting officer's liaison with an enlisted man, glimpses of a transport ship floating on an African river, murmured lines from the weird sisters in *Macbeth*, snippets of a harlequin woman and her companion in an unidentified northeast African landscape, shots of the two companions draped listlessly over the bases of heavy industrial rigging. Using these disparate pieces, viewers must ask what the murder has to do with the military, with sex, with gender, with industry, with nature, with racial difference, with international relations, and so on.

The necessity for such critical viewing begins with the film's dreamlike imagery, lack of chronology, and stylistic bricolage. *Bloody Child* opens with a lurid sunrise beneath which two figures materialize out of the darkness, closing in upon a third. The film cuts to an Arab woman unlocking a chained gate, then back to the figures in the desert, then to a jungle clearing. Sibilant voices on the sound track murmur lines from *Macbeth* over the image track: "When shall we three meet again / In thunder, lightning, or in rain?" (1.1.1). The film returns obsessively to the desert scene; to the sergeant thrusting the face of the suspect into the bloody body of his alleged victim; to marines waiting (for an ambulance? for more police?) after the arrest has been made; to scenes of drunken marines entertaining themselves lewdly in a country-western bar. The film jumbles the chronology of these fleetingly perceived places and events thoroughly: scenes of the cars leaving precede scenes in which they arrive; the alleged murderer appears seated in the car before the arresting officers put him there; the sergeant thrusts the suspect's face into his wife's bloody body before he forces the suspect into the car where the body lies. In addition to creating a filmic world that constantly gestures *through* the visible to the mysterious, invisible silences and significances inhabiting the visible, this kind of scrambling undermines any sense of narrative tension so that the viewer cannot derive pleasure from any dramatic buildup and release surrounding the murder or the capture of the murderer.

In this way, the film avoids giving the viewer a prurient narrative pay-off when a woman gets killed or a killer gets caught. By decentering these acts—acts that occupy central positions within conventional stories about violence—*Bloody Child* deemphasizes the notion of woman-as-victim and asserts that the mind of an individual killer is unimportant next to the totality of cultural influences surrounding his killing. Hence, spectators never see the actual murder, never enter the mind of the murderer. As Jonathan Rosenbaum notes, "*The Bloody Child* doesn't proceed like a crime story in any ordinary sense; the focus is on the arrest rather than the crime, which is never shown. We're taken into the lives of the captain and other soldiers . . . but not into the life or mind or motivations of the murderer, who's never heard and is seen only from behind or from a distance" ("Arresting Images"). By omitting considerations common to conventional crime dramas, Menkes's film ushers the spectator toward unconventional avenues of thought and feeling about violence.

Conventional crime drama, like newspaper accounts, whether of war or individual acts of murder, often fail to plumb the complexities of how violence permeates and thus alters the individual and collective psyche because both forms of representation restrict themselves largely to the visible: who did what to whom when, where, and why. From the *Los Angeles Times*, for instance, readers learn only that a marine killed his wife. By heightening ambiguity through cinematic experimentalism and allegorical devices, *Bloody Child* explores the less obvious aspects of this act, the psychic states antecedent to and induced by violence. The film's nonlinear structure and use of surrealist strategies suggest that violence can be understood as a condition of consciousness and culture, as opposed to an individually perpetrated event.

The film's most obvious allegorical device resides in its characterizations. With the partial exception of the Captain, its characters, all nameless, do not emerge as individuals. The Captain constitutes only a partial exception because, while the film does portray her personal life to some extent, it features the same actor as Captain, Arab woman, harlequin woman, and woman in the forest, turning her into an everywoman. Tierney-Tello cites such characterization as a hallmark of postmodernist allegory. While postmodernist texts, she notes, may not be "single, sustained allegories," they often use "such allegorical techniques as abstraction, incorporation of commentary and interpretation, [and] the *use of personifications rather than realistic protagonists* [emphasis mine]" (17). The portrayal of an abstraction, of course, necessitates a nonrealist characterization. In Jungian terms, abstractions conceived as characters are called archetypes, and *Bloody Child* pursues its metaphysical inquiries through archetype.

In an interview with Holly Willis, Menkes offers an archetypal reading of the sullen, pained-looking women who haunt her films. The filmmaker describes this figure as the spectral presence of that facet of the female psyche ravaged psychologically by patriarchal stricture. Menkes remarks,

> Women [in the United States] are supposed to look and act in a very specific way that could be summarized as "friendly and fuckable." Also, we have to have perfect, flawless skin, which we can simulate by applying makeup. Well, why do we have to cover up? Cover up what? You see, it's all that pain and rage from not being seen at all, from being forced into this very unnatural

shape. In *Magdalena Viraga* and *Queen of Diamonds* it is this wounded figure which appears, unveiled. She's sort of straight out of the menstrual hut, and she's not cleaned up. (Willis 12)

The wounded-woman figure appears in *Bloody Child* as well—the mascara-smeared woman staring unhappily into the mirror as the sound track intones "Mirror, mirror, on the wall," the harlequin woman, the woman at the chained gate. This allegorical apparition, in addition to figuring an aspect of the female unconscious, overturns patriarchal cinematic conventions by transforming woman from erotic spectacle to subject unto herself. *Bloody Child* thus does what Mulvey predicted a feminist avant-garde would do: effect a "constant return to woman, not indeed as a visual image, but as a subject of inquiry, a content which cannot be considered within the aesthetic lines laid down by traditional cinematic practice" ("Film, Feminism" 125). This break with much commercial cinematic tradition—the casting of woman as subject instead of object—alone constitutes a political act. Further, however, the allegorical figure of the wounded woman implies that patriarchal culture scars women psychospiritually and immobilizes her sociopolitically. The wounded woman refuses to be "friendly and fuckable," insisting instead on parading her unhappiness, eschewing and actively undermining the role her culture asks her to play. Her makeup, instead of rendering her an erotic object, mars her beauty and makes her fearsome—a woman made grotesque by the accoutrements designed to enhance her.

The archetypal functions of the wounded-woman figure are echoed elsewhere in the film. Critical consensus about *Bloody Child* hovers about the notion that the soul of the murdered wife haunts the scene of the arrest and that the image of the woman in the jungle pictures the Captain's unconscious response to the victim and the arrest. The image may just as legitimately be read as an externalization of the Captain's interior response to her subject position in a more generalized sense, and it just as easily represents the interiority of other characters or may even be, as the critic Lea Russo suggests, "the ghost of our collective unconscious, inflicting pain on ourselves and the world" (qtd. in Thomas, "*Child*"). Certainly, however, the jungle image—a woman kneeling among dense green palms, tracing letters across her sand-covered arm—might also suggest a neutral, possibly peaceful, metaphorical space within the Captain's consciousness (Tinka Menkes plays both women).

The meanings evoked by this dream image have all the indeterminacy of reference that Deborah Madsen attributes to postmodern allegory; this is its power (*Allegory in America* 4). Within the captain's consciousness, the image—which the sound track embellishes with lines from *Macbeth;* fragments of Christian liturgy; moaning, crying, laughing—seems to encompass both anxiety, mourning, and a desire for or memory of a serenity, playfulness, and peace connected with a feeling of being at home in a preindustrial natural environment. The clipped, strained dialogue among the marines and the thickly textured aural collage of the jungle scene contrast the Captain's brisk external efficiency with her melancholic inner spaces where both extraordinary and quotidian brutalities (the murder versus the marines' brusque treatment of each other) lodge as sorrow, emotional withdrawal, and longing. The abstract condition represented by the jungle sequences, however, has wider application than the Captain's individual consciousness.

The dreamlike quality of these sequences connects them with the other dream elements of *Bloody Child,* as against the cinema verité style of the sequences near the military base (the arrest, revelries inside the country-western bar, the motel). These other dreamlike elements include the harlequin woman, a lone female flaneur in an unidentified African city, and the harlequin woman sans harlequin outfit, with an African companion, posed lethargically or mournfully in various urban locales. These women, portrayed by one actor, provide a commonality connecting the military base sequences and the African sequences; her presence in Africa forges a link between both of these and the African footage from which she is absent: the pristine jungle lake (in which at one point she appears swimming), the robed man at the river, the transport ship floating on the river. Menkes describes her artistic intentions for these shots in an interview with *American Cinematographer:* "My initial cinematic concept for the African footage was for a fractured female character . . . to be positioned within a variety of evocative African milieus; I wanted to connect the West's destructive relationship with Africa to that which the dominant Western culture has to women. All of my images were to be dreamlike and iconic to evoke the *feelings* created inside of us, or more specifically, inside of me, by external political and social realities" (A. Thompson 16).

The spectator confronting these "dreamlike and iconic" images must puzzle out their interrelations. To make sense of the film, the viewer must examine, in addition to the connection between the murder and the jungle footage (what has individual violence to do with nature?), the connection between the murder and the African footage (what has it to do with U.S. involvement in Africa?); between the murder and the scene of the two companions lying on the industrial rigging (what has it to do with industry and environment?); between the murder and the transport ship (what has it to do with international trade?); and so on. These disparate images, implying that all *are* connected without specifically articulating the relationships, invite the spectator to view violence as permeating all domains and to pursue necessarily subjective, associative reflections grounded in the particulars of each image.

The harlequin woman appears seated on a crowded bus, lying on a meager cot before a bare wall, and posing with an African companion on a stage holding a large religious icon. The harlequin, traditional trickster figure from commedia dell'arte, retains no playfulness in *Bloody Child*. Her harlequin suit, not particolored, but stark black-and-white, lends a wry turn to this archetypal personage, who becomes an abjectly ridiculous figure. Hardly an amiable buffoon, this harlequin woman, so jarringly out of place, bears silent witness to crowding, poverty, and environmental pillage. Like the lines from *Macbeth* that pervade the sound track, reminding spectators that "Fair is foul, and foul is fair" (1.1.11) and nervously evoking that time "When the hurly-burly's done / When the battle's lost and won" (1.1.3), harlequin woman offers a sullen, silent, judging commentary upon all she sees unfolding, an "incorporation of commentary and interpretation" Tierney-Tello posits (17) as central to postmodernist allegory.

The nature of the commentary reaches beyond logocentric verbal assessments of the action, however. The harlequin communicates her judgments not through words but through her dejected, pained expressions and postures. Inexplicably, she appears in street clothes as well, maintaining the same watchful, silent presence. She sits next to a young boy at a Greek Orthodox service, gazing up at some unidentified religious image or vision; she crouches with an African companion against a bare wall, waiting, head buried in her knees; she lies uncomfortably, sweating in the sun, across the bases of some industrial rigging—possibly oil storage or electrical towers. In every guise, she embodies inarticulate pain, unhappiness, and disapproval. The oppressive atmosphere surrounding her is relieved only by periodic cuts to the jungle sequences, featuring the sand-covered woman or the secluded body of water—small spaces of greenery and relative ease amidst the inhospitable places and human interactions populating the film.

The film's two modalities—the dreamlike and the verité—meet in the image of a magnificent stallion appearing suddenly at the arrest scene. Jonathan Rosenbaum writes, "The film proceeds in scrambled, patchwork fashion, moving ceaselessly between realism (the desert and bar) and poetry or myth (the forest and *Macbeth*) until a beautiful black horse trots improbably through the landscape where the cars and soldiers are waiting for back-up. Then the distinctness starts to blur" ("Arresting Images"). The stallion, in addition to demonstrating the painful disjunction of the natural/wild/mythic and the military-industrial world (beauty seems so out of place there), brings the iconic resonance of the African sequences to the harsh world of the military base and the brutal murder. Looking beyond the grubby dailiness of the desert and bar scenes allows spectators to plumb American military culture for its underlying psychospiritual dramas: the absences and evacuations of feeling that are a condition of military life.

For Menkes, this drama extends far beyond particular international conflicts. Unlike some politically engaged films, which clearly revolve around specific conflicts, *Bloody Child* locates itself in time quite subtly, preferring to probe the sociocultural, psychospiritual conditions underlying not just the Gulf War but violence as an overarching force or response. Spectators might easily miss the lines in the film that reference the gulf conflict. During the bar sequences, bits of banter reveal the historical moment but remain only parts of an extremely textured image track and cacophonous sound track. One of the men exclaims indignantly, "A third-world fuckin' country!" Another responds, but only part of his response can be heard: "Just protectin' our interests? What the fuck have they ever done for us?" A little later, someone sneers, "Fuckin' Iraqis!" In addition to capturing realistically a fairly routine brand of political discourse in America, this sequence invokes the gulf conflict without delimiting the scope of the film, through which Menkes clearly means to explore the sources and ramifications of violence at the level of the unconscious or iconic. She achieves this largely by repeating certain scenes and images, drawing their resonance out by accretion.

Amidst scenes of routine interpersonal cruelty, drunken homosocial bonding, and emotional isolation and stasis, three images stand out: the murderer, unable to wash the blood off his hands; the sergeant, forcing the murderer's face into the dead body of his wife amid a torrent of cusswords; and the murderer after this ordeal, silent and quivering as if in shock, face covered with blood. In the first image, the marine appears at a blood-filled sink, feverishly rubbing his forearms in the blood, trying unsuccessfully to wash it off, a visual manifestation of Lady Macbeth's psychotic delusion of the "damn'd spot" that will not "out" (5.1.35). In operating through intertext like this, allegory manages to multiply the meanings attendant upon an image. Lady Macbeth's guilt extends beyond the murder of the king to the litany of further violence the cover-up requires. Her "damn'd spot" represents an accumulation of violences and cruelty, a ruthlessness borne of ambition and power that now has infiltrated her whole being. Similarly, the murderous marine has more blood than his child-wife's on his hands, a fact that the ideological apparatuses supporting the American military would have the public forget. In point of fact, American soldiers do not just die for their country, they *kill* for it. A soldier recently returned from Persian Gulf combat has the blood of civilian women, children, and men on his hands along with that of enemy soldiers and his own comrades. Though he has committed legal violence, in the mythopoetic space of nature and the unconscious, killing is killing. When the murderer, brutalized by his arresting officers, sits trembling and speechless in the police vehicle, it is impossible to tell whether his shellshock-style mental breakdown stems from criminal behavior or a soldier's daily routine. The wife murder, and the spot that will not out, proceeds, the film suggests, from a long chain of events.

As *Bloody Child* demonstrates, violence issues from violence. It is not restricted to particular incidents and individuals but is an energy dominating large sectors of culture. From subtler violences, like the erasure of all individuality through uniform clothing, haircuts, and postures, to the more physical violence of barroom brawls between enlisted men, to the demeaning manner in which superior officers treat underlings, violence pervades military life. This violence erupts notably when the sergeant interrogates the suspect, grasping him by the hair and shoving his face into the bloody body, goading, "Do you like that? Do you fuckin' like that?" The sergeant's screaming rage, which conflates the realm of professional obligation with the realm of primal brutality, contains curiously sexual innuendos. He asks the suspect, "How does that smell?" and "How do you like that pussy?" and "Does that make your dick hard?" His vituperative lexicon betrays a confused misogyny even as it purports to communicate outrage over the woman's death, evincing the strain of hatred for women that riddles paternalistic concern for them. These myriad psychological violences, *Bloody Child* illustrates, cannot be separated from acts of violence that register on women's (and men's) bodies.

Taken together, the fragmented and surreal images of *The Bloody Child* do indeed explore, as the subtitle suggests, an interior of violence. This interior view de-emphasizes the physical aspect of violence and shows how its psychospiritual dimensions reach into everyday behavior and international policy, affecting other countries, other cultures, and the environment. Menkes's holistic, ecofeminist views, traceable in articles, interviews, and press materials for her films, lead her to construct a postmodern allegory precise enough to evoke a palpable sense of horror and grief, flexible enough to evoke the totality of an ecofeminist perspective, and challenging enough to engage the spectator's critical awareness. Writing rather elliptically in *Variety,* Godfrey Cheshire remarks that the "pic's poetic approach disturbingly evokes a pervasive tapestry of psychic and actual violence by examining a couple of its threads. There are political and feminist ramifications here, surely, yet pic leaves it to the viewer to decipher—or supply—them" (15).

With its own ellipticism and allegorical maneuvers, *The Bloody Child* invites viewers to consider violence as a vast network of connections encompassing criminality, the military, industry, imperialist-capitalist opportunism, patriarchy, misogyny, race relations, and environmental ruin. Perhaps notable here is Menkes's deployment of postmodernist aesthetic forms—fragmentation, allusion, allegory—to overtly political and spiritual ends; *The Bloody Child* shows that postmodernism can involve claims to truth and value even as it decenters or problematizes the notion of meaning. In "The Will to Allegory," Paul Smith observes that modern and postmodern allegory entails an "authoritative claim to meaning" (106–7). Smith considers this reactionary but as Tierney-Tello rightly asks while discussing Smith's analysis, "is such a will to meaning essentially reactionary?" (20). In the case of *Bloody Child,* with its critique of military, American/patriarchal culture, environmental irresponsibility, and Western intrusions into less industrialized nations, the will to meaning is politically *progressive,* even radical.

5

Lourdes Portillo, Rea Tajiri, and Cheryl Dunye

At twenty-one, Lourdes Portillo assisted on a documentary film production and realized she had found her life's calling. She trained in San Francisco at the National Association of Broadcast Engineers and Technicians and graduated from the San Francisco Art Institute in 1978. Since then the Mexican-born, Chicana-identified Portillo has produced and directed a series of award-winning documentaries, funded by American Film Institute Filmmakers awards, National Endowment for the Arts grants, and grants from the Corporation for Public Broadcasting, the National Latino Communications Center, and the Rockefeller Foundation, among others. She has also received a Guggenheim Fellowship. While her work includes politically motivated films that focus on social injustice, such as *Las Madres: The Mothers of Plaza de Mayo* (1986), a film that, in addition to winning twenty other awards, garnered an Academy nomination for best documentary in 1985, Portillo consistently challenges the adage that all documentaries deal "with injustice." Her critically acclaimed *La Ofrenda: The Days of the Dead* (1988), *The Devil Never Sleeps/El diablo nunca duerme* (1994), and *Corpus: A Home Movie for Selena* (1999) make use of experimental documentary forms to explore dream states, desire, Latino fan culture, and other topics that address cinematic representations of Chicanos, Latinos, and Mexicans in U.S. visual culture. Her highly acclaimed *Senorita Extraviada* (2002) brings to public attention the unsolved murders of hundreds of women—*maquiladoras*—in Ciudad Juarez.

Rea Tajiri, a third-generation Japanese American, received a B.A. and an M.F.A. from the California Institute of the Arts in Los Angeles. In 1991, she wrote, produced, and directed her first film, *History and Memory*, which immediately received numerous awards, including the Distinguished Achievement Award from the International Documentary Association and the Best Experimental Video Award at the Atlanta Film and Video Festival. *History and Memory* has since been shown on PBS and at numerous film festivals, art museums, and universities around the world. Tajiri followed it with *Passion for Justice* (1993), a documentary on the human rights advocate Yuri Kochiyama; *Strawberry Fields* (1997), a narrative feature; and *Little Murders* (1998), a digital video musical. Tajiri has received awards and funding from the Rockefeller Foundation, the Corporation for Public Broadcasting, the National Endowment for the Arts, and the New York Foundation for the Arts.

Cheryl Dunye, born in Liberia in 1966, grew up in Philadelphia. She received a B.A. from Temple University and an M.F.A. from Rutgers in the early 1990s. Her filmography includes the short, experimental works *Janine* (1990), *She Don't Fade* (1991), *Vanilla Sex* (1992), and *Untitled Portrait* (1993). The filmmaker coined the term "Dunyementary" to describe the evolving genre in which she works—a combination of fiction, documentary, experimental video, and autobiography. Following *The Potluck and the Passion* (1993) and *Greetings from Africa* (1994), Dunye moved to feature production. Her 1996 *Watermelon Woman*, funded in part by a National Endowment for the Arts grant, got a theatrical release and generated controversy when right-wing members of Congress, flustered by a love scene between two women, questioned its funding. HBO produced and aired Dunye's second feature, *Stranger Inside*, a narrative set in a female prison, about a mother and daughter who have been separated. Dunye, who has received numerous awards, fellowships, and funding from sources such as the Rockefeller Foundation, recently completed her first studio feature, *My Baby's Daddy* (2004).

KATHLEEN McHUGH

History and Falsehood
in Experimental
Autobiographies

The media artists Lourdes Portillo, Rea Tajiri, and Cheryl Dunye
have each used autobiographical formats to expand the political reach of
their experimental filmmaking. Though their films represent experiences
of "difference," all refuse the rhetoric of pathos.[1] Instead they make use of
their own autobiographical histories to reorient self-expression from assertions about identity to questions about representation and epistemology. In
so doing, they work within two distinct but overlapping traditions, thereby
transforming them. The first is the tradition of autobiography, both literary
and cinematic, and the second is that of identity politics. These filmmakers
return to some of the concerns of classical literary autobiographies in order
to expand the formalist understanding of avant-garde cinematic autobiography articulated in the 1970s. Yet they also challenge identity politics. Though
each filmmaker could be said to possess an identity marked by multiple
differences, all three women avoid reifying these differences as features of
a fixed identity. Rather they draw from a generic tradition, autobiography,
which has, from its inception, been both necessarily concerned with *and*
fundamentally suspicious of self-representation and its flawed relationship
to truth and knowledge.

I examine Portillo, Tajiri, and Dunye because their reliance on these two
traditions systematically discredits our most illusory but persistent social
distinction, that between public and private, a distinction that has structured
the understanding of gender and other differences in the United States.[2] As
an alternative, they use their "selves" experimentally, explicitly relating interiority, affect, and an individuated sense of self to the material world, its ap-

paratuses, and its social relations. In effect, by reconstructing, inventing, and sometimes overtly fictionalizing these relations, these artists actually *historicize* them. They do so by transgressing the usual affective, personal conventions that contain "authentic" self-representation within the private, thereby making manifest the public rhetorics, institutions, and conventions to which the self is subject.[3] While I will focus on Portillo, Tajiri, and Dunye, other female media artists such as Janice Tanaka, Su Friedrich, Vanalyne Green, and Lise Yasui also work in this mode. In order to appreciate fully the intervention that these filmmakers effect in critical understandings of autobiographical avant-garde film, it is important to consider briefly what the cinema inherits from and what it initially excludes from the literary tradition.

Revelation, Ribbons, and Self-Representation

Autobiography, from Augustine to its recent emergence as a privileged genre for identity politics, demonstrates the crucial importance of the self in Western epistemology and the dependence of both self and epistemology on social, religious, and political infrastructures and institutions. Significantly, long before "relativism" became a touchstone of cultural politics, the Western tradition of autobiography and its constructions of the self had been predicated upon insinuations of truth and fiction and a profound mistrust of the representational capacities of language. In Augustine's *Confessions*, there is a very pronounced concern for the relationship between classical knowledge, together with the institutions and careers that supported that knowledge, and the ideological and institutional development of a belief system (Catholicism) that would challenge it. Augustine's text, which has been designated the origin of the genre in the West, invents a mode of self-representation predicated on a sinning, misguided self whose ruminations effectively wed classical rhetoric to the Judeo-Christian tradition.[4] Augustine transforms classical rhetoric from an objective discourse to a subjective one by subsuming it within Christian theology through the narrative agency of a sinning self who confesses. Predicated on his experience of conversion and revelation, his brilliantly paradoxical work employs the conventions of debate, rhetoric, and classical knowledge to articulate the certainty of not-knowing, non-mastery, of what that knowledge cannot comprehend. In effect, he uses language and rhetoric to prove the existence of meanings that exceed their expression. But his rhetorical transformations are always articulated in relation to the state, to educational and religious institutions, and to his profession as an orator. Thus he serves as an apt patron saint of contemporary performance, experimental features, and video art in which artists more or less invent themselves for political, communitarian, and epistemological purposes.

Jean-Jacques Rousseau secularizes confession and establishes the humanist subject's relation to knowledge as a relation to the mysteries of (him)self. Rousseau vests his confessions in establishing his difference and uniqueness within the varied political, social, philosophical, and economic milieux in which he lived. To do so he articulates a profoundly self-conscious, profoundly unreliable self; his confessions interiorize not-knowing and establish it as an attribute of the individual's relationship to himself. Although Rousseau does relate foibles of his character to conventions of politesse and self-presentation that dominated social interactions in his lifetime, his autobiography departs from Augustine's in positing that the authenticity of the self precedes and transcends external sources and institutions.

From these origins, three defining features of autobiography emerge. First, Augustine invénts a mode of narration—confession—predicated on a sinning but very articulate self that has significant epistemological, religious, and institutional consequences; second, the rhetorical capabilities of language are essential to the distinction he establishes between the presentable and the unknowable, with those capabilities both opposed and essential to the expression of the truth. Third, in Rousseau, this emerging mode of knowing and not-knowing the self becomes interiorized and secularized, but it is still associated with paradoxes concerning truth and expression. That is, Rousseau claims both authenticity and singularity for his text *because* it is contradictory and inconsistent and *because* part of his proof of the truth of his text is that he lies and confesses his lies. Here I refer to the famous incident in which Rousseau, having stolen a ribbon from his employer's daughter and been found with the evidence, lies and accuses another servant, Marion, of having given it to him. Recounting this event, he asserts that it is his desire to be relieved of the burden of guilt that he has shared with no one and that has haunted him ever since that has led him to write his confessions.[5] Thus, what Augustine and Rousseau share is that their respective productions of truth are, in each case, dependent upon sins, errors, and duplicity related to both the self and to language and its expressive capacities.

This genealogy provides an important context for considering the understanding of autobiography in classical avant-garde film criticism and theory. While for both Augustine and Rousseau, the narrative agency of very differently conceived selves allows each of them to transform the epistemological truths of his historical moment, in Augustine these transformations are much more overtly linked to social and religious structures and institutions than they are in Rousseau. Though P. Adams Sitney, who codifies the film genre in an article entitled "Autobiography in the Avant-Garde Film," cites the example of both writers, he seems particularly influenced by the example of Rousseau. Sitney's determinations cast the understanding of experimental cinematic autobiography toward a modernist formalism that is significant for what it excludes: women, feminism, and identity.

History by Flicker and Symbol

In the late 1970s, as the classical avant-garde was breaking apart, its histories began to be written. P. Adams Sitney embarks upon one such history, his lengthy "Autobiography in the Avant-Garde Film," by objecting to the insistence with which the term "personal" had been applied to most independent avant-garde films made during the previous twenty years. Seeking to elicit the "meaningfulness" from this "epithet," he asserts that structural similarities in the works "of several major artists" in the last decade have prompted him to "a generic and historical analysis" of autobiographical film (199). Sitney writes this seminal piece on cinematic autobiography during the period (1977–78) in which the classical avant-garde and radical cinema gives way to a cinema politicized in relation to identity, especially evident in feminist filmmaking and theory (James, *Allegories* 304–14). Laura Mulvey has already written "Visual Pleasure and Narrative Cinema" (1975) and women are making a range of films, including autobiographical works. In this historical context, what Sitney includes must be considered in relation to what he excludes. Accordingly, the project of Sitney's piece emerges as an attempt to locate autobiography in formalist concerns while avoiding issues having to do with identity.

In his introduction, Sitney enumerates the qualities of "true" autobiographical film, among which the most important are, first, "the quest for a cinematic strategy which relates the moments of shooting and editing to the diachronic continuity of the film-maker's life" and, second, the generation of metaphors from the inevitable failures "involved in trying to make language (or film) substitute for experience and memory" ("Autobiography" 200). While the first renders the autobiographical endeavor resolutely formalist, the second clearly follows in the tradition of literary autobiography's suspicion of representation and its capacity to apprehend truth. Sitney's commitment to a self-reflexive formalism, especially in relation to autobiography, is attuned to key influences of his historical moment, particularly that of the Yale critics. In his acknowledgments to *Visionary Film*, Sitney states that throughout the writing of that text, he was constantly reading the work of Maurice Blanchot, Paul de Man, Geoffrey Hartman, and Harold Bloom. Significantly, de Man wrote extensively on autobiography during this period, one very widely read piece focusing on Rousseau's *Confessions* and his later *Reveries of the Solitary Walker*.[6] The article begins from the premise that all autobiography has "a referential reading-moment" and ends by arguing that such a moment is merely a "delusion," that "[t]here can be no use of language which is not, within a certain perspective thus radically formal, i.e. mechanical" (de Man 278, 294).

In a very similar move, Sitney initially mentions, in the second paragraph of his article, autobiography's claims to "extra-textual veracity." This concern is progressively displaced, such that Sitney's final declaration is that "autobiographical cinema per se . . . confronts fully the rupture between the time of cinema and the time of experience and invents forms to contain what it finds there" ("Autobiography" 246). That is, as a genre, avant-garde autobiography turns from the specificity and question of the extratextual referent to overarching, generalized meditations on the nature of cinema, the impossibility of representation, and the conundrums of existential and cinematic temporality.[7]

Such critical substitutions or displacements—as from the "personal" as (extratextual) epithet to the true self-reflexive formalism of autobiography— condition Sitney's choice of filmmakers *and* his analyses of their work, his choices delimiting not only what he does see in this work but also what he cannot. To illustrate his theses, Sitney makes use of the very differently realized examples of autobiography in the films of Jerome Hill (*Film Portrait,* 1970), Stan Brakhage (*Scenes from under Childhood,* 1967–70; *The Weir-Falcon Saga,* 1970; *Sincerity,* 1973), Hollis Frampton (*Nostalgia,* 1971), George Landow (*Wide Angle Saxon,* 1975; *Remedial Reading Comprehension,* 1970; *Institutional Quality,* 1969; *New Improved Institutional Quality,* 1976), and James Broughton (*Testament,* 1974). Beyond the fact that they are all authored by white men, Sitney's selections also function to recuperate to the formalist project works that are more expressive of gay identities (Hill and, to a much greater extent, Broughton) and to assimilate to autobiography works that are insistently formalist and whose status as autobiography is somewhat questionable (Frampton and Landow). In a very revealing move, Sitney prefaces his remarks on Landow with the statement that Landow's

films "are actually hardly autobiographical in the sense I have been elaborating here: they do not represent diachronical reflection in any manner";
but as a series of inter-referential texts, they do represent "the moment of
artistic vocation" ("Autobiography" 232). Thus for Sitney, the camera's eye
and what it records displaces the artist's self and life as the true subject of
cinematic autobiography.

Sitney's generic criteria of formal self-reflexivity and the foreclosure of
the extra-diegetic become most difficult to argue in the case of Brakhage and,
secondarily, Broughton. Sitney spends almost half the article on Brakhage's
intensely personal film texts, insisting that the filmmaker's longstanding interest in the cinema's capacity to represent his own perceptions and personal
vision is actually a meditation on the cinema itself. He asserts, "Brakhage is
not a practicing psychologist but a film-maker, and although he may sometimes deny it, considerations of the ontology of cinema consistently take pre-
cedence over the observation of phenomena in his work" ("Autobiography"
215). But then there is the problem of Brakhage's wife, Jane, who consulted,
collaborated, and picked up the camera on, as well as serving as the subject
of, many of Brakhage's autobiographical films. If Brakhage's studies in (his
own) perception are to equal or to merely stand for the ontology of cinema,
gender difference(s) in perception becomes a crucial problem (a double ontology) in relation to both the film text and its spectator.

Sitney resolves the question of gender difference through a very ellipti-
cal argument about Brakhage and flicker effects. In one of the article's only
considerations of women, he invokes Brakhage's own writing about his attempts to incorporate his wife's vision, and therefore the vision of women
per se, into his filmmaking. In the passage, Brakhage refers to the research
of the kinesiologist Ray L. Birdwhistell (which Sitney has never been able to
locate) to assert:

> Every woman in the world . . . has a certain specific, different visual possibil-
> ity than any man: one of them is that women are trained . . . to move their
> eyes while the eyes are closed: and all of boy babies (and therefore—men) are
> trained by the same mothers to never move the pupils of their eyes during
> a blink or while the eyes are closed. Certainly it's mysterious when you con-
> sider that a woman for the first time in her life, confronting her son, begins
> to hold her eyes steady while blinking and closing them (which she has never
> before done in her entire history as a woman . . .): she does this specifically
> with her son without knowing why or even knowing that she does it so he'll
> have that specificity of sight, as distinct from any daughter. There's an infi-
> nite number of differences in what all women share very closely as distinct

from any man, in sight: and I'm concerned to get simply the woman's view
into the work. (qtd. in Sitney, "Autobiography" 225)

Whereas other film scholars treat those films in which Jane Brakhage actually takes up the camera (James, *Allegories* 38–39), Sitney relies on this extraordinary passage to relegate women's difference in vision to a biological
determinism that strongly implies that only men can use the camera. The
question then becomes how men can incorporate women's vision. Sitney
concludes that Brakhage does so by his use of flicker effects: "The unar-
ticulated principle behind Brakhage's theory could be expressed thus: the
mnemonics of watching the flicker effect is universal; so a sufficiently schematic representation of the mnemonic response will induce a personal and
proportional reaction in every viewer" ("Autobiography" 228). The formal
schema of the flicker effect subsumes difference within the universal. Every
spectator will be either man or (m)other.

This part of Sitney's argument can be usefully compared with his reading
of Broughton's *Testament,* specifically his reading of the filmed procession
the filmmaker stages down the street of his hometown, Modesto, California.
Garbed in a birdlike feathered costume and carried on a litter under the ban-
ner "In Memory of James Broughton," the filmmaker was attended by his
students, also costumed, and a "nearly naked youth, in silver body paint, with
a long goat-like phallus, which he rubs against an immense egg, representing the poet." Sitney argues that this sequence represents "the moment of
poetic incarnation," an argument that relies on his reading this image, this
performance (in a place called *Modesto* no less), as symbolic ("Autobiography" 241–42). He thereby reinstates an age-old gender distinction, affiliating
women with the biological and men with the symbolic, while completely
ignoring elements of Broughton's scene whose referents cannot be successfully subsumed under considerations of the ontology of cinema.

Thus the generic foundations of avant-garde autobiography are clearly
predicated on a suppression of the extra-diegetic and all particularities of
identity in favor of a formalism that clearly does not apprehend all aspects
of even the work to which Sitney applies it. Women's cinema and feminist
film theory insist upon the significance of the personal and the extra-diegetic, but it is precisely that insistence that excludes them from this genre
as defined by Sitney.

In another critical formulation of cinematic autobiography, "Eye for I:
Making and Unmaking Autobiography in Film," Elizabeth Bruss takes a
more general approach. Her article is her contribution to a 1980 collection

of essays otherwise devoted to literary autobiography. She commences her argument with the assertion, "[T]here is no real cinematic equivalent for autobiography." This literary genre does not translate readily to film, she says, because "[t]he unity of subjectivity and subject matter—the implied identity of author, narrator, and protagonist on which classical autobiography depends—seems to be shattered by film; the autobiographical self decomposes, schisms, into almost mutually exclusive elements of the person filmed (entirely visible, recorded and projected) and the person filming (entirely hidden; behind the camera eye)" (297).

Exploring autobiography as a particular speech act, Bruss carefully measures film's capacity to fulfill those parameters—"truth-value," "act-value," and "identity-value"—that "give classical autobiography its peculiar generic value" (299). Drawing her examples primarily from art cinema and European auteurs (again, all white men)—Federico Fellini (8 ½, The Clowns, Satyricon, Amarcord), François Truffaut (400 Blows), Jean Cocteau (Testament), Conrad Rooks (Chappaqua), Kenneth Anger (Fireworks)[8]—she determines that "[s]uch films cannot produce the old self-knowledge (nor the old self-deceptions) of classical autobiography, but they can do something else: they can take identity beyond what one consciousness can grasp, beyond even what the unaided consciousness can encompass. . . . Film also challenges the presumed integrity of the perceiving subject" (318–19). Because of all the technologies (lighting, editing, and so on) mobilized to represent the autobiographical subject in film, Bruss argues that we cannot and do not understand this subject as preceding or preexisting its representation but rather as generated or invented by it. She concludes by asserting that the representational technologies of film and video apprehend, as literature cannot, the very different condition of human subjectivity as it exists today in relation to these very technologies and in complex "social interdependencies" (320).

Though these critics and other historians of the American avant-garde have consistently noted the affiliation of this mode of film production with personal and autobiographical self-expression, the character of this affiliation and of its self-expression have changed. While both Sitney and Bruss emphasize the importance of the cinematic apparatus in their formulations of filmic autobiography, Bruss insists on both social context and representational technologies as influences that alter human subjectivity and our perceptions of it. Her essay comes much closer than Sitney's to apprehending the relation of much autobiographical work to history in contemporary feminist experimental cinema.

Stealing the Ribbon

Media artists Lourdes Portillo, Rea Tajiri, and Cheryl Dunye are implicated in the history of avant-garde film and of women's cinema but are also "other" to these traditions. In their autobiographical films, they each take up formalist considerations and suspicions of representation and each relates the process of her filmmaking to her own life. In their uses of temporality, however, they replace "time" with "history" as the representational conundrum that drives and shapes their autobiographical meditations. Personal and private aspects of their lives therefore never serve as the pretext for abstract meditations on representation and the self. Rather all three filmmakers pointedly historicize their bodies, their experiences and their desires, placing them in very specific social and political locations and interdependencies.

The allegories of reading that each perpetuates make use of the indexical, material veracity of cinematic representation in a way that takes up but completely alters the stake of Rousseau's ribbon. That is, each filmmaker lies and ultimately reveals that she lies, but each lies by inventing a ribbon (of film) from a history that is not there, that was not recorded, that never existed. Their prevarications use the referential function of the cinema to testify to representational gaps and flaws that are inherent both to cinematic representation per se and to its historical applications as well. That is, each filmmaker assumes the formalist and self-reflexive tenets of the genre but uses them to indicate how and why these determinants are not and have never been enough.

History and Melodrama

Lourdes Portillo's *The Devil Never Sleeps/El diablo nunca duerme* begins with a reverie illustrated by two images, water and a religious icon: "When I dream of home, something always slips away from me just beneath the surface—the faces of my family, old stories, the land, mysteries about to be revealed. And sometimes I dream of Santa Rita, the patron saint of Chihuahua." Her meditation is interrupted by an event: "It all started when I received a message that my favorite uncle had died." Rumors in the family are flying. After a frustrating call to her uncle's widow, played "live" on the sound track over images of a graveyard, Portillo resolves "to go to Mexico and find out what really happened." Thus Portillo takes up her camera to investigate or document the reality of an event ("what really happened"), an endeavor that is specifically posed against the insufficiency of memories and dreaming, where "something always slips away."

From the first, the image track serves or documents the sound track. The narration presents itself and the filmmaking as immediate and contemporaneous with the investigation Portillo undertakes, an investigation that involves interviews with Uncle Oscar's family, friends, business associates, and the detective who looked into his death. These sequences, which make up the present tense of the film, are augmented by two other types. The first uses anecdote, still photographs, home movies, maps, and reenactments to render the interrelated histories of her Uncle Oscar, her family, and northern Mexico. The second, sometimes subsumed within the other two, documents the modes in which we tell stories, preserve memories, understand, document, and communicate events and construct what we take to be "true" histories. These sequences range from a shot of a bronzed shoe that serves as a memento of one of Portillo's deceased relatives to the repeated cutaways to televised melodramas that are being broadcast within the diegesis.

Portillo intercuts all three types of footage in the film's lengthy introduction that frames her subsequent investigation in very specific ways. Images of satellite dishes, phones, a hand writing her uncle Oscar's name on a gravestone, a television screen playing a melodrama, a map, and the Mexican flag all insist on the diverse kinds of mediation involved in any kind of information or knowledge. Following the title shot, we see images of a map locating her hometown, the Mexican flag, the sky, while we hear a song from the Mexican revolution written for Pancho Villa, who, like Portillo, was a northerner. These designations of location and nation are replaced by footage of a window, a door, the facade of a house, and finally a keyhole and the crack in a door through which the camera peers.

"Everything we left behind is now gone," Portillo recounts of her immediate family's move from Mexico, "except my memories." Moving from geography, nation, and history to the personal, Portillo both marks and complicates her status as Chicana and an American citizen. Chihuahua, Mexico, is her "home" but it is no longer familiar to her. It has become an enigma, a closed window, a gate, a keyhole. These images, signifying both access and obstacle, resonate with the film's investigatory structure. But they also, together with the map and the flag, signify borders, barriers, between nations and between abstract and literal edifices of historical and personal containment and identity. Portillo's camera looks in, signaling her complicated and liminal relationships with identity, nation, and home.

But some things have *not* changed. As we see several images of a building's exteriors and then a proscenium inside, Portillo remarks that the cinema, the first place she saw a film, is still the same. She muses, "All those years, I would immerse myself in melodrama and in that magical darkness I found what would obsess me for the rest of my life—the movies." Photographs of Pancho Villa and of Emiliano Zapata in his coffin, then of tourists photographing cathedrals, follow as Portillo observes: "History is followed like melodrama here. The passion for great heroic figures as legends is what people hold on to. The provinces have long been the stronghold of conservative values. In Chihuahua, which I soon found out, these values were a thin veneer of respectability covering over the sordid details of my uncle Oscar's death." In this crucial sequence, Portillo identifies the overarching trope of her film— the alignment of history and melodrama.[9] She exists both within this tradition and location and outside of them, as she, like the tourists, has come to Mexico with her camera to document her experience, then to return home.

The images and information that make up the introduction of Portillo's film skillfully weave together the disparities with which the subsequent narrative will be concerned: events and their myriad representations; dreams, memory, and other media of recording and communication; Mexico and the United States and Portillo and her family's existence within and between them; and finally the insinuation of the cinema's capacity for storytelling, documenting, and investigating that will constitute Portillo's autobiographical film.

In the film that follows, Portillo makes use of traditional documentary strategies of truth-telling: narrating anecdotes as we see family photos; recounting the agricultural, industrial, and economic history of northern Mexico within which her uncle Oscar flourished and amassed a fortune; interviewing family and friends about his life and death. But she complicates the very narrative she "finds herself" telling as she tells it. Uncle Oscar's second wife, many years his junior and poor before he married her, has alienated the family. Many believe that she had him killed. Portillo documents this story while also attempting to document her Aunt Ofelia's side of the story. Ofelia will not appear on camera, so Portillo records what seem to be three different phone calls with her. The call that begins the film is followed in the middle by a lengthy conversation with visuals depicting Portillo with a sound crew and recording equipment capturing Ofelia's voice. This repeated footage resonates with the other images Portillo returns to again and again—cutaways to the ubiquitous telenovelas airing during the day. These serve as a form of diegetic commentary, casting doubt on Portillo's documentation as she produces it.

In the final section of the film, Portillo makes a "confession," even as she includes evidence that casts doubt on Ofelia's guilt, pointing to suicide instead. Speaking in Spanish, she inquires of a confessor, "If I believe someone is guilty of murder and I listen in on their phone calls is that a sin?" Also speaking in Spanish, the priest basically says yes. Portillo's confession must be translated via subtitles into the language of the narration. It thereby becomes ironic—literally double-voiced. Portillo, who has narrated the film in English up to this point and appeared only in the corners of frames, now occupies the linguistic milieu of the story as (guilty) subject. Further, this confession can be retrospectively understood only in light of the credits that reveal that an actress, Soco Aguilar, has performed all of Ofelia's recorded phone conversations. In addition, the film's narration was written not by Portillo but by Olivia Crawford and Laura del Fuego. In a *New York Times* review of this film, Stephen Holden noted that the film's conclusions "are too vague and scattered for her spadework to dig up a compelling drama." But this is precisely Portillo's point, which she explicitly asserts at the end of the film: "I came back to Mexico with the naïve idea that if I pursued all the clues, found out all the facts that I would uncover the truth, just like in the movies. Did Uncle Oscar commit suicide or was he killed by a hired assassin?" Her film compels its spectator to experience what she finally observes, that there are no clear solutions, only glimpses of truth.

Portillo, by incorporating diegetic telenovelas as a stylized form of commentary within her "documentary," suggests that no matter what the capacities of a medium (film, photography) for rendering truth, the modes of narration and understanding that permeate any culture will shape and mediate any search for history ("what *really* happened"). She complicates this message even further by littering her film with simulations. She reenacts the drowning of her uncle's tractor, using a toy tractor; she infers the causes of Oscar's first wife's cancer by depicting a huge tomato, incorporating the sound of a crop-dusting airplane, and then sprinkling powder on the tomato. But the most dramatic and reflexive simulations are her aunt Ofelia's phone calls and her own narration. Portillo articulates this narration as her immediate commentary on her investigation, which is depicted by the film as simultaneous with the filmmaking. Yet the credits reveal this narration, which provides the logic for the visual sequences, as scripted—that is, produced after the fact. Further, we have never heard Ofelia's actual voice, just that of an actress simulating her, speaking her lines. This post-film information dramatically recasts the meaning of the sequences that depict Portillo on the phone with her aunt, recording her voice, depicting the sound crew, the microphones, the tape-recorder, the telephone wires as we presumably hear a recorded conversation. What the film invites us to experience "as it happened" is revealed to be a retrospective reenactment or a fabrication; even Portillo's sin was a lie. What the film ultimately documents is film's capacity to simulate immediate documentation. But Portillo suggests, in a vertiginous and ludic conceit, that our faith in facts, in truth, and the representation of both in one all-encompassing history with an all-knowing author and reader, is our most compelling and ongoing engagement with melodrama.

Spectacles and Specters

The opening to Rea Tajiri's video *History and Memory* is significant for what it withholds: the image. Instead, a lengthy scroll of text, white letters on black background headed by the date, "December 7, 1961," describes an aerial shot of a man and woman that is *not* there as an image. This scroll is followed by another, in parentheses and italics, that grounds this absent shot, the absent image, in a very specific historical context and perspective: "The spirit of my grandfather witnesses my father and mother as they have an argument about the unexplained nightmares their daughter has been having on the twentieth anniversary of the bombing of Pearl Harbor, the day that changed the lives of 110,000 Japanese Americans who shortly after were forced by the U.S. government to sell their property, homes, cars, possessions, leave their communities, and relocate to internment camps." In this sequence, history is conjoined with an impossible perception; a visual framing (overhead—a crane shot? A zoom?) wedded to, explicated by, a metaphysical conceit. We are going to hear a ghost story, a horror story, a history lesson structured by the absence and impossibility of certain images.

Near the end of this scroll, we hear Tajiri's voice talking about a fragment, an image she has always had in her mind. The image, of her mother standing at a faucet filling a canteen with really cold water, appears on the screen for a couple of seconds, as Tajiri says, "The sun's just so hot, it's just beating down and there's this dust that gets in everywhere and they're always sweeping the floors." The image Tajiri shows us is her invention, her recreation of a memory she could not possibly have had. She remembers an experience her mother had before she was born, a memory her mother does not have. Though the image is referentially and logically false, Tajiri's film will articulate a context in which its lack of a referent will document the historical truth of memories that do not exist for a history that *did* happen.

Thus, in its opening minutes, Tajiri's film refers to complicated relationships involving history, witnessing, dreaming, memory, and visual documentation based on her family's and many other Japanese Americans' experience of trauma in the aftermath of Pearl Harbor. Systematically referencing and telling the official story through the various modes in which it was represented, Tajiri undercuts and devastates the veracity of the historical record by assessing it in relation to the stories and images that it withholds or that do not exist.

Tajiri is led to unearth these stories by puzzling and logically inexplicable behaviors in her own generation. What of her memory of her mother at the faucet in the camps? And what of the nightmares she began having on the anniversary of Pearl Harbor? And what of her sister's curious behavior, the filming of which opens the film proper, of following a boy on whom she had a crush through the park every day after school. Tajiri's voice-over tells us this was a phase her sister went through in high school and notes: "Rather than talk to him, she told me, she preferred to take his picture." Intercut with film stills of famous fictional couples—Elizabeth Taylor and Montgomery Clift, Rock Hudson and Dorothy Malone, actors playing Jack and Jackie Kennedy in Dallas—black-and-white footage depicts Tajiri's sister attempting to pose her reluctant subject. Tajiri explains that her sister had a box full of pictures of movies stars that she would pore over. She wonders "where my sister's habit of observing others from a distance came from." We see the stills. Her sister craves images but they are all of white people. Her desire is not for the Japanese American boy but for his image.

Subsequently, under the caption "History," Tajiri shows us footage from a newsreel entitled "Attack on Pearl Harbor." On the sound track she muses, "There are things which have happened in the world while there were cameras watching, things we have images for." A clip from *From Here to Eternity* follows, again under the caption "History," as Tajiri continues, "There are other things that happened while there were no cameras watching which we restage to have images of." Two more clips, one taken from captured Japanese footage from *Hawai Mare Okino Senjo Eigwa* and the last from a John Ford documentary on Pearl Harbor, illustrate Tajiri's final observations on images and events: "There are things which have happened for which the only images that exist are in the minds of the observers present at the time while there are things that have happened for which there are no observers save for the spirits of the dead." These meditations, aligned with the anecdote about her sister, subtly confound "private" issues of desire and sexuality with "public" concerns of history, documentation, and witnessing. Narrative and documentary film, photographs and film stills solicit and suture private desires and identities within public imaginings as in the instance of Tajiri's sister, but they extend beyond entertainment to world historical events. Yet what Tajiri's film is concerned with are the images, both fictional and documentary, which are withheld, whose effects—on her sister's desires, on her own dreams—are registered and interconnected by their absence.[10]

Tajiri renders this concern by contrasting publicly recorded and disseminated historical accounts of Pearl Harbor and the subsequent internment of Japanese-Americans with the memories and records of those whose lives were uprooted, their constitutional rights abrogated, their homes and possessions lost. She represents these different perspectives in the sound, image, and text tracks of her film. A clip from Curtiz's *Yankee Doodle Dandy* (1942) featuring the song lyric "We're one for all, all for one" in the war effort prefaces Tajiri's narrative of her mother's and father's entire families being interned while her father was serving in the U.S. Army. Tajiri's ongoing voice-over and the voices of her aunts, her father, her brother, and her mother radically alter the meaning of what we are seeing on the screen. Later in the text, for example, over rare camp film footage, we see smiling Japanese Americans digging ditches and performing other daily activities as Tajiri remembers "living in a family full of ghosts. I could remember a time of great sadness before I was born." The lie of the smiles, of the "home movies" in the camp, is revealed by an impossible memory whose assertion we nevertheless immediately recognize as the truth. Tajiri continually documents the effects of an intergenerational memory whose temporality completely confounds the logical and contemporaneous relationship we take to exist between an event, its experience, and its representation. She begins her film with the puzzling memories and behaviors of her generation, only to trace their causes to the experiences of her parents, experiences they have not told her about and, in the case of Tajiri's mother, do not remember.

Tajiri's script inverts the usual hierarchy between public history and private memory in relation to truth. But she enacts this inversion in a film that consistently undercuts its own referential function and locates the truth in what we are not seeing, in images that exist not as documentation but as fiction, and finally in experiences of which there is no recollection. The end of the film consists of video footage depicting Tajiri literally re-searching her mother's lost memory of the camps—that is, she visually retraces her mother's journey there, videotaping the trip, as we hear her mother's voice on the sound track saying, "I don't remember this. I don't remember how we got there." Tajiri asserts the truth of memory over that which we understand as history by documenting the memories her mother *does not* have.

Tajiri then ends the film, having explicated the elusive image with which she began it—that of her mother filling a canteen with water at a faucet. She has been living with this picture and now she has given it a story. She made this image for her mother, made a memory neither of them had in a history that was stolen from them. Tajiri brings a ghost into the world of representation, placing it into struggle with the official story by giving it epistemological status that ultimately outweighs its (false) ontological one.

Making History

Cheryl Dunye's *The Watermelon Woman* tells the story of a lesbian experimental filmmaker named Cheryl searching for details about an elusive African American film actress named Fae Richards. Using the conceit of fandom and star culture, Dunye collapses public and private history as they relate to media, documentation, and desire in such a way as to challenge the distinctions between fiction and nonfiction, autobiography and fantasy, actuality and invention.

The film opens at a wedding reception in Bryn Mawr, the first shot of Tamara, Cheryl's friend and business partner, standing in front of the camera with a light reflector, saying "Where do you want it?" Random shots of the reception and the guests—African American, Jewish, generic Anglo—follow, the scene thereby avoiding a simple black/white binarism. We hear Cheryl giving directions to Tamara, who walks in and out of the frame with equipment. Paid by a dour-faced, white matron on camera, Cheryl and Tamara have the first of many arguments, this one about money. Cheryl has taken money from Tamara's cut for a payment on their camera. When Tamara protests, Cheryl remarks, "You remember what Rose [Troche] and Gwen [Turner] said in the *Go Fish* book: 'if you want to make a film, you have got to make sacrifices.'" To which Tamara responds, "I'm not into making sacrifices . . . I need cash today!"

Though an apparently anomalous set piece, played for comedy and perhaps also to underscore how independent, avant-garde filmmakers get the bills paid, this "making-of-the-wedding-video" scene provides an excellent entrée to Dunye's subsequent autobiography of desire. It serves to introduce one of Dunye's overarching concerns: the pervasive and persistent ways that media interacts with and also rigorously circumscribes expressions of personal desire. Wedding videos, as James Moran notes, "cross all categories of ethnicity, gender, sexuality and age" yet nevertheless all tell "largely the same story" (360). Dunye starts from this "same story," retelling it from its most proscribed perspective, that of the videographer, whose image, voice, and sensibility must *never* appear in the ritualistic narrative she is paid to reproduce (Moran 367). Dunye positions this heteronormative story as incidental to the one she will recount. Her film is about (her) filmmaking—the money, labor, research, collaboration, and desire involved—and its relationship to history and visibility. Her reference to *Go Fish* signals these concerns, as well as the history of lesbian feature filmmaking, while also coyly referencing the mixed diegesis that *Watermelon Woman* will employ. Though Cheryl Dunye appears as herself in the film, Gwen Turner, the star of *Go Fish,* plays Diana, Cheryl's fictional girlfriend.

In the film's third sequence, Dunye directly addresses the camera, identifying herself as a filmmaker, then backtracking, "I'm working on being a filmmaker." She wants to make a film on black women "because our stories have never been told." She decides, on camera, to make a film about a beautiful black actress she has seen, credited only as "The Watermelon Woman" in a film called *Plantation Memories.* "I'm going to find out what her real name is, who she was and is, everything I can find out about her. I'm just going to tell you all about her." Like Portillo, Dunye articulates her project as an investigation that her camera will document. Yet whereas Portillo's film seeks to record "what really happened," Dunye's will pursue the elusive object of the filmmaker's desire: there is "something in her [the Watermelon Woman's] face, the way she moves."

The remainder of the film interconnects various kinds of footage: narrative sequences depicting Cheryl and Tamara's interactions with friends, lovers, each other, as they work on the project; interview footage, live, simulated, and fictionalized, of people giving opinions, information, and contextual information on Fae Richards (the Watermelon Woman); repeated sequences of Cheryl's direct address to the camera; scenes of the streets and skyline of Philadelphia. In the search for Fae Richards, Dunye documents race films, black theaters, and nightlife in Philadelphia and references the names of other African American actresses.

The film also features cameos by an array of African American and Anglo lesbian and gay writers, musicians, and critics, among them, Toshi Reagon (African American lesbian singer/songwriter), Brian Freeman (actor from the performance troupe Pomo Afro Homos), Cheryl Clark (African American lesbian poet), Sarah Schulman (lesbian novelist), and Camille Paglia (eccentric cultural critic). This casting continues the work of historical documentation the film performs throughout, referencing aspects of and artists involved in queer cultural expression—novels, poetry, performance, and music. Also, in using these artists, who appear either as themselves or as fictional characters, the film articulates different readings and levels of familiarity for its audience based upon queer and ethnic culture and media savvy.

Yet Dunye evades reifying any particular identity or position in the complicated interactions that make up her "personal" life in the film. Tamara, her best friend and partner, constantly clocks "the girls" and enjoys gay porn. She wants to match Cheryl up with another African American woman (Yvette) who is clearly not her type. She also takes an instant dislike to Diana and Annie, both of whom are white, and she accuses Cheryl of getting involved with Diana because she wants to be white. But the film ultimately verifies Tamara's analysis of Diana's fetishistic interest in Cheryl as correct. In the interactions and differences between its characters, the film refuses to make any doctrinaire statements about identity positions or desires but rather depicts how difference(s) marks conflicts, jealousies, desires, and denial.[11]

Dunye skillfully constructs this autobiography as one in which her "moment of artistic vocation" is inseparable from her search for Fae Richards, whose life uncannily turns out to mirror aspects of her own, but with a twist. Dunye makes a film about an African American actress involved with a white woman director while she is also having a relationship with a white woman, Diana. Neither relationship lasts, and Dunye's relationship with Diana is depicted significantly as incidental to her roles as filmmaker, star, and director of *The Watermelon Woman*. That is, her desire for the Watermelon Woman, her desire for her film, exceeds her desire for Diana.

As with Portillo's film, Dunye's involves us in a search that, despite promising leads and tantalizing bits of information, ultimately proves disappointing, with incomplete results. In the film's stunning final sequences, Dunye reappears, her words resembling Portillo's: "I thought it was going to be easy. I thought I was going to be able to use the camera to document my search for Fae. But instead I'm left empty-handed, except for this package from June." Addressing the woman who was probably Fae Richard's lover and companion for the last twenty years of her life, Dunye says of Fae Richards: "I know that she meant the world to you but she also meant the world to me. . . . What she means to me, a twenty-five-year-old black woman, means something else; it means hope, it means inspiration, it means possibility, it means history. And most important, what I understand is that I'm going to be the one who says I am a black lesbian filmmaker who's just beginning but I am going to say a lot more and have a lot more work to do."

The beginning and end of the film mark Dunye's transformation from "working on" being a filmmaker to "being" a black lesbian filmmaker. Yet she affirms her working identity in a particularly paradoxical context. She announces, "Anyway, what you have all been waiting for, the biography of Fae Richards, Faith Richardson." As she narrates Fae's biography, stills, photos, and film clips illustrating her narration, the biography is intercut with the credits, which reveal that an actress has played Fae Richards and that the documentary footage, the clips, the evidence all document a woman who never existed. Lest the spectator miss the inference of the credits, Dunye also includes a quote, "Sometimes you have to create your own history. The Watermelon Woman is a fiction."

This sequence, structured as a palimpsest, crystallizes the brilliant interplay between history and desire cumulatively articulated by the whole film. Dunye's direct address, together with the search structure of the narrative, insinuates the spectator in its protagonist's goals. By this point in the film, we *want* Fae Richards to exist. The final credit sequence formally demonstrates the dilemma: what do we choose to pay attention to, to believe in—the evocative black-and-white images, this impossible, compelling narrative or the documentation of the credits? Dunye not only chronicles her own search, her own desire for mirroring, for a history, for origins; she also compels the spectator to experience that desire *even as* she certifies it as a fantasy. Her closing sequence provides a resonant analog to the one that opened the film. In each, Dunye underscores the production process, the mediation involved in any scenario of desire, whether it is of the "same story" or of the one never told. Her wedding video carefully reveals what is left out of such productions—behind-the-scenes conflicts, staging, planning and attendant annoyances, and the desperation and boredom on the faces of some of the guests. At film's end, the biography of the Watermelon Woman captures what the wedding ceremony represses, the structure of desire. Her film thus sketches two modes of historical discourse, one of which simply documents facts and events. The second one puts desire into the picture and thereby has an elusive object that cannot be pinned down or verified. Once again the absence of the referent, the fiction of the images, testifies to, documents the reality of a history that has not been written, recorded, or, in this case, even existed.

* * *

In Portillo, Tajiri, and Dunye's autobiographical work, each filmmaker is looking for something, wants something that is not there: dreams, phantom images, desire. Portillo wants to know and to make a film about "what really happened" to her uncle Oscar and how he died. Rea Tajiri seeks her mother's lost experience in and her absent memories of the internment camps. Cheryl Dunye wants to find a history, images of her own desire. Each of their searches leads them to encounters with public institutions of various sorts, but the most significant in each case is the media. Each filmmaker creates an image for what they cannot find, what is impossible to document, and it is precisely their creation and confession of these false images that expresses the truth of their autobiographies. As in Rousseau, the lies told by their ribbons of film testify to the truth of what is not there: their desire, their history, stories of what really happened, whose absent reality can only be certified by falsehood, simulation, and invention.

NOTES

1. Julia Lesage's essay on women's autobiographical filmmaking has informed my approach in this piece. See her "Women's Fragmented Consciousness in Feminist Experimental Autobiographical Video," in *Feminism and Documentary*, ed. Dianne Waldman and Janet Walker (Minneapolis: University of Minnesota Press, 1999), 309–23.

2. I consider how gender was constructed as the preeminent social difference in America via the doctrine of separate spheres as a way of defusing and domesticating other, primarily racial and class, differences in *American Domesticity.*

3. Scott MacDonald's "Avant-Gardens" in this collection traces a lineage of women filmmakers whose work provides a wonderful complement to the filmmakers I discuss. The women filmmakers he considers resolutely focus on the domestic and its importance, refusing to trivialize it, as patriarchal discourses have so often done, or to critique it, as feminism has done.

4. The sacrament of confession was not codified until 1215 by the Lateran Council. Georg Misch's extensive *A History of Autobiography in Antiquity* (Cambridge, Mass.: Harvard University Press, 1951) convincingly makes the case that Augustine's innovation was not that of autobiography per se but of the confessional mode of self-scrutiny, which dictated a philosophical understanding of his life in relation to "its direction, its ends and aims, its meaning." See part 3 chapter 3, "The Confessions of St. Augustine," 625–67.

5. The incident with the ribbon occurs at the end of book 2 of the *Confessions.* See Paul de Man's extensive discussion of this incident and its significance in "Excuses" (*Allegories* 278–301).

6. Originally published as "The Purloined Ribbon," in *Glyph: Johns Hopkins Textual*

Studies 1 (1977): 28–49, the piece was included by de Man as the last chapter, entitled "Excuses (Confessions)," of his *Allegories of Reading.*

7. Sitney writes: "What makes autobiography one of the most vital developments in the cinema of the late Sixties and early Seventies is that the very making of an autobiography constitutes a reflection on the nature of cinema and often on its ambiguous association with language" ("Autobiography" 202).

8. Lucy Fischer's "Passion, Politics, and Production in *The Tango Lesson*" in this volume asserts that female directors always revise the established canon of the cinema. Potter's autobiography certainly constitutes a very interesting revision of autobiographical film-making in European art cinema.

9. Rosa Linda Fregosa calls Portillo's film a "melodocumystery," aptly capturing the generic boundaries the film crosses. See her "Devils and Ghosts, Mothers and Immigrants: A Critical Retrospective of the Works of Lourdes Portillo," in *Lourdes Portillo: The Devil Never Sleeps and Other Films,* ed. Rosa Linda Fregosa (Austin: University of Texas Press): 81–101.

10. See Abe Mark Nornes, "Our Presence Is Our Absence: History and Memory," *Asian America: Journal of Culture and the Arts* 2 (Winter 1993): 167–71.

11. Laura L. Sullivan makes this point in "Chasing Fae: *The Watermelon Woman* and Black Lesbian Possibility," *Callaloo* 23:1 (2000): 451–52.

6

Sally Potter

As an independent British filmmaker with ties to numerous other arts, Sally Potter is the reigning "Renaissance woman" of the current cinematic avant-garde. In the 1970s she studied dance at the London School of Contemporary Dance and later joined Strider, an innovative dance company led by Richard Alston. In the years to follow, she formed her own company with Jacky Lansley, the Limited Dance Company. While she had made films since her teenage years, in this period she combined her interests in cinematography and dance, creating *Combines* (1972), a three-screen work exhibited at The Place, a contemporary dance theater in London.

Potter soon branched out into the area of performance art. She authored and appeared in several solo shows and in large-scale theatrical productions (e.g., *Mounting: Death and the Maiden* and *Berlin*) in collaboration with Rose English. Potter is also a lyricist and singer and has performed with numerous bands. She worked with the composer Lindsay Cooper on a song cycle entitled "Oh Moscow," which she performed throughout Europe and North America. She collaborated with David Motion on the sound track for *Orlando* and does the vocals for her own composition on the sound track of *The Tango Lesson*.

Potter turned primarily to the cinema in 1978 with her release of a short film, *Thriller* (1979), a reworking (from a feminist/theoretical perspective) of Puccini's opera *La bohème*. Her short film *The London Story* (1980) followed. After this, she made her first feature film, *The Gold Diggers* (1983), shot by an all-female crew and starring Julie Christie. The film concerned the "circulation of gold, women and money" (lycos.com). Potter then focused on documentary, making a four-part series for Britain's Channel 4 (*Tears, Laughter, Fear, and Rage* [1987]) and a work on Soviet women filmmakers entitled *I Am an Ox, I Am a Horse, I Am a Man, I Am a Woman* (1988).

In 1992, Potter released *Orlando*, an internationally financed film starring Tilda Swinton and based upon Virginia Woolf's famous novel. The film brought worldwide attention to Potter and earned her two Academy Award nominations and twenty-five international awards, including the Felix, given by the European Film Academy. Following *Orlando*, Potter wrote four screenplays. Two of them have been produced, *The Tango Lesson* (1997), which has won numerous prestigious prizes, and *The Man Who Cried* (2000).

LUCY FISCHER

Passion, Politics, and Production in *The Tango Lesson*

Introduction: "Dancing Through the Mine Field . . ."

When Sally Potter came of age as a filmmaker in London of the 1970s, she did so within the force field of two powerful cultural movements: that of structural film and that of feminist theory. From the former, she inherited an appreciation for experimental cinema of a conceptual bent; and, from the latter, she gained an understanding of the ways in which issues of gender might be integrated into works of art.

When her first major film, *Thriller,* was released in 1979, it was immediately hailed by scholar E. Ann Kaplan as a groundbreaking "feminist theory film," a work "concerned with demystifying representation so as to make women aware that texts are producers of ideology" (*Women and Film* 138). Such films were said to be highly self-reflexive (drawing attention to the cinematic apparatus) and to deal with questions of female subjectivity and women's history (138–39). *Thriller,* clearly, conformed to this new genre, with its deconstruction of traditional melodrama (specifically the libretto of Puccini's *La bohème*), and its analysis of the tragic role of the heroine in literature and theater (153–54).

At first glance, Potter's film *The Tango Lesson* (made in 1997) seems a far cry from the stern and ascetic *Thriller.* For rather than dissect a patriarchal form like opera, she engages another—the tango. Moreover, instead of rejecting melodrama, she relishes it, since *The Tango Lesson* concerns her passionate and tumultuous love affair with dancer Pablo Veron. If *Thriller* conceived itself as classical opera's antagonist, *The Tango Lesson* imagines itself as the Hollywood musical's alter ego.

But, with a film as sly and complex as Potter's, we should not jump to rash conclusions about its relative conventionality. And, with a title like *The Tango Lesson,* we should not precipitously dismiss its pedagogical potential. For, ultimately, Potter's movie is a "theory film" for the nineties—one that has learned the lessons not only of tango, but of feminism as well.

In 1980, Annette Kolodny wrote an essay on feminist literary theory entitled "Dancing through the Mine Field" a phrase by which she meant to reference the perils and politics of working in her area. It is this kind of dangerous ideological "dance" (as well as the Latin variety) that Potter choreographs in *The Tango Lesson.* But if Potter's work is a revised "theory film," what suppositions does it rework? If it provides us lessons in more than the tango, what cultural curriculum does it endorse?

Lesson One: The Female Author

> There was an absolute explosion after I finished doing the press tour of *Orlando.* . . . I got back to my table and sat down and thought, "Now what?" I reached for my pencil and there was this wild explosion of ideas that had accumulated over the endless period of focusing on *Orlando.*
>
> —Sally Potter

It is useful to return again to Potter's formative years in the 1970s. At the same time that *Thriller* was released, American scholars Sandra Gilbert and Susan Gubar wrote *The Madwoman in the Attic,* a work that considered the status of the female writer in the nineteenth century. Focusing on the etymological connection between the words "author" and "authority," Gilbert and Gubar conclude that "it is no wonder that women have historically hesitated to attempt the pen . . . [a]uthored [as they are] by a male God and by a godlike male" (15). Engaging in further word play, Gilbert and Gubar ask, "If the pen is a metaphorical penis, with what organ can females generate texts?" (7).

As though self-consciously to raise this issue, *The Tango Lesson* begins with black-and-white footage of a table which holds a blank sheet of paper. In close-up, Potter's hand lifts a pencil and begins to write. Abruptly, the image shifts to color footage of a female model, dressed in red, who is fired upon by a gun. The image then returns to black-and-white and depicts a blank page on which Potter writes the word "rage." Immediately, she crumples the sheet and discards it. As though to imply her frustration in writing (and need for escape), the next sequence presents Potter in Paris, entering a theater in which the tango is to be performed. It is here that she first encounters dancer Pablo Veron. What this segment succinctly communicates is the female author's conventional difficulty with creation—a dread and blockage that propels her toward flight. Significantly, Potter has attempted to compose with a pencil, a more tentative implement than a pen.

When Potter returns to London, she again confronts her tabula rasa. As she sharpens her pencil, the screen erupts with Felliniesque color images of a drama in which high-fashion models are fired upon during a photography session. When the image returns to that of Potter in black-and-white, she seems frustrated in writing, and relaxes by taking a few tango steps. In the next sequence, she enters a London night spot for ballroom dancing.

In a later segment, she again confronts a blank sheet of paper, but is distracted, by a stain on her table. After some intervening color footage of the fashion thriller narrative, Potter kneels on the floor and examines a crack in the wood planking. Her act again suggests female writer's block, this time masked by obsessive-compulsive behavior which focuses on the minutia of domestic space. As the drama continues (and not only Potter's floor but ceiling disintegrates), we are reminded of the Gothic genre and of the decaying house in which the literary heroine often finds herself. Here, we would seem to have The Fall of the House of Potter—whose collapse seems tied to her disquiet with artistic creation. At a contractor's suggestion, Potter vacates her crumbling London abode (while he tears it up). She travels to Buenos Aires to pursue her "double life" as a tango dancer. Clearly, A Room of Her Own has proven a troubled site.

Lesson Two: Pleasure or Pain

The magic of the Hollywood style at its best . . . arose . . . from its skilled and satisfying manipulation of visual pleasure.

—Laura Mulvey

Significantly, in bolting to Argentina, Potter leaves behind an aborted film scenario. Entitled *Rage* (shown to us in fleeting, garish vignettes that contrast with the other black-and-white segments), it seems a quasi-experimental work (which draws upon themes from films like *The Eyes of Laura Mars* [1978]) and concerns a group of models murderously pursued by a demented, legless fashion designer. At a meeting with Hollywood executives, Potter (with calculated pretension) calls it a "treatise on beauty and the glamorization of death" (while they crassly deem it "Carnage on the Catwalk"). Although in the late seventies, such a narrative might have been novel (bespeaking the newly voiced feminist "rage" at a voyeuristic culture of female objectification), by now it seems clichéd and hackneyed—which is, precisely, the point. On some level, Potter abandons not only a screenplay entitled *Rage,* but the very emotion that it signifies. Thus, in trekking around the world in pursuit of the tango, she is choosing pleasure over pain—an amorous "last tango in Paris," instead of a grim "dance of death."

In so doing, Potter questions feminist doctrine of the 1970s which, suspicious of visual pleasure, called for the forging of a new type of art. As Laura Mulvey wrote in her seminal 1975 essay, "It is said that analysing [*sic*] pleasure, or beauty, destroys it. That is the intention of this article. The satisfaction and reinforcement of the ego that represent the high point of film history hitherto must be attacked" ("Visual Pleasure" [1992] 748). Clearly, in the intervening years (between 1975 and 1997), the feminist community had shifted its stance on this issue. In 1982, a provocative conference, "Towards a Politics of Sexuality," was held at Barnard College and produced an anthology, *Pleasure and Danger,* in which the alleged "puritanical" nature of the contemporary women's movement was questioned. As Carole S. Vance wrote in an introduction: "To focus only on pleasure and gratification ignores the patriarchal structure in which women act, yet to speak only of sexual violence and oppression ignores women's experience with sexual agency and choice and unwittingly increases the sexual terror and despair in which women live" (1). As she remarks, the intent of the conference was not to weaken the critique of danger but "to expand the analysis of pleasure" (3). The titles of several essays in the collection illustrate how the subject was foregrounded: "Seeking Ecstasy on the Battlefield" (by Ellen Carol DuBois and Linda Gordon), "The Taming of the Id" (by Alice Echols), "*Variety:* The Pleasure in Looking" (by Bette Gordon), and "No More Nice Girls" (by Brett Harvey). In a similar vein, Lynne Segal, in *Straight Sex: Rethinking the Politics of Pleasure,* voices her regret that the women's movement has turned away from a validation of "women's rights to sexual pleasure and fulfillment" to embrace a "bleak sexual conservatism" (xii). Even feminist historical studies, like that of Lauren Rabinovitz on Chicago, examined turn-of-the-century mass amusements to demonstrate how they "addressed the relevance of female identity formation to pleasure seeking" (*For the Love of Pleasure* 178).

Not only had Mulvey's seminal essay challenged visual pleasure, it had called for the renunciation of popular narrative in favor of a "politically and aesthetically avant-garde cinema" ("Visual Pleasure" [1992] 748). Once more, in the decade following the publication of her tome, feminist critics disputed her rejection of classical form—attempting to locate gaps and fissures in mainstream works that voiced female rebellion, or offered women a position from which to "redeem" their love of traditional texts. Mulvey herself, in a piece entitled "Afterthoughts on 'Visual Pleasure and Narrative Cinema,'" revised her earlier posture, admitting that the female spectator can assume multiple viewing positions, some of which allow her the satisfaction of identifying with the male hero (29–38). In a related move, Jackie Stacey in *Star Gazing* (1994) interviewed female movie fans to document their pleasure in identifying with favored screen actresses (127). Similarly, in *Loving with a Vengeance* (1982), Tania Modleski defended the values of televised soap opera—arguing that serial melodrama addressed woman's role as mediator of the family circle. Likewise, Pam Cook viewed the stylistic contradictions (expressionism vs. realism) of *Mildred Pierce* (1945) as self-reflexively surfacing the schizoid role of women in patriarchy ("Duplicity" 68–82). Finally, I asserted that, despite its aura of standard *grand guignol*, the horror film *Rosemary's Baby* (1968) articulated valid concerns experienced by pregnant women (*Cinematernity* 73–91). In the spirit of such feminist revision, Potter rejects her scenario for *Rage* (a film she admits she did not want to make) and moves from the confines of experimental cinema to the broader realm of modernist narrative. In so doing, she frees herself from her artistic demons.

Thus, retrospectively, Potter's uneasiness in writing seems reasonable. It is not that the female author has made no progress since the nineteenth century (the era which Gilbert and Gubar study). Rather, it is that to write one must remain true to oneself rather than craft a text according to cultural expectations (the "ladylike" novel or the "politically correct" screenplay). As an earlier epigraph makes clear, however, the "real" Sally Potter faced no writer's block in conceiving *The Tango Lesson*. Rather, it came to her as a "wild explosion of ideas" upon the completion of *Orlando* (1992).

Lesson Three: Through the Looking Glass

Before the woman writer can journey through the looking glass toward literary autonomy . . . she must come to terms with the images on the surface of the glass.

—Sandra Gilbert and Susan Gubar

In actually having *lived* a variant of the love story she performs and dramatizes (her off-screen romance with Pablo Veron), Potter's impetus in making *The Tango Lesson* is more than theoretical. By allowing a version of her affair to be restaged within the film, she squarely enters the autobiographical realm (Monk 54).

Critics responded quite differently to Potter's gesture. Claire Monk saw *The Tango Lesson* as existing "perilously on the knife edge between reality and fiction," but praised the director for taking a "significant personal risk" to make "a film which is mostly intriguing and affecting rather than embarrassing" (54). David Rooney, on the other hand, thought that *The Tango Lesson* ran "to self-indulgent extremes," and predicted that people would either "adore" or "abhor" it (he clearly falling into the latter camp).

In metaphorically violating the "180-degree rule" and moving from *behind* to *before* the camera, Potter breaks the normal pattern for female film artists who, typically, move from screen star to director (as did Jeanne Moreau, Ida Lupino, and Barbra Streisand)—and not the other way around. Finally, in using the autobiographical mode within a film about gender politics, Potter utilizes what Kathleen McHugh terms in this volume "a privileged genre for identity politics [that] demonstrates the crucial importance of the self in Western epistemology and the dependence of both self and epistemology on social, religious, and political infrastructures and institutions" (108).

Lesson Four: Dance and Film

> My notes to myself say things about writing as dancing, dancing instead
> of writing. The notes say that my body has been involved on the pages.
> —Sally Potter

In making *The Tango Lesson* (and assuming the role of actor/director), Potter not only connects with the auteur tradition of figures like Welles and Chaplin, she joins with those whose legacy is dance and film. On one level, this establishes ties between her work and that of other avant-garde women artists. Maya Deren, Yvonne Rainer, Amy Greenfield, Doris Chase, and Kathy Rose have all made experimental films that highlight their own status as dancer/cineaste (see Fischer, "Shall We Dance?" and "The Eye for Magic"). But Potter's focus on dance also links her to the mainstream cinema. We should not forget that some of the *first* appearances of woman on film in the late 1890s involved dance, be it Fatima the belly dancer, Loie Fuller the skirt dancer, or Annabelle the butterfly dancer.

Clearly, given the association of dance with visual spectacle, it has attached most easily to the female body, which was already culturally marked for that purpose. Significantly, when women began to direct films, they sometimes critiqued this assumption. A classic work, in this regard, is Dorothy Arzner's *Dance Girl Dance* (1940), which attacks the entertainment industry for casting women as burlesque queens rather than as ballerinas (see Fischer, *Shot/*

Countershot 148–54). But rather than assume the canonical feminist position (of rage against dance's enlistment of the female body in visual spectacle), Potter tends to complicate the issue. For if, at moments, in *The Tango Lesson*, she approximates Maya Deren, at others, she resembles Ginger Rogers, who rendered a tango-like "Carioca" in *Flying Down to Rio* (1933).

Thus, at times, Potter allows for the sensual pleasures of conventional ballroom dancing, despite the problematic politics of its discourse. For, as Sally Peters notes, "Though chaos may rage in male/female relations in the larger culture, the landscape of the ballroom is infinitely . . . ordered" (147). That "order" traditionally identifies the male role as one of "strength and dominance" and the female role as one of "grace and submissiveness" (157). Yet, many progressive women would confess to experiencing a sense of exhilaration in watching Fred and Ginger dance—perhaps because of Rogers's feisty persona, or Fred's genteel masculinity. Clearly Potter, too, feels the pull of the musical's seduction and rejects the claim that such choreographed fantasy must be entirely retrograde.

Hence, throughout the film, her camera moves fluidly and elatedly along with the dancers, becoming a kinetic third partner to them. Furthermore, certain sequences pay loving homage to the Hollywood musical. In one, she and Veron dance by the mist-laden Seine, in a scene that could be from *An American in Paris* (1951). In another, they tango in a thunderstorm, in a moment reminiscent of *Singin' in the Rain* (1952). Finally, in another segment, Veron tap dances on a mantel in his apartment, paying debt to the comic bricolage characteristic of the musical. Potter's attraction to the sensuality of dance (and the challenges of filming it) is apparent in the following statement. As she notes: "You can't really film the experience of dancing, at least not directly. You may get the surface of it, but you don't get anything that resembles the incredible feeling in the body that dance gives you" (qtd. in MacDonald, "Interview" 195).

Lesson Five: Tango Argentino

[T]he tango embrace . . . is the embrace of dominators and dominated (class-, race-, and gender-wise) struggling with and clinging to each other; trying to hold each other in place while dancing displacements.

—Marta Savigliano

While all of ballroom dancing has its ideological discourse, tango has a particular rhetoric. Conceived in Argentina in the late nineteenth century, tango has its roots in the dance of African enslaved exiles in the Rio de la

Plata region (Savigliano xiv). Not only was the dance, originally, associated with the racial Other, it was linked to the lower classes and to the culture of brothels and slums (Taylor 2).

Tango evinced a particular sexual politics that was associated with a male-oriented subculture (Savigliano 12). As Marta Savigliano observes, "the dilemma of macho pride ... haunts the tango" (44). There are two traditional styles of the art form: the ruffianesque and the romantic. It is the former and older brand that is most tied to the aggressive male posture. In the archetypical tango plot (expressed in the song lyric), the *compadrito* (a "whiny ruffian") and the *milonguita* ("a rebellious broad") perform "gender stereotypes and heterosexual dynamics that [are] disturbing and unsettling for the bourgeois patriarchy, given its fixation with ... respectability" (Savigliano 47).

Because of its sexual politics, the tango was immediately marked by controversy. As Savigliano remarks: "The worldwide popularity of the tango has been associated with scandal: [it involves] the public display of passion performed by a heterosexual couple, the symbol of which is a tight embrace and suggestive, intricate footwork" (11). But a sense of outrage also attached to the dance's racial overtones: "Tango opened a place for itself among *les dances brunnes:* [along with] the Afro-American cake-walk, the Brazilian maxixe, and the apache" (Savigliano 111).

Eventually, the tango gained popularity with the Argentine middle and upper classes, as a sense of its disrepute was replaced by an aura of exoticism. Its popularity spread to Europe as part of what Savigliano terms the "world economy of Passion." As she notes: "Exoticism is an industry that requires distribution and marketing" (3). Especially struck by the tango's impact was Paris of the early 1900s, where dancers first performed the tango in Montmartre cabarets (Savigliano 109). By 1913, organized protests against the dance had been launched by civic and religious groups (Savigliano 109). Nonetheless, Paris became the "manager" of the tango; it "reshaped its style and promoted it to the rest of the world as an exotic symbol of heterosexual courtship" (Savigliano 122).

London also experienced tango fever. Turn-of-the-century England held "tango teas" and, in 1913, Gladys Beattie Crozier published an instruction manual called *The Tango and How to Do It*. As Savigliano remarks: "London and Paris ... became rather complementary, promoting the tango as a social dance and a stage *diva*, respectively. Paris, the capital of pleasure, developed the spectacular scenarios of the revue and the music halls.... London ... devoted its efforts to the social dance industry. Assuming England's role as the 'workshop' of the world, English dance-masters not only codified dance styles in manuals but also aggressively promoted the sport of dancing" (129–30). (Decades later, of course, Andy Warhol would mock such dance instruction in his piece *Dance Diagrams: Tango* [1961].) Meanwhile, in America, avant-garde dancer Ruth St. Denis choreographed a "Gringo Tango" which she performed with Ted Shawn at the Academy of Music in Newburgh, New York, in 1924 (Savigliano 134).

Given the dance's male-orientation, Savigliano remarks that "[a]t first glance, tangos seem to offer women two [unacceptable] positions. They can be either the object of male disputes or the trigger of a man's reflections. In either case, it is hard for a woman to overcome her status as a piece of passional inventory" (48). Yet Savigliano and others have noted the dance's qualified assertion of male dominance. In the tango ballad (which is part of a composite aesthetic of song and dance), "Teary-eyed men talk about how women (mis)treated them" (Savigliano 55). These lyrics are "male confessions" of weakness (Savigliano 55) and have been called "the lament of the cuckold" (Taylor 7). Significantly, when Pablo and Sally discuss her directing him in a film, he balks at the notion of playing a melodramatic scene: "Suppose I don't want a tear down my face," he says. "What else don't you want to do?" she sardonically replies.

What is especially interesting here is the focus on *male* (rather than *female*) melodrama, since women have often been associated with the form. For Peter Brooks, heroines (not heroes) are the classic melodramatic protagonists (symbols of innocence wronged, misprized, and abused). Furthermore, it was precisely this histrionic female role that Potter had dissected in *Thriller*. Thus, her interest in the lachrymose male subject of the tango ballad seems logical—challenging, as it does, the melodramatic paradigm.

If men are, ultimately, not that strong in tango discourse, then women are not that weak. Savigliano calls the *milonguita* a "femme fatale" and sees "a whole array of manipulative stratagems, deceptive behaviors, and strategies for subversion . . . allocated in tango—women's hands" (109, 57). Hence the art form engages in the "blatant exposure of . . . insurgency on the part of the victimized heroine" (71). As Savigliano notes: "Women's participation in tango, whether as characters . . . or as audience members, presents a dilemma. Tango has avoided giving any straight answers about women, perhaps because they were/are seen as the pawns of the tangueros' male wars. . . . [I] question the hegemony of the macho message" (69).

Lesson Six: Two to Tango

> I had wondered why my seeking out of tango practices in Buenos Aires
> had taken on a dimension so compelling that sometimes I found myself
> abandoning all other activities to sleepwalk to another shabby dance hall.
>
> —Julie Taylor

But what has the history and politics of tango to do with Sally Potter? It seems significant that she lives in London and first meets Veron in Paris, thus, negotiating two European capitals with strong historic ties to tango. Similarly, as one of many foreign tango devotees in Buenos Aires, she joins a long tradition of pilgrims who come to the city to study dance (Taylor 33). Julie Taylor remarks how people in Buenos Aires "walk in, right off the street, to . . . unlikely places and begin to dance" since "it is normal to go about ordinary business . . . with a pair of extra shoes just in case the opportunity to dance presents itself" (14).

Clearly, as a contemporary feminist, Potter would be especially interested in the sexual dynamics of tango. In the beginning of the film, when she first studies with Veron, she seems entirely under his spell—hanging on his every word, capitulating to his every choreographic command. Her subservience, of course, coincides with her growing ardor for him. By the drama's end, Potter has come to dismiss Veron's complaint that she "does too much" in dancing, and chastises him for "dancing like a soloist." Furthermore, she complains of having to "walk backwards," in executing the tango, which seems to have a political as well as spatial meaning. Hence, Potter invokes the rebellious spirit of the *milonguita* who saves tango from male domination. Potter, ultimately, extends her power by enlisting Veron for a role in her own film, thus reversing the positions of teacher and student, director and performer. As she proclaims: "It doesn't suit me to follow; it suits me to lead and you can't deal with that." Significantly, scholar Beatrice Humbert argues that tango's popularity in Europe at the turn of the century promoted women's liberation: "Tango opened a venue for women to exhibit sensuality in public. . . . [T]ango showed and performed the strong changes in gender roles that were under way at the time, conflictively joining voting demands, dress reforms, and the recent scientific findings in birth control as well as the psychoanalytic incursions in female sexuality" (qtd. in Savigliano 127).

A certain female power can even be found in the gaze associated with tango. As Taylor confesses, when she first frequented Buenos Aires dance halls, she was perplexed that no men asked her to tango. Her Argentinian girlfriends finally informed her that her gaze discouraged their approach. Evidently, she had immediately lowered her eyes whenever a potential male partner looked at her. As she recalls: "In a concerned fashion, the women around me explained that I needed to hold the other person's gaze to transmit acceptance of his invitation. This proved far more easily explained than performed. . . . Dropping my eyes was a reflex I did not know how to control" (39).

This need, in the dynamics of tango, for a strong (versus reticent) female gaze seems especially relevant for Potter, a filmmaker whose craft relies on the act of observation. Significantly, when she first witnesses Veron dance in a Paris theater, the camera focuses on her looking. To make parallels to cinema even sharper, he and his partner throw shadows against a white wall, like projected images upon a screen. Significantly, by the end of the drama, Potter's gaze has empowered her to move from the audience to the stage, thus, entering theatrical space herself.

One also recalls that, in the fragments we have seen of her defunct film *Rage,* there are two close-up shots of women's feet. In one image, a model in stiletto heels trips and falls on some stairs. In another, a woman in toe shoes walks, uncomfortably, on point. Significantly, when Potter arrives in Buenos Aires, the first thing she does is purchase a pair of sturdy tango shoes. Unlike the footwear depicted in *Rage,* these are shoes which empower, rather than constrain (despite their high heels).

If critics accused Potter of a certain melodramatic excess in *The Tango Lesson,* they should know that her stance borrows from the dance's aesthetic. As Savigliano notes, "Tangos . . . are public displays of intimate miseries, shameful behaviors, and unjustifiable attitudes. In tango, intimate confessions are the occasion for a spectacle" since "the personal is the political" (61). Moreover, the pathos of tragic love is also part of the tango's staple rhetoric, for "Tango is . . . a spectacle of traumatic encounters," a story of meetings "between those who should never have met" (iv–xv). As though to mock this melodrama, when Sally and Pablo say goodbye at the Paris airport, they execute a series of campy, overblown gestures on parallel moving sidewalks.

Finally, in dividing her film between dance numbers and narrative segments, Potter mimics tango's dual-track discourse of dance and song—elements which are quite separate and contradictory. One does not dance to music with lyrics; and the emotions of a tango ballad run counter to those of the choreography. As Taylor explains, "The passive woman and the . . . physically aggressive man [in the dance] contrast poignantly with the roles of the sexes depicted in the tango lyrics" (10). It is this complexity (of both art and romance) that Potter attempts to capture in her film.

Lesson Seven: Colonizing the Tango

Tango became exotic for the ones "up" who were looking "down."

—Julie Taylor

The female gaze is not the only one at issue in the tango. For, as Savigliano notes, "In tango, the [L]atin . . . couple dances for the bourgeois colonizing gaze. French, British, U.S. colonizers and their local allies have been key in shaping the . . . meaning of the tango steps" (76). According to this reading, Potter can be seen to occupy the questionable position of a privileged European who usurps and appropriates a foreign cultural artifact. For, as Taylor remarks, "Tango became exotic for the ones 'up' who were looking 'down'" (74).

To its credit, Potter's film makes oblique reference to this issue. In one Buenos Aires tango parlor, someone inquires suspiciously whether she is English, as though to suggest that she is out of place there. A cab driver is equally skeptical of her devotion to the dance, remarking that one must first suffer to comprehend the tango. Clearly, he sees her empowered national status as precluding any sensitivity to the form.

Attention to the issue of colonization helps elucidate an otherwise enigmatic aspect of the film. In conversations between Potter and Veron, the question of being Jewish is raised. It first arises one night as they sit and talk. Veron inquires whether Potter believes in God and she says that, although she is an atheist, she still "feels like a Jew." He confesses that he is also Jewish. Sharing this intimacy inexplicably brings tears to their eyes. Later on, Potter proceeds to tell him a so-called Jewish story about the ancient Jacob wrestling a stranger who he determines is an angel or God. Later, the couple stand beneath a painting of that biblical scene and enact the role of Jacob and his antagonist as portrayed on the canvas. We recall here that, upon meeting Veron, Potter remarked that he moved "like an angel." In yet another scene, Potter lies in bed reading Martin Buber's *I and Thou*, thus linking her love affair with a spiritual search. Finally, in a closing segment of the film, the couple sits in a synagogue, listening to religious chants, Veron wearing a yarmulka. When they leave, he says he is not at home in temple, but confesses that he fears being "without roots" and "disappearing without a trace" (anxieties also ascribed to the Jewish people). Just how central these exchanges concerning Judaism are to the film is emphasized when, later, in discussing Veron's performance in her upcoming movie, Potter talks of staging the very scene of their original conversation about religion.

What these suggestive but fragmentary conversations manage to do is to highlight tango's links to marginalized or colonized peoples—be they Jews or blacks. Similarly, this thematic foregrounds the dance's attraction to the Other—be it Veron (whose Jewish family immigrated to Argentina some time in the past) or Potter (who journeys there today). For, as Savigliano notes, "The history of tango is a history of exiles" (xiv). Here we should recall that in addition to having its own historic Jewish population, Argentina was a site to which Jews fled in the era of World War II.

Lesson Eight: Celluloid Tangos

In the period of the early twenties, technical advances in the electrical media of phonographs and moving pictures give the tango a broader audience than was possible earlier.

—Donald Castro

In *Shot/Countershot: Film Tradition and Women's Cinema,* I argued that female directors, to some degree, all revise the established canon—one that has been predominantly authored by men. If we apply that framework to Sally Potter's *Tango Lesson,* certain classic films demand the spotlight.

We recall that an early screen idol gained popularity through his rendition of the tango. I am, of course, speaking of Rudolph Valentino—an actor who induced an erotic frenzy in his female fans, yet another scandal associated with the dance. In *The Four Horsemen of the Apocalypse* (1920), a scene takes place in a seedy Buenos Aires café. Valentino (playing Julio Desnoyers, the dissolute grandson of a wealthy Argentinian) stares intensely at the dance floor while smoking a cigarette. Dressed in full gaucho regalia, with whip in hand, he approaches a couple. Winking at the woman (who seems to be an aging prostitute), he chases her partner away, then grabs her to dance. In a shot which follows, Valentino's magnetic allure is emphasized as the couple tangos straight toward the audience, with the camera retreating at their approach. Julio is part French, and, when his family inherits money, they travel to Paris. There, he finds a city crazed for the tango. As an intertitle tells us: "The world was dancing. Paris had succumbed to the mad rhythm of the Argentine tango." People attend "tango teas" and take dance lessons, and Julio soon builds a reputation as a skilled instructor.

Clearly, in the narrative of *The Tango Lesson,* we find reverberations of *The Four Horsemen.* Like a film from the 1920s, it is shot in black-and-white. Like Julio Desnoyers, Potter (a fellow European) travels between Paris and Buenos Aires. Furthermore, she falls in love with a handsome, Valentino-like tango instructor who aspires to act in films. (In one scene, we see Veron reading a book about Marlon Brando.) If the story of Jacob and the angel figures allegorically in *The Tango Lesson,* the parable of the angel of prophecy is invoked in *The Four Horsemen* (in relation to the coming world war). But if, in *Horsemen,* the tango is a dance which, as Julio's mother asserts, nice girls must avoid, in Potter's film, woman delights in Dirty Dancing.

In so doing, Potter becomes identified with the male/libidinous stance—a fact that is emphasized by her rapture in watching Veron. Not only is she depicted gazing at him in the audience of a Paris theater, but she is represented that way as he later dances in his apartment. Furthermore, toward the end of the film, when he rebels at her position as film director, he accuses her of having become camera-like in her perception of him. She responds by claiming that she loves him "with her eyes" and "with her work." Thus, it is Veron (as opposed to Potter) who is mostly "looked at" in the film, thereby being located in the traditional female role. Here, we are reminded that Valentino was often charged with effeminacy and disliked by a male public which was suspicious of him as the object of female erotic fantasy.

Potter's interest in gender fluidity is apparent not only in her film *Orlando,* but in various statements she has made. For example, in one interview, she notes that her "own sexual history is . . . complex." As she continues, "I don't have a singular sexual identity. . . . I'm more interested in the idea of claiming identities then throwing them away, and of melting identities, as gender melts" (qtd. in MacDonald, "Interview" 218). Perhaps this is why there is a theme of doubling in *The Tango Lesson,* by which Potter and Veron are equalized. When they enact the drama of Jacob and the angel, we are reminded that Potter had said that Jacob was merely fighting himself. Significantly, when they assume that pictorial posture, they also look like a couple in a tango embrace. The final sequence of the film bears out this doppelganger motif, as we hear Potter sing: "You are me and I am you. One is one and one are two."

Lesson Nine: Shot/Countershot

> The text is . . . a multi-dimensional space
> In which a variety of writings, none of them
> original, blend and clash. The text is a
> tissue of quotations drawn from the
> Innumerable centres of culture.
>
> —Roland Barthes

If we turn now to the contemporary cinema, we find that it is no longer the case that women directors alone must address an alien, established canon.

For, by now, their work has entered the mainstream. Significantly, a year after Potter's film emerged, a male director made a work so similar that it had to be viewed in relation to hers. I am speaking of Carlos Saura, whose *Tango* (1998) was directly compared to Potter's film in a review by Janet Maslin.

Clearly, Saura had already done significant work in the dance film genre, having made *Carmen* (1983) and *Flamenco* (1995). Like *The Tango Lesson*, his movie concerns a dancer making a film about the tango. Here, the protagonist is not a stand-in for the director but a fictional character named Mario Suarez (Miguel Angel Sola). Mario is divorced from one dancer in his company, though he is still captivated by her. Soon, however, he falls in love with another performer, a young woman named Elena (Mia Maestro), who is the girlfriend of a gangster. The film toys with the ambience of film noir and with the tensions of love, jealousy, murder, and retribution. Though *Tango* has far more plot than Potter's movie, it is equally self-reflexive. In the opening of the film, in a scene paralleling that of Potter at her writing table, we see Mario's hands holding a pen (not a pencil) and reviewing pages of a film script from which his movie is to be shot. Furthermore, most of the dance sequences (which take place in a cavernous rehearsal hall) are done in abstract, shadowed tableaux that are entirely synthetic.

What is, perhaps, most noteworthy about *Tango* (in relation to Potter's work) is its complete male orientation—with Mario identified with tango's *compadrito*. Saura's film is represented as entirely Mario's fantasy, with many of the scenes superimposed over images of him reclining in bed, as though dreaming or imagining. While Potter largely eschews the tango lyric (which is identified with the remonstrative *tanguero*), Saura wallows in the music's anguish—a stance that conceives the male as a victim of female perfidy. As an opening song croons: "How could I know that her affection would cause me all the troubles that it did?"

Finally, Mario relishes the role of male director/impresario. An opening voice-over queries: "Who is Mario Suarez, the hero of our story? That's not as important as what happens to him." It is clear that Mario has functioned as Svengali to his former wife and, again, gleefully assumes that role with the young Elena—launching her dance career by featuring her in his production. While Maslin compares *Tango* to Bob Fosse's *All That Jazz* (1979), we might also liken it to Federico Fellini's *8½* (1963)—the paradigmatic tale of the male artist/lover. While Potter downplays the violent aspects of tango lore in favor of its romantic side, Saura highlights the dance's cultural associations with machismo and brutality. In one tango number, two *compadritos* fight over a woman (played by Elena). When she is stabbed, we are unsure whether the deed is part of the fictional script or a bloody retaliatory act ordered by her mobster beau.

While Potter focuses on the personal meaning of tango, Saura makes his meditation overtly political. Hence, one of the final dance numbers choreographs the tango within a scene of political torture, thus referencing the tragic fate of Argentina's "disappeared." (Earlier, someone had remarked that the police played tango music to drown out the sound of screaming prisoners.) As though to inoculate himself against criticism of this move, Saura scripts into the narrative a woman who complains that such numbers do not belong in a musical.

Lesson Ten: Conclusion

Clearly, *The Tango Lesson* is a highly pedagogical and theoretical work. In the course of its narrative, it provides a treatise on the female author—portraying both the perils and glories of writing. At the same time, it questions rigid binaries that have haunted feminist thinking—those between sexual pleasure and oppression, those between male and female roles. Moreover, the film invokes (in the course of its modernist romance) the history of the tango as well as of the musical film. Finally, in the intertextual conversation that later developed between Potter's work and that of Carlos Saura, we find a representation of opposing stances toward the tango—ones that starkly conform to cultural notions of masculinity and femininity. Thus, the two films together constitute the perfect cinematic tango "couple" (*compadrito* and *milonguita*), locked in creative embrace. While in the traditional dynamic, it has been the female artist who has had to respond to the male's prior authorial statement, now it is the male director who must suffer "the anxiety of influence." Thus, in closing, we might return to the opening of *The Tango Lesson* and the image of Potter's dreaded writing desk. For it turns out to be not simply a symbol of the problematics of female authorship but an emblem of how the tables have turned.

7

Yvonne Rainer

Born in San Francisco (1934), Yvonne Rainer moved to New York to become an actor, but in 1957 she began studying modern dance. Subsequently she studied at the Martha Graham School and with Ann Halprin, James Waring, Merce Cunningham, Carolyn Brown, Judith Dunn, and Viola Farber. She choreographed and performed her first piece, *Three Satie Spoons,* in 1961 at the Living Theater in New York. She began a productive, successful association with the Judson Dance Theater. Then Rainer left performance in 1972 to pursue filmmaking.

From 1972 to 1996, she produced seven films that combine her interest in the body and bodies in motion with women's material and emotional circumstances. Rainer's film practice examines the affective and psychic consequences of women's everyday existence—including what Rainer calls the "shared emotions" of relationships—using her own life "as a sort of mythic source." The shift from dance to cinema allowed Rainer to explore emotion in its most populist and extravagant form: melodrama. Yvonne Rainer's use of melodrama in avant-garde films enables her to dramatize private and public moral dilemmas. Rainer's melodramas, ironic nonstories about women struggling for public voice, make melodrama politically progressive.

Especially concerned with issues of performance and identification, Rainer distances the spectator from the performer with complex editing techniques that disrupt narrative flow. Her first three films, *Lives of Performers* (1972), *Film about a Woman Who . . .* (1974), and *Kristina Talking Pictures* (1976), include dances Rainer produced years before and explore abstract principles of duration and continuity while portraying the emotional lives of performers.

In *Journeys from Berlin/1971* (1980), *The Man Who Envied Women* (1985), and *Privilege* (1990), Rainer unravels complex questions of identity and sexuality. In these renderings of women's lives from girlhood to menopause, Rainer probes the most intimate space of the self, the unconscious, offering insights into psychological conflicts complicating women's identity. The director's film MURDER *and murder* (1996) features largely linear narrative. The excessive distancing strategies of her earlier work disappear as bodies onscreen perform the erotic play of sexual romance. However this is not an ordinary love story; it is a romance between two middle-aged women. Thus, even when utilizing more familiar aesthetic forms, Rainer experiments with content and conventions of representing women's bodies.

PATRICIA LEVIN

Yvonne Rainer's Avant-Garde Melodramas

Yvonne Rainer's turn to feminism came several years after her work had already been embraced by feminist film theorists as a model for feminist filmmaking. The move to engage explicitly with feminist politics necessitated a reconceptualization of her longtime interest in minimalism and the so-called neutral body. In some ways we might see minimalism as both a break with the transcendental space of most modernist art and a return to realizing the potential charge of the mundane, or the arbitrary, as in Duchampian readymades. Minimalism repositioned the viewer and reintroduced the significance of both space and time in the form of presence by dismissing distancing devices. In this way minimalism privileges the complexity of phenomenological experience, perception, and presence. Elsewhere, I have argued that as Rainer attempted to use her minimalist aesthetics, conceiving bodies as "neutral" doers in her earlier films, the narratives produce a psychical disjunction and audio-visual incoherence. Encouraged by the choreographed structure and melodramatic mode of Rainer's films, both of which are already excessive, the narratives and performances produce effects similar to hysteria. The trauma of minimalism's neutral doer, embodied in the gendered trajectory of film history and reception, brings about slippages of excess. In these early works we can see Hal Foster's concept of deferred action at work; the significance of a sexed and gendered body emerges in anticipation of Rainer's subsequent embracing of a feminist critique.

Despite the filmmaker's public reluctance to identify herself with feminism, her viewers certainly recognized feminist dimensions in Rainer's first three films; and over time Rainer increasingly came to identify herself overtly with feminism as her career progressed. Thus, the move from minimalism's neutral body to a sexed and gendered subject parallels Rainer's ongoing analysis of her own position as an artist who happens to be a woman and of the cultural politics of her time. Her earlier films attempted to establish the possibility of a neutral doer in a field saturated with sex. *Lives of Performers, Film about a Woman Who* . . . , and *Kristina Talking Pictures* took minimalism's conceptualization of the abstract subject to its limits, pushing Rainer to question minimalism's unexamined embracing of phenomenology and instigating her turn to sexual politics. As feminism elaborated its concerns with subjectivity as constructed through language and institutions of power—both of which are thoroughly sexed and gendered—Rainer also made the connection and adopted the same concerns.

In *Journeys from Berlin,* for example, one of Rainer's characters defiantly exclaims, "[M]y cunt is not a castrated cock." This statement, with its brute directness and provocative force, bespeaks the filmmaker's interest in contemporary theory: psychoanalytic, feminist, and film. With these words, Rainer identifies theoretical tendencies to situate women in the abject position of Other against whom men can be favorably defined and against whose imagined "lack" men can experience fantasies of wholeness and plenitude. Rainer embraces theory with a vengeance, using it, turning it on itself, and unsettling it. I call this appropriation and deployment of various theoretical voices—a central strategy of the filmmaker's development as an artist, thinker, and self—Rainer's "ventriloquism."

The earlier films, while derived from Rainer's personal experiences, maintain emotional distance through a conceptual focus on performers, conceived as neutral doers. In her four films produced in 1980 or thereafter, Rainer personalizes her narratives, moving away from the abstracted lives of performers to examine the lives of everyday women. As always, her own life serves as "mythic source" book, but an added intimacy emerges as Rainer embraces the feminist manifesto "the personal is political." In *Journeys from Berlin/1971, The Man Who Envied Women, Privilege,* and MURDER *and murder,* Rainer unravels complex questions of identity and sexuality in private and public spaces. By examining women's lives from girlhood to menopause, Rainer peruses intimate spaces of self and unconscious, offering insights into psychical conflicts within female identity. Simultaneously, she mines the field of cultural politics and uses ventriloquism to explore representations of women in public discourses. In these films, Rainer's analysis of "femininity" in psychoanalytic theory, along with her exposition of how mass culture represents women, departs from and criticizes the supposedly nongendered, nonspecific subject of minimalist art.

True to her background (Rainer's parents were anarchists) and avowed political orientation, Rainer becomes a habitual anarchist in her films, using the avant-garde to break the patriarchal mold of that modernist institution by asking questions that exceed the traditional rhetoric of its masculinist soldiers, moving beyond its boundaries into the maverick arenas of gender and sexuality. She asserts her differences as both artist and woman. Before our eyes, in these films, we see the disjointed, bumpy spectacle of femininity in crisis. Rainer's personal examination of her status as a woman/artist compelled to self-scrutiny positions her "to look herself in the mouth" and to find her own voice by mouthing the voices of others, critically. Through a cinematic ventriloquism, Yvonne Rainer "speaks" her *self* into being.

Rainer's Ventriloquism

In 1981, Rainer wrote "Looking Myself in the Mouth" to describe her theoretical and practical relationship to narrative. Her title underscores the importance of vision and its connection to language, a connection Rainer's work has long explored by interweaving verbal texts and images. The title also rightly emphasizes Rainer's critical fascination with her own work. The article, structured like her films, entails a collage of appropriated quotations taken from important contemporary theorists. Rainer "dances" in, around, and through the appropriated texts, addressing and commenting on ideas expressed in the quotations. Rainer makes explicit in this essay the impossibility of escaping the tyranny of narrative, character identification, and various effects of narrative in conventional cinema. She summarizes her position in the following: "This text has been concerned with the necessity for problematizing a fixed relation of signifier to signified, the notion of a unified subject, and, specifically, within the codes of narrative film practice, the integrity of the narratological character. Any such problematizing, calling into question, or 'playing off' of the terms of signification of necessity involves an unfixing of meaning, a venturing into ambiguity, an exposing of the signs that constitute and promulgate social inequities" ("Looking Myself in the Mouth" 96).

Interestingly, this essay outright positions the artist as ventriloquist ("Looking Myself in the Mouth" 86), echoing her cinematic use of appropriated texts, film clips, music, and images. Might Rainer's ventriloquism be a manic performance of her own battle with narrative conventions? The phrase "looking myself in the mouth" suggests how significant Rainer's obsessive self-analysis and engagement with critical theories of the subject are to her post-seventies work. Rainer's ventriloquism, in incorporating the words and images of others, highlights the processes of identification she critiques in her turn to feminism.

Autography

As someone reminded me recently, I've already written
my autobiography in my films.

—Yvonne Rainer

Journeys from Berlin/1971, The Man Who Envied Women, Privilege, and MUR-
DER *and murder* examine the signifying spaces of women's everyday existence, elaborating negotiations of private desire as well as figurations of the feminine in the public sphere. Rainer's films combine appropriated critical texts with fictionalized elements of autobiography; thus her films become a filmic variation on *écriture feminine.* Formally avant-garde, they thwart numerous film conventions and yet they are melodramas. Relentlessly political, they pose questions about women, subjecthood, body, and identity in private and public spheres. Rainer grounds her investigations of femininity in specifics, with special attention to the problematic of the body, not as a biological entity, but as the psychically constructed image that provides a location for and imageries of unconscious processes like desire and fantasy. Whereas in the filmmaker's estimate, the feminist aspects of her earlier films remained secondary to their formal concerns, each of the four films discussed here deals with the explicitly feminist project of rendering feminine notions of desire and language on film. Rainer elaborates a new syntax for this project, speaking the female body differently by way of a consciously performed ventriloquism. Her halting, even inarticulate, mouthing of others' words enacts what Mary Ann Doane has called "the greatest masquerade of all," a "woman speaking (or writing, or filming), appropriating discourse" ("Woman's Stake" [1991] 172). In fact, Rainer is a consummate ventriloquist, convincingly performing the words of others through the belly of her films.

In *Journeys from Berlin/1971, The Man Who Envied Women,* and *Privilege,* Rainer makes the body disappear, sublimating it into texts that write the feminine body by fragmenting traditional narrative conventions: image and text rarely coincide in these films. Rainer's early attempt to impose a neutral doer—by downplaying the body and privileging text as expressive instrument—created a psychical disjunction in her early films. In those films the conflict between body and narrative in play with the expressionistic aesthetics of melodrama produced highly visible hysterical symptoms on the bodies of performers and in the film body itself.

Rainer's writerly approach to filmmaking might best be discussed in terms of autography, as defined by the feminist literary theorist Jeanne Perreault. Autography traces the discursive boundaries of identity in its elaboration of a "self." As such, it is a form of self-invention that Perreault sees as an important aspect of contemporary feminist textual practice. Autography differs from autobiography in that it does not necessarily follow the unfolding of life events; rather, it makes writing itself an aspect of the selfhood the writer experiences and brings into being (Perreault 4). Autographical texts can be seen as constructions of an evolving "self" that assert "a highly indeterminate feminism and an equally indeterminate notion of selfhood" (Perreault 7). Perreault explains:

> As women write themselves categories of difference (inner, outer, body, world, language) do not disappear, but take shape as "I" and in relation to "I." The shifts in relations between personal, body-specific identity and communal or ideological identity (the I who says we) both maintain ongoingness and require discontinuity. To the extent that "I" and "we" are imbricated in feminist autography, tracing the modulations of representation is the crux of feminist thought. The texts that are effected anticipate and extend the problematic of subjectivity. The feminist "self," then, exists in the particulars of feminist texts and not in any particular kind of text. Like all writing, feminist self-writing is informed by the experiences of the everyday, of the body, of the sites of contact with and isolation from the read-about and lived-in worlds. But that world as the writer lives it can be imagined, felt, and recognized only from the writing. (7)

Perreault's account well describes how Rainer's films produce her "self" via textual appropriation. Rainer's ventriloquism works out narratively like visual collage, her strategic application of others' critical voices helping to construct her own. The words may be fragments of others' voices, but they become her words through appropriation. And like the autographies Perreault describes, Rainer's films depend on the reader/spectator's response to make coherent the incoherence of her cinematic bricolage. In this way, Rainer practices constant dialogue with her "self" and her audience as she produces a "self" that is never fixed or finally conceptualized. Rainer's films are ongoing discursive productions that necessitate viewer participation.

The three films made during the 1980s constitute fragments of a larger exploration of Rainer's "life." Each represents a chapter in the life of "a woman," a staged and interrogated reminiscence in which real life experiences and abstract theories collide to produce art. Rainer herself has characterized this as "a tendency to transform theory into narrative" by interpolating what she calls "concrete experience in the form of a first-person pronoun and progressive verb" and by becoming "Artist as Ventriloquist" ("Looking Myself in the Mouth" 66–67). In these films, another kind of body emerges, a subject whose sex, gender, ethnicity, class, and age matter. Rainer closely examines these bodies, exploring how institutions and mass culture shape and represent them. Rainer is remaking herself, taking ever further her critique of minimalism's nonspecific body. As she inhabits a feminist stance, she asserts the significance of sexed and gendered bodies in life and art, not as flesh bodies but as interpolated narrative constructions.

Examining the following films, I trace the figure of the hysteric in Rainer's work. In her earliest films the hysterical body appears as a result of a crucial disjunction; later, Rainer consciously plays on the significance of that body. Hélène Cixous has described the hysteric as a "body transformed into a theatre for forgotten scenes," further explaining that she "relives the past. . . . unties familiar bonds, [and] introduces disorder into the well-regulated unfolding of everyday life" (Cixous and Clement 5). A boisterous and imperious presence, the hysteric maintains a visible presence in each of Rainer's films. When she is not present, the filmbody itself performs her symptomatic displays in disjunctive, stuttering, or silent pantomimes created with editing techniques and melodrama. The three films from the 1980s make use of the hysteric, who, though physically absent, remains, paradoxically, to recall events and represent through her symptoms and discourse the repressed past of patriarchal history. In what follows I trace the hysteric's legacy: the ways Rainer elaborates private crises of women in the public sphere. These works also reveal the artist struggling to claim her identity as an artist whose specificity as a subject also matters.

Travelogues of Emotion

Among the many revealing moments in Yvonne Rainer's complex, enigmatic film *Journeys from Berlin/1971* (1980), a girl's voice is heard off screen reading the following while an aerial view of Stonehenge fills the screen space: "I saw my ego staring me in the face. I ceased to listen to what they were saying because I saw that what I had been saying did not come from myself. What is my self and what is my ego? Who is the I and the self and the ego? Show me this monster who claws my senses and I will rend him to pieces" (Rainer, *Films* 163).

In characteristic fashion, Rainer visually punctuates the paradox of the girl narrator's self-questioning by picturing Stonehenge, which, like the unconscious that the girl seeks to know, remains an enigma. This pun illustrates Rainer's propensity for irony, compulsive self-questioning, and therapeutic analysis. *Journeys*, like her other films, uses ventriloquism to pursue its inquiries. The girl's questions—"What is my self?" and "Who is the I and the self and the ego?"—define the larger problem of subjecthood that recurs thematically throughout Rainer's oeuvre. This moment in the screenplay also reveals Rainer's ambivalence about psychoanalysis, an institution of power/knowledge that she both interrogates and utilizes. *Journeys* probes the politics of consciousness as it attempts imaginatively to render the unconscious on film. It marks the beginning of Rainer's political move to examine the theories, experiences, and terrains of women's social relations in everyday life.

Journeys from Berlin/1971, an anomaly within Rainer's corpus, is simultaneously the most distanced and personal film Rainer has made. For *Journeys* Rainer uses lip-sync audio. While this technique unfurls multiple narratives, it entails less fragmentation and less intrusive editing than her previous projects. *Journeys from Berlin/1971* also proves visually compelling in a way her other films aren't. There occur moments of serene cinematic beauty, glimpses of domestic interiors that pay homage to Vermeer, fragments of sepia-tinted aerial footage that recall Leni Riefenstahl, and an approach to visuality at once poetically elegiac and rigorously documentarian. The film's haunting visual images aid the narrative at times but, in typical Rainer fashion, they also silently compete with complex discourses on the sound track that narrate the anxiety of private life as it bleeds into public/social spaces. Rainer here attempts to narrate the most personal, private spaces of a life, a site necessarily off screen and unspeakable: the unconscious.

So *Journeys from Berlin/1971* examines topographies of the unconscious, landscapes of repressed private desire, and feelings mapped onto public terrains of political belief and action. The main motifs are the psychoanalytic session—the private talking cure—juxtaposed with an examination of the life of Ulrike Meinhof, a political dissident recast as ordinary criminal by the right-wing state apparatus in postwar West Germany. These two narrative tracks intertwine with a third track of a young girl reading from her journal.

The psychoanalytic session expresses Rainer's fascination for therapeutic self-analysis while the Meinhof narrative, based on the dissident's journals and letters, becomes a modern-day paradigm for a secular hagiography. From all three emerge an examination of private and public narrative space. The girl reading her journal entries serves as a bridge to the other two narrative tracks. As in a psychoanalytic session, private thoughts are revealed and analyzed. In form they reiterate the main source for the Meinhof narrative, the journal. With each narrative track, Rainer explores the role of women in contemporary life through an obsessive examination of the boundaries of private and public space, ultimately suggesting that "real" life is lived in the interstices between the two.

Rainer poses a problem for our consideration: just how do we inhabit our lives, our memories, our histories, the spaces where the private and public merge? *Journeys from Berlin/1971* unfolds as a meditative, polymorphous mapping of the unconscious; image-memories roll by as dream sequences and narrative threads spin tales that fuse fiction with autobiography and history. Rainer thus makes unconscious process visible to the spectator, while "real" life happenings remain invisible and off screen. *Journeys from Berlin/1971* reveals so much about the interior workings of the unconscious that it removes the spectator from the traditional place of voyeur, the external viewer caught in the seductive cinematic mechanisms of identification. Instead, Rainer positions the spectator at the core of the images and narratives in a nonplace, the no place of the unconscious, a nonspecific here, there, and everywhere.

The film begins with a blackened screen. We are aurally aware that the opening sequence takes place in the most private space of a home, the bathroom. We hear bath water, splashes and draining, followed by the subtly perceptible towel drying of a body. Such quiet domestic sounds squarely situate the invisible mise-en-scène—one that will always be off scene—as private space. Within this invisible place, the most public dilemmas will be enunciated by an unseen, unnamed couple—the film's He and She. Rainer uses appropriated sources to piece together a dialogue that co-opts the genre of domestic melodrama, for this segment of *Journeys* features passages of the private narratives of women who gave up their domestic desires for their political beliefs.

Immediately, then, viewers encounter one of the three dominant narratives: the ongoing conversation between the invisible man and woman. This track consists of conversations about women anarchists, especially Ulrike Meinhof. Meinhof's story, constructed through recited fragments taken from journals and letters, illuminates the trauma of a private commitment to an unauthorized ideology, a woman's transformation into a public political figure and, eventually, her vilification by institutionalized power. Rainer's ventriloquist uses of Meinhof require voice-over narration and scrolling text that relate Meinhof's transformation from wife and mother into political activist. During the exposition of Meinhof's story, the invisible He and She engage in mundane domestic duties—preparing dinner, for example—while talking about radicalized political action and debating the ideologies informing such activism. He and She speak their dialogue against the scrolling texts, sketching the contemporary West German political scene. Visually, their conversations are peppered with views of a city street from an open apartment window or desolate industrial landscapes glimpsed from the window of a moving train. The film, while offering up these images of public space and proliferating the language of politics, makes viewers privy to the couple's domestic space only through the audio track.

The off-screen voices and mundane domestic sounds, juxtaposed with the images of public space, emphasize the contrast as well as the inseparability of private and public. The public lives of female anarchists, retold as the couple read directly from the historical journals left by these women, reiterate dilemmas faced by women who become politically active—the clashes and (con)fusions of public and private that can be maddening to navigate. By leaving private experience and domestic life mostly inferred and only sometimes seen, and by foregrounding the altogether visible spaces of public movement and action, Rainer mirrors in film form the conflict of public/private that women face. Domestic, social, and political spheres merge in the He/She segments, making literal the tense and shifting interconnections between the personal and the political.

Splintering the narrative of the never-seen He and She is the psychoanalytic session, presented in full public view, sometimes in a gallery space, sometimes in a large warehouse, always with an audience present in the background, mysteriously obscured by the overall darkness of the large spaces. With this conceit Rainer captures Peter Brooks's concept of the melodrama of psychoanalysis. Brooks observes that "melodrama exteriorizes conflict and psychic structures producing what we might call the melodrama of psychology" (35–36) and follows up by claiming that "psychoanalysis can be read as a systematic realization of the melodramatic aesthetic, applied to the structure and dynamics of the mind" (201). Rainer uses a "melodramatic aesthetic" in *Journeys* and later films to make vivid interior feminine dramas of becoming. In *Journeys*, the analyst is by turns a man, a woman, or a boy. The patient is always the same woman, her back to the camera. In the screenplay notes, Rainer describes these character configurations as embodying "the enormous space that contains the 'essential relationships': patient to therapist, daughter to parent, mother to child, person to person, spoken fantasy to filmic illusion, interior to light of day, individual to society" (*Films* 148). By making hyperbolically public the ordinarily intimate space of therapy, wherein patient and analyst engage in the confession of analysis, Rainer makes visible the conflicts and alienation of the many selves who make the "I" of the self.

The session, presenting an individual struggle writ large, showcases the melodrama of self-absorption—the conflicts of personal good and evil, the fervent desire to know oneself, the aspiration to transcend self and serve the greater good. This melodrama issues from the never-to-be-resolved conflicts arising from self-examination, which Rainer performs in the film and in her life. Self-examination, the film suggests, is essential to the formation of the sociopolitical self: we must "know what our personal struggle is . . . to get to the other side of it" because as the film's She cautions, "[p]ouring unexamined personal rage—or whatever—into social action" will inevitably "foul things up somewhere along the line" (Rainer, *Films* 147). Social commentary. Perverse humor. And Rainer reiterating the impossibility of removing the personal from the social.

The third narrative thread, the Girl reading her journal, utilizes additional dimensions of melodrama and figures another aspect of the journey to active sociopolitical subject. The Girl, in her excessive sincerity, naïveté, and ingenuousness, configures an innocent voice of optimism and hope. Unmarked by the wary cynicism of the other voices, she stands as keystone figure of moral imperative. She is the virtuous ingenue: an essential element of traditional melodrama. The girl's clear language, lacking affect even as it indulges an exaggerated desire to ponder every life action and expression, articulates the central question that *Journeys* poses about the complex nature of subjectivity: "What is my self and what is my ego? Who is the I and the self and the ego?" Throughout the film the Girl thoughtfully reads excerpts from her journal, which detail her observations, feelings, and experiences. Significantly, her intimate thoughts stand in contradistinction to the journals read by He and She, which seem more critically distant, historical and, at first, more overtly political. The Girl's more directly personal voice constitutes a third register in this psychical melodrama. Her desire to get to the bottom of things, to really understand herself, is as urgent as the archaeological impulses expressed by others in this complicated drama, but hers is the language of private space, the language of the interior.

Together, these narrative threads form a multilayered drama that examines the significance of self-analysis, the drive for self-knowledge, and the connection of these processes to public sociopolitical projects. Foucauldian in its examination of the inextricable relationship of knowledge and power, *Journeys* deploys critiques of various institutions, targeting especially the institution of psychoanalysis, which Rainer both needs and reviles. Employing various forms of confession—the intimate conversation, the psychiatric session, the journal—Rainer represents strategies women use to analyze and evaluate themselves. At the same time, she charts the dangers of institutional or state systems of control that use these same forms, showing how regimes of knowledge/power can become devices of psychological warfare. Rainer writes, "Psychiatry, like imperialist science in general, is a means, not an end. Psychiatrification as a device. . . . of psychological warfare, aims to persuade the destroyed fighter of the pointlessness of revolutionary politics, to destroy the fighter's credibility. At the same time it is a police tactic" (*Films* 168). Yet this institution remains for Rainer a fascinating theater that blends private and public; it compels her to draw from its stages source material that fuels her excavation of unconscious process and the formation of self.

Journeys thus highlights Rainer's consistent focus on a female will to self-knowledge that lies embedded in public theaters of power/knowledge and that sits at the heart of both melodrama and psychoanalysis. This will to self-knowledge grows from a desire to discover personal significance and self-value in a sociopolitical landscape fraught with fluctuating and multifaceted structures of power. The determination to focus on this journey of self-articulation constitutes the first step in Rainer's movement toward an increasingly specific female subject.

Eyes Wide Shut

In *The Man Who Envied Women* Yvonne Rainer presents additional dramas of everyday existence by juxtaposing personal action against the larger social field. An excessively confessional film, *The Man Who Envied Women* again features the psychoanalytic session as a theater for articulating the melodrama of personal significance and moral value. *Journeys* represents the innocent narrative voice of a girl reflecting on her life experiences and an examination of domestic life, albeit portrayed through the intellectual/political banter by a model heterosexual couple. *The Man Who Envied Women* presents a hardball, sock-it-to-you world of academic intellectualism and urban gentrification alongside the story of a collapsed marriage. It is a story of theory meeting practice, of abstract ideas meeting lived "reality": Michel Foucault and Fredric Jameson meet the Steering Committee of Artists' Call Against U.S. Intervention in Central America and No More Nice Girls.

The theory is spouted by Jack Deller, a phallocentric mouthpiece whose name is a play on "tell her," which he does, nonstop, throughout the film. Jack Deller's theory-speak contrasts with the more informal voices of various invisible women: the always off-screen heroine/narrator Trisha and two nameless women (played by Yvonne Rainer and Martha Rosler) who engage in pointed conversation and commentary. While *Journeys* remains an intimate yet politically inflected melodrama, *The Man Who Envied Woman* plays like a Woody Allen melodrama; but its appeal aims at a specialized group of urban artists, theorists, and feminists who are both its performers and likely audience.

Jack Deller is an over-the-top characterization of all that is wrong with theory made into jargon. His academese epitomizes language for language's sake—a narcissistic game of word-play that patronizing academics indulge. Deller pontificates from a rostrum in a classroom that doubles as newly renovated loft. A privileged urban gentrifier, he inhabits a space surrounded by walls of books and graced by a NordicTrack, emblem of his bourgeois status and virtual life. Lines from Freud and Lacan erupt from his mouth in a lecture about semiotics, Lacanian *lack*, and the cinematic apparatus. Ironically, two actors portray him, a gesture that both accentuates and critiques the problematic of identification already addressed by Rainer in earlier work. Deller, an accomplished name-dropper, invokes the top-ten critical theorists of the moment throughout the lecture. He talks and talks but doesn't listen. Lost in the world of academic-speak he is cut off from "real life," living instead in the abstract world of the theoretical end-game. When not talking, Jack is often seen wearing headphones, a barrier that sustains his isolation from ordinary conversation. Deller embodies the voice of male privilege masquerading as sensitive feminist, intellectual, daddy, voice of authority, manly man. He uses knowledge of theory as a tool of seduction. At one point, a female character remarks, "A feminist is a man who's found a new way to meet broads" (Rainer, *Films* 182). In the end, though, Rainer will illustrate how theory "simply has no teeth" (210).

Juxtaposed with the parodic examination of theory through the character Jack Deller are a number of other narrative voices that represent the power of active, engaged, and thoughtful analysis; here, theory may be invoked but always self-reflexively. The powerful voices of theory come from off-screen women—Trisha, Rainer, and Martha Rosler—as well as the very visible Jackie, a sexy French feminist theorist.

The highly specialized language of theory is interspersed with vignettes of women in coffee shops or on the street, whose private conversations reiterate the concerns of the film's main narratives. These vignettes represent daily lived manifestations of the theoretical "he said/she said" narrative. When viewers first meet Trisha, Jack's wife (who, paradoxically, never appears on-screen, so she is present in voice but absent physically), she has experienced a difficult week: "I split up with my husband and moved into my studio. The hot water broke and flooded the textile merchant downstairs; I bloodied up my white linen pants; the Senate voted for nerve gas; and my gynecologist went down in Korean Airlines Flight 007. The worst of it was the gynecologist. He was a nice man. He used to put booties on the stirrups and his speculum was always warm" (Rainer, *Films* 173).

Trisha's narrative weaves private concerns together with issues and events preoccupying the larger social community. She may privilege those events that immediately touch her, but unlike Jack, whose stultified prose removes him from lived reality, Trisha communicates her frustrations and disappointments directly, with ironic awareness. She is as competent as Jack in using theory as discourse, but unlike Jack, she understands theoretical discourse as a specialized tool. Like any tool, when used inappropriately, it becomes useless, or even harmful. Theory in the domain of intimate relationships can act as a smokescreen that prevents real communication between husband and wife. Tricia avoids this. She lives in the world and makes connections that Jack seems incapable of imagining.

In the public world of politics and social action, the film suggests, the wide array of theoretical "isms" proves a seductive, but ultimately specious, mode of exchange. During one encounter in a narrow corridor outside a party for liberal do-gooders, Jack and Jackie recite theoretical commentaries while performing a "minimalist song and dance of seduction, ambivalence, attraction and withdrawal—via exchanges of gaze, gesture and moves" (Rainer, *Films* 210). This spectacle calls attention to the fussy impotence of theory. Jackie, the French bombshell theorist—the feminine counterpart to Jack—remarks, "Theory as watchdog is a poor creature: not because it is nasty or destructive, but for attacking the analysis of confrontations, it simply has no teeth" (210). Through Jackie, with her sexy French accent, Rainer both performs and critiques the cultural currency of contemporary French thought among academics and artists.

When Jackie identifies one of the consequences of the "freudo-marxist marriage presided over by language" as "the systematic evacuation of certain questions—political, economic, and above all historical" (Rainer, *Films* 210), Rainer expresses a concern that the rhetoric of theoretical abstraction threatens the effectiveness of significant political critique and real action. Finally, in response to Jack's extended recitation of Michel Foucault on the nexus of power/knowledge, Jackie retorts, "The world of theorization is a grim one, haunted by mad scientists breeding monsters through hybridization, by the haunted ghosts of a hundred isms, and the massive shadow of the subject surging up at every turn" (211). This trenchant critique of the uses and abuses of theory further elaborates Rainer's growing concern for the specificity of the subject.

Rainer's distrust of Critical Theory—of rhetoric for rhetoric's sake—doesn't, however, prevent her from plumbing the depths of theory's seductions. Her ventriloquism is always self-reflexive. Rainer has been seduced by the lure of psychoanalysis in the past, and now fueled by feminist scholarship, with eyes wide open, she's determined to expose how critical theories have produced a neutered subject, made women and difference disappear into the complex jargon of theory-speak. At the film's conclusion Trisha summarizes the dangers of theory's appeal: "If a girl takes her eye off Lacan and Derrida long enough to look, she may discover she is the invisible woman" (Rainer, *Films* 215). How, then, does one fight against the patriarchal oppression and cultural imperialism embedded within theory?

That's easy. You make use of "the master's tools." Woman may be culturally invisible—an invisibility Trisha's physical absence performs in this film—but she can practice strategies of presence anyway. Visibility requires that we put ourselves into words. For Rainer, echoing Perreault's formulations regarding autography, to be heard is to be seen: "[T]he claiming of speech exerts a measure of control that the grammar of 'being seen' disallows" (Perreault 25). In *The Man Who Envied Women* Rainer makes women heard and therefore "seen" by embracing the politics and theories of feminism. She responds to feminism's rallying cry—its call to self-awareness as a foundation for thinking about how personal life and a sense of selfhood connect to a larger social fabric of public actions. *The Man Who Envied Women* unveils Rainer's explicit commitment to the sexual politics of feminism, a pronounced ideological turn. It also represents Rainer's rejection of the concept of neutral (nongendered) subjectivity promoted both by the patriarchal avant-gardists of the art world and by the critical theorists of the academic world. *The Man Who Envied Women* is an explicitly political film; its elucidation of privilege in patriarchal culture foreshadows Rainer's next foray into the cultural politics of gender and sexuality.

Menopause

Not a new woman, not non-woman or misanthrope, or anti-woman, and not non-practicing Lesbian. Maybe unwoman is also the wrong term. A-woman is closer. A-womanly. A-womanliness.

—Yvonne Rainer

In *Privilege,* which features a film within a film, Rainer, in taking on menopause, makes a quantum leap toward a specific, gendered, female body-subject; along the way, her investigation of female sexuality enters the contentious terrains of race and class, further arenas for articulating subjecthood as a phenomenon inflected by myriad material conditions. The film's narrative focus on menopause echoes one of the subplots in *The Man Who Envied Women.* In an unexpected, telling moment in the earlier film, Yvonne Rainer appears on screen, lips painted fiery red, affect hyperbolized to the point of clownishness or hysteria, kneeling down to face the camera in close-up. She removes her glasses and announces, "Will all menstruating women please leave the theater?" This Bakhtinian moment of disruption, immediately following a line referring to "themes resonating around politics and sexuality," triggers a brief commentary by Trisha about women and sexual desirability. Trisha remarks: "In our culture a woman is sexually desirable only as long as her sexuality can inspire fear. For the heterosexual male, woman is dangerous because she menstruates. The mystery and power of menses evoke in him the fear of castration. Man's loss of sexual interest in the menopausal, or no longer menstruating, woman goes hand in hand with the waning of his terror of her. Because she no longer has the potential to harm him, she no longer has the power to make him afraid. Anger and contempt now replace fear" (Rainer, *Films* 197). Here, Trisha points out how women have fallen into believing the illusion that patriarchal culture projects about the "origin" of personal power. The loss of power associated with menopause presupposes a belief that women are valuable only while they are fertile, fertility being the only time and form of privilege they enjoy.

Privilege, like *Journeys* and *The Man Who Envied Women,* uses the confessional aspect of melodrama, a mode of expression that provides a fictional system for articulating psychical conflict and making sense of lived experience. The film explores the loss and recovery of female selfhood and explicates ways men and patriarchal institutions victimize women. These issues play out through a double trajectory of recollection and documentation. While the so-called documentary imparts statistics and clinical research about menopause, it also tells stories. Interviews with numerous older women are intercut with reminiscences by Jenny, one of the film's central characters. Both forms of testimony operate as a melodramatic device for expressing emotion. They perform the melodrama of psychical conflict during menopause—a critical juncture in the lives of women, who at this time experience loss in biological and psychological terms.

As Jenny laments: "Aging has been such an emotional subject for me. No one ever told me how many hours of the day I'd spend mourning for . . . what? Myself? I don't know what . . . some part of me" (MacDonald, *Screen Writings* 281). The recovery of selfhood follows a demystification of menopause that includes an acknowledgment that sexual power and desirability, as prescribed by culturally sanctioned stereotypes, are limiting standards of value that, at best, offer women marginalized social roles as wife/mother. Undoing the hegemony of those values and roles makes life after menopause potentially liberating. But accessing such understanding requires travel back in time—in Jenny's case through a "*hot* flashback," a different kind of confessional, during which she recounts a particular premenopausal moment in her life as a sexually desirable woman. In her telling remembrance, Jenny identifies forms of privilege associated with race, class, and sexual orientation.

Jenny's *hot* flashback takes place as Yvonne Washington (Rainer's black alter ego?) interviews Jenny for a documentary about menopause. Jenny cautions Yvonne that in talking about menopause, "We'll just be reducing women to their biological processes all over again. Anatomy is destiny. When you're young they whistle at you, when you're middle-aged they treat you like a bunch of symptoms, and when you're old they ignore you" (MacDonald, *Screen Writings* 280). Yvonne turns Jenny's comment around and points out that patriarchy, not biology, poses the problem: "When you talk about biology and 'them,' you're confusing biology with patriarchy. Just because some men invoke *our* biology for their own advantage doesn't mean *we* have to go along with them" (281). This remark enunciates the institutional nature of any form of privilege, which always confers or withholds power and control.

Rainer uses high-contrast black-and-white to evoke film noir and heighten the visual appeal of the *hot* flashbacks. The familiar look gives these scenes a visual impact that differentiates them from the rest of the film—actually video-8. The flashbacks, Rainer observes, invoke "clichés of anxiety which that kind of lighting and mise-en-scène produce" (qtd. in Easterwood et al. 232). This visual strategy constitutes another example of Rainer's using the expressive capabilities of melodramatic convention to sharpen the film's emotional edge. These sequences both heighten and unmask the film's emotional illusionism. Some of the reverse shots reveal the studio setting and production equipment. These moments rupture and complicate the flashbacks, introducing the potential for memory to be understood as fictive, contrived.

Early in Yvonne's exchange with Jenny, race enters the conversation. Jenny, ever the liberal bohemian artist, wonders why Washington, an African American, wants to interview her. Jenny is, after all, white: "What about black women? Do you have any black women lined-up? White women have been interviewing one another for years" (MacDonald, *Screen Writings* 281). Yvonne replies, "Let me worry about that. Just because I'm African-American doesn't mean I can't deal with anything but so-called 'black-problems'" (282). As this conversation demonstrates, Jenny recognizes the problem with essentializing women as bodies limited by biology but remains unable to see Yvonne functioning outside a framework of race-specific interests. Jenny is therefore sensitive to issues related to sex and gender but blind to the problematic of essentializing race and class. *Privilege* thus uncovers blind spots that progressives retain regarding the workings of representation; it mimics concerns raised by women of color about feminism. The memory Jenny shares will illuminate other blind spots: Jenny's, those belonging to other characters in this political melodrama, and Rainer's.

Jenny thinks back to an earlier time in her life (a time when "men still whistled" at her) and recalls an incident she has never shared with anybody. She begins narrating the incident, which includes a rainbow cast of characters: Brenda, a lesbian; the Puerto Rican couple Carlos and Digna; their African American friend Stew; and an upper-class white male prosecutor named Robert. All of these characters reveal their own biases through their respective encounters with one another. As disenfranchised individuals— excepting Robert—each stands outside the safety net of privilege. However each assumes a position of privilege during these encounters, even if it is limited in scope and duration. Rainer makes these moments of privilege— moments when privilege is assumed or enacted—quite clear. In doing so, she calls attention to the tenuous, socially constructed nature of privilege;

privilege fluctuates, and to be maintained it must be constantly assessed and deployed. Thus, privilege becomes a tango of power and control: as one person asserts control and position, another resists or acquiesces, in ongoing interplays. In these complex, changing relationships, Rainer underscores Michel Foucault's notion that "relations of power-knowledge are not static forms of distribution" but rather "they are matrices of transformations" (*History of Sexuality* 99).

While Brenda recognizes her marginalized position as a white lesbian living in a predominantly heterosexual society, Carlos and Stew, as men of color, see skin color as the primary marker of privilege. Digna, on the other hand, sees herself doubly oppressed because of her sex and skin color. Jenny, a straight, menopausal woman, feels invisible because of her age and perceived loss of sexual desirability. After a sudden epiphany, Jenny shares, "My biggest shock in reaching middle age was the realization that men's desire for me was the linchpin of my identity" (MacDonald, *Screen Writings* 317). When Brenda and Carlos interact, their feelings of alienation and exclusion become reconfigured in relation to each other. Brenda feels the privilege of her skin color while Carlos attempts to assert the privilege of his heterosexual masculinity. When Carlos assaults Digna and the police intervene, Digna gets diagnosed as crazy and is locked up at Bellevue: again, privilege influences the interactions.

Digna is perceived as a classic hysteric. Her biology has predisposed her to a diagnosis of insanity while Carlos's privilege supports his veneer of sanity. Jenny may feel invisible, but Digna *is* invisible to the other characters. Ironically, she masquerades throughout most of the film as the hyperbolic figure of Carmen Miranda. Her masquerade, excessively visible and recognizable, only further emphasizes Digna's invisibility as a woman of color. The Carmen Miranda conceit exemplifies further how Rainer uses melodrama's expressionistic aesthetic; her hyberbolic figures insist on legibility. In this over-the-top costume, Digna shadows Jenny (and her upper-class lover, Robert) around town, providing a running commentary about class prompted by astute observations of power differentials between Jenny and Robert.

In addition to detailing processes of self-examination and self-formation on the part of the characters, the film's reflexivity follows with interest similar processes on the part of its makers. As the credits roll, the film presents numerous shots of the wrap party, at which actors, crew, and interviewees for the film-within-the film mill about talking and celebrating. An important coda unfolds, with Rainer reaffirming her anarchist political commitments. Rainer is heard in voice-over interviewing obviously "menopaused" women about anarchism and feminism. Audrey, a woman in her seventies, thought-fully articulates the kind of liberation, the reward for surviving menopause, alluded to earlier in the film:

> The notion that anarchism is a philosophy and it's a way of life and a way of interpreting what happens around you stays with you forever whether you're actively involved in something or not. I'm certainly not very actively involved . . .
> Y.R.: But it has sustained you.
> Audrey: It has sustained me. (MacDonald, *Screen Writings* 325)

I read this final remark as Rainer's own reaffirmation of her activism as an artist committed to critical intervention and wry commentary on the social conditions of women's daily lives.

Rainer's clever layering of these stories about privilege also allows her, per-haps inadvertently, to remark on her own. As artist/filmmaker, Rainer has the privilege of voicing ideas about any number of distressing sociopolitical problems. Her visible status as a member of an artistic community gives her a powerful forum for opining publicly about the politics of representation, racial inequality, class bias, and the implicit heterosexism (even her own) that pervades contemporary culture. More than a story about menopause and its physical and social discomforts, *Privilege* self-consciously enacts and explores privilege itself.

During this decade, Yvonne Rainer's life and work confirm Perreault's notion that "women's senses of self in the world are modified in the pro-cess of an evolving feminist consciousness" (130). Rainer's feminist turn has taken her toward understandings of sexual, race, class, and gender differ-ences that saturate with specificity the subjects and bodies in her films. Her formal interventions arise from a generalized interest not merely in avant-garde disruption and narrative fragmentation but in explicit feminist cri-tique and self-evolution. Rainer does not just make melodramas, she uses melodrama's expressionistic aesthetics as a feminist strategy of formal and narrative intervention. Rainer's now intentional representations of the hys-terical body challenge cinematic conventions that portray the female body as pure surface or image.

In traditional cinema the spectator's participation hinges on his or her perception of spatial coherence: fragmentary images acquire a logical con-sistency because they are subordinated to a causal sequence of narrative events. Rainer breaks up spatial coherence by playing on the hysteric's de-sire to overidentify. Rainer's hyperboles, mode of address, formal structuring, anti-narrativity, and ventriloquist appropriations destroy any coherence that would sustain excessive identification between viewer and characters. These formal strategies also illustrate structurally Perreault's notion that the female subject consists of intersecting narrative selves that generate an ongoing process of self-invention. This ever-evolving, multifaceted, specifically embodied female subject is precisely how Yvonne Rainer conceptualizes subjectivity during the 1980s. Rainer's ventriloquism captures both the complexity of the subjecthood she envisions and the specificity of women in their everyday existence.

With an explicit feminist twist, *Journeys, The Man Who Envied Women,* and *Privilege* reimagine the "woman's film." A master of irony and parody, Rainer enunciates female subjectivity using melodrama's hysterical body in all its somatic splendor. Rainer's particular deployment of the hysterical body, "in which the body is transformed into a text—enigmatic but still decipherable" (Doane, *Desire to Desire* 40), spotlights the problem of representation and its relationship to the feminine body. Further, Rainer draws from her own experiences and feelings to produce inventive melodramas of selfhood. As autographies, her films dramatize the ongoing movement of female self-development. In *Journeys from Berlin/1971,* Rainer explores how our multiple "selves" link private and public, demonstrating once again that cornerstone of feminist ideology: the personal is political. Its stories of personal action and public accountability illustrate the search for moral significance, value, and self that undergirds female self-development. Parodying Woody Allen's comedic portrayals of neurotics, *The Man Who Envied Women* reformulates Freud's observations and turns the tables, asking, "What do men really want?" This explicit feminist turn evidences further shifts in Rainer's concept of the subject and anticipates the full-scale plunge into the politics of subjectivity and body seen in *Privilege.* Not surprisingly given the rigor and dynamism of the filmmaker's inquiries, *Privilege* contains the narrative seed for Rainer's next project.

Yvonne Washington asks Jenny a pointed question: "Jenny, there's one thing I'm curious about. Did you ever make it with Brenda?" In response, Jenny exclaims: "Hell, no. I was terrified of women." This teasing question, sprung at film's end, guarantees viewers they can expect much more on the topic of lesbian relationships. Her emerging interest in homosexuality, an underdeveloped (even a blind spot?) but consistent presence in each of Rainer's previous films, surfaces, however tangentially, in Brenda's story. Rainer's own coming out parallels her growing interest in the stories of lesbians; her newfound desire comes under scrutiny in her most *straight*forward and fleshed-out narrative film to date, MURDER *and murder.*

A Love Story Goes Queer and Narrative Goes Straight

Following from my new sexual status, to "call myself" a lesbian is not only a statement of sexual preference, it is a way of pointing to where I—and others like me, for the same, also different, reasons—live: outside the safe house, on the edge, in the social margin.

—Yvonne Rainer

Yvonne Rainer's long-time creative exploration of self-discovery comes full circle with MURDER *and murder.* Gone are the excessive distancing strategies of jump cuts, intertitles, voice-overs, and nonacting actors. Now Rainer has gone narrative. She tells a story—really two stories—in a relatively straightforward manner. Melodrama returns, however, in the form of the carnivalesque, enhanced by brilliantly saturated color film, slapstick, and overdetermined music. Significantly, Rainer finally allows bodies to perform erotically the play of sexual romance. Of course these bodies are not just any bodies, but the usually invisible bodies of middle-aged lesbians, perhaps the most "Othered" others in cinematic history.

The bodies of a cancer survivor and an HIV-positive drag queen appear here as well—incarnations of that physicality Bakhtin terms the "grotesque," the messy, vulnerable, unidealized body. MURDER *and murder,* a delightfully coherent narrative film about two middle-aged lesbian lovers, features an intertwining second narrative detailing Rainer's own battle with breast cancer. Just as Rainer turns queer she goes straight, once again turning away from whatever expectations we might have of the avant-garde and whatever illusions we might ordinarily require from a love story. In going narrative, though, Rainer still avoids the predictable and opts for the unfamiliar, much-suppressed presence of the lived lesbian body—this time her own.

Peter Brooks describes the eruption of the previously suppressed into visibility as an intensely dramatic moment. He writes, "And when there is . . . a piercing of repression—a return of the repressed—the result is the melodrama of hysteria and hallucination" (175). Brooks's conception helps us understand elements at work in Rainer's film—in particular her manipulations of difference, temporality, and narrativity, issues Rainer has addressed over the years but explores freshly in this film. MURDER *and murder* is, in fact, a return for Rainer. Here, Rainer returns to narrative as an unfolding story and to the body as fully material, all the while experimenting with issues of time. Rainer's self-conscious probing of her own sexuality and sexual identity in MURDER *and murder* evidence a need to return to what had been repressed: certain conventions of language and the body. As she recognizes her desire personally, she becomes impelled to represent that desire, to make it speak and appear, despite the dominant culture's drive to keep it invisible.

To make the lesbian body appear, she embraces narrative in its conventional, *straightforward* form; and she fleshes out the bodies she seeks to represent. As usual, for Rainer, there is no middle ground. Her narrative lines ascend to the hyperbolic heights of emotion that melodrama demands, both when stretching around the love story and presenting Rainer's own battle with breast cancer. In true melodramatic form, MURDER *and murder* creates a confrontation between good and evil, using an "us-versus-them" mentality, unabashedly enacting the historical ritual of melodrama, which purports to highlight innocence and purge villainy. The heroines of this story, Doris and Mildred, are postmenopausal lesbian lovers, and the murderous villains are homophobia and cancer.

The title, MURDER *and murder,* announces the focus of both story lines. Rainer's screenplay explains:

> There is Murder and then there is murder. Murder by homophobia; murder by social and legal abuse, repression and stigma. Murder by DDT, PCBs, dioxin, by 177 organochlorides stored in our fat, breast milk, blood, semen and breath, by nuclear tests conducted in the 1950s. Murder by electromagnetic fields. Murder by breast cancer. And how must lesbians murder in order to survive? As children we fantasized Murdering our sisters, our mothers, our newly born siblings. As adults we must learn to tolerate and work through the fantasized murders of our lovers. Thoughts can be murderous, but thoughts don't kill. (Rainer, MURDER *and murder* script 60)

These are serious topics, but Rainer infuses her drama with a humor that bites as it tickles.

Bakhtinian Carnival

> [M]elodrama's mode must be centrally, radically hyperbolic, the mode of bigger-than-life, reaching in grandiose reference to a nominal realm.
> —Peter Brooks

Rainer's film appropriates Mikhail Bakhtin's notion of the carnivalesque to examine the murderous effects of stigma, repression, legal abuse, and toxic chemicals. The carnivalesque presents a world turned upside down, in which the low inhabits the position of the high and boundaries, both institutional and fleshly, are transgressed. It makes use of ambivalent yet mocking laughter to emphasize the resulting stark contrasts. In MURDER *and murder* Rainer uses contrasting images, ambiguities, and indeterminacy to effect a carnivalesque juxtaposition of high and low. Her two main characters are a professor and a performer. The rigors of critical theory contrast with the banality of garden-variety performance art and mind-numbing statistics. The settings shift from SoHo loft to Coney Island—gentrified domestic haven and public circus space. The use of relatively conventional narrative—straight narrative progression—contrasts with unconventional content, the love story of two postmenopausal women.

Rainer's project, viewed in relation to the carnivalesque, raises interesting questions regarding the representation of Bakhtin's "grotesque body" within the realm of feminist politics. "For Bakhtin, the grotesque body represents a powerful force," writes Michelle Hirschorn. "It is a body that is always in process, it is always becoming, it is a mobile and hybrid creature, disproportionate, exorbitant, outgrowing all limits, obscenely decentered and off-balance, a figural and symbolic resource for parodied exaggeration and inversion" (131). MURDER and murder presents the lesbian body as grotesque in this sense, and unruly. In an interesting twist on carnival's notion of the grotesque, this same body (evoked by Rainer's own body) marks multiple sites of abjection; here appears the medicalized, scarred, desexualized, postmenopausal woman. MURDER and murder also presents viewers with the body of an HIV-positive drag queen, who happens to be an overweight African American. MURDER and murder thus offers a virtual parade of the polymorphously perverse and abject.

MURDER and murder is also Rainer's first erotically charged film. Rainer's earlier repression of the erotic or sexual body, a purposeful political choice, arose from the filmmaker's aversion to certain uses of narrative. As Thyrza Nichols Goodeve explains, the erotic body for Rainer has at times been "'bad' because it was seen as something that enthralled the spectator in vicarious experience and wiped out his/her critical faculties" (62). Throughout this film, however, Mildred and Doris engage in a sensually palpable, flirtatious badinage and erotic foreplay. Without a doubt, MURDER and murder, as love story, celebrates mature lived sexuality. The film includes, for example, scenes of lovemaking, of toes exploring breasts and playing with nipples, even an exclamation extolling the pleasures of "eating pussy," all played out in reel time. The characters are never severed from their voices; visual images are synchronized with the sound track, giving depth and definition to the characters.

MURDER and murder thus has the visual feel of three dimensions rather than the flat, compressed space of Rainer's previous works. There is a depth of space and meaning that is suggested not just in the visual look of the film, with its oblique camera angles and varied use of motion, but especially in the nuanced performances of its main characters, Mildred (Kathleen Chalfant) and Doris (Joanna Merlin). Rainer's turn to the materiality of bodies and their varied appearances emphasizes the particularities of flesh and its cultural meanings. The embodied presence of these actresses defines a multilayered screen space as lived space, never before embraced by Rainer.

Clearly, Rainer's decision to take a less fragmented approach to narrative and to emphasize bodily erotics is political, as she explains in the following: "This is such a rarely represented kind of relationship—older women *and* lesbians. I can't think of a single film dealing narratively with older lesbians, and by 'older' I mean in their 50s and 60s. It seemed necessary to make the relationship more 'credible,' at least more recognizable, via the conventions of shot/reverse shot and extended scenes with almost classical structure in terms of development and climax" (qtd. in Goodeve 62).

As Rainer implies, the very representation of these bodies as erotic is experimental. Along similar lines, Teresa de Lauretis has written eloquently about the need to make culturally marginalized bodies visible. De Lauretis discusses what she calls "the conditions of visibility," the formation of subjective vision and social visibility, or what she elaborates as "being and passing, representation and spectatorship" ("Film and the Visible" 223). The conditions of visibility, in other words, amount to "what can be seen, and eroticized, and on what scene" (223). The questions "How do I look?" "How do I appear?" and "How do I see?" seem deceptively simple. They are, however, critically important to theorizing the conditions of vision and the modes of representation for feminist and lesbian cultural theorists. Rainer's celebration of mature lesbian love and mature lesbian bodies helps alter the conditions of visibility for female bodies. Conditions of visibility, obviously, heavily affect issues of lesbian representation and spectatorship; lesbian subjectivity and desire have frequently been either invisible or visible only through a heterosexual matrix and pathologized as freakish or monstrous. In light of the history of the representation of lesbians, Rainer's attention to lesbian bodies invokes the grotesque body as a disturbing presence. She also plays with representation by making visible the physical similarities of the lesbian couple, thus articulating sameness as difference. In addition to evoking the carnivalesque via the grotesque body, Rainer's lesbian love story turns melodrama topsy-turvy.

Mildred, who is in her mid-fifties, speaks directly to the camera at one point about falling in love with Doris: "I knew this wasn't going to be easy.

But I also knew what I wanted." The imagery of a roller-coaster ride, coming at critical moments in the story, figures metaphorically the wild rides and up/down work of relationship building. In a point-of-view shot with the characters' backs to the camera, the riders—Jenny and Mildred at a younger age—view the archival footage unfolding before them, and viewers share in the thrill as the two flail and shriek with the unpredictable twists and turns. The imagery evokes the scary ups and downs of all relationships and positions the viewer to experience the discomfort and excitement.

Heightening the drama are the interwoven narratives of Rainer's own battle with breast cancer and Doris's diagnosis of breast cancer. In addition to statistics, Rainer uses humor to enliven a pivotal scene of the film, where all the previously introduced pathologies converge—ripe for Rainer's forceful left hook. As Doris and Mildred dance around the ring clinching and fighting in full regalia and arguing about food, laundry, and the condition of the loft, the camera pans down to reveal the floor, which is stenciled with statistics on breast cancer. The crowd roars approval at the spectacle taking place center ring. The scene shifts to a medium close-up of Rainer wearing a fight robe and sitting ringside next to Jenny and young Mildred, who are eating hotdogs and guzzling beer. With hands bandaged in bright red, Rainer appears to be the next contender in this parodic battle of domesticity. Then, boldly, she removes her robe to display what she has been hiding. "Alright, I've been putting this off," she confesses and slips off the left side of the robe to reveal a flat, mastectomied chest with its diagonal slash of a scar, like a fallen exclamation mark.

With her embodied presence Rainer literally makes a spectacle of herself by visually flaunting the body in pieces as the grotesque body. She recites her history of biopsies and surgeon recommendations while brandishing cardboard signs to explain the difference between Murder by homophobia and murder by social and legal abuse, repression, and stigma. This is a strategic political gesture. In her exposure she lays bare her flaws while at the same time inviting us to see the power in this calculated loss of boundary. Until this scene, the statistics about breast cancer had been disembodied and abstract. Now Rainer's very physical being, with its awkward movements and vulnerable wounds, establishes the significance of the marked body, whether that mark be determined by sex, skin color, age, or gender performance. For the first time in her film practice she has produced a more naturalistic narrative; rather than disrupt it with excessive editing techniques she uses her own scarred and unruly body to disturb its coherence.

Throughout the film, then, we are confronted by the so-called grotesque as it is manifested in the lesbian body, the postmenopausal woman, the breast cancer survivor, and the African American HIV-positive drag queen. These are the underrepresented bodies of contemporary cinema and Rainer makes good use of them to articulate the subversive effects of the carnivalesque. Her own performance invokes the archetypal figure of the circus clown, a funny but perversely wise figure in this film, rhetorically similar to Shakespeare's fools.

In this film, then, Rainer troubles Judith Butler's notions of the performative by explicitly emphasizing the significance of corporeality and introducing a critically complex vision of subjecthood in which bodies do matter. Rainer has moved from figuring the body as a neutral doer to a disembodied voice to a fully material and specific fact, inseparable from lived experience.

Rainer has not really redefined melodrama so much as she has made exquisite use of its expansive mode. She has achieved subversive effects in her treatment of melodrama not because she avoids its conventions but because she meets those forms head on, appropriating them and turning them around in startling ways. She has found ways to play on melodrama's excess by using its hysterical and carnivalesque qualities to give meaning and significance to women's everyday lives. In MURDER *and murder* Rainer challenges traditional cinematic conventions by making a film about disease and lesbian desire without resorting to any spectacle of victimization. Mildred and Doris, even Jenny and young Mildred, are rendered powerfully visible, empathetic characters. We enjoy them, laugh with them, and cry with them.

For once Rainer has allowed us to identify with her characters and there is a real pleasure in that gesture. It acknowledges the limited opportunities for lesbians to see themselves on screen. Perhaps even more dramatic is Rainer's significant presence in this film as the tuxedo-wearing director. She self-consciously claims her right to be visible at the film's beginning when she first appears railing against the privileges assumed by her fellow director Stanley Kubrick. Her onscreen presence is important because she humanizes the abstract statistics about breast cancer, her awkwardness and vulnerability bringing viewers closer both to her and her subject matter—Murder by DDT, PCBs, and dioxin and murder by social and legal abuse, repression, and stigma.

She has drawn her characters in flesh and blood with all flaws and idiosyncrasies visible—precisely because they are not abstract entities. Just like us, they are of the world. The film ends with an image that perfectly embodies the ubiquitous melodramas of everyday existence that Rainer's films have so persistently elaborated over the years. In a darkened kitchen Mildred and

Doris sit opposite one another eating chicken soup. In its stark ordinariness, this image of a couple so obviously in love powerfully performs an utterly subjective vision of desire. It is a simple scene that quietly draws our attention; with this final silent image before us nothing else need be said. Sometimes words are not enough.

8

Safi Faye
and Trinh T. Minh-ha

Safi Faye was born in Dakar, Senegal, on November 22, 1943. After attending the Rufisque Normal School, she received her teaching certificate in 1963. She subsequently studied filmmaking in Paris during the 1970s. Faye received a Ph.D. in ethnology from the University of Paris in 1979 and earned an additional degree in ethnology from the Sorbonne in 1988. She began making films in the early 1970s with a short film, *La passante* (1972), in which she also acted. Subsequently, Faye secured financing for her first feature, the classic *Kaddu Beykat* (*Letter from My Village*, 1975), which won the prestigious Georges Sadoul Prize, as well as the International Critics Award at the Berlin Film Festival in 1976. Faye's career as a pioneering cineaste was launched. The enthusiastic reception of *Kaddu Beykat* confirmed Faye as the foremost feminist ethnographic filmmaker of sub-Saharan Africa. One of Faye's most famous works, *Selbe et tant d'autres,* a thirty-minute 16 mm color sound film from 1983, documents the role women play in many African cultures, tending home and family, sometimes while men sit in the shade and watch women perform daily domestic tasks. Faye's cinematic and editorial style has been influenced by the controversial ethnographic filmmaker Jean Rouch, in whose *Petit à petit* (1970) Faye appeared as an actor. Like Rouch, Faye trains the camera's seemingly impassive gaze, steady and fixed, on her protagonists. Faye does, however, acknowledge her role as director, albeit without introducing herself as a character within the work. In recent years, Faye's work has been the subject of numerous retrospectives around the world, and her newer films, *Selbe et tant d'autres* (1983) and *Mossane* (1996), have consolidated her reputation as an original, uncompromising ethnographic filmmaker.

Trinh T. Minh-ha was born in Vietnam in 1953 and settled in the United States in 1970. Minh-ha was an ethnographer before she became a filmmaker, and she worked for three years doing field research in Africa for the University of California, Berkeley, in the early 1980s. Openly critical in her writing of the colonial impulses of ethnography, she enacts a richly ambiguous relationship with the discipline through her films, which explore the cultures of marginalized groups while working to subvert the traditional strategies and poses of ethnographic film. Her many films include *The Fourth Dimension* (2001), *A Tale of Love* (1995), *Shoot for the Contents* (1991), *Surname Viet Given Name Nam* (1989), *Naked Spaces: Living Is Round* (1985), *Reassemblage* (1982), and *Calligraphy* (1981). Her films have won numerous awards, including the Blue Ribbon Award for best experimental feature at the American International Film Festival and the Golden Athena award from the Athens International Film Festival for *Naked Spaces* in 1985, as well as awards from the Berlin and Bombay International Film festivals for *Surname Viet Given Name Nam* in 1991. Frequently screened around the world in retrospectives and museums, Minh-ha's work delicately blends ethnographic and personal concerns, cutting across the traditional boundary maintained in documentary between filmmaker and subject.

Trinh T. Minh-ha has become increasingly interested in abstract political commentary in her films, particularly *A Tale of Love,* which was shot in a studio in 35 mm and codirected by Jean-Paul Bourdier. Influenced by collagists and other experimental cineastes of the 1960s, she creates a laboratory for political discussion within her works. Although she differs from Faye in style and approach, Minh-ha concerns her work with the female body and with issues of subjectivity, race, and class that surround that body in a postcolonial world.

GWENDOLYN AUDREY FOSTER

Experiments
in Ethnography

The Francophone filmmaker Safi Faye and the Vietnamese-born
filmmaker Trinh T. Minh-ha contribute to a tradition of experimental documentary filmmaking that avoids the objectifying, colonialist tendencies of
much documentary and ethnography. In fact, no available critical paradigm
adequately describes how these filmmakers reinvent documentary form by
combining self-reflexive gestures with innovative narration. Using these
strategies, Faye and Minh-ha emphasize the bodies and subjectivities of African and Asian women. These filmmakers make the body central to their
work, connecting body to subjectivity and letting the presence of the body
problematize narration, so that the narration cannot pretend to suppress or
contain difference. As part of their repertoire of strategies for representing
female bodies, Faye and Minh-ha both engage in what the feminist anthropologist Allison Jablonko terms "haptic learning, learning through bodily
identification" (182): they facilitate direct, visceral moments of identification
among their own bodies, the bodies of the women onscreen, and the bodies of viewers, emphasizing how perception and understanding arise within
and through the body.

Moving across the boundaries of visual pleasure, both scopic and haptic,
Faye and Minh-ha carve out a space for the skin and body—uncontained and
uncontainable vessel of subjectivity. In the works of both artists, the body
becomes emphatically present in its capacity to feel, perceive, communicate,
and apprehend. Contemporary theory does little to elucidate how such explorations of embodiment affect the workings of documentary practice. As
the film theorist Jennifer Barker explains, "the body as excess presents such

a problem for current theories ... that posit narration as cohesive, unambiguous *containment* of different and contradicting voices within the text"
(68). Faye's *Selbe et tant d'autres* and Minh-ha's film *Reassemblage* allow us
to assess the shortcomings of current theory for analyzing experimental
documentaries by women; the films also demonstrate how the emphatic
presence of the body complicates and rehabilitates narration, permitting
documentary form to present without appropriating, represent without
containing, or explore without conquering.

   Selbe et tant d'autres is a thirty-minute film that follows the daily rou-
tines and rituals of Senegalese women and one woman in particular: Selbe.
Faye converses with Selbe, who simply tells her story while working inces-
santly, cooking, cleaning, and selling, in order to provide for her family. Men
remain largely absent from the film, because in this region, men leave for
temporary jobs in the city. For the most part, viewers watch the body of
Selbe. An extraordinary example of cinema verité, *Selbe* portrays women's
space and women's subjectivity using strategies unusual for documentary
film. Like other Francophone women ethnographers, Faye addresses routine
assumptions behind narrative theory and ethnographic theory, as well as
larger issues regarding the representation of difference. One obvious way
she does this is to let Selbe herself speak to the camera. By facilitating the
self-representation of a speaking African subject, Faye cautiously avoids the
traditional ethnographic objectification and silencing of African subjects,
thereby rendering haptic space, women's space, and female subjectivity with
great care in her film.

   Also, *Selbe* celebrates excess, featuring excesses of female subjectivity, pain,
pleasure, work, and routine. Selbe's body compels viewer attention powerfully throughout the film: Selbe's gaze into the camera; the plentiful images
of Selbe's laboring hands, feet, arms, and shoulders; her bold, strong, accomplished gestures. Because of Selbe's intense physicality, charisma, and
spirituality, the film demands a new way of looking. In its focus on the
body, *Selbe* prompts us to rethink the way we experience the body in the
spectacle of film, the apparatus of film. Specifically, a film like *Selbe* inverts
the implied objective-subjective power relationship of documentary film
spectatorship, giving the film's subject the power to shape viewer perception. Kristin Thompson acknowledges this tendency for film to reorganize
perception in her essay on cinematic excess. Thompson writes that "each
film dictates the way it wants to be viewed" and suggests that in eliciting
viewer responses, a film's excesses can renew film's "ability to intrigue us by
its strangeness" (141). Thompson adds, "It can also help us be aware of how

the whole film—not just its narrative—works upon our perception" (141). As an example of cinematic excess and savvy about the embodied nature of representation and viewing, *Selbe* renews the ability of documentary form to induce a productive identification between viewer and subject.

Film reception theory tends to underemphasize the role of the body in film viewing—the fact that viewers experience film through and with the body. Borrowing from ethnography and phenomenology, I would like to revisit some principles of film reception to pave the way for my reading of *Selbe,* in particular my assertions about how Faye handles the portrayal of Selbe's subjectivity and difference. Much film theory assumes, for instance, that introduction of the film apparatus necessarily obliterates subjectivity, that the film "captures" and therefore objectifies and negates the subject. This is one way of looking at film, of course, and certainly many ethnographies and documentaries conform to this schema; but perhaps in formulating such a universalizing concept, we have neglected the possibility that the film apparatus could provide opportunities for salutary political interventions and expanded air time in the public sphere for subjectivities and bodies too little visible in Western culture.

There are, however, alternative conceptions of the relationship between cinema and subjecthood. Jean-Louis Baudry, for instance, proposes that theorists have been so intent on the characteristics of the film image that they have not noticed that the apparatus "in its totality includes the subject":

Almost exclusively, it is the technique and content of film which have retained attention: characteristics of the image, depth of field, offscreen space, shot, single-shot sequence, montage, etc.; the key to the impression of reality has been sought in the structuring of image and movement, in complete ignorance of the fact that the impression of reality is dependent first of all on a subject effect and that it might be necessary to examine the position of the subject facing the image in order to determine the raison d'être for the cinema effect. (312)

Baudry, then, understands film reception to be dependent on how the filmed subject operates upon the apparatus and the viewer, ascribing to the filmed subject a certain degree of agency and power. Henri Bergson offers a similar conception, allowing for the possibility of agency and vibrancy in the filmed subject by placing the subject "halfway between the 'thing' and the representation" (9). *Selbe* exemplifies that subject position in cinema of which Baudry and Bergson speak. Figuring the body as it does, *Selbe* addresses viewers across and through their own haptic zones, their own capacities to learn and experience with and through their bodies as they identify with the body onscreen. Thus, the viewer's own experience of body meets Selbe's experience of Selfhood within the space of embodiment, allowing for an interpenetration and negotiation of haptic space and, therefore, a bridge across the divide between self and other.

Paul Ricoeur has also written about the body's role in the perception and negotiation of otherness and difference. Ricoeur says:

> the metacategory of one's own body overlaps with the passivity belonging to the category of other people; the passivity of the suffering self becomes indistinguishable from the passivity of being the victim of the other (than) self. . . . . In a sharp-edged dialectic between praxis and pathos, one's own body becomes the emblematic title of a vast inquiry which, beyond the simple mineness of one's own body, denotes the entire sphere of *intimate* passivity, and hence of otherness, for which it forms the center of gravity. (51)

Ricoeur thus locates otherness in a "center of gravity" arising from the body of the perceiving self but inseparable from the other. In terms of cinema, this means that both viewer and viewed actively constitute the images and effects made manifest in the act of viewing: the divide between subject and object is neither firm nor clear nor impenetrable. The vein of film theory that *Selbe,* with its deployment of excess and its emphasis on the body, calls into question locates the center of gravity strictly in the critic's ontological space, discounting any performative rupture across the filmic apparatus. *Selbe* demonstrates that such ruptures can occur, which means that film can perform a kind of fluid identity negotiation wherein the filmed subject helps construct both her own self-representation and the viewer's perception of her. This understanding of the relationship between viewer and viewed affects the whole notion of perception in cinema. Perhaps this collaborative vision of cinematic perception is what Christian Metz was hinting at when he wrote "*The fact that must be understood is that films are understood*" (59). Since the body, which exists largely beyond conscious control, constitutes the site of perception, the film apparatus cannot fully control the experience of the viewer or the effects of the viewed on the viewer.

Some film theorists and anthropologists have opened avenues for thinking about how the body's role in perception might work to unsettle the colonizing capacities of the film apparatus and traditional notions of a subject/object divide. Jennifer Barker, for instance, argues that Western objectifying critical film discourse is "challenged by the presence of the physical body, which threatens non-compliance with, even subversion of, the film's organized system of meaning-production" (58). Barker uses the term "bodily irruptions" (57) to describe how bodies onscreen can defy both the critic's and the filmmaker's attempts to organize meaning in a particular direction. *Selbe* accomplishes a steady stream of such irruptions by highlighting so determinedly Selbe's physical presence. Michael Taussig also credits the body's role in constituting perception, subjectivity, and thought when he asks, "Might not the mimetic faculty and the sensuous knowledge it embodies be precisely this hard-to-imagine state wherein *the senses therefore become directly in their practice theoreticians?* (98). Taussig, in fact, rereading Walter Benjamin's famous and oft-quoted work on subject-object relations in spectatorship, goes as far as suggesting that the camera can "create a new sensorium involving a new subject-object relation and therefore a new person" (24).

Before considering this notion, we need to revisit Walter Benjamin's thoughts on the ritual nature of artwork—in this case, film—at the service of the aura as it is embedded in the fabric of tradition. Benjamin's notion of the aura helps enrich a cross-cultural reading of Faye's Senegalese film because we must keep in mind, as Benjamin cautions, that "to pry an object from its shell, to destroy its aura, is the mark of a perception whose 'sense of the universal equality of things' has increased to such a degree that it extracts it even from a unique object by means of reproduction" (225). For Benjamin, and many others, artworks in the service of ritual and artwork can and should "never entirely [be] separated from its ritual function" (226). Critically privileging the *ritual* nature of film, then, opens a whole realm of possible meaning to cross-cultural film studies. In the case of *Selbe*, it restores to us a sense of the ritual or sacralizing nature of Selbe's performative acts. Whether she is cooking, caring for her children, collecting mussels to sell in order to support her family, throwing pottery, interacting with others, or telling her story, she ritualizes and sacralizes her everyday experience. The ritual nature of film, in this case, becomes deeply significant. For far from destroying the original, or "decaying" Selbe's own aura, uniqueness, or subjectivity, Safi Faye's film can be seen as, "meeting the beholder halfway" (Benjamin 222)—meeting the viewer between cultures, across and between subjectivities. Because of the bodily identifications between viewer and Selbe, an intersubjectvity emerges; the film extends Selbe's agency, visibility, and voice.

Despite my optimistic rereading of Walter Benjamin here, and despite my desire to read cross-culturally, I acknowledge the problem of filmic (re)production. Are we looking only at a copy, a simulacrum of Selbe's body, Selbe's culture, Selbe's subjectivity? Are we limited in our ability to enter into Selbe's experience because of the decay of the aura or, more precisely, because of the nature of film itself, as a reproducer of culture and ritual? The distance between "the 'thing' and the representation," as Bergson puts it, is palpable. It is worth quoting Benjamin on this distance as it is present in the aura:

> The definition of the aura as a "unique phenomenon of a distance however close it may be" represents nothing but the formulation of the cult value of the work of art in categories of space and time perception. Distance is the opposite of closeness. The essentially distant object is the unapproachable one. Unapproachability is indeed a major quality of the cult image. True to its nature, it remains "distant, however close it may be." The closeness which one may gain from its subject matter does not impair the distance which it retains in its appearance. (245 n. 5)

The problematic of this distance inevitably affects cross-cultural readings of African women's films. Consider for example N. Frank Ukadike's response to *Selbe*. Ukadike credits Faye for conveying "female subjectivity" (114) yet complains that the film "depicts the men as village parasites—totally indifferent to familial bonds" (113). While I thoroughly agree with Ukadike's point on the depiction of female subjectivity, I do not see *Selbe* as misandrist. While it is quite apparent, as Ukadike notes, that the men in *Selbe* do not help women in the daily chores, Faye handles this fact compassionately, indicating that Serer men are undergoing terrific hardships of their own: lack of employment or long days in the field (in some cases) and also debilitating apathy and depression. In short, Faye acknowledges multiple sociocultural factors that explain why the men don't help the women. There is also, of course, the matter of traditional gender divisions in Serer culture, and no doubt these would be far more easily read by an African (and particularly a Serer) audience. In this case, I submit that the reproduction of images is not decaying the aura of the subject, but that critical intervention is prying the object from its shell, ignoring African tradition. I run this same risk, of course, but I hope to delimit the nature of my cross-cultural reading by discussing Selbe herself as subject. This seems in keeping with Safi Faye's project, considering that it is Selbe who maintains a constant screen presence as self and speaker, acting and performing ritual functions while inhabiting her body and in so doing moving her uncontainable subjectivity through scopic and haptic zones of experience—hers and the viewer's.

Safi Faye's statements in an interview with Angela Martin emphasize her status as an observer-participant; a storyteller who presents "documents"; and an artist who believes less in the categories of "fiction, documentary and ethnology" (A. Martin 18) than in the importance of maintaining and recording traditional African culture and the presentation of the individual subject. Faye explains:

> What I try to film is things which relate to our civilisation—a civilisation and a social organisation that one can differentiate from others. In a word: a typically African culture. And it's good that the inhabitants of a district are enabled to speak. OK, they're the problems, the sequences of daily life, but for me that's a very important choice. Because I don't know if my children will have the opportunity to see what I've seen, or what I try to know. It's for this reason that I make films about reality. A reality that has a tendency to disappear. Why? Because the old people, the carriers of history, of Africa, are disappearing . . . we become culturally assimilated and we only know through writing and through films what our past and our society were. And I try to make films not in the usual sense, but documents. . . . I give people a voice; they are enabled to speak about their own problems, to show their own reality, and I take a position within that. I situate myself on one side or another; my voice criticises what is open to criticism or I provide some small explanation, but that's all. And I'm paving the way for the possibility of future self-expression because it is only they who can appropriately speak about their problems. (A. Martin 18)

Faye thus circumscribes her role as filmmaker, endeavoring to act as facilitator for texts and documents created as much by the African subjects appearing in her films as by the filmmakers and viewer reception. The desire to give people a voice, however, can be distinctly problematic in ethnography. As Bill Nichols notes:

> The anthropologist/filmmaker usually disappears behind the optical vantage point when camera and filmmaker preside—a behind-the-scenes perspectival equivalent of the film frame's vanishing point. This disappearance, once valorized as part and parcel of observational respect for one's subjects but subsequently criticized as a masquerade of self-effacement that also effaces the limitations of one's own physicality in favor of omniscience and omnipotence, transforms first-hand, personal experience into third-person disembodied knowledge. ("Ethnographer's Tale" 64)

Safi Faye's films enjoy a reputation for avoiding the traps of traditional ethnography because of her presence, sometimes on-camera but mostly off-camera, as interviewer and observer-participant. Though Selbe herself does most of the talking, we can *hear* Faye's presence in the form of questions and comments. Thus the filmmaker keeps her own mediating presence explicit and avoids the pose of omniscience or omnipotence that Nichols criticizes.

Relationships among narration, body, subjecthood, and the presentation of knowledge become painfully evident upon comparing Faye's original to the American print, which contains an annoying British female voice-over. The voice-over, appropriating Selbe's actions and attempting to control viewer reception with "authoritative" commentary, threatens to disembody Selbe's knowledge and subjectivity. This voice-over serves as a reminder of colonialist film practice that does violence to the colonialized Other. Not only does it almost completely destroy the filmmaker's intentions, but it keenly demonstrates how disembodied knowledge destroys the authority of others. The delivery of the British woman's voice-over is terribly downbeat and is completely at odds with Selbe's own strong, determined temperament. The voice-over exemplifies the disembodied voice described by Bill Nichols: it is this voice that denies the subject's own voice and subjectivity.

The British female voice-over judges and objectifies Selbe, making tragedy (in the guise of feminism) while from Selbe's point of view there is survival and competence. Far from appearing as a speaking subject, Selbe is reduced to a colonialized Other and her life gets read through the prism of Western feminism. Such a demeaning appropriation of Selbe's circumstances certainly supports Aihwa Ong's assertion that "for feminists looking overseas, the non-feminist Other is not so much patriarchy as the non-Western woman" and that when Western feminists look cross-culturally, they often "establish their authority on the backs of non-Western women" (372). Examination of Faye's original reveals that for Faye, Selbe is not an objectified presence. In fact, Selbe has a powerful presence and gaze of her own.

Selbe's gaze amounts to that "black womanist" gaze defined by bell hooks as a form of "oppositional gaze." Faye emphasizes the oppositionality of Selbe's gaze, filming Selbe speaking directly to the camera while "staring" at both filmmaker and viewer. So there are multiple oppositional gazes at work, and these multiplications or magnifications of oppositionality break down the distance automatically presumed between spectator and spectacle. Mark Reid comments on Faye's construction of an oppositional gaze, observing that

> Faye does not agree with the closed status of the male gaze but views the male gaze as a matter of who is behind, who is in front of, and who belongs to the audience that participates in this relationship. In *The Passerby*, a 10-minute narrative film, she disrupts the male gaze upon female body parts by giving the female object a transitive quality and, thereby, both reversing the source

of the gaze and providing an "other" meaning. A series of shot-reverse shots and point-of-view shots decenters the authority of the male point of view, as well as its discourse, and exposes the polyvalent quality of the male gaze. Thus, as early as 1972, Faye was constructing a black womanist gaze to resist dominant viewing relationships. (65)

Reid's reading shows how filmmakers and filmic subjects can operate outside the subject/object mode often posited by film theory, improvising powerful strategies for exercising agency and showcasing their own subject-hood. Of course, vision, enacted through the gaze, is only one of the senses that allows Selbe's body to exceed the filmic apparatus and achieve a sense of haptic or embodied subjectivity that is shared with the viewer. As Trinh T. Minh-ha affirms, "[W]e write, we think and feel—with our entire bod-ies" (*Woman* 36) and "thought is as much a product of the eye, the finger, or the foot as it is of the brain" (39), which means that the body with all of its faculties becomes engaged in the filmic exchange. Safi Faye's camera moves with the body of Selbe. Viewers respond to Selbe's feet, working arms, gath-ering shoulders, and various facial expressions, experiencing through Selbe's body her spiritual and psychological resilience.

Selbe's gestures also convey her vitality. Gilles Deleuze writes about the importance of female gesture—or *gest*—to filmic representations of women. Deleuze suggests, "The states of the body secrete the slow ceremony which joins together the corresponding attitudes, and develop a female *gest* which overcomes the history of men and the crisis of the world" (196). This inde-fatigable female *gest* is ever-present in *Selbe,* in Selbe's mannerisms, move-ment, form, and bodily function. She has evolved a veritable language of expressive gestures that communicate the quality and history of her experi-ence. Writing about the relationship between gesture and memory, David MacDougall suggests that gestures may be read in anthropological terms as "signs of memory" wherein "a day's work or a short trip can now speak of a life's journey" (262). Selbe's gestures bespeak a life of capable labor and a sense of competence and determination, especially as she moves through her routine of *colportage*—the transportation of items from place to place in order to peddle them as merchandise.

The feminist cultural anthropologist C. Nadia Seremetakis discusses the wonderfully rich metaphorical dimensions of colportage, reading in it an extension of the body's material performance of memory, self, and culture. Memory moves not only through the body, Seremetakis claims, but also through objects and spaces:

Colportage has nothing to do with completed appearances and geometric closures; rather, in ornamenting the everyday with the sensibility of the different it cuts up the edifice of the routine and prosaic, it forms fragments and animates broken up pieces of multiple realities in transit. This is the migration of sensory forms via material artifacts, and the memory they leave behind. The traffic of exotic matter here is both literal and symbolic, actual and remembered; the transport (*metaphora*) of artifacts and narratives from one historical or cultural site to another is their metaphorization. Therefore colportage and its engagement with what can be shifted and altered is neither nostalgic nor realist. (220)

In Selbe's case, the self is grounded in objects like pottery, cleaning implements, and containers, as well as in the village itself, with its female spaces. Migrating from place to place through colportage, the material artifacts of Selbe's physical world represent the dispersal of her experience, memories, and activities. Subjectivity becomes, in this metaphorical view, a moving chain of sensory signifiers, a collection of experiential memory fragments. The images of Selbe cleaning clay in water, throwing pots, moving through the village present subjectivity as "a contraction of the real," to use Bergson's phrase, an accumulation of memories and experiences embedded, embodied, and symbolized in the material circumstances, artifacts, and activities of a life (34). In following Selbe's body and detailing the material circumstances and artifacts of her life, Safi Faye figures forth the body and subjectivity that remains inextricable from female living space; Trinh T. Minh-ha's films provide a similar exploration of female subjectivity through body and physical space.

Trinh T. Minh-ha restructures the colonial gaze that traditionally establishes an objectifying relationship between viewer and viewed. Minh-ha's films have often been critically received (and reduced) as "anti-ethnographies" or "anti-documentaries," films that deconstruct the tendency of documentary and ethnographic film practice to reduce third world "subjects" into flattened out figures of sublimated desire and lack. But Minh-ha's irony and deconstructive impulses question the critical enterprise as well, resulting in a thoroughly ambiguous and paradoxical approach that critiques traditional ethnography while resisting efforts to package this critique as evidence of any reified analytical position. The voice-over in *Reassemblage* criticizes "the habit of imposing a meaning to every single sign," as if to outwit any attempts to reduce the film to a limited, Euro-identified, critical category. Nevertheless, *Reassemblage* conducts its own critical activity, contemplating documentary form and gesturing in particular toward its colonialist gaze and posture toward African women. Critique of documentary and ethnography, however, which one would expect from a filmmaker whose writing explores postcolonial issues, constitutes only one type of border crossing accomplished by *Reassemblage.*

It would indeed be reductionist to attempt to identify the "subjects" of Minh-ha's film. I mean instead to "speak nearby" some of them, feeling acutely aware of my habit of "imposing a meaning to every sign." As a filmmaker and performance artist myself, I appreciate the performative quality of the film's structure—its jump cuts, black leader, silence on the track, non–eye matches, bursts of repetitive voice-overs, and disarming close-ups. These experimental techniques, reminiscent of French New Wave filmmakers like Jean-Luc Godard, allow *Reassemblage* to reflect continually on its own operations. Like the line "This is a film found on the scrapheap," which injects a measure of reflexivity into Godard's *Weekend,* Minh-ha, in voice-over, interrupts *Reassemblage* with the question, "A film about what, my friends ask." This Godardian moment shifts *Reassemblage* from documentary to document, a poetic attempt to speak nearby the "subject": Senegalese women. Speaking nearby this subject is all a sensitive critic can do.

In *The Woman at the Keyhole,* Judith Mayne invokes Minh-ha's complex relation to ethnography, noting that Trinh T. Minh-ha "questions the very possibility of seizing the reality of Senegal through such a visual documentation" (212). Using voice-over, close-up, fragmentation, and repetition, Minh-ha deconstructs traditions of the colonialist documentary and critiques Western notions of a unified "third world feminine." Documentarists and ethnographers have portrayed a "primitive" or "third world" female Other from the perspective of "mastery" and intrigue. The "objective" documentary perspective serves to intensify this intrigue, shrouding the non-Western subject in otherness. Robert Flaherty's *Nanook of the North,* the progenitor of the documentary-ethnographic form, demonstrates the flattening effects many documentaries have on their subjects. *Nanook* offers viewers little more than a sort of vague astonishment over the material conditions of Nanook's life. The film does little to convey Nanook's actual personhood—a sense of identity, subjectivity, creativity, inner agency. And if Nanook seems underdeveloped and flatly represented in terms of his personhood, still less so is Nanook's wife. This flattening effect mars many documentaries about African women as well. Who are the "subjects" of documentaries about Africans? Evidencing and addressing Minh-ha's discomfort with traditional ethnographic film, *Reassemblage* uses experimental form to highlight the maddening capacity of documentary and ethnography to reduce African women to their physical surfaces. Numerous close-ups of the faces and bodies of African women recall this lamentable habit of the documentarist. The visual barrage of African female breasts—so prominent in documentary and ethnographic photography—makes the black female body a self-less object, a marker of otherness and lack in ethnographic, medical, and clinical discourses. As if to literally remap the marker of the female breast, which also conjures the Western patriarchal positioning of breast as fetishized object, Trinh uses excessive repetition to reframe this image beyond the borders of Western voyeuristic film practice and, in the process, exposes our habit of imposing a meaning on everything.

While viewers gaze at the breasts of Senegalese women, the image gazes back at viewers and the sound track disarms reductionist critical impulses. The film's self-reflexive, performative gestures continually reposition the female body and female subjectivity for the viewer. The sound track, for example, contains an African tale that underscores African women's subjective space in oral storytelling tradition, thus recontextualizing the breast as signifier in non-Western terms. Through the story of woman (depicted as fire) we learn of the signifier of woman as the possessor of fire, that which destroys and at the same time regenerates: "Only she knew how to make fire. She kept it in diverse places. At the end of the stick she used to dig the ground with, for example, in her nails or in her fingers." Through this story, and its juxtaposition with images of the body, the female body becomes a transcendent signifier that rejects meanings defined by medical literature, psychoanalytic literature, and the gaze of the ethnographer and documentarist. Later in *Reassemblage,* the voice-over returns to fire as a symbol of women's embodied presence: "The fireplace and woman's face. The pot is known as a universal symbol for the mother, the grandmother, the Goddess." According to the performative logic of *Reassemblage,* the breast no longer reveals (perhaps never did reveal) femaleness: "Nudity does not reveal the hidden in its absence." The body "has no eye" yet "it records."

In addition to repositioning the image of the breast through repetition, juxtaposition, and sound track, *Reassemblage* also critiques the so-called "mastery" of the documentary film over the "subject" through nontraditional use of voice-over. The disembodied voice-over of the documentary film is critiqued in *Reassemblage* as an "eternal commentary that escorts images." Trinh T. Minh-ha lets *images* escort the commentary in *Reassemblage,* transforming object into subject. Senegalese women's voices also reverberate throughout the sound track, which, as Judith Mayne points out, underscores and celebrates "the significance of oral traditions" (216). Both filmmaker and the Senegalese women contribute to the film's oral collages;

these voices speak in a dissonant yet poetic unity on the sound track. Mayne reads the collagist sound track as a rejection of any presumed unity of "third world subject." Mayne also suggests that in *Reassemblage,* "the very division between the voice and the image suggests the possibility of another kind of observation, one resistant to the dualities of 'West' versus 'Third World'" (216). *Reassemblage* thus revolutionizes spectatorship, unsettling traditional semiotic and symbolic uses of the female body and blurring or reversing the traditional subject/object boundaries of ethnographic film. Minh-ha thus achieves a film that can "demand a new means of perception on the part of its spectators"—an achievement Ann Daly considers central to feminist creativity (245).

Minh-ha's filmmaking thus exposes some of the core myths undergirding traditional ethnography and documentary. In addition to questioning habitual representations of the female body and the subject-object divide, Minh-ha's film questions a core metaphor of documentary practice: the lens as captor. The "objective" documentarist has "captured" nothing more than a mere signifier of his own subjectivity reflected in the eyes of his subject. *Reassemblage* drives home this point in a voice-over aside stating that the ethnographer is sleeping next to his switched-on tape recorder, missing his opportunity to "capture his subject." The film thus reveals the mimetic capacity of ethnography as flawed. "To copy reality reduces reality and the copy becomes a veiled substitute," states the voice-over. *Reassemblage,* with such self-reflexive, performative gestures, becomes a film-poem and film-essay that "speaks nearby" African female subjecthood. The film's playful dissonance of images, sound, and signifiers embraces what Adorno celebrated as "the determinate and indeterminate [that] remains ambiguous even after they have been synthesized" (181); in attempting to synthesize the plenitude of determinate and indeterminate images and relationships on screen, the active spectator engages with active subjects that assert their subjecthood through the medium of cinema.

In the films of Safi Faye and Trinh T. Minh-ha, then, female bodies and women's spaces serve to articulate female subjectivity and difference as active, powerful phenomena in a cinematic domain purged of the power relations typically at work in ethnographic and documentary film. The works of both filmmakers emphasize the body's presence with profound resonance and forcefulness, enhancing its aura and using its power to mark the vitality of female subjects who cannot be contained within the reductive, limiting, subject-object configuration and symbolic landscape of Western patriarchal documentary. These filmmakers are carving out the beginnings of a feminist vision in experimental ethnographic and documentary film.

9

Faith Hubley
and Caroline Leaf

Motivated by a lifelong commitment to social justice, Faith Hubley began her career in Hollywood in the 1940s, working her way up from messenger to script clerk at Columbia, then moving on to work as a freelance editor of educational films and documentaries. As a result of the blacklist, she and her husband, John Hubley, an animation director, moved to New York in the 1950s. The couple began collaborating on groundbreaking animated films, which Hubley called "personal films," while supporting their family with work in advertising. Although husband and wife did not share directing credit until 1973, they were equally instrumental in creating their Oscar-winning *Moonbird* (1959), among other landmark works. After John Hubley's death in 1977, Faith Hubley continued to experiment with animation techniques—combining them with her intensifying commitment to women's issues, which had begun with films such as *WOW* (*Women of the World*) (1975). *The Cosmic Eye* (1986), a feature-length animated film, combines the best sampling of Faith Hubley's solo work, with segments focusing on the environment, children's issues, and goddess mythology. Faith Hubley died in 2002.

After studying visual arts at Harvard, Caroline Leaf joined the National Film Board of Canada. As is common for films from the NFB, Leaf's films feature sophisticated animation techniques while remaining accessible to children. Leaf's work consistently reflects Canada's multilingual culture. *The Owl Who Married a Goose* (*Le mariage du hibou*) grew out of Leaf's work with Native American folk tales. In this film the design resembles Native art and the characters speak in untranslated, unsubtitled Inuit. In her 1976

Oscar-nominated *The Street*, Leaf tries another technique—painting under the camera. The resulting watercolor-like images enable characters and locations to fluidly transform themselves from one shape to another as the main character comes of age. *Two Sisters* (1990) calls forth a new visual style based on an incredibly laborious technique. Scraping the black off each frame of 70 mm film by hand, Leaf reveals the colors beneath. Scratched directly onto film stock, the lines shimmer because they cannot fall exactly where they had in the previous frame. Her technical inventiveness makes her a significant figure in the animation field.

AMY LAWRENCE

Two Sisters

From the 1970s on, there has been an explosion of work by women in the field of independent animation. While women have worked in studio animation since the early twentieth century, it was the conjunction of independent filmmaking and the feminist movement that led numerous women to begin making their own films in this period. Two of the best known independent animators, Faith Hubley and Caroline Leaf, exemplify the dramatically different career paths women have taken, including the range of working methods and funding available to women animators who choose to work outside the studio system. In this essay I will focus on how Hubley's and Leaf's position outside "industrial animation" encourages experimentation with form, and how each woman's choice of technique makes literal her views of sisterhood. This will be demonstrated in two animated films, Faith and John Hubley's *Windy Day* (1968) and Leaf's *Two Sisters* (1990).

In *Windy Day* and their other independent films, John and Faith Hubley experimented with a loose, fluid style that was at odds with the hard-edged opacity of traditional cel animation. They also created a collaborative model of film production that eventually expanded to include their children. By tape-recording their children making up stories during playtime, the Hubleys were able to introduce an improvisatory ethos to their films unprecedented in animation. Hubley herself identifies this as "our contribution . . . using improvisation—to liberate animation from itself" (McGilligan 13).

Caroline Leaf entered the field from a different direction, becoming an animator while studying visual arts at Harvard followed by a period at the National Film Board of Canada, where government support gave artists a steady salary, access to equipment, and freedom to experiment. Like Hubley, Leaf has little use for cel animation, preferring images created under the camera. Working under the camera requires a fulltime commitment of a camera and space for the course of the production (for these films, several months to over a year). Her best-known film, the Oscar-nominated *The Street* (1977), based on a Mordecai Richler story, is done with painting under the camera, a technique that mixes Vaseline with paint so the image remains liquid during shooting. The Oscar-nominated *The Owl Who Married a Goose* (1974) uses sand animation to imitate tribal art.

Despite their different backgrounds, Hubley's and Leaf's interests converge on the issue of familial sisterhood (as opposed to the political ideal of sisterhood). We shall see how their experimental techniques encompass everything in this relationship from the humorous to the horrific.

In the introduction to the 1985 book *The Sister Bond,* Toni McNaron writes, "The relationship between sisters, like that between mothers and daughters, comes to us shrouded in silence and ignorance" (5). In an anthology published ten years later, Patricia Foster asserts that "since feminism proposed a new family of sisters, few writers have looked closely at the issues which unite and disrupt real sisters" (4).

In a sociological study of sibling relationships, Francine Klagsbrun found the initially reassuring circumstance that "[o]n almost every scale of closeness … sisters topped the charts for intimacy and warmth toward one another" (296). Such closeness, however, often makes it difficult to forge an individual identity. As Klagsbrun notes, "When sibs are of the same sex, a special kind of identification takes place between them, and a special struggle goes on against that identification" (79).

The danger of too much closeness quickly becomes clear. Foster, for instance, announces that her book was written to address this very question, "Who am I if I am not my sister?" (3). As a five-year-old, Foster offered to merge with her six-year-old sister.

> "I'm you," I said to her one night.
> "We're me," she agreed. . . .
> "Sometimes I'm me," [Foster countered].
> "No, you're not," her sister replied. "We're always me." (2)

The problem of sororial closeness is that it can never escape issues of dominance. Domination between siblings is almost always linked not to gender but, as the films show, to birth order. The older child often feels forced into a role of responsibility while the younger feels dominated; the older resents not being respected for all the helpful advice that the younger regards as criticism and proof of bossiness.

Windy Day

The 1968 film *Windy Day* can be seen as the girls' version of John and Faith Hubley's 1959 Oscar-winning *Moonbird*, which stars their two sons. In both films the older child wants to carry out a grand project and needs the younger child's cooperation. The children provide the voices while their parents make their imaginary worlds come alive visually. In responding to parameters established by the children's spontaneous story spinning and idea sharing, the Hubleys introduce considerable improvisation into animation and allow child minds to evolve the thematic content of the work. Interestingly, this thematic content becomes a complex exploration of the shifting power dynamics of sisterhood.

As *Windy Day* opens, two girls are playing in a meadow. Emily, the older girl, is primarily concerned with social roles, concocting stories about princes, damsels in distress, and marriage. As she recounts them, the field behind her sprouts childlike drawings of castles and dragons. Emily becomes Prince Valiant, her dress turned into a doublet and tights. Because it is her play, Emily gets to do all the active things while her little sister, Georgia, waits. (Emily has since become a well-known animator; Georgia is a member of the band Yo La Tengo.) Emily's control of their play narrative, however, does not last indefinitely.

Despite the age difference (Emily is ten or twelve and Georgia is around five), Georgia is very assertive when it comes to expressing her displeasure at being cast in her sister's fantasy. The first lines we hear establish the tensions in their relationship as well as their parity.

Emily says, "Georgia. We have to do the play now." And Georgia says, "No."

"*Yes*," Emily says, "I wanna do the play."
"You do, but I don't wanna do the play so I'm not gonna do the play."
"But Georgia, we *have* to."
"No, we don't have to."
The sisters' banter here makes clear the competition and negotiation that underlies their relationship. This competition and negotiation is informed by the intersubjective closeness of sisterhood. According to Klagsbrun, the ability "to think about one another's thoughts and feelings" makes siblings "more

adept at playing pretend games with each other" (354). Their knowledge of each other enables siblings to engage in collaborative fantasy that requires them to negotiate their roles and desires within the imagined scenario. As a result of these negotiations, a joint fantasy can suddenly be vetoed by either party. For instance when Emily as the prince proposes to Georgia on bended knee—"Please, Polly, you *do* want to marry me"—Georgia replies curtly, "I don't. Marry your wife." Certainly, the younger sister manages to hold her own within the power dynamics percolating through their fantasy world.

Where Emily's dreams center on gender roles and marriage, Georgia focuses on animals and mommy/baby issues. At one point Georgia hijacks the story (and by extension the film) by making up "another play" about kangaroos and giraffes taking their babies for a ride. Having allowed Georgia her imaginary excursion, Emily takes back control of the narrative, which, in fairy-tale fashion, must end in marriage. While the film could end in this classic way, there is a break as the film's tone shifts, and once again Georgia asserts herself and her concerns into the play.

The older sister gently tries to change the subject to how babies are born, telling Georgia she was a seed in her mommy's tummy. Georgia, however, insists on bringing the subject back to death. "Then what happened to the seed, it died. That's what it did, it died." Emily counters, "But the seed is the baby and you're the baby, and then you grow up." Taking logic where she wants it to go, Georgia concludes, "But then when you finish growing up, you die."

The mood lightens only when a bell rings to summon them home. Skipping through the woods, they embody siblings Klagsbrun writes about known as Hansels and Gretels, who "find security" and "discover that they can make their way through frightening forests . . . by depending on each other" (299). Back home the sisters wait alone outside on the deck as the film tries to balance a mood of hope with the specter of mortality. The light fades as they wait, giggling and shivering in the breeze, becoming silhouettes.

In addition to infusing animation technique with elements of improvisation by using a found sound track, the Hubleys' film breaks new ground for experimental film in terms of content. In highlighting play with gender roles, sororial intersubjectivity, and negotiated power, *Windy Day* dramatizes the fluctuating, experimental, and fledgling emergence of each sister's sense of self. Part of this sense of self includes an ability to speak, command attention, and wield power in the intensely close relationship developed by sisters within a family structure. Struggling to articulate and inhabit a singular space for self within shifting power dynamics suggested and intensified by birth order, the sisters vie for control of their collaborative narrative—a process that reflects at the level of play the tension-filled complexity of female self-development within the context of sisterhood. Both nourishing and threatening, validating and undermining, sisterhood becomes a space wherein the emergent female subject encounters both challenges to and support for her evolution into a powerful, capable, singular subject.

Two Sisters

Leaf's *Two Sisters* is much darker than the Hubleys' film, literally and narratively. While Hubley's girls negotiate their different desires, the women in *Two Sisters* submerge their differences. In fact it is difficult to distinguish one from the other at first. As Patricia Foster writes, "If sisters do not go through the process of separation, their stories are diminished, reduced, the anxiety palpable in what gets repressed" (8). Leaf's claustrophobic world of sisterhood is filled with the danger of physical and psychological violence.

Unlike *Windy Day* where the bright watercolor style and emphasis on transparency minimize any potential for serious conflict, inside the home of the two sisters darkness is coupled with extreme camera angles that make it impossible to get completely oriented. Two hands brush someone's hair. Two legs stretch out and rest on a stool. A cup appears out of the blackness, then a pot materializes to pour coffee. In these scenes we see bits and pieces of bodies, hands, hair, legs, but no whole self. We also see the body's relation to objects (the coffeepot, the comb). What is *not* made clear is that there are in fact *two* bodies; how they come to be separate is the film's central conflict.

The opening scenes are marked by humming and tapping sounds, enveloping vocal and kinetic rhythms undifferentiated by dialogue or lyrics. This whirl of sound suggests an all-absorbing closeness between the sisters that is reminiscent of Julia Kristeva's notion of *chora,* an imaginary, preverbal space that Kaja Silverman calls an attempt to "abolish the opposition of inside and outside," a rejection of the outside world in favor of an "image of unity" (*Acoustic Mirror* 100, 102). Although they are adults, sisters Marie and Viola are trapped in a mutual dependency, an emotional dyad that allows neither sister space for individuation. When Viola's writing goes well, Marie brings out a mirror and says, "Look at yourself." Viola backs into the darkness, a state that hints at dread—perhaps concerning family secrets. The older sister, Marie, maintains the status quo, telling Viola she sees "no change at all" and keeping Viola trapped within the constricting space of their connectedness. In order to find her own identity and not be defined by her sister, Viola must separate from her sister.

Throughout the film there is an intense struggle between light and dark, presented originally in gendered terms. A man opens the door allowing light to burst in. Confronted by an outsider, Viola does something astonishing. She shows him (and us) her severely disfigured face. When he gasps, she laughs and turns on her heel like a gleeful child who has dared something outrageous. Viola's willingness to show herself in all her stunning single-ness—imperfections and all—demonstrates a strong desire to assert a sense of self in the landscape of her sequestered life.

Marie instantly recognizes that the true threat is not the intruder but Viola's urge to have her own identity. She also quickly discerns the method whereby individuation will disrupt the sisterly unity: it is language, the sym-bolic, that breaks the imaginary unity of the chora. The man tells Viola, "I've read everything you've written. Every word." Marie confirms the danger this represents when she turns on Viola and says, "You send your stories out and this is what washes up." Viola's language thus serves as her link to the out-side world and the medium through which she experiences and expresses her own individuated subjecthood. Marie is obviously threatened by Viola's process of individuation.

In a frenzy of cleaning, Marie tries to interrupt or drown out their con-versation and locks the door when they try to leave. Her last weapon is her first, threatening Viola with the world's horror if Viola were to venture out. "You don't want to go out there. You're a freak. We're sisters, Viola. Let me make lunch and everything will be like it was before." As Viola steps outside with the man, into the blinding light, Marie closes the door behind her and locks it.

Leaf's technique in this film is extreme even by animation standards. In contrast to the spontaneity of the Hubleys' film and the fluidity of her own earlier work, the technique Leaf pioneered here is incredibly laborious. Leaf scrapes the black off each frame of 70 mm film by hand, revealing the colors beneath. By scratching the image directly onto film stock, Leaf literalizes the idea of scratching out an existence or an identity. The lines shimmer because they cannot fall exactly where they had in the previous frame. As a conse-quence, the image is always in the process of being swallowed by darkness. Leaf thus manages to enact in her creative process and capture in film form the tenuous, difficult, seemingly endless process of carving out an individual self from the undifferentiated darkness of the psychospiritual imbroglio that is family life.

Although outside Viola basks in sunlight, her facial disfigurement and humped back do not miraculously disappear. The painfully overexposed white light threatens to burn out Viola's image as violently as the darkness threatens to suffocate her. No resounding victory of individuation here: emerging selfhood is represented visually as blindingly painful. Nor does the film end with the inevitability of heterosexual romance. Viola's own actions have established her identity. The film resolves its extremes of light and dark by positing a middle way.

Autographing her book and saying goodbye to her male fan, Viola returns home to Marie, having in effect renegotiated their familiar roles. As Marie moves to close the door, Viola says, "Leave it open." As Viola returns to her writing, Marie dusts the keyboard of Viola's computer and sets a chair in front of the open door, keeping an eye on the outside. As Marie hums, Viola taps the keys, showing how the symbolic and the choric can coexist.

Although they have very different tones and offer starkly contrasting depictions of sisterly relationships, both Hubley's and Leaf's films are built around the issue of how to negotiate sisterhood: to be close without merging, separate without breaking apart, to have a balance that is equally positive for older and younger sisters. For Hubley, the sisters' relationship helps them prepare to face life. In Leaf's film, Viola braves the world in order to be strong enough to learn how to live with her sister. Taken together, these films use animation to draw a complex portrait of how self and subjecthood emerge in the emotionally charged environment of sisterhood.

10

Marie Menken,
Carolee Schneemann,
Marjorie Keller,
Anne Charlotte Robertson,
and Rose Lowder

Marie Menken played a range of roles in the New York art scene from the 1940s through the 1960s. She and her (gay) spouse, the poet and filmmaker Willard Maas, made their Brooklyn Heights apartment a salon and haven for young artists and writers, including Andy Warhol, Edward Albee, Marilyn Monroe, Stan Brakhage, Norman McLaren, P. Adams Sitney, and Truman Capote. Menken was a painter, but when she was given the pawn ticket for filmmaker Francis Lee's camera when Lee went into the army, she became dedicated to the new medium: "I just liked the twitters of the machine, and since it was an extension of painting for me, I tried it and loved it. In painting I never liked the staid static, always looked for what would change with source of light and stance, using glitters, glass beads, luminous paint, so the camera was a natural for me to try—but how expensive" (qtd. in Mandell). Menken found ways of working inexpensively and developed an aesthetic that abjured the high-tech continuities of the commercial cinema. During the 1940s and 1950s, Menken's little films pioneered more flexible, more expressive uses of the handheld camera, gestural camerawork that at the time seemed a form of cinematic action painting.

Menken's films include evocations of fellow artists Isamu Noguchi (*Visual Variations on Noguchi*, 1945), Kenneth Anger (*Arabesque for Kenneth*

Anger, 1961), and Piet Mondrian (*Mood Mondrian,* 1963); "notebooks" of city scenes like *Notebook* (1962–63), *Go! Go! Go!* (1962–64), *Lights* (1964–65); and "recyclings" from film and television like *Wrestling* (1964), which "wrestles" with a telecast of a wrestling match, and *Hurry! Hurry!* (1957), which recycles imagery of human sperm struggling to impregnate eggs into a bizarre dance of death. (Dating of Menken's films can be only approximate; her informality and her tendency to do several versions of films make dating difficult.) Menken also acted in films by others: she served as subject and cameraperson for Willard Maas's *Geography of the Body* (1943) and acted in Warhol's *The Life of Juanita Castro* and *Bitch* (both 1965), as well as *Chelsea Girls* (1966).

Menken made other contributions as well. Stan Brakhage remembers that "it was Marie who worked, bringing home the money. For all of their married life she worked for Time-Life; and every evening, five and sometimes six days a week, Marie trudged up to the Time-Life Building for the night shift, to pick up all the overnight cables from whatever state or country she was handling that night, and held that job for thirty years. She would come home at two or three o'clock in the morning and drink herself into sleep" (*Film at Wit's End* 46). Menken died on December 29, 1970, at the age of sixty; Maas died four days later.

* * *

Carolee Schneemann's filmmaking has always been an extension of her work in other media. Like Menken, she began as a painter (an abstract expressionist) and an assemblage artist (her constructions often evoke the works of Joseph Cornell and Robert Rauschenberg), but she is best known as one of the formative performance artists. During the sixties and seventies, she was a leader in liberating the body, with such classic performances as *Meat Joy* (1964), *Water Light/Water Needle* (1966), and *Interior Scroll* (1975), in which she removes a scroll from her vagina and reads the text on the scroll. Her book *More Than Meat Joy* (1979) documents her performance career through 1979. Early paintings and assemblages, along with more recent collages and assemblages, appear in *Schneemann, Early Work, 1960–1970* and *Carolee Schneemann—Recent Work,* catalogs for shows at the Max Hutchinson Gallery in New York in 1982 and 1983, respectively.

By the time she made *Fuses* (1967), Schneemann was using filmmaking to combine painting, collage, and performance. For a year, she and her partner James Tenney performed sexually for and with the camera; and Schneemann subsequently painted, scratched, and collaged on the filmstrip as a means of revealing dimensions of the psychic experience of sex not evident in the photographed imagery. Schneemann says that *Fuses* responds to Stan Brakhage's birth film, *Window Water Baby Moving* (1959): "I had mixed feelings about the power of the male partner, the artist subsuming the primal creation of giving birth as a bridge between male constructions of sexuality as either medical or pornographic. . . . I know that Stan and Jane passed the camera back and forth, but I was still very concerned that the male eye replicated or possessed the vagina's primacy of giving birth. The camera lens became the Os, the aperture out of which birth was 'expressed'" (qtd. in Haug 26).

Fuses is the first of three films that comprise Schneemann's *Autobiographical Trilogy*. In *Plumb Line* (1971) Schneemann attempts a cinematic exorcism, attempting to rid herself of the psychic wounds of a painful love relationship; in *Kitch's Last Meal* (1973–76), her Super 8, two-projector (one slightly larger image projected above another) domestic epic, Schneemann depicts her relationship with the filmmaker Anthony McCall over a period of months, at the end of which they no longer live together. In more recent years, Schneemann has used video more often than film. She continues to perform and lecture on performance. A two-hour version of *Kitch's Last Meal* was exhibited as part of Big As Life: An American History of 8 mm Film.

∗ ∗ ∗

By the time of her death in 1994, at only forty-four years, Marjorie Keller had established herself as a major contributor to alternative film, in several arenas. Her book *The Untutored Eye: Childhood in the Films of Cocteau, Cornell, and Brakhage* (1986) was a substantial contribution to the literature about alternative media. Keller founded and edited the journal *Motion Picture* and was professor of art at the University of Rhode Island. She was also an accomplished filmmaker who produced twenty-one films between 1969 and 1988—the most widely viewed being *Misconception* (1977) and *Daughters of Chaos* (1980).

Misconception is one of a series of remarkable avant-garde films that depict human birth and has also been considered a response to Stan Brakhage's *Window Water Baby Moving*. When Keller was asked to film the birth of her niece, she agreed; but unlike Brakhage, whose film sings the miracle of the birth of his first daughter, Keller presents her sister-in-law's birth as a physical and psychic struggle. Made during the heyday of seventies feminism, *Misconception* construes childbirth as both mystery and political challenge for all concerned: mother, father, child, and filmmaker. Keller evokes adolescence in *Daughters of Chaos,* combining her own footage with reworked home movies from her childhood.

Considered a master of small-gauge (8 mm and Super 8) filmmaking—she was represented by ten films in Big as Life: An American History of 8 mm Films, sponsored by the Museum of Modern Art and the San Francisco Cinematheque, in 1998–99—Keller used filmmaking to negotiate her personal life, not by suppressing the painful realities of domestic life, as most home movies do, but by using filmmaking to plumb the complexities of family. In *The Answering Furrow,* one of her last films, Keller celebrates her achievement of domestic contentment with her husband, P. Adams Sitney, and their two daughters.

*   *   *

Filmmaking has been a lifeline for Anne Charlotte Robertson in an unusually direct sense: her adult life includes a struggle with bipolar syndrome, and filmmaking allows her to express this struggle and succeed as an artist despite it. Inspired by the small-gauge guru Saul Levine, Robertson's teacher at the Massachusetts College of Art; by Carolee Schneemann's *Kitch's Last Meal;* and by Jonas Mekas's diary films, Robertson began what has become her monumental *Diary* on November 3, 1981, and has lengthened and reworked it ever since. *Diary* documents Robertson's struggles with bipolar syndrome, weight, vegetarianism, and a range of other personal issues, as well as the pleasures of gardening, extended family, and daily life. Robertson has also finished dozens of short films—including *Melon Patches* (1994)—many of them diaristic but separate from *Diary.*

In 1988, the American Museum of the Moving Image presented *Diary,* which was at that time approximately forty hours long, half-hour by half-hour, in a small gallery Robertson decorated with childhood artifacts and inhabited while the museum was open. Throughout the weeklong screening, Robertson introduced reels of the diary and provided spontaneous commentary. Sections of *Diary* have been shown throughout North America in the original Super 8. In more recent years, half-hour sections of *Diary* have been released on video cassette. Robertson received a Guggenheim Fellowship in 2002, and in recent years the accomplishments of her *Diary* and other films have been widely recognized and honored.

*   *   *

Rose Lowder has been an important force in the European alternative film scene since the early 1980s, both as filmmaker and codirector of the Archives du film expérimental d'Avignon, in Avignon, France, which she and her partner, Alain-Alcide Sudre, established in 1982 to collect, preserve, and showcase landmark "experimental film." Born of British parents living in Peru, and trained as a painter, Lowder had her first experiences as a filmmaker at the BBC in London, where she was an assistant editor from 1965 to 1967. She worked on a variety of programs but notes "editing was about the only thing women were allowed to do" (qtd. in MacDonald, *Critical Cinema 3* 223). She moved to France with Sudre and settled in Avignon, where they began to present screenings during Avignon's famous annual summer theater festival.

Lowder has always preferred the term "experimental film" since, unlike many filmmakers, she sees her films as experiments. Her earliest experiments involved film loops that allowed her to explore the frame-by-frame production and perception of imagery. She discovered that she could construct an image on the retina using bits of individual film frames: "There's a lot of talk about the smallest unit of cinema being the frame, but in fact that's not the case at all" (qtd. in MacDonald, *Critical Cinema 3* 219). By the late 1970s Lowder was finishing discrete films, many of which provide beautiful, distinctive evocations of French landscapes and cityscapes, especially in and around Avignon. Generally, her films are precisely scored in advance (indeed, the scores are artworks in their own right) but shot quickly: each hundred-foot roll of 16 mm film is exposed, frame by frame, on a single day. Each day's shooting becomes a module and may be combined with other modules to make a more sustained film.

Lowder has also worked to make the work of other experimental filmmakers available to audiences throughout France. In 1989, for example, she and Sudre organized a French tour of Canadian experimental films and filmmakers and produced *The Visual Aspect: Recent Canadian Experimental Film* (Avignon: Editions des archives du film expérimental d'Avignon), a collection of essays by filmmakers and scholars. In 1987 she finished her Ph.D. thesis, "Le film expérimental en tant qu'instrument de recherche visuelle: Contribution des cinéastes expérimentaux á une démarché exploratoire" (Experimental film as an instrument of research: The contribution of filmmakers to an experimental approach) at the University of Paris and Nanterre.

SCOTT MacDONALD

Avant-Gardens

Yes the sowing of a seed seems a very simple matter, but I always feel as if it
were a sacred thing among the mysteries of God. Standing by that space of blank and
motionless ground, I think of all it holds for me of beauty and delight, and I am filled
with joy at the thought that I may be the magician to whom power is given to summon
so sweet a pageant from the silent and passive soul. I bring a mat from the house
and kneel by the smooth bed of mellow brown earth, lay a narrow strip of board
across it a few inches from one end, draw a furrow firmly and evenly in the
ground along the edge of the board, repeating this until the whole bed
is grooved at equal distances across its entire length.

—Celia Thaxter, *An Island Garden*

During the summer of 1993, I had the good fortune to attend a National Endowment for the Humanities Summer Institute, "Hudson River
Valley Images and Texts: Constructing a National Culture in Nineteenth-
Century America," during which I was able to indulge my growing fascination with nineteenth-century American landscape painting.[1] As the weeks
of the institute passed, it became increasingly obvious to me that the early
depiction of American landscape—at least by European Americans—was
even more fully the province of male painters than I had imagined. Finally,
assuming that there *must have been* an under-recognized woman painter
or two who had contributed to the early-to-mid-nineteenth-century visual
surveying of American spaces (the way Susan Fenimore Cooper had contributed to the early history of American Nature Writing with her exploration
of Cooperstown in *Rural Hours* [1850]),[2] I asked Margaretta Lovell, one of
the NEH scholars, "How did women contribute to the imaging of American
landscape during the eighteenth and nineteenth centuries?" Lovell responded,
"They were probably cultivating real gardens." Of course, like so much do-

mestic labor, early American domestic gardening has been little chronicled, with the notable exceptions of Celia Thaxter's garden on the Isle of Shoals off the coast of New Hampshire, which was documented by Thaxter's own *An Island Garden* (1894), a book on the pleasures and challenges of gardening, illustrated with paintings by the American impressionist Childe Hassam, and Emily Dickinson's gardens, the subject of Judith Farr's *The Gardens of Emily Dickinson* (2004).

During the twentieth century the depiction of American landscape was at least as fully the province of cinema as of painting, though serious commitment to place as filmic subject, rather than as background for melodramatic action (in the western, most obviously), became the province of independent cinema, and in recent decades, of a generally under-recognized tradition within avant-garde filmmaking. While this modern interest in cinematically depicting landscape is less clearly gendered than was nineteenth-century landscape painting, the gender distinction in the nineteenth century between surveying the American scene and cultivating real gardens seems subtly echoed by a distinction between depicting extensive landscape scenes, primarily by men (I'm thinking, for example, of Bruce Baillie's *To Parsifal* [1963], Larry Gottheim's *Horizons* [1973], much of James Benning's and Peter Hutton's work), and depicting or evoking the domestic garden, frequently by women. None of the men or women filmmakers in this tradition has received widespread recognition; as was true in the nineteenth century, however, the contributions by women have been even more fully overlooked and undercelebrated than those of men.

In general, the films discussed here can be seen as using the traditional idea of the garden as an implicit and sometimes explicit critique of the ways in which modern commerce, including modern commercial film and television, compromises our willingness and ability to engage the particulars of place by endlessly marketing a rootless movement across the landscape in service of material accumulation. In each of the films I discuss, the domestic or domesticized garden or "garden" is envisioned as a safe space within which the spirit can be nurtured despite the demands of an outer world whose focus and velocity tend to be determined by men. As will be obvious, however, I am less interested in promulgating a theory about women, or women filmmakers, than in honoring the cinematic exploration of five filmmakers who have struggled, by various, sometimes intersecting routes, toward film practices and products that defy central tendencies in the male-dominated history of cinema.

Glimpse of the Garden (1957)

There was a very lyrical soul behind that huge and very often sad bulk of a woman, and she put all that soul into her work. The bits of songs that we used to sing together were about the flower garden, about a young girl tending her flower garden. Marie's films were her flower garden. Whenever she was in her garden, she opened her soul, with all her secret wishes and dreams. They are all very colorful and sweet and perfect, and not too bulky, all made and tended with love, her little movies.

—Jonas Mekas's *Village Voice* obituary for Menken and Willard Maas, January 14, 1971

Probably no woman who has had as significant an impact on American cinema as Marie Menken has remained as little celebrated. Except for several of her colleagues of the 1950s and 1960s—Stan Brakhage, Jonas Mekas, and P. Adams Sitney—virtually no one has been interested in assessing her films and their impact on others; and only Brakhage has written as much as a chapter on Menken. Indeed, Sitney's "greatest regret" as chronicler of American avant-garde filmmaking of the post–World War II era is that he did not include Menken's work in his *Visionary Film* (1974, 1979).[3] Menken was not a prolific filmmaker. Eighteen films are currently in distribution, nearly all of them quite short, including most of the films that established and maintained her reputation at least among avant-garde filmmakers of her era: *Visual Variations on Noguchi* (1945), *Hurry! Hurry!* (1957), *Glimpse of the Garden* (1957), *Arabesque for Kenneth Anger* (1961), *Eye Music in Red Major* (1961), *Bagatelle for Willard Maas* (1961), *Notebook* (in various versions, from 1961), *Go! Go! Go!* (1962–64) (these last two are compilation pieces made up of several mini-films).[4] Only her portrait of Warhol, *Andy Warhol* (1965), runs more than fifteen minutes.

Menken's contribution to film history is twofold: several of her films repay careful engagement as complex, finished works; and Menken's *approach* to filmmaking was a pivotal influence on filmmakers who themselves have had considerable impact on modern avant-garde film. Of her earliest films, *Glimpse of the Garden* may be the best for revealing both dimensions of this impact. *Glimpse of the Garden* is a response to the Long Island garden of Dwight Ripley, an ex-lover of Menken's husband, Willard Maas. According to Brakhage, Ripley "was an alcoholic who . . . had become very dependent on Marie. She came to love him deeply, long after Willard was through with him and they were great friends. Dwight was a painter, and, as well, was passionately involved in gardening" (*Film at Wit's End* 44).[5] Ripley's extensive garden was full of rare imported plants; it included outdoor expanses of plantings and a greenhouse. As her title suggests, Menken's little film (4 minutes, 47 seconds) creates a counterpoint to Ripley's garden, both in scope and implicitly in the style with which Menken engages the garden spaces. While Ripley's garden reflects the organization and regular maintenance necessary for keeping a wide variety of plants alive, Menken's film feels off-hand, free-form, nearly spontaneous.

Not that *Glimpse* is disorganized. Menken edited the film's sixty-odd shots into rhythmic clusters that play off one another in a variety of formal ways,[6] within an overall structure punctuated by two brief shots of Ripley's greenhouse reflected in his pond (filmed with the camera upside down so that the greenhouse is seen right-side up): the first, approximately two minutes into the film; the second, near the end. The various clusters of imagery seem to enact a catalog of ways in which a camera can "glimpse." Early in the film, for example, two rightward pans with mounted camera across the pond and nearby rock gardens lead into a series of brief images of particular plants, which are followed by two clockwise pans from a tripod and then by a long, handheld traveling shot along a line of bushes, ending as the camera pans up a tree and back down to the garden where a series of very brief shots moves us successively closer to a bush with orange flowers—possibly a Roxana (*Potentilla nepalensis*). Each of these visual strategies is echoed during the second half of the film. The middle of the film explores the greenhouse, beginning with a continuous handheld pan that moves to the right across potted plants; then after an ambiguous, relatively still image of a yellow plant, a second pan moves to the left, echoing the first. Menken's visual imagery is accompanied by a sound track of birdsong from a phonograph record. No attempt is made to synchronize the sound and image. At most, one might conjecture that Menken hoped some of her more free-form camera movements might evoke the birds that must have flitted around the garden. Indeed, the obviously prerecorded bird sounds (sometimes distorted by the transfer to optical sound) seem a wry comment on the idea of nature, roughly in keeping with the implicit self-reflexivity of Menken's moving camera.

Despite the evident care in Menken's editing, however, and despite her topic—which offered her the possibility of a conventionally beautiful film—Menken's response to the Ripley garden is at least quirky and often abrasive. If her friends and colleagues recognized the quality of *Glimpse of the Garden*, most viewers then and now would, I'm sure, be skeptical of Menken's film. An audience ready for a film about a beautiful garden, or about nature, would be likely to find *Glimpse* lacking not only the smooth, generally predictable rhythms normally associated with the idea of filmically rendering a beautiful space, but the quality cinematography one expects of the competent nature photographer. Indeed, by the time the viewer reaches the final section of *Glimpses,* and several conventionally beautiful shots of flowers, these images seem surprising: most viewers would wonder why Menken didn't work harder to create *consistently* well-photographed, beautiful images and would assume the answer was either laziness or incompetence. The fact that several of the earliest shots in the film reveal that the camera gate had not been cleaned—bits of dirt are clearly visible at the upper left edge of the frame—would seem to confirm such a conclusion.

Menken would be quick to point out that her films are not aimed at a general audience, or at an audience interested in conventionally capable depictions of nature; like Gertrude Stein, Menken made film for herself and a few friends. When asked in 1963, "Who is your audience?" she responded, "Mostly people I love, for it is to them I address myself. Sometimes the audience becomes more than I looked for, but in sympathy they must be my friends. There is no choice, for in making a work of art one holds in spirit those who are receptive, and if they are, they must be one's friends" (qtd. in Mandell 47).[7]

If we respond to *Glimpse of the Garden* as Menken's friends—and if one has seen *Go! Go! Go!* and *Notebook,* one is inclined to give her the benefit of the doubt—we can use the very abrasions of Menken's little film as an opening into the complex sensibility that informs it. No one who knew Menken and Maas doubted they were serious artists; indeed, by the 1950s *Geography of the Body* (1943), for which Menken did much of the camera work (she also appears in the film), was justifiably recognized as a landmark avant-garde film. And they were artists at the center of the New York scene of that era: visitors to their apartment included such notables as Marilyn Monroe and Edward Albee (Menken recalled later, "Albee used to come here every time to eat and just sit and sit and listen while Willard and I argued. Then he wrote *Who's Afraid of Virginia Woolf.* That's supposed to be me and Willard arguing about my miscarriage" [qtd. in Jacoby 122]) and many major contributors to independent film, including Norman McLaren, Kenneth Anger, Stan Brakhage, and Andy Warhol (Menken would have a starring role as an addict in Warhol's 1966 film *Chelsea Girls*).

Even if Menken was not a first-rate cinematographer by professional standards, she surely knew the difference between a beautiful image and an underexposed one, and she fully understood the implications for viewers of her compositions ("As a painter of some experience, I can frame immediately with no deliberation of arrangement" [qtd. in Mandell 48]). The logical conclusion is that in *Glimpse* Menken was exploring an aesthetic somewhere *between* a commitment to conventional forms of beauty (exemplified, of course, by the flowers in Ripley's garden and by the garden itself) and what Patricia R. Zimmermann describes as "reinvented amateurism": "Since the 1950s . . . the American avant-garde has appropriated home-movie style as a formal manifestation of a spontaneous, untampered form of filmmaking" (146). Near the end, *Glimpse* provides a series of quite beautiful close-ups of flowers—enough to place the less-than-beautiful images into relief as another *option*, or set of options, for rendering the scenes offered by the garden: that is, she provides conventionally beautiful images, but *not too many*.

In fact, Menken's film seems to hover between a variety of possibilities, each of which, pursued too enthusiastically, might have rendered the result less fully a work of art that she and her friends could respect. On one hand, the film seems childlike (the bold, painted credits evoke children's art); on another, sophisticated (the witty irony of her use of canned bird sounds with the garden, itself a kind of "canned" reality). Some shots seem dedicated to a reasonably realistic rendering of the Ripley garden; and yet, at certain moments, Menken's freewheeling camera moves her imagery in the direction of abstraction—evoking the gestural dripping and/or brushwork of Pollock and DeKooning.[8] Her decision to accept imagery in which dirt from the camera gate is visible seems the epitome of artistic nonchalance, even laziness; and yet *Glimpse of the Garden* is quite heavily edited and in a manner that makes this heavy editing obvious. Finally, *Glimpse,* like other Menken films, is a response to another person's work (in *Visual Variations on Noguchi,* Menken responds to the sculptures she saw in Isamu Noguchi's studio; in *Arabesque for Kenneth Anger,* she responds to Anger's *Eaux d'artifice*);[9] but it is not really an imitation of the original and it's not an homage. *Glimpse* is a self-expressive engagement with Dwight Ripley's garden—a kind of after-the-fact collaboration. It is *her* film as fully as it's *his* garden.

To put it simply, Menken's work, and *Glimpse* in particular, is the result of her attempt to be a serious artist without being pretentious (or self-effacing) and a working-class woman without being anti-intellectual or disdainful of aesthetics. In *Glimpse of the Garden* Menken seems to reveal a filmmaking process and practice that is innocent of the corruptions of capitalism—her film is a defiantly little film, of virtually no commercial value—*and* of the class sensibilities of communism: she may be a working-class filmmaker, but *Glimpse* is defiantly individual; it is aimed at a coterie audience, and it luxuriates in a wealthy friend's hobby. I'm reminded of comments by Jonas Mekas, Menken's friend and admirer and fellow Lithuanian, in his *Lost Lost*

Lost (1976): "Oh let my camera record the desperation of the small countries. Oh how I hate you, the big nations . . . you always think that you are the only ones, and others . . . should only be part of you and speak your language. Oh come, come, the dictatorship of the small countries."[10] Menken's aesthetic seems a version of this sensibility: just as Mekas could (in the 1970s) see the "small countries" as innocent of the immense crimes of the "major nations," Menken's film creates a cinematic Edenic space—a psychic garden, as well as a literal one—not compromised or colonized by the "big countries" of cinema history. In this garden, as Mekas would suggest in his obituary, Menken was able to grow a variety of "flowers," some more impressive than others.

Further, Menken's way of being a filmmaker became puissant for the filmmakers who knew her and her films, which were clearly the seeds for filmmaking projects far more ambitious than her own. Among the filmmakers for whom Menken's work was pivotal are Stan Brakhage and Mekas, themselves two of the most powerful forces in the modern evolution of independent film. For these men, Menken was important for her general approach to making art. Brakhage called Menken "a 'natural,' her world the world of openings. . . . It is the ideology, if you can call it that, of Marie's working processes which have influenced my work. She made me aware that I was freer than I knew, that those chains were daisy-chains, those locks free flowing hair, etc." (qtd. In Haller, *Brakhage Scrapbook* 92–93). Mekas's enthusiastic embracing of Menken's approach seems to have instigated an expansion of the notebook form Menken was exploring in *Notebook* and *Go! Go! Go!*, first in his *Film Magazine of the Arts* (1963) and subsequently, in the epic film "diary" originally known as *Diaries, Notes and Sketches* (also known as *Walden*)—now, simply *Walden*—filmed 1964–68, edited 1968–69) and the many diaries that have followed.[11]

More specifically, both Brakhage and Mekas (and, no doubt others) were formally influenced by Menken's freeform camera work, the stylistic embodiment of her general attitude and approach, first in *Visual Variations on Noguchi* and later in *Glimpse of the Garden*. Brakhage: "'Visual Variation on Noguchi' liberated a lot of independent filmmakers from the idea that had been so powrful up to then, that we have to imitate the Hollywood dolly shot, without dollies—that the smooth pan and dolly was the only acceptable thing. Marie's free, swinging, swooping handheld pans changed all that, for me and for the whole independent filmmaking world" (*Film at Wit's End* 38). Mekas: "Brakhage and Menken represent the spearhead of . . . a film poetry free of obvious symbolism and artistic or literary influences, a poetry where the filmic syntax achieves a spontaneous fluidity. . . . The structure of Menken's filmic sentences, her movement, and her rhythms are those of poetry" (46–47).[12]

In fact, Brakhage and Mekas were so committed to Menken's work that when Amos Vogel refused to show or distribute Brakhage's *Anticipation of the Night* (1958) and Menken's *Glimpse of the Garden* at Cinema 16, Brakhage refused to let Vogel show his other work, an incident that seems to have been pivotal in Mekas's subsequent formation of the New American Cinema Group and the Film-makers' Cooperative.[13]

If Menken's films are not currently in the forefront of the critical discourse about independent cinema, the influence of her early work remains pervasive. The "little film" she did so much to legitimize remains one of the options for avant-garde filmmakers from Brakhage to Jennifer Reeves. And 16 mm, 8 mm, Super 8, and video cameras, having been loosed from their Hollywood moorings, gesture from within the work of many film/video-makers, and even from commercial film and television. Menken's individual films may have flowered only briefly, during the late 1940s through the mid-1960s; but her approach remains a perennial, if under-recognized, influence on contemporary media-making. She seems sure to reemerge, however, not simply because of the accomplishments of her films and their considerable influence, but because the story of the life Menken and Maas shared—a heterosexual woman married to a sexually active, uncloseted gay man (whose response to Menken's accomplishments was at best ambiguous)—and the psychic toll it took seems to beg for a biographer. Indeed, within the context of this complex relationship, Menken's discovery of a mode of film practice that allowed her moments of psychic release from the traumas of the everyday and opportunities to have her own relationships with her husband's lovers—in the case of *Glimpse of the Garden,* to spend some moments merging Dwight Ripley's Eden with her own Edenic practice—is all the more poignant.

Fuses

For the economically lucky, emotionally/sexually confused generation that came of age in the late 1950s and early 1960s, Eden *was* Edenic because Adam and Eve were naked there "and were not ashamed." That the biblical Eve and Adam didn't actually have sex in the Garden (Adam doesn't "know" Eve until Genesis 4:1, after the Expulsion) didn't matter: if they were nude together and were not ashamed, they clearly lived in a sexualized state we could only dream of, a state of sensual freedom that was only alluded to in commercial film romances like *A Summer Place* (1959, directed by Delmer Daves), where sex, at least between young people, was at best furtive and dangerous to one's name and future. Indeed, it was not for the better part of the decade that film history would produce a film that matched our sense of what Eden ought to be like, and that suggested that a man and woman, living in the real world now, could experience, on a day to day basis, the central fantasy of our adolescence. The film, Carolee Schneemann's *Fuses* (1967), has become one of the quintessential sixties films—though it was controversial then and has remained controversial, for a variety of different reasons, ever since.[14]

For *Fuses,* Schneemann and her partner, the composer James Tenney, recorded their sexual activity over a period of months; and Schneemann, who realized early on that the simple filming of sexual activity did little to capture her or their psychic experience during sex, worked the resulting imagery in a wide variety of ways: she painted the filmstrip, etched into the emulsion with a razor blade and a toothbrush, bleached portions of it, batiked it. Indeed, she became so involved in layering imagery on the filmstrip that, "It was a horrible shock, one of the worst," after three years of work, "to be told by the film lab that *Fuses* in its collaged layers was too thick to run through the printer!" (qtd. in Haug 47). The finished film is, as several commentators have recognized, a remarkably textural experience that reveals sex as more fully an experience of touch than of visual spectacularity.[15] And, to return to the idea of sexuality *as* Garden of Eden, the sex depicted in *Fuses* is not seen as a series of acts that take place within the confines of a physical garden; rather, the lovers' sexual intimacy *is* an Edenic state from which the world around them acquires new meaning and is transformed.

Within Schneemann's abstract-expressionist design, a variety of imagery in addition to the sex itself is visible. There are frequent images of Schneemann's cat, Kitch, who is this film's spirit of place. Kitch is alert to her surroundings, but in an entirely nonjudgmental way: sex is something that, of course, is going on in her world. And there are frequent images of a window (often Kitch is sitting in the window) that simultaneously allows light into the room and allows us to see out, though we see only the leaves of nearby trees and, in winter, a bit of snow-covered yard.[16] If it is clear that this lovemaking has a life that spans the seasonal cycle, it is also obvious that the life of the lovemaking proceeds regardless of what the season is. While we do see a few images of life away from sexuality—several shots of Tenney driving; one brief passage of crossing the George Washington Bridge into Manhattan; and, at the end, images of Schneemann running on a beach—most of these images confirm the rural surround implicit outside the window. In many instances, Schneemann develops explicit comparisons between the nature outside the window and the "nature" inside. At one point a close-up of Tenney's scrotum and testicles is followed by a close-up of a cluster of grapes hanging from a vine; and "there's a close-up of my 'bush.' Then the clouds over a silhouetted bush—the sun setting behind the shrub. I loved discovering those associations" (qtd. in Haug 45).

The connection between the nature outside the window and the sexual intimacy inside is confirmed, first, by the fact that Schneemann provides little sense of the indoor space she and Tenney are living in: we see that they are often on a bed; at Christmas time we see a decorated tree (just before we see the lovers' bodies decorated with Christmas lights). But we are generally more fully aware of the natural surround outside the home than we are of the indoor spaces: cinematically, the lovers are juxtaposed with nature, not with the conventional accoutrements of domesticity. Second, in addition to the several means of working the surface of the filmstrip already mentioned, Schneemann often experimented with more direct, visceral means: at times, she hung strips of film outside during rain and electrical storms to see how such natural events might impact the filmstrip; she even put strips of film in a bucket of her own urine. And throughout her work on the film, "I was working in a very dusty space. Every day another bunch of spiders had crawled over the table there. The cat was in my lap. . . . given the physical conditions I worked in and my own temperament, what I made could never be pristine. . . . I felt that all my images had to be available to the natural kinds of damages that would occur in my working situation" (qtd. in MacDonald, *Critical Cinema* 138–39).

However, while *Fuses* does work within the tradition of the Garden, Schneemann's Eden defies the biblical Eden in a variety of ways and counters the pervasive American tradition of visualizing New World nature, in Annette Kolodny's words, as "a maternal 'garden,' receiving and nurturing human children" (*Lay of the Land* 45). If Western sexual politics has depended on the second creation story, where Eve is created after Adam as a helper, in Schneemann's Eden the woman and the man are sexual equals (as Adam and Eve are in Genesis 1), *partners* in sexual pleasure; and this equality is expressed visually in a variety of ways.[17] Schneemann and Tenney do not enact a frieze of sexually-politically charged "positions" and even when one or the other is "on top" (what would often during the 1970s/1980s be understood as a vestige of the sexual politics of domination), Schneemann prints the image both right-side up and upside down: in a sexually political sense, there is no "up" or "down" in this interaction; both man and woman give and take pleasure. Even when Schneemann alludes to the artistic tradition of the nude, as she does, for example, in a slow pan of herself in a reclining position, this relatively conventional image is balanced with images where the camera pans Tenney's body in the same way: *both* bodies are at times objects of an erotic gaze on the part of the viewer, the camera, and implicitly of Schneemann and Tenney; and neither body is frozen by this gaze: "I had to get that nude off the canvas" and away from "art history's conjunction of perceptual erotica and immobilizing social position" (qtd. in Haug 30). While an immobilizing, scopophilic gaze has been as fully a part of film history as of art history, Schneemann's combined activity as both sexual partner and filmmaker was, and remains, a feminist response.[18]

If the sexual equality of the man and woman in Schneemann's Eden conforms more fully to the Eden of Genesis 1, however, *this* Eve defies the Creator in Genesis in a most crucial way: God's first demand of the newly created man and woman is to be fruitful and multiply, but Schneemann's Eden is clearly childless. In fact, Schneemann claims that Stan Brakhage's *Window Water Baby Moving* (1959) instigated her decision to make *Fuses;* her mixed feelings about Brakhage's birth film led Schneemann to balance Brakhage's paean to motherhood with a film in which sexuality/eroticism was definitely not a means to the end of fruitfulness/multiplication.[19] In this sense, *Fuses* is a reimagining of the Genesis Eden, from Eve's point of view. Both creation stories suggest that at least the primary, and perhaps the only, creativity available to woman is the creation of children; but *Fuses* argues that if "God created man in his own image, in the image of God he created him; male and female he created them" (Genesis 1:27 [RSV]), then women, like men, should be honored not simply for the creation of children, but as God-like creative beings in general, capable of original creation as well as of the replication of the species. In Genesis 2 and 3, the serpent is condemned for beguiling Eve by appealing to her desire for wisdom. As *Fuses* makes clear, however, Schneemann is committed to the wisdom of women, not just about childbirth and child rearing, but also—and despite the norms of 1950s and early 1960s America—about all aspects of life, including sexuality. If the serpent has often been read as a stand-in for the phallus, Schneemann is not only not "beguiled" by this "serpent," she accepts him into herself: one of the earliest recognizable sexual images in *Fuses* is Schneemann putting her mouth over Tenney's penis.

Fuses reverses the trajectory of the Eden story. Adam and Eve are driven from the Garden as a result of their desire for knowledge and freedom, into the drudgery of toiling in the Earth and the pain of childbirth, and, in

Christian mythology, they cannot regain Paradise except through a second dispensation—a sacrificing of the things of this world in the name of Christ. By means of their love, Schneemann and Tenney are able to transform their everyday world back into an Eden, a place where love—as expressed not through self-sacrifice but through physical unification—exists unendingly between the lovers, and the seasons outside their window fly by, as if the lovers exist in a timeless world. Schneemann does not till a literal garden in *Fuses:* we do not see her gardening in the imagery; and while she did, in at least one instance, use the filmstrip as a garden "bed" in which to grow mold (*Vietflakes*, 1965), she doesn't do that here.[20] But her reworking the filmstrip was an attempt to move a technological medium, a quintessential product of the Industrial Revolution, in the direction of the organic.

As a young painter, Schneemann struggled with the question of how to represent the complex experience of sitting in a landscape, simultaneously trying to see its structure and to be a living part of it. In *Fuses,* Schneemann uses the filmstrip as a space in which she can represent the fusion of her physical and psychic life during lovemaking, but, more fundamentally, where she can attempt a fusion of the traditionally gender-distinct realms of technology and biology. By painting and etching over and across the precise, individual spaces of the frames, Schneemann fuses the preordained, technological regularity of the filmstrip with expressive gestures that develop from her biological rhythms, dramatized *in* the film by both the sexual rhythms of the lovemaking and by the imagery of Schneemann running on the beach.[21] Like the ocean and like other women, Schneemann is on a lunar cycle of ebbs and flows that endlessly resists the assemblyline structures of modern history, structures that seem dedicated to the suppression of the erotic and the organic in the interests of the production of endless forms of redirected desire and the multiplication of industrial products dedicated to the momentary illusion of relief from our fallen state.

The Answering Furrow

Marjorie Keller's *The Answering Furrow* seems as fully indebted to Marie Menken, and perhaps to *Glimpse of the Garden,* as any Mekas or Brakhage film. I know of no place where Keller makes a specific connection between her garden film and Menken's, but she does make a historical claim for Menken's cinematic style: "Menken opened a [William Carlos] Williams-like poetic dailiness to film. Williams's attention to detail—poetry as a series of close-ups—is analogous to Menken's cinematic style, which Brakhage has radically extended" (qtd. in James, *To Free the Cinema* 87). In *The Answering Furrow,* and in her other films, Keller has extended it as well.

In *The Answering Furrow* Keller uses her father's vegetable garden in York-town Heights, New York, as an emblem of her connection—as daughter and as filmmaker—with European spiritual and aesthetic traditions thousands of years old. The four sections of *The Answering Furrow* overtly echo Virgil's *Georgics;* each section begins with a text (as is true in Virgil's paean to pastoral life) that describes the imagery the viewer is about to see:

> *Georgic I*—The annual produce first seen in spring—The furrowed earth ready for planting—The distribution, support and protection of young plants—The implements of the garden.

> *Georgic II*—The life of Virgil is recapitulated in summer, with a digression on the sacred—The sheep of Arcadia—The handling of bees—The pagan lion of Kea.

> *Georgic III*—The skill and industry of the old man in autumn—Ancient custom and modern method—The use of implements of the garden.

> *Georgic IV*—The compost is prepared at season's end—The filmmaker completes *The Answering Furrow* with the inclusion of her own image.

Keller's attitude toward the literary father of this film, like her attitude toward her biological father (and toward *The Answering Furrow* itself), is one of deep respect, qualified with a wry good humor, evident even in her use of these descriptions to introduce sections of a relatively brief (27 minutes), 16 mm film.

As is clear in Keller's introductory texts, *The Answering Furrow* is organized seasonally, from spring through summer into fall, though there are other organizational trajectories as well. "Georgic I" (4 minutes, 39 seconds, including the text and the pause before the imagery of the garden commences) is organized into clusters of hand-held shots, accompanied by environmental sounds, first of birds and then of distant church bells, that feel in synch with the visuals though they were recorded separately. These clusters of shots—of the plowed garden; of deep-green plants growing in furrows and along a fence and, later in the season, guarded by strips of aluminum foil, cat masks, and pinwheels to frighten away birds and rabbits—begin in lower-light conditions, making the imagery grainy, though by the end of the section, as summers nears, the imagery is brighter and clearer. The fact that the individual clusters are separated from one another by moments of darkness suggests that the filmstrip is a metaphor for the gardening furrow. As the seeds germinate in darkness as a result of the action of sunlight, the "furrow" of Keller's filmstrip in spring reveals a series of isolated images—also created by the action of light—that fill out the cinematic furrow by summertime.[22]

Near the conclusion of "Georgic I," we see a blue-headed rake; a small, yellow, gas-driven tiller; and a red wheelbarrow (perhaps an allusion to the famous William Carlos Williams poem, "The Red Wheelbarrow")—the "implements of the garden." On one level, these modern tools seem to clash with the serious tone of this georgic, which is maintained by the tolling of the bells, though like the quirkiness of this gardener's means of dissuading birds and rabbits from eating the seeds and young plants, the bright-colored modern implements evoke humor in the American tradition epitomized by Washington Irving's "Rip Van Winkle" and "The Legend of Sleepy Hollow." Irving's interest in creating a mythic past for the young American nation by inventing obviously tall tales and claiming considerable historical evidence for their factuality was a way of simultaneously admitting that great cultures must have traditional mythic tales, while recognizing that, whenever these stories are created, they are the fabrications of real people. If Irving cannot supply his American mythic tales with sufficient age to render them classic, he can offer his unpretentious, good humor as a replacement. Similarly, Keller knows she's not likely to match the remarkable, classic accomplishments of Virgil; but the bright colors of her father's garden implements add a good-humored American exuberance to her classic theme: bright primary-colored plastic and metal may seem the opposite of the pastoral, but in fact they are the American means for maintaining the Virgilian tradition, and judging from the success of this garden, they work reasonably well.

"Georgic II" is the longest section of The Answering Furrow, though Keller's textual description develops the slightly mock-heroic quality subtly evident in "Georgic I." "Georgic II" certainly cannot "recapitulate" the life of Virgil, but it does provide a multilayered evocation not only of the great Roman poet's life and work, but of the Greco-Roman classic tradition in general. "Georgic II" reviews a trip Keller took that included France (St. Remy en Province), Italy (Mantua, Rome, Brindisi), and Greece (Arcadia, the island of Kea); a further, implicit location is evident on the sound track of "Georgic II," a recording of "Ambrosian Chant" by Cappella Musicale del Duomo di Milano. These locations do, very roughly, suggest the life of the Roman poet, who was born in Mantua, educated in Milan and Rome, used Arcadia as the mythic location for his earliest poems, the Eclogues, and died in Brindisi, after setting out to visit Greece (on the voyage he caught the fever that killed him) presumably to research Greek locations for a final revision of *The Aeneid*. Keller's imagery of sheep certainly recalls Virgil's dedication to the pastoral; and a stunning, golden, slow-motion passage of a beekeeper and his bees is an allusion to a well-known passage in Virgil's *Georgics* on bee-keeping, not only in its subject matter but in the beauty of Keller's imagery. These evocations of Virgil are humorously confirmed by a glowing, golden image of a pat of "Virgilio Burro" (Virgil-brand butter).

On another level, Keller's trip—especially within the larger context of her "Georgics" I, II, and IV—suggests an American odyssey: Keller leaves her father's garden in Westchester County (in New York State), travels the Mediterranean, and, in the end, finds her way back home. If she doesn't undergo the trials and tribulations of Greek or Roman heroes, she presum-ably does hear a "siren's song" (the chant) and feel its (monastic) allure; and while she confronts no cyclops, she does see the (stone) pagan lion of Kea. While Keller's imagery of Europe is often lovely, however, the further east and into the classical past she goes, the less fruitful the landscape seems: the mountainous terrain in Greece seems particularly dry and inhospitable (this is emphasized by what appears to be a vertical band of overexposure on the film). As a result, when the filmmaker returns to her father's New York garden, in "Georgic III," its lovely autumnal colors and obvious pro-ductivity are all the more obvious. Keller reminds us of a paradox familiar to nineteenth-century American writers: this American garden may be part of a very young nation, but in its simplicity and unpretentious engagement with the earth, in its very youth (which is confirmed by the appearance of a young girl child in the garden), it declares its kinship with the pastoral ori-gins of the great classic cultures.[23]

A parallel relationship is evident on the sound track of "Georgic III," which begins with the tolling of the bells and with the sounds of chirping insects and continues with a passage from Charles Ives's Sonata for Violin and Piano #4 ("Children's Day at the Camp Meeting"). Heard first during the textual introduction of "Georgic I," the Ives piece represents a distinctive contribution to American music—indeed, according to some commenta-tors, Ives was "the first important distinctively American composer," whose work "anticipated some of the most radical developments of twentieth-cen-tury music (dissonance, polytonality, polyrthythm, and experimental form)" (Grout 644). The obvious dissonance of the violin in the repeated Ives pas-sage, which is heard a third time in Keller's brief fourth "Georgic" (1 minute, 59 seconds), is a key to her own aesthetic as it is embodied in this film.

"Georgic IV" begins with Keller tending to the garden in late fall, flashes back briefly to imagery from her European trip (as if she is remembering it while she works), then concludes with Keller preparing the compost at season's end. On the most literal level, she is carrying on her father's work, maintaining the fertility of the garden he has established. At the same time, since this activity also "completes THE ANSWERING FURROW," clearly Keller means for us to see gardening as a metaphor, not just for filmmaking, but for a particular tradition of filmmaking that may have begun in Europe but has flowered in America: what is generally called avant-garde filmmaking.[24] Throughout her tragically short life, Keller was devoted to this history in virtually every way possible: in addition to her filmmaking, she was a writer, an editor, a teacher, and a programmer. The Answering Furrow suggests that she saw her position in regard to the commercial film industry as analogous to the way Virgil positioned himself in relation to larger cultural developments.

Coming of age in the generation after Augustus had ended the Roman civil wars, Virgil argued, especially in The Georgics, for a return to traditional agriculture and a movement out of the overly crowded urban centers of power. By 1985, Keller—like many of us—may have seen herself moving out of what had been a volatile period of American cultural "civil wars" and interested in reaccessing the possibility of fruitful domesticity and spiritual connection. And just as small-gauge (16 mm and Super 8) filmmaking had allowed Keller in the 1970s to mount her own critique of the American gender politics marketed in mainstream media, it now allowed her to argue, at least implicitly, for the necessity of familial connection and for a simpler, deeply considered life. While those whose understanding of cinema is determined by mass-market film and television are sure to find The Answering Furrow too informal or "unprofessional"—in a dissonant relationship to the smooth, marketable continuities of the mainstream—the film's unpretentious, hand-crafted subtlety speaks with considerable elegance, with poetry, to those willing to cultivate a more complex, broad-ranging cinematic sensibility.

Melon Patches, or Reasons to Go On Living

Like Menken, Schneemann, and Keller, Anne Robertson uses the particulars of her domestic surround as the raw material for her films; but in her case, the relationship between life and filmmaking is both more consuming and, in at least one sense, more intense. The crucial fact of Robertson's personal life, and of her epic *Five Year Diary,* which has now been growing for more than twenty-five years, is the bipolar syndrome with which Robertson has been struggling, both at home and in mental hospitals, throughout most of her adult life. Making her film diary and reworking it into individual reels of diary film—to use the distinction David James developed for his discussion of Jonas Mekas, one of Robertson's cinematic mentors[25]—has been not only the central activity of her life, but one of her most effective means for managing the ravages of her disability: filming, editing, and showing her films has become a celluloid lifeline, providing coherence and continuity amidst the demands of the sometimes self-destructive voices she hears. Working in Super 8, the quintessential domestic film gauge of the 1970s and 1980s, Robertson documents her own recoveries and relapses, both visually and vocally; her bipolar rhythm is expressed directly in her commentary and, indirectly, in her depiction of her own experience and the life around her. The only periods of Robertson's life *not* documented in *Five Year Diary* are her hospitalizations: for legal reasons, of course, cameras are not allowed in mental hospitals.

In recent years, the advent of video, combined with the precariousness of Super 8 (fewer and fewer exhibition sites are willing and able to show Super 8 film; Kodak no longer manufactures Super 8 sound filmstock though, like other Super 8 devotées, Robertson stockpiled filmstock before Kodak ceased its manufacture), has led Robertson to release portions of the *Diary* on VHS. As of 2004, much of *Five Year Diary* is available on video,[26] along with two cassettes of shorter films including the subject of this discussion: *Melon Patches, or Reasons to Go On Living* (1994). While Robertson does not consider *Melon Patches* part of *Five Year Diary,* it is closely related to the *Diary,* not only because it uses many of the same sorts of imagery, but because its meaning and impact are to a considerable degree a function of its relationship to Robertson's ongoing project.[27]

Each reel of *Five Year Diary* is introduced by the same opening credit and includes a variety of visual and vocal gestures that have remained motifs throughout the project, including two auditory tracks (on one, Robertson comments on what we're seeing, the way many of us "narrate" our home movies when we show them to friends and family; the other presents the more troubled voice of Robertson's disorder as she records it on tape or in sound Super 8); time-lapse imagery of Robertson in her apartment;[28] visual and/or auditory references to *Dr. Who,* the British sci-fi series starring Tom Baker, with whom Robertson has been romantically obsessed since the seventies; imagery of the backyard of her family home in Framingham, Massachusetts, just outside of Boston, where her mother lives (in recent years Robertson has lived there, too), and in particular of a gazebo where Robertson has always dreamed of being married; imagery of the obsessive eating, drinking, and smoking with which Robertson struggles; her related obsession with her weight; and documentation of two gardens: one a community garden where Robertson has regularly grown her own organic produce; the other, behind the Framingham house.

Gardening is a special activity for Robertson—one that often provides a gauge of her current sense of her life. Early in reel 23, her tenuous hold on psychic stability is reflected in her desire to liberate the root vegetables in her refrigerator by re-planting them in the community garden. Reel 76 begins with the line, "it was the end of the gardening season"—a fitting preview to the disillusionment with Tom Baker that occurs when she travels to Chicago to attend a Tom Baker conference. Robertson's agony at the shocking loss of her three-year-old niece, Emily (in reel 80), is reflected by her use of garden flowers to represent, on one hand, the fact that Emily was "the flower in our lives," and on the other, the impossible paradox of the loss of the child in the spring, and in the flower of her youth.

The films that reveal Robertson at her happiest are also much involved with gardening. The most obvious instance is *Melon Patches,* in which gardening becomes a metaphor for sanity and for connection with family. While *Melon Patches* is (at 28 minutes, 10 seconds) approximately the same length as the individual *Diary* reels, it has its own structure and, at least overtly, reveals little of the psychic struggle dramatized in the *Diary.* With a single exception, there is no explicit representation of breakdowns or bipolar syndrome; the focus is consistently on Robertson's pleasure in growing melon seedlings from seeds, planting the little seedlings in the two gardens, frequently looking in on the growing melons (often, she reveals them to us as if they were secret treasure shared with intimate friends), and finally harvesting and eating the melons with her mother. About halfway through *Melon Patches* Robertson begins the whole process a second time—in black-and-white we see her, again, growing seedlings from seeds, planting the seedlings, looking in on the melons; the implication seems to be that this is an annual process, a yearly ritual. At the end of the second season, the melons are shared not only with her mother but with members of her extended family, including several nieces and nephews. The imagery was recorded during successive years, 1990 and 1991.

The sound track of *Melon Patches* is much simpler and less troubling than the sound tracks of the reels of *Five Year Diary.* During the first part of the film, we hear a baby playing nearby and at times apparently *with* the tape-recorder microphone during what seems a quiet morning; later, we hear baby sounds with traffic in the background and the sound of the parents talking with the baby—"Tape recorder," says the mother, "It's a machine." During the second half of the film, and the second growing season, we hear an older child—or the same child, a year older—talking with her mother and father as they read a book and sing "Teddy Bears' Picnic." At the very end, there are just the sounds of nearby sparrows and distant traffic.[29] The auditory pervasiveness of children throughout the film suggests, of course, that the melon seedlings and growing melons are Robertson's children. As she says in reel 80 of *Five Year Diary,* "I had no children; all I had was a garden"; but near the end, the round faces of the babies of Robertson's siblings come to seem a different sort of melon crop; and family life itself—particularly the years with young children—is envisioned as an Edenic moment. Judging from *Five Year Diary* in general, it is virtually the only Edenic moment in Robertson's experience.

For those familiar with *Five Year Diary,* and for Robertson herself, *Melon Patches* is all the more poignant because of its subtle references to her more usual, troubled experience. These references include several passages of time-lapse imagery of Robertson smoking (typically, the pixilation gives her smoking a somewhat hysterical edge) and one shot of her taking some pills. There is also the frequent appearance of the gazebo in her mother's backyard: within a family context, Robertson's dream of her own marriage and family seems, now that she's forty-five, a nostalgic, impossible fantasy, as Robertson is well aware. The only solutions seem to be frustration and anger, which move her toward further hospitalization, and those forms of creativity that are available to her: gardening and filmmaking. Gardening is clearly a pleasure in itself *and* a metaphor for the ongoing, yearly "growth cycle" of *Five Year Diary.* In *Melon Patches* Robertson takes this metaphor one step further: the lovely developing spheres of the melons are a metaphor for *this* Edenic film and the psychic and familial wholeness it represents for Robertson.

She may never find an Adam with whom she can have children, but the little Edens she cultivates do matter. It is obvious in *Melon Patches* that Robertson's gardening contributes to the experience of her extended family—we see them enjoying the melons—and the gardens also seem to attract her nieces and nephews, whom she films amidst the plants. Robertson's filmmaking also adds to the experience of her extended family, the way home movies, and more recently home video, have always added to the sense of family; and further, since Robertson's filmmaking is a bridge to a world beyond the domestic (*Five Year Diary* documents trips to New York City for shows at Anthology Film Archives and the New York Film Festival, to San Francisco, and to other screening venues), one can only infer that the family recognizes that *Five Year Diary* and its satellite shorter films embed them within a larger cultural arena.

During the 1950s and 1960s, at least in the United States, amateur film became virtually synonymous with home movies—not surprising during an era when the nuclear family was seen as "the only social structure available for the expression of common shared experiences that could shore one up against alienation and isolation."[30] Robertson's "home movies" are powerful because they simultaneously confirm and critique home-movie conventions. Robertson may idealize the nuclear family as fully as any home-movie maker, but she does so from a position to the side of that institution. She idealizes what she cannot achieve, and the poignancy of her films is a function of the fact that the longer she films, the more fully the combination of aging (with all the difficulties aging still brings women in our youth-oriented, image-obsessed society) and bipolar syndrome place this ideal beyond her grasp.

Or to put this in terms provided by *Melon Patches* itself, we need only be alert to the film's opening sequence—and the single exception, mentioned at the beginning of this discussion, where Robertson refers directly to her disability. Immediately following the credits we see—as if in the first person—Robertson's closed hands held out in front of her. The hands open to reveal pills: specifically, the Trilafon she uses to control her bipolar swings. The hands close and when they reopen, they reveal cantaloupe and watermelon seeds. The gesture is evocative of traditional magic tricks—and, of course, the incorporation of magic into cinema—but within Robertson's film, and within her epic chronicling of her adult struggle to achieve something like a "normal" happy life, the transformation of pills into seeds is an act of hope and a fitting opening to the lovely reprieve of *Melon Patches*—one of the very few reprieves in the many hours of Robertson's filmmaking—from the relentless unending fall from innocence chronicled in her work.

Toward an Ecological Cinema

By the time Rose Lowder bought her own 16 mm camera, she had spent years working with loops of 16 mm film, trying to determine whether the smallest unit of film structure was the single frame—as the Austrian Peter Kubelka had theorized,[31] concluding finally that "that's not the case at all," that in fact "pieces from different frames can make up what you're seeing on the screen" (qtd. in MacDonald, *Critical Cinema 3* 219). Lowder's researches into the microcosmic units of cinema continued after 1977, once she was shooting her own imagery (for those early experiments she had used various film leaders and had worked directly on strips of clear celluloid: punching holes through frames, scratching and/or drawing lines along the filmstrip, and trying other techniques). While some of her earliest films use relatively long, continuous shots, others involved a painstaking process of recording imagery a single frame at a time, refocusing from one focus point to another within a single framed space, according to precisely organized "scores." This particular approach came to fruition in a triad of films, each of which focuses on a different kind of garden.

For *Rue des teinturiers* (1979), Lowder set up her camera to look out the balcony window of the second story of her house in Avignon, through her tiny balcony garden, at the rue des Teinturiers across the way.[32] Over a period of months, she recorded this space, using a range of focus points so that, in some instances, elements of the street are in focus through the blur of nearby leaves, while at others, the leaves are clear and the distant street is a blur. Of course, since the focus point changes in virtually every frame, the resulting experience creates a continual retinal collage that suggests the perceptual immensity of even the tiniest space and the myriad intersections between Lowder's cinematic plan, the activities on an Avignon street, and the various changes in light, breeze, color—some of them predictable, others outside of Lowder's control—occurring in the balcony garden. In a sense, the little garden and Lowder's camera provide an analogy: each becomes a medium between Lowder's inner world (her domestic space, her plan for the film) and the space of the world outside; just as Lowder organized the garden to provide a tiny but effective "screen" between the busy street and her private space, the finished film is meant to screen out (if the reader can forgive the pun), at least for a moment, the usual commerce of film narrative and conventional exploitation of space.

Much the same procedure was used to make *Retour d'un repère* (Recurrence, 1979), in which Lowder explores a portion of a public park in Avignon, and *Champ provençal* (Provençal Field, 1979), for which she filmed a peach tree in a Provençal orchard on three separate occasions (April 1, April 16, and June 24). In all three instances, Lowder uses her painstaking, even obsessive procedure to expand what for most filmmakers—and especially commercial directors—would be a minimal bit of setting into a substantial film experience.[33] Beginning with *Les tournesols* (The Sunflowers, 1982), however, Lowder began to shift her tactics. *Les tournesols* is a brief (3 minutes) film of a field of sunflowers, photographed from a wide variety of focus points within the camera's field of vision. While the film certainly maintains its gaze on a single scene for far longer than any commercial film would, Lowder's single framing of the field seems to energize the field, condensing the subtle movements of the sunflowers that occurred during a period of hours into a comparatively brief cinematic moment. That the film's energizing of the field seems particularly reminiscent of Van Gogh's sunflower paintings, which were painted in nearby Arles, was not Lowder's conscious intent: "I didn't go out to make a Van Gogh film, and never imagined that I had, because the brush strokes of Van Gogh . . . are so far removed from the kind of work I had to do to make the film" (qtd. in MacDonald, *Critical Cinema* 3 238–39).

In the years after *Les tournesols*, Lowder's "minimalism" became less and less an attempt to reveal the complexity of tiny local spaces by expanding them cinematically, and more and more an attempt to explore what might be accomplished by condensing events that took place over the period of a day into a single, limited duration of film. While the early films often explore the deep space of a single composition, recent films explore time more fully than space. In *Impromptu*, Lowder focuses on three trees and a field of poppies, each location filmed on a different day in a different way and strung together to make the finished film: "In the case of the first tree in *Impromptu* [a tree in a courtyard in Avignon], I just exposed one frame, left the next one black, exposed the next, left the next one black. Then I wound the film back, to exactly the same place . . . and then . . . exposed the second, fourth, sixth frames" (qtd. in MacDonald, *Critical Cinema* 3 237).[34] In the resulting imagery of the tree, the space remains constant, but the time is reconstructed so that during any one second we see twelve frames filmed during one sustained moment during the day, interspersed with twelve frames filmed at a later time during the same day; and since various natural factors—the light, the breeze, the shadows—are continuously undergoing more or less dramatic changes of their own, the resulting intensification of time within the space of the frame causes the tree to shimmer and quiver in such an unusual way that when Lowder concludes this first roll with a few seconds of normal motion, the normal motion looks as mysterious and surprising as the intensely worked passage that precedes it. Subsequent passages of *Impromptu* focus on a peach tree in an orchard near Avignon, a field of red poppies, and the peach orchard itself; in each instance, Lowder energizes a limited space by condensing and reorganizing the hours it took to make the imagery into the brief, seemingly continuous durations of the finished film.

Lowder's urge to explore the spaces and times of life in and around Avignon, and especially to condense experience into minimal cinematic durations, culminated in *Bouquets 1–10,* ten one-minute minifilms, made during 1994 and 1995. Even more than the earlier films, the *Bouquets* are meant to provide a cinematic model for ecological awareness: for Lowder, the relationship between her filmmaking and commercial filmmaking is analogous to that between organic farming and industrial farming:

> *MacDonald:* But do you see your concentration in your films as a kind of cinepolitics? You eat organically; you don't own a refrigerator. Is your decision to work frame by frame a kind of environmental statement?
>
> *Lowder:* In opposition to big-budget TV or cinema footage, yes. A developed society doesn't have to be a wasteful society. Take the example of organic farming. To survive today in France, an organic farmer has to be much more technically knowledgeable than an industrial scale farmer. The traditional farmer will be comparatively uneducated on the whole and will have technological sales representatives come along and tell him what to do, and when to do it. To reduce the number of people working on a farm, you need a tremendous amount of heavy equipment. You depopulate the countryside; you do very little manual work; and you produce a tremendous amount of food—too much, so much you have to throw some of it away (the government pays you to throw it away so that the prices stay up). Now if you look at the organic farmer, besides having to have more education, he or she will have to do more manual work. The field will need to be dug up by hand, or by more gentle machines, three or four times. The organic system requires that people are brought back to work on the land. Actually, in organic farming, there are more pieces of machinery, but smaller, more precise, and designed to accomplish particular tasks.
>
> As an artist—to come back to your question—it's the same choice. You can work in a very precise way and make very particular decisions about everything you do. When I worked in the Industry, we sometimes had a sixty-to-one shooting ratio. I worked in one television company where I was throwing away sacks and sacks of stuff every day. In the Industry, the only things that count are the ones you sell. . . .
>
> . . . I don't propose that things change all at once—that would be unecological—but hopefully things could change in an ecological direction by gradually moving toward a world that is more in the interests of everyone. (MacDonald, *Critical Cinema 3* 236)

The idea of digging up a field by hand, more than once, describes Lowder's procedure in a variety of her films, and especially in *Impromptu* and in sections of *Bouquets 1–10,* where our field of vision is created by Lowder's planting—on our retinas—images made by moving along the furrow of the film and exposing individual frames to light, several times. The unusually high energy of the landscapes in *Impromptu* is analogous to the high energy achieved by an organic diet.

Like Lowder's earlier films, *Bouquets* is arranged formally, like a carefully planned formal garden. Each *Bouquet* is exactly one minute long and is separated from the *Bouquet* that follows by six seconds of dark leader punctuated by a single frame of a single flower in close-up.[35] Each *Bouquet* begins with the title, spelled out one letter at a time, and ends with "Rose Lowder" and a completion date, spelled out a single letter or number at a time. Within any particular *Bouquet,* Lowder explores a range of visual possibilities of working one frame at a time, sometimes creating effects familiar from *Impromptu, Les tournesols,* and other earlier films, sometimes creating powerful, strobelike flicker effects. While earlier Lowder films tend to arrange successive frames that have a clear compositional relationship to one another, however, gaps between successive frames in *Bouquets* are often so considerable that viewers tend to be seeing several kinds of spaces simultaneously: one triad of successive frames in *Bouquet 10* (1995), for example, reveals a close-up of a yellow lactuca perennis, followed by a long shot of the artificial lake near the French Alps created by the Serre-Poncon dam on the Durance River (completed in 1960, the dam flooded two villages, leaving only a hilltop church—in center of frame—above water level), followed by a close-up of a yellow hieracium. Another triad (in *Bouquet 7*) reveals a Provençal skyscape, a close-up of a tiny waterfall, and a tree in a courtyard. Lowder's consistent interplay among multiple spaces has the opposite effect of her articulation of multiple focus points in *Rue des teinturiers:* the earlier film expands a minimal physical space into an expanded cinematic space; each *Bouquet* condenses a considerable number of small, medium, and large spaces into a single multilayered cinematic experience.

Not only do particular moments within individual *Bouquets* sometimes create "retinal bouquets"—more literally, when successive frames reveal a succession of different flowers, and always figuratively, since Lowder is almost always gathering the "flowers" of the physically beautiful region in which she lives—but the series of minifilms, as the title suggests, is conceived as a bouquet: a bouquet of *Bouquets.* Like a conventional bouquet of flowers, this one is designed not just for a single look but to be savored over a period of time. Certainly the visual density and the distinctive visual design of each individual *Bouquet* (*Bouquets 1–10* is silent) can sustain, indeed demands, multiple viewings, the way an individual flower can sustain attention to its particulars. And the cluster of films involves so many different images of so many different places, presented in so many ways, that few viewers can summon the energy necessary to see the entirety of what Lowder has done during any single viewing. Fortunately, this cinematic bouquet has a life span considerably longer than a real bouquet—though, as Lowder's title also implies, each *Bouquet* she has presented to us is fragile, not only in the obvious sense that we can't hold on to its complex imagery for long, but in the sense that like all objects in the material world, any particular film (and especially, every color film) is subject to decay the moment it leaves its creator's hands. *Bouquets 1–10* requires that we gather our (cinematic) rosebuds while we may.

* * *

Given the limited sample of films and filmmakers discussed here, I hesitate to tender anything like a conclusion; and yet, the films do reveal a number of—forgive me—fertile parallels. Most obviously, all the films I've discussed are defiantly unpretentious, and part of their defiance involves the filmmakers' choices to honor domestic spaces and aspects of domestic dailiness considered too mundane or too "personal" for big-budget melodrama and even for most documentary and avant-garde cinema. Indeed, viewed from the perspective of 2005, the defiance of these filmmakers relates not only to forms of filmmaking we would identify as historically patriarchal, but to those feminist responses to traditional cinema that have been so pervasive in film/video discourse and literary discourse about film during the past quarter century.

Judging from what we know of these women, all of them were/are powerful people, in the thick of the ideological currents of their moment—that is, actively political in a variety of ways. But as filmmakers, they have chosen, to use Emerson's phrase, to do *their* work,[36] regardless of how it might look—aesthetically, ideologically—to those who presume to be defining the limits of personal expression. That many men, especially those in power, define the domesticity that supports their professional lives as beneath serious attention, and that many feminists expose domesticity as a patriarchal trap inimical to the full creative potential of women and therefore of society at large—these are or were realities obvious to these filmmakers, not just in theory, but in the widespread resistance and denigration of their work by many of those around them. But however fully they ventured beyond the traditionally "proper place" for women in their professional lives, they all seem to have shared one conclusion: that we cannot live outside a domestic sphere and that therefore, given the inevitability of the domestic, surely it is progressive to model ways of cinematically exploring and revealing the domestic without reducing it to sterile metaphors in the service of either patriarchy or justifiable feminist fury. For these filmmakers, at least during the production of these films, domestic space and domestic life could be, *had to be,* recognized as containing not only psychic and social limits, but the possibility of the Edenic—if we were to achieve fulfilling lives, day by day, in a more humane society.

NOTES

The epigraph that opens this essay is from Celia Thaxter, *An Island Garden,* with pictures and illuminations by Childe Hassam (Boston: Houghton Mifflin, 1894), 27–28. The original Thaxter text, including the Hassam imagery, was published in a facsimile edition in 1998.

1. This NEH Institute was designed and hosted by H. Daniel Peck and the American Culture Program at Vassar College.

2. Two versions of Cooper's *Rural Hours* have been published: the shorter, revised version that Cooper published in 1887 (Syracuse University Press, 1968), and the original, complete version, published in 1850, newly edited by Rochelle Johnson and Daniel Patterson (University of Georgia Press, 1998). Cooper's exploration of the seasonal cycle in Cooperstown is now recognized—along with Thoreau's *Walden* (1854) and *A Week on the Concord and Merrimack Rivers* (1849)—as one of the prime instigators of what has become known as American Nature Writing.

In the spring of 2002 I was fortunate to see the show All That Is Glorious: Paintings from the Hudson River School at the Nevada Museum of Art in Reno (the show, which ran from February 10 through June 30, was a collaboration of the Nevada Museum of Art and the Westmoreland Museum in Greensburg, Pennsylvania). All That Is Glorious included paintings by four women: Julie Hart Beers, Eliza Greatorex, Abigail T. Oakes, and Laura Woodward.

3. In the preface to the second edition of *Visionary Film,* published by Oxford University Press in 1979, Sitney admits that "Marie Menken's work deserves a chapter, not the brief passing reference I gave it in 'The Lyrical Film' [Sitney's chapter 5]. But five years ago I did not understand how crucial her teasingly simple films were in their dialogue of camera eye and nature" (xi). The third edition of *Visionary Film,* published in 2002, includes discussion of several Menken films.

4. I am using the dates assembled by Robert A. Haller for Brakhage's *Film at Wit's End* and for *First Light,* a catalog, edited by Haller, for a film series sponsored by Anthology

Film Archives in 1998. Menken's records are currently unavailable to scholars, and they may never become available. As a result, dating her films, some of which she showed in multiple versions over a period of years, is not as easy as it should be.

5. In his 1963 reminiscence "The Gryphon Yaks," Maas explains, "Marie's last real contact with Dwight . . . was when Dwight was getting over the DTs. . . . Dwight recovered and was never fun again. Marie says she did not and has been fun ever since" (53). Menken's *Dwightiana* (1957) was made during this moment.

6. When I last counted shots, I came up with sixty-two (plus two opening credits and "The End"), though a passage of sporadically lit close-ups near the end makes distinguishing separate shots difficult.

7. The interview/article indicates that Leslie Mandell was assisted by Paul [P. Adams] Sitney, of *Filmwise*.

8. A 1967 *Time* review of the new avant-garde cinema described Menken's camera work in *Lights* (1964–65): "She slashes at her subject with a camera as an action painter slashes at his canvas" (*Time*, February 17, 1967, 99).

9. P. Adams Sitney compares *Eaux d'artifice* and *Arabesque for Kenneth Anger* in "Marie Menken: Body and Light."

10. Menken was born (in 1910) in New York City to immigrant Lithuanian parents. According to Mekas, he and Menken "used to sing some old Lithuanian songs together, some of which she still remembered from her mother" (Mekas 414).

11. When I asked Mekas about Menken's influence, Mekas responded, "Oh, yes. I liked what she did and I thought it worked. She helped me make up my mind about how to structure my films" (MacDonald, *Critical Cinema 2*, 91).

12. Marjorie Keller discusses some of the specifics of Menken's influence on Mekas in "The Apron Strings of Jonas Mekas," 86–88.

13. Brakhage discusses this incident in MacDonald, *Cinema 16* 298–300. P. Adams Sitney discusses it in MacDonald, *Critical Cinema 4* 26–28. The arrival of Mekas and the New American Cinema—with its commitment to the particular vision of specific filmmakers, rather than the "potpourri" approach to cinema exhibition evident at Cinema 16—changed, for better and/or worse, the nature of avant-garde exhibition, distribution, and production and was one of the factors that led to the demise of Cinema 16, the most successful film society in American history.

14. Schneemann discusses the evolution of audience reception of *Fuses*, at least insofar as she's experienced it on tour, in MacDonald, *Critical Cinema*, 140–42, and in Kate Haug's interview with Schneemann, 26–29.

15. See David James's elegant discussion of "the touch of her [Schneemann's] hand on the film's flesh," in *Allegories of Cinema*, 320, and Bruce Elder's exploration of Schneemann's work in *A Body of Vision*, 233–76.

16. The use of window as metaphor for the camera has been pervasive in American avant-garde film: distinguished instances include Maya Deren's *Meshes of the Afternoon*, Stan Brakhage's *Window Water Baby Moving* (1959), and Michael Snow's *Wavelength* (1966), as well as *Fuses*.

17. In the first creation story (Genesis 1:1–31, 2:1–3), Eden is created separately from humankind. Actually, in the earlier creation story Eden is not mentioned: God creates the

heavens and the earth in six days and places man and woman in charge of the creation. In the second creation story (Genesis 2:4–25; 3:1–24), God first breathes life into man, having formed him from the dust; then he plants a garden in Eden and places man there, to till it and keep it, and finally creates Eve from Adam's rib so Adam will have company. In both stories, God makes clear that man and woman should be fruitful and multiply (Genesis 1:28) and that they are to become one flesh (Genesis 2:23), but sexual pleasure and love, in the conventional, modern sense of the words, are not mentioned.

18. I am alluding of course to Laura Mulvey's "Visual Pleasure and Narrative Cinema" and the substantial literature it has inspired. According to Schneemann, "Mulvey talked to me about the rupture *Fuses* made in pornography—how important *Fuses* was in an erotic vision. It was going to change the whole argument and discussion of filmic representation of sexuality and . . . then she couldn't touch it! Mulvey has never mentioned my films" (qtd. in Haug 28).

19. Schneemann has also expressed reservations about the way Brakhage's camera usurps the female birth function: "the male eye replicated or possessed the vagina's primacy of giving birth. The camera lens became the Os [mouth] out of which the birth was 'expressed'" (qtd. in Haug 28).

20. Stan Brakhage grew mold on the filmstrip for several films, including *Dog Star Man* (1962–64) and *Song 14* (1966, 1980).

21. R. Bruce Elder argues, correctly, that *Fuses* avoids the usual orgasmic rise-to-climax and denouement structure of narrative; but the pulsation built into the overall structure of the film—periods of energetic sexuality are followed by moments of calm—suggest a sexual as well as a daily rhythm, whether one wants to imagine the rhythm as emblematic of multiple orgasm within a single sexual moment, or a series of orgasms during a longer sexual interchange. See Elder, *A Body of Vision*, 235–36.

22. A different, but related "furrow" is suggested by Keller's presentation of her title at the bottom of the frame: the line of verbal text is imaged as a furrow—and of course adequate verbal "plantings" do constitute a "field."

23. The child "reads" as Keller's daughter and the "old man's" granddaughter, though the girl cannot be one of Keller's daughters (who were born after the film was shot) and is more likely to be one of Mr. Keller's many great-granddaughters.

24. For useful attempts to see the interconnections of European and American avant-garde film history, see Curtis's *Experimental Cinema*, LeGrice's *Abstract Film and Beyond*, and Rees's *A History of Experimental Film and Video*.

25. See David James's "Film Diary/Diary Film." James distinguishes between Jonas Mekas's ongoing diaristic record of the sights and sounds of his life and his decision to transform this record into individual "diary films" that can stand on their own as works of art. In the late 1990s Mekas became a supporter of Robertson's work; in several telephone conversations with me, Robertson mentioned that Mekas told her that *her* films are the *real* diary films.

Another crucial influence for Robertson is Carolee Schneemann's diary of her domestic life with Anthony McCall, *Kitch's Last Meal* (1973–76). Robertson talks about the impact of Schneemann's work on hers in our interview: see MacDonald, *A Critical Cinema 2*, 215–16.

26. Available VHS tapes include reel 22—August 23–September 1, 1982 (24:00 minutes), *A Short Affair (and) Going Crazy;* reel 23—September 1–December 13, 1982 (26:04 minutes), *A Breakdown (and) After the Mental Hospital;* reel 31—August 19–28, 1983 (24:36 minutes), *Niagara Falls;* reel 71—February 3–May 6, 1990 (27:02 minutes), *On Probation;* reel 76—October 30, 1991–March 28, 1992 (28:10 minutes), *Fall to Spring;* reel 80—May 14–September 26, 1994 (26:49 minutes), *Emily Died;* reel 81—September 27, 1994–January 29, 1995 (25:03 minutes), *Mourning Emily.*

27. The optimum screening situation for *Five Year Diary* is probably the one arranged by David Schwartz at the American Museum of the Moving Image in 1988: Robertson presented her domestic epic in a small gallery space decorated with objects from her own apartment. Robertson lived in the gallery space during museum hours for eight successive days, projecting the film and providing commentary for interested spectators. However, since few exhibitors are willing to make this level of commitment to an independent film, and since most potential viewers are likely to see *Five Year Diary* on VHS, I am confining my references to those reels currently available.

28. The narrating track on the VHS reels of *Five Year Diary* is one version of what is, in live presentations of the film, Robertson's in-person commentary. From Robertson's point of view, this represents an unfortunate compromise, since ideally, the commentary should be different each time the particular reel is presented—a way of reflecting how her own ongoing experiences and events around her continually recontextualize the earlier visual/auditory material of each diary reel (phone conversation with Robertson, August 11, 1999).

29. There is no way for viewers to know whether we are hearing one child at various ages, or several children. In fact, four children's voices are heard on the track: those of Robertson's nephew, Michael, in the first passage; a niece, Emily, above the traffic; another niece, Renata, talking with her mother; and finally niece Elena singing "Teddy Bears' Picnic."

30. I am quoting Patricia Zimmermann's paraphrase of a passage in Jezer's *The Dark Ages* (223–25) in her *Reel Families* (133).

31. See Kubelka's well-known essay "The Theory of Metrical Film." Kubelka uses his own early films as examples of "metrical structure" based on the assumption that the essential "articulation of cinema" takes place "*not between shots but between frames*" (141). Lowder's researches became her Ph.D. dissertation at the University of Paris and Nanterre.

32. Lowder has lived in France since 1973. She has an extensive knowledge of independent cinema from many parts of the world, in part because of her work as an archivist and programmer at the Archives du film expérimental d'Avignon.

33. In the case of *Retour d'un repère,* this expansion was itself extended, first, in *Rapprochements* (1979), a two-projector film in which two prints of *Retour d'un repère* are projected, one on top of the other ("to see if I could make a brighter film" [qtd. in MacDonald, *A Critical Cinema 3,* 234]), and in 1981, in *Retour d'un repère composé,* a fifty-nine-minute reworking of the same material.

34. The title of *Impromptu* refers to the fact that Lowder had been asked to screen the

film before she considered it finished, and it refers also to a series of accidents that occurred during and after the shooting.

35. The flowers are those that "happened to be on our balcony when I decided to introduce a pause of black in between each *Bouquet* with a single flower as punctuation"
(Lowder, letter to the author, September 8, 1998): a red pourpier (portulaca or purslane);
a white snap dragon; a small sunflower; a magenta portulaca; a yellow-orange marigold;
a white arum lily (of the araceae family); a black-centered, yellow-petaled rudbeckia; a
yellow-orange portulaca; and a white arum lily.

36. The phrase from paragraph 10 of Emerson's "Self-Reliance" is, of course, "But do
your thing, and I shall know you. Do your work, and you shall reinforce yourself."

Filmography

The entries below include the following information about each film:

> *Title,* with another director, country, date, run time,
> format, sound/silent (distributor; see list following
> filmography for abbreviations)
> USA unless indicated
> color unless indicated
> sound unless indicated
> aka = also known as
> b&w = black and white
> 16 mm = sixteen millimeter
> dv = digital video
> qt = quicktime
> v = video
> Super 8 = Super 8 millimeter

Ahwesh, Peggy (1954–present)
(peggy@echonyc.com; www.hi-beam.net/mkr/pa/pa-bio.html)
> *Corner Film,* 1978, 5 min, Super 8
> *Interactions: Bridge Climb, Mill Siting, Snow Clearing, Crypt Crawl,* 1980–82, Super
> 8/v
> *The Edge of Space, The End of Time,* 1981, 30 min, Super 8
> *The Pittsburgh Trilogy: Verité Opera, Para-Normal Intelligence, Nostalgia for Para-*
> *dise,* 1982–83, 56 min, Super 8/v
> *Ode to the New Pre-History,* 1984–87, 25 min, Super 8/v (CC)
> *From Romance to Ritual,* 1985, 20 min, Super 8/v (CC, FCNY, EAI)
> *Philosophy in the Bedroom,* 1987, 10 min, 16 mm (FCNY, EAI)

I Ride a Pony Named Flame, 1988, 20 min, 16 mm (EAI)
Martina's Playhouse, 1989, 20 min, 16 mm (CC, FCNY, EAI)
The Deadman, made with Keith Sanborn, 1990, 40 min, 16 mm (CC, FCNY, EAI)
Strange Weather, 1993, 50 min, v (CC, FCNY, VDB, EAI)
The Scary Movie, 1993, 9 min, 16 mm (CC, FCNY, EAI)
The Bataille Lexicon, 1994, 5 min, 16 mm
The Color of Love, 1994, 10 min, 16 mm (CC, FCNY, EAI)
The Fragments Project, 1985–95, 60 min, Super 8/v (EAI)
Trick Film, 1996, 5 min, 16 mm (FCNY)
Magnetism, Attraction and Repulsion, Deep Sleep, Auto Suggestion, Animal Magnetism, Mesmerism, and Fascination, 1996, 15 min, quicktime
The Trilogy of Plato's Cave, 1996, 25 min, 16 mm/v (CC, FCNY)
The Family Crisis/Frankensteina, 1996, 16 min, Super 8/v
The Vision Machine, 1997, 20 min, 16 mm (CC, FCNY, EAI)
Nocturne, 1998, 30 min, 16 mm (CC, FCNY, EAI)
73 Suspect Words and *Heaven's Gate,* 1999–2000, 8 min, qt (EAI)
She Puppet, 2001, 17 min, dv (FCNY, EAI)
The Star Eaters, 2003, 24 min, dv (EAI)
Certain Women, made with Bobby Abate, 2003, 72 min, dv

Akerman, Chantal (1950–present)

Saute ma ville, aka *Blow Up My Town,* Belgium, 1968, 13 min, 35 mm, b&w
L'enfant aimé, ou je joue à être une femme mariée, aka *The Beloved Child, or I Play at Being a Married Woman,* Belgium, 1971, 35 min, 16 mm, b&w
Hotel Monterey, 1972, 65 min, 16 mm
La chambre 1, aka *The Room, 1,* 1972, 11 min, 16 mm
La chambre 2, aka *The Room, 2,* 1972, 11 min, 16 mm
Hanging Out Yonkers, unfinished, 1972, 90 min, 16 mm
Le 15/8, codirected with Samy Szlingerbaum, 1973, 42 min, 16 mm
Je tu il elle, aka *I You He She,* Belgium, 1974, 90 min, 35 mm, b&w
Jeanne Dielman, 23 quai du Commerce, 1080 Bruxelles, Belgium, 1975, 200 min, 35 mm
News from Home, USA/France/Belgium, 1976, 85 min, 16 mm
Les rendez-vous d'Anna, aka *Meetings of Anna,* France/Belgium/Germany, 1978, 127 min, 35 mm
Dis-moi, aka *Tell Me,* made for French TV, 1980, 45 min, 16 mm
Toute une nuit, aka *All Night Long,* France/Belgium, 1982, 89 min, 35 mm/v
Les années 80, aka *The Eighties,* France/Belgium, 1983, 82 min, 35 mm/v
Un jour Pina a demandé, aka *One Day Pina Asked,* made for French TV, 1983, 57 min, 16 mm
L'homme à la valise, aka *The Man with the Suitcase,* made for French TV, 1983, 60 min, 16 mm
J'ai faim, j'ai froid, aka *I'm Hungry, I'm Cold,* France, 1984, 12 min, 35 mm, b&w
Family Business: Chantal Akerman Speaks about Film, made for British TV, 1984, 18 min, 16 mm

New York, New York bis (lost), 1984, 8 min, 35 mm, b&w

Lettre d'un cinéaste, aka *Letter from a Filmmaker,* made for French TV, 1984, 8 min, 16 mm

Golden Eighties, aka *Window Shopping,* France, 1985, 96 min, 35 mm

La paresse, aka *Sloth,* made for omnibus film *The Seven Deadly Sins,* France, 1986, 14 min, 35 mm

Le marteau, aka *The Hammer,* France, 1986, 4 min, v

Letters Home, France, 1986, 104 min, v

Mallet-Stevens, France, 1986, 7 min, v

Histoires d'Amerique, aka *American Stories/Food, Family and Philosophy,* Belgium/France, 1988, 92 min, 35 mm

Les trois dernières sonates de Franz Schubert, aka *Franz Schubert's Last Three Sonatas,* France, 1989, 49 min, v

Trois strophes sur le nom de Sacher, aka *Three Stanzas on the Name Sacher,* France, 1989, 12 min, v

Nuit et jour, aka *Night and Day,* Belgium/France, 1991, 90 min, 35 mm

Le déménagement, aka *Moving In,* made for French TV, 1992, 42 min, 35 mm

D'est, aka *From the East,* Belgium/France, 1993, 107 min, 35 mm

Portrait d'une jeune femme de la fin des années 60, à Bruxelles, aka *Portrait of a Young Girl in the Late 60s in Brussels,* made for French TV, 1993, 60 min, 35 mm

A Couch in New York, 1996, 104 min, 35 mm

Chantal Akerman par Chantal Akerman, episode of *Cinéastes de notre temps,* made for French TV, 1996, 63 min

Sud, aka *South,* 1999, 71 min

La captive, aka *The Captive,* 2000, 118 min

De l'autre côté, aka *From the Other Side,* 2002, 103 min

Demain on déménage, aka *Tomorrow We Move,* France/Belgium, 2004, 110 min

Avery, Caroline (?–present)

Son(n)tag Platz, 1982, with *Big Brother,* 1983, 11 min, 16 mm (CC, FCNY)

Big Brother, 1983, with *Son(n)tag Platz,* 1982, 11 min, 16 mm (CC, FCNY)

Snow Movies, 1983, with *Fourth of July,* 1988, 11 min, 16 mm (CC, FCNY)

First of May, 1984, and *Flap,* 1983, 5.5 min, 16 mm (CC, FCNY)

Pilgrim's Progress, 1985, 9 min, 16 mm (CC, FCNY)

Cross Road, 1985 and *Midweekend,* 1988, 9 min, 16 mm (CC, FCNY)

Miniatures: I, Steve; II, Owen, 1985–88, 10 min, 16 mm (CC, FCNY)

Mr. Speaker, 1986, 45 sec, 16 mm (FCNY)

Ready Mades in Hades, 1986–87, 7 min, 16 mm (CC, FCNY)

Midweekend, 1988, with *Cross Road,* 1985, 9 min, 16 mm (CC, FCNY)

Dancer for the Coronation, 1988, 8 min, 16 mm (CC, FCNY)

Fourth of July, 1988, with *Snow Movies,* 1983, 11 min, 16 mm (CC, FCNY)

The Living Rock, 1989, 9 min, 16 mm (CC)

Cassandra, 1989, 2.5 min, 16 mm (CC)

Simulated Experience, 1989, 45 sec, 16 mm (CC)

Benning, Sadie (1973–present)

Living Inside, 1989, 4 min, v (VDB, WMM)

Me and Rubyfruit, 1989, 4 min, v (VDB, WMM)

A New Year, 1989, 4 min, v (VDB, WMM)

If Every Girl Had a Diary, 1990, 6 min, v (VDB, WMM)

Jollies, 1990, 11 min, v (VDB, WMM)

A Place Called Lovely, 1991, 14 min, v (VDB, WMM)

Welcome to Normal, 1991, 19 min, v (VDB, WMM)

It Wasn't Love, 1992, 20 min, v (VDB)

Girl Power (Part 1), 1992, 15 min, v (VDB)

The Judy Spots, 1995, 13 min, v (VDB)

German Song, 1995, 5 min, v (VDB)

Aerobicide, 1998, 4 min (VDB, WMM)

Flat Is Beautiful, 1998, 56 min, v (VDB)

Sadie Benning Videoworks, Volume 1, includes *Jollies, If Every Girl Had a Diary, Me and Rubyfruit, Living Inside, A New Year,* 1989–90, 35 min, v (VDB, WMM)

Sadie Benning Videoworks, Volume 2, includes *Girl Power (Part 1), It Wasn't Love, A Place Called Lovely,* 1991–92, 49 min, v (VDB, WMM)

Sadie Benning Videoworks, Volume 3, 1995–98, 1:10 min, v (VDB, WMM)

Borden, Lizzie (1958–present)

Regrouping, 1976, 80 min, b&w

Born in Flames, 1983, 90 min, home video

Working Girls, 1986, 93 min, home video

Love Crimes, 1992, 85 min, home video

Red Shoe Diaries, "Juarez" episode, 1992, 30 min, v

Inside Out: Tales of the Unexpected, 1992, 89 min, v

Let's Talk about Sex, 1994, 35 min, v

Bute, Mary Ellen (1906–83)

Rhythm in Light, 1934, 5 min, 16 mm, b&w

Synchronization, 1934 (lost)

Synchromy No. 2, 1935, 5 min, 16 mm, b&w

Dada (Universal Clip), 1936, 3 min, 16 mm

Escape, 1937, 4 min, 16 mm

Parabola, 1937, 9 min, 16 mm

Spook Sport, 1939, 8 min, 35 mm

Tarantella, 1940, 4 min, 16 mm

Polka Graph, 1947, 4 min, 35 mm

Color Rhapsodie, 1948, 6 min, 35 mm

Pastoral, 1950, 6 min, 16 mm

Abstronic, 1952, 5.5 min, 35 mm

Mood Contrasts, 1953, 6.5 min, 16 mm

Imagination, 1958, 2 min, 16 mm

RCA: New Sensations in Sound, 1959, 3 min, 35 mm
Finnegan's Wake, 1967, 92 min, b&w

Campion, Jane (1954–present)
An Exercise in Discipline—Peel, aka *Peel,* 1982, 9 min, 16 mm (WMM)
Passionless Moments, 1983, 13 min, 16 mm, v, b&w (WMM)
Mishaps of Seduction and Conquest, 1984, v
A Girl's Own Story, 1984, 27 min, 16 mm (WMM)
After Hours, 1984, 26 min, 16 mm (WMM)
Dancing Daze, TV series, 1986, 6 episodes, 50 min each
Two Friends, made for TV, 1986, 76 min, 16 mm
Sweetie, 1989, 97 min, home video
An Angel at My Table, 1990, 158 min, home video
The Piano, aka *Leçon de piano,* France, 1993, 121 min, home video
The Portrait of a Lady, 1996, 135 min, home video
Holy Smoke, 1999, aka *Holy Smoke!* 2000, 115 min, home video
In the Cut, 2003, 119 min, home video

Chenzira, Ayoka (?–present)
(contact@redcarnelian.com; www.ayoka.com)
Syvilla: They Dance to Her Dream, 1979, 25 min, 16 mm (TWN, WMM)
Hair Piece: A Film for Nappy-Headed People, 1985, 10 min, 16 mm (TWN, WMM)
Secret Sounds Screaming: The Sexual Abuse of Children, 1986, 30 min, v (TWN, WMM)
Fire out of Fire, 1987, 7 min, v (WMM)
Zajota and the Boogie Spirit, 1988, 18 min, 16 mm
The Lure and the Lore, 1988, 15 min, v (TWN)
MOTV (My Own TV), 1993
Alma's Rainbow, 1994, 85 min,

Child, Abigail (?–present)
(achild@mindspring.com)
Some Exterior Presence, 1977, 8 min, 16 mm (CC)
Peripeteia 1, 1977, 9 min, 16 mm (CC)
Daylight Test Section, 1978, 4 min, 16 mm (CC)
Peripeteia 2, 1978, 12 min, 16 mm (CC)
Ornamentals, 1979, 10 min, 16 mm (CC, FCNY)
Pacific Far East Lines, 1979, 12 min, 16 mm (CC)
Is This What You Were Born For? 1981–89, 56 min, 16 mm/v (CC), seven-part series:
Prefaces (Part 1), 1981, 16 mm/v (CC, FCNY, VDB)
Both (Part 2), 1988, 16 mm/v (CC, FCNY, VDB)
Mutiny (Part 3), 1982–83, 16 mm/v (CC, FCNY, VDB)
Covert Action (Part 4), 1984, 16 mm/v (CC, FCNY, VDB)

Perils (Part 5), 1985–86, 16 mm/v (CC, FCNY, VDB, WMM)
Mayhem (Part 6), 1987, 16 mm/v (CC, FCNY, VDB, WMM)
Mercy (Part 7), 1989, 16 mm/v (CC, FCNY, WMM)
Below the New: A Russian Chronicle, 1989, 30 min, 16 mm (FCNY)
Swamp, 1991 (1989–90?), 35 min, v (CC)
Eight Million, 1992, 24 min, v (CC)
B/Side, 1996, 37 min, 38 min, 16 mm, b&w&c (CC, FCNY)
Surface Noise, 2000, 18 min, 16 mm, b&w&c (CC, FCNY)
Dark Dark, 2001, 16min, 16 mm, b&w (CC)
Where the Girls Are, 2002, 4.5 min, 16 mm, available from artist
The Milky Way, 2003 (installation), 16 mm, available from artist
Cake and Steak 2003–4, 16 mm (CC)
The Future Is Behind You, 2004, 16 min, 16 mm (CC)

Citron, Michelle (?–present)
(citron@northwestern.edu; www.rtvf.nwu.edu/faculty/)
Self Defense, 1973, 4 min
April 3, 1973, 1973, 3 min
Integration, 1974, 8 min
Parthenogenesis, 1975, 25 min
Secretary Tapes, made with Fina Bathrick, 1976, five 30-min tapes, v
Birth Tapes, 1977, 60 min, v
Daughter Rite, 1978, 55 min, 16 mm (WMM)
Claire Zeisler Textile Artist, 1979, 31 min
Mother Right, 1983, 25 min, v
What You Take for Granted, 1983, 75 min, 16 mm (WMM)
Great Expectations, made with Michael Hyde and Gordon Quinn, 1988, 15 min
Pandora, feature-length screenplay, 1996
Bent Love, feature-length screenplay, 1997
As American as Apple Pie, CD-ROM, interactive narrative, part of a larger work,
    Home, made with Annette Barbier, project director, 1999
Cocktails and Appetizers, 2002, CD-ROM

Clarke, Shirley (1925–97)
Dance in the Sun, 1953
In Paris Parks, 1954, 13 min
Bullfight, 1955
A Moment in Love, 1957, 11 min
Brussels Loops, 1958, 22 min
Bridges-Go-Round, 1958, 4 min, 16 mm (CC, FCNY)
Skyscraper, 1959, 20 min
A Scary Time, 1960
The Connection, 1961, 110 min, b&w
The Cool World, 1963, 125 min, b&w

Robert Frost: A Lover's Quarrel with the World, 1964
Portrait of Jason, 1967, 105 min, b&w
Trans, 1978, 9 min
One-2-3, 1978, 6 min
A Visual Diary, 1980, 6 min
Tongues, 1981–82, 45 min (EAI)
Savage/Love, 1981, 25 min (EAI)
Performance, 1982, 7 min
The Box, 1983, 4 min
Ornette Coleman: A Jazz Video Game, 1984, 4 min
Ornette: Made in America, 1985, 85 min

Cuevas, Ximena (1963–present)
Ala Manera de Disney, 1992, 3 min, v (VDB)
Corazon Sangrante, 1993, 4 min, v (VDB)
Medias Mentiras/Half Lies, 1995, 37 min, v (VDB)
Cosi fan tutte, Mexico, 1996, v
Cuerpos de Papel, aka *Paper Bodies* 1997, 4 min, v (VDB)
Noche de paz, Mexico, 1998, v
El Diablo en la Piel, aka *Devil in the Flesh,* 1998, 5 min, v (VDB)
Cama, aka *Bed,* 1998, 2 min, v (VDB)
Alma Genela, aka *Soulmate,* 1999, 2 min, v (VDB)
Baba de Perico, 1999, 2 min, v (VDB)
Calzoda de Kansas, aka *Kansas Avenue,* 1999, 2 min, v (VDB)
Contemporary Artist, 1999, 5 min, v (VDB)
Destino, aka *Fate,* 1999, 2 min, v (VDB)
Estamos Para Servile, aka *We're Here to Serve You,* 1999, 3 min, v (VDB)
Hawaii, 1999, 2 min, v (VDB)
Help, 1999, 2 min, v (VDB)
Natural Instincts, 1999, 3 min, v (VDB)
Televisión, 1999, 3 min, v (VDB)
La Puerta, 2000, 5 min, v (VDB)
La Tombola, 2001, 7 min, v (VDB)
Staying Alive, 2001, 3 min, v (VDB)
Estamos Para Servile, aka *We're Here to Serve You,* 2002, 1 min, v (VDB)
Colchones Individuales, aka *Single Beds Volume 1: Desolacion,* 2002, 18 min (VDB)

Dash, Julie (1952–present)
(http://geechee.tv/)
Working Models of Success, 1973
Four Women, 1977, 4 min, 16 mm (TWN)
Diary of an African Nun, 1978, short, Super 8
Illusions, 1982, 34 min, 16 mm, b&w (TWN, WMM)
Relatives, made for TV, 1990, short

Praise House, 1991, 25 min, v (TWN, WMM)
Daughters of the Dust, 1991, 114 min, home video
Breaths, made for TV, 1994, short
Women: Stories of Passion, TV series, 1997, 27 min
Subway Stories: Tales from the Underground, segment "Sax Cantor Riff," made for TV, 1997, 80 min
Funny Valentines, made for TV, 1999, 108 min
Incognito, made for TV, 1999
Love Song, 2001, made for TV, 90 min
The Rosa Parks Story, made for TV, 2002, 97 min

Davis, Zeinabu Irene (1961–present)
(zdavis@weber.ucsd.edu; http://communication.ucsd.edu/people/f_davis.z.html)
Filmstatement, 1982
Re-creating Black Women's Media Image, 1983, 28 min
Crocodile Conspiracy, 1986, 13 min, 16 mm (TWN, WMM)
Sweet Bird of Youth, 1987
Cycles, 1989, 17 min, 16 mm, b&w (WMM)
Trumpetistically, Clora Bryant, 1989, 5 min, 16 mm & v
Kneegrays in Russia, 1990, 5 min
A Powerful Thang, 1991, 57 min, 16 mm (WMM)
A Period Piece, 1991, 4 min, v (WMM)
Mother of the River, 1995, 28 min, 16 mm, b&w (WMM)
Compensation, 1999, 95 min, 16 mm, b&w (WMM)

de Hirsch, Storm (?–2000)
Aristotle in *Cine-Songs Program*, n.d., 3.5 min, Super 8, silent (FCNY)
Charlotte Moorman's Avant-Garde Festival #9, n.d., 10 min, Super 8, silent (FCNY)
Deep In The Mirror Imbedded, n.d., 14 min, Super 8, silent (FCNY)
Ives House–Woodstock, in *Cine-Songs Program*, n.d., 11 min, 16 mm (FCNY)
Malevich at the Guggenheim, in *Cine-Songs Program*, n.d., 5 ¾ min, Super 8, silent (FCNY)
Newsreel: Jonas in the Brig, n.d., 5 min, 16 mm, silent, b&w (FCNY)
The Recurring Dream, in *Cine-Songs Program*, n.d., 3 min, Super 8, silent (FCNY)
A Reticule of Love, in *Cine-Songs Program*, n.d., 3 min, 16 mm, silent (FCNY)
Silently, Bearing Totem of a Bird, in *Cine-Songs Program*, n.d., 6 min, Super 8, silent (FCNY)
Journey around a Zero, 1963, 3 min, 16 mm, b&w (FCNY)
Divinations, 1964, 5 min, 16 mm (FCNY)
Goodbye in the Mirror, 1965, 80 min, 16 mm, b&w (FCNY)
Peyote Queen, 1965, 9 min, 16 mm (CC)
Sing Lotus, 1966, 14 min, 16 mm, (FCNY)
Cayuga Run—Hudson River Diary: Book I, 1967, 18 min, 16 mm (CC, FCNY)
Shaman, A Tapestry for Sorcerers, 1967, 12 min, 16 mm (FCNY)

Trap Dance, 1968, 2 min, 16 mm, b&w (FCNY)
Third Eye Butterfly, 1968, 10 min, 16 mm(FCNY)
The Tattooed Man, 1969, 35 min, 16 mm (CC, FCNY)
An Experiment in Meditation, 1971, 18 min, 16 mm, silent (FCNY)
September Express, 1973, 6 min, 16 mm, silent (FCNY)
Wintergarden—Hudson River Diary: Book III, 1973, 5 min, 16 mm (FCNY)
River Ghost—Hudson River Diary: Book IV, 1973, 9 min, 16 mm (FCNY)
Lace of Summer, 1973, 4 min, 16 mm, silent (FCNY)
Geometrics of the Kabbalah, 1975, 11 min, 16 mm (FCNY)

Deren, Maya (1917–61)
(www.mayaderen.org)
Meshes of the Afternoon, codirected with Alexander Hammid, 1943, 14 min, 16 mm silent (sound version with Teiji Ito score made by Deren in 1959), b&w (FCNY, WMM)
The Witch's Cradle, 1943, 13 min, 16 mm (FCNY)
At Land, 1944, 15 min, 16 mm, silent, b&w (FCNY, WMM)
A Study in Choreography for the Camera, 1945, 4 min, 16 mm, silent, b&w (FCNY, WMM)
Ritual in Transfigured Time, 1946, 15 min, 16 mm, silent, b&w (FCNY, WMM)
Meditation on Violence, 1948, 12 min, 16 mm, b&w (FCNY, WMM)
Medusa (unfinished), 1949, 10 min, 16 mm
The Very Eye of Night, 1958, 15 min, 16 mm, b&w (WMM)
Haiku footage, 1959–60, 58 min, 16 mm
Divine Horsemen: The Living Gods of Haiti, shot by Deren, compiled and edited by Teiji and Cherel Ito, 1985, 52 min, b&w (FCNY, WMM)

Dulac, Germaine (1882–1942)
Les soeurs ennemies, France, 1915, 35 mm, silent, b&w
Venus Victrix, aka *Dans l'ouragan de la vie*, France, 1917, 35 mm, silent, b&w
Géo, le mystérieux, aka *La vraie richesse*, France, 1917, 35 mm, silent, b&w
Ames de fous, aka *Ames d'hommes fous*, France, 1918, 35 mm, silent, b&w
La cigarette, France, 1919, 35 mm, silent, b&w
Le bonheur des autres, France, 1919, 35 mm, silent, b&w
La fête espagnole, aka *Spanish Fiesta*, France, 1919, 35 mm, silent, b&w
Malencontre, France, 1920, 35 mm, silent, b&w
La belle dame sans merci, France, 1920, 35 mm, silent, b&w
La mort du soleil, aka *The Death of the Sun*, France, 1921, 35 mm, silent, b&w
La souriante Madame Beudet, aka *The Smiling Madame Beudet*, France, 1923, 35 mm, silent, b&w
Gossette, France, 1923, 35 mm, silent, b&w
Le diable dans la ville, France, 1924, 35 mm, silent, b&w
Ame d'artiste, France, 1925, 35 mm, silent, b&w
La folie des vaillants, France, 1926, 35 mm, silent, b&w

L'invitation au voyage, aka *Invitation to a Journey,* France, 1927, 35 mm, silent, b&w
Le cinéma au service de l'histoire, France, 1927, 35 mm, silent, b&w
Antoinette Sabrier, France, 1927, 35 mm, silent, b&w
La coquille et le clergyman, aka *The Seashell and the Clergyman,* France, 1927, 35 mm, silent, b&w
Thèmes et variations, France, 1928, 35 mm, silent, b&w
Princesse Mandane, France, 1928, 35 mm, silent, b&w
Disque 957, France, 1928, 35 mm, silent, b&w
Danses espagnoles, France, 1928, 35 mm, silent, b&w
Celle qui s'en font, France, 1928, 35 mm, silent, b&w
Étude cinégraphique sur une arabesque, aka *Arabesque,* France, 1929, 35 mm, silent, b&w
Je n'ai plus rien, France, 1934, 35 mm, silent, b&w

Dunye, Cheryl (1966–present)
(www.cheryldunye.com)

Wild Thing: A Poem by Sapphire, 1989, 8 min
Janine, 1990, 10 min, v (EAI)
She Don't Fade, 1991, 24 min, v, b&w (EAI)
Vanilla Sex, 1992
Untitled Portrait, 1993, 3 min, v, b&w (EAI)
The Potluck and the Passion, 1993, 30 min, v (EAI)
Greetings from Africa, 1994, 8 min, 16 mm, b&w&c
The Watermelon Woman, 1996, 90 min, 16 mm, b&w&c
Stranger Inside, made for TV (HBO), 2001, 97 min
My Baby's Daddy, 2004, 99 min

Duras, Marguerite (1914–96)

La musica, France, 1966, 80 min, b&w
Détruire, dit-elle, aka *Destroy, She Said,* France, 1969
Jaune le soleil, France, 1971, 100 min
Nathalie Granger, France, 1972, 83 min, b&w
La femme du Gange, France, 1973, 100 min
India Song, France, 1975, 120 min
Son nom de Venise dans Calcutta désert, France, 1976, 120 min
Des journées entières dans les arbres, aka *Entire Days among the Trees, in the Trees,* France, 1976, 95 min
Baxter, Vera Baxter, France, 1976
Le camion, aka *The Lorry,* aka *The Truck,* France, 1977, 80 min
Le navire night, France, 1978, 95 min
Les mains négatives, France, 1978, 14 min
Cesarée, France, 1978
Aurélia Steiner, France, 1979, 28 min

L'homme atlantique, France, 1981, 41 min
Agatha et les lectures illimitées, France, 1981, 90 min
Il dialogo di Roma, Italy, 1982, 62 min
Les enfants, France, 1984, 94 min

Faye, Safi (1946–present)

La passante, Senegal, 1972
Kaddu Beykat, aka *Lettre paysanne,* aka *Letter from My Village,* Senegal, 1975, 90 min, b&w
Fad'jal, aka *Grand-père reconte,* Senegal, 1979, 108 min
Selbe, 1983, 30 min, 16 mm (WMM)
Mossane, Senegal/Germany, 1996, 105 min

Finley, Jeanne (?–present)
(jeannecfinley@earthlink.net; http://www.hi-beam.net/mkr/jfjm/)

I Saw Jesus in a Tortilla, 1982, 3 min, v (VDB)
Deaf Dogs Can Hear, 1983, 5 min, v (VDB)
Beyond the Times Foreseen, 1984, 10 min, v
Risks of Individual Actions, 1985, 11 min, v
Common Mistakes, 1986, 13 min, v (VDB)
Accidental Confessions, 1987, 5 min, v
So, You Want to Be Popular? 1988, 18 min, v (VDB)
Against a Single Match, the Darkness Flinches, 1988, 18 min, v
At the Museum: A Pilgrimage of Vanquished Objects, made with John Muse, 1989, 23 min, v (VDB)
Involuntary Conversion, made with John Muse, 1991, 9 min, v (VDB)
Nomads at the 25 Door, made with John Muse, 1991, 43 min, v (VDB)
A.R.M. around Moscow, made with Gretchen Stoeltje, 1994, 57 min, v (VDB)
Conversations across the Bosphorous, 1995, 42 min, v (VDB, WMM)
The Adventures of Blacky, 1997, 6 min, v (VDB)
Based on a Story, 1998, 44 min, v (VDB)
Time Bomb, 1998, 7 min, v (VDB)
O Night without Objects, made with John Muse, 1998, 60 min, v
Loss Prevention, made with John Muse and Doug Dubois, 2000, 17 min, v (VDB)
Language Lessons, 2002, 9 min, v (VDB)

Fonoroff, Nina (?–present)

Big Story, 1984, 10 min, 16 mm (CC)
Some Phases of an Empire, 1984, 9 min, Super 8 (CC)
Department of the Interior, 1986, 8.5 min, 16 mm, b&w (CC)
A Knowledge They Cannot Lose, 1989, 17 min, Super 8 (CC)
Accursed Mazurka, 1994, 40 min, 16 mm (CC)
The Eye of the Mask, 2004, 40 min, 16 mm (CC)

Friedrich, Su (1954–present)
(sufried@princeton.edu; www.sufriedrich.com)
> *Hot Water,* 1978, 12 min, Super 8, b&w
> *Cool Hands, Warm Heart,* 1979, 16 min, 16 mm, silent, b&w (CC, WMM)
> *Scar Tissue,* 1979, 6 min, 16 mm, silent, b&w (CC)
> *I Suggest Mine,* 1980, 6 min, 16 mm, silent, b&w
> *Gently Down the Stream,* 1981, 14 min, 16 mm, silent, b&w (CC, WMM)
> *But No One,* 1982, 9 min, 16 mm, silent, b&w (CC)
> *The Ties That Bind,* 1984, 55 min, 16 mm, b&w (CC, WMM)
> *Damned If You Don't,* 1987, 42 min, 16 mm, b&w (CC, WMM)
> *Sink or Swim,* 1990, 48 min, 16 mm, b&w (CC, WMM)
> *First Comes Love,* 1991, 22 min, 16 mm, b&w (CC, WMM)
> *Rules of the Road,* 1993, 31 min, 16 mm (CC, WMM)
> *Lesbian Avengers Eat Fire Too,* made with Janet Baus, 1994, 60 min, v
> *Hide and Seek,* 1996, 65 min, 16 mm, b&w (WMM)
> *The Odds of Recovery,* 2002, 65 min, 16 mm (WMM)
> *The Head of a Pin,* 2004, 21 min, v (sufriedrich.com)

Geiser, Janie (1957–present)
(geiser@calarts.edu)
> *Babel Town,* 1992, 7 min, 16 mm (CC, FCNY)
> *The Red Book,* 1994, 11 min, 16 mm (CC, FCNY)
> *The Secret Story,* 1996, 9 min, 16 mm (CC, FCNY)
> *Immer Zu,* 1997, 9 min, 16 mm, b&w (CC, FCNY)
> *Lost Motion,* 1999, 11 min, 16 mm (CC, FCNY)
> *The Fourth Watch,* 2000, 10 min, 16 mm (CC, FCNY)
> *Spiral Vessel,* 2000, 7 min, 16 mm (CC, FCNY)
> *Ultima Thule,* 2002, 11 min (further information unavailable)
> *Terrace 49,* 2004, 5.5 min (further information unavailable)

Godmilow, Jill (1943–present)
(Jil.Godmilow.1@nd.edu; http://www.nd.edu/~jgodmilo/)
> *Tales,* made with Cassandra Gerstein, 1971, 70 min
> *Antonia: A Portrait of the Woman,* 1974, 58 min
> *Nevelson in Process,* made with Susan Fanshel, 1977, 28 min
> *The Popovich Brothers of South Chicago,* 1977, 60 min (FM)
> *The Odyssey Tapes,* 1978, 30 min
> *Far from Poland,* 1984, 106 min, 16 mm, b&w (WMM, FM)
> *Waiting for the Moon,* UK/France/US, 1987, 88 min (FM)
> *Roy Cohn/Jack Smith,* 1995, 88 min, 16 mm (FM)
> *What's Underground about Marshmallows: Ron Vawter Performs Jack Smith,* 1996, 60 min (FM)
> *What Farocki Taught,* made with Gloria Jean Masciarotte and Ted Mandell, 1997, 30 min, v (VDB)
> *The Loft Tapes: Student Films from Notre Dame,* 1999, 110 min (FM)

Gomez, Sara (1943–74)
Ire a Santiago, 1964
Excursion a Vueltabajo, 1965
Guanabacoa: Crónica de mi familia, 1966
Y tenemos sabor, 1967
En la otra isla, 1968
Una isla para Miguel, 1968
Isla del tesoro, 1969
Poder local, poder popular, 1970
Un documental a proposito del transito, 1971
Atención pre-natal, 1972
Ano uno, 1972
Sobre horas extras y travajo voluntario, 1973
Spielfilm, 1974
De cierta manera, aka *One Way or Another,* Cuba, 1977, 78 min, b&w
Che comandante amigo, 1977
Patria libre o morir, 1978
Al final de tan corto camino, 1978
Ingola construye, 1978
Vi festival internacional de ballet, 1978
La infancia de Marisol, 1979

Hammer, Barbara (1930–present)
(bjhammer@aol.com; www.barbarahammerfilms.com)
A Gay Day, 1973, 3 min, 16 mm (CC)
I Was/I Am, 1973, 7.5 min, 16 mm
Sisters! 1973, 8 min, 16 mm (CC, FCNY)
Dyketactics, 1974, 4 min, 16 mm (CC, FCNY, WMM)
Jane Brakhage, 1974, 10 min, 16 mm, b&w (CC)
Menses, 1974, 4 min, 16 mm (CC, FCNY)
Women's Rites, or *Truth Is the Daughter of Time,* 1974, 8 min, 16 mm (CC, FCNY)
X, 1974, 8 min, 16 mm (CC)
Psychosynthesis, 1975, 8 min, 16 mm (CC)
Superdyke, 1975, 20 min, 16 mm (CC)
Moon Goddess, made with Gloria Churchwoman, 1976, 15 min, 16 mm (CC)
Women I Love, 1976, 27 min, 16 mm (CC, WMM)
The Great Goddess, 1977, 25 min, 16 mm (CC)
Multiple Orgasm, 1977, 6 min, 16 mm, silent (CC)
Double Strength, 1978, 20 min 16 mm (CC, FCNY, WMM)
Eggs, 1978, 10 min, 16 mm (CC, FCNY)
Haircut, 1978, 6 min, 16 mm
Home, 1978, 12 min, 16 mm (CC)
Sappho, 1978, 7 min, 16 mm (CC)
Available Space, 1979, 20 min, 16 mm (CC)
Dream Age, 1979, 12 min, 16 mm (CC)

Our Trip, 1980, 4 min, 16 mm (CC, FCNY)
Arequipa, 1981, 10 min, 16 mm, silent, b&w&c (CC, FCNY)
The Lesbos Film, 1981, 30 min, 16 mm (CC)
Machu Picchu, 1981, 15 min, 16 mm (CC)
Pictures for Barbara, 1981, 10 min, 16 mm (CC)
Pools, made with Barbara Klutinis, 1981, 8 min, silent, b&w&c (CC, FCNY)
Sync Touch, 1981, 12 min, 16 mm (CC, FCNY, WMM)
Audience, 1982, 33 min, 16 mm (CC)
Bent Time, 1982, 22 min, 16 mm (CC, FCNY)
Pond and Waterfall, 1982, 15 min, 16 mm, silent (CC, FCNY)
New York Loft, 1983, 9 min, 16 mm, b&w (CC, FCNY)
Stone Circles, 1983, 10 min, 16 mm, b&w&c (CC, FCNY)
Doll House, 1984, 4 min, 16 mm, b&w&c (CC)
Parisian Blinds, 1984, 6 min, 16 mm, silent, b&w&c (CC)
Pearl Diver, 1984, 5 min, 16 mm (CC)
Tourist, 1984–85, 4 min, 16 mm, b&w&c (CC)
Optic Nerve, 1985, 16 min, 16 mm, b&w&c (CC, FCNY)
Wouldn't You Like to Meet Your Neighbor? 1985, 15 min, ¾" Umatic (CC)
Snow Job: The Media Hysteria of AIDS, 1986, 8 min, v, b&w&c (CC)
No No Nooky T.V., 1987, 12 min, 16 mm (CC, FCNY)
Place Mattes, 1987, 8 min, 16 mm, b&w&c (CC, FCNY)
Bedtime Stories I, II, and *III*, 1988, 33 min, v, b&w&c (CC)
    Bedtime Story I: The Wet Dream
    Bedtime Story II: The Erotic Intellect
    Bedtime Story III: Clip, Grab, and Paint
Endangered, 1988, 18 min, 16 mm (CC, FCNY)
The History of the World According to a Lesbian, 1988, 16 min, v (CC)
Two Bad Daughters, made with Paula Levine, 1988, 12 min, v (CC)
Hot Flash, 1989
Still Point, 1989, 9 min, 16 mm, b&w&c (CC)
TV Tart, 1989, 10 min, v (CC)
Dr. Watson's X-Rays, 1990, 21 min, v, b&w&c (CC)
Sanctus, 1990, 19 min, 16 mm, b&w&c (CC, FCNY)
Thanatos, 1990, 9 min, v, silent, b&w&c (CC)
Vital Signs, 1991, 9 min, 16 mm, b&w&c (CC)
Nitrate Kisses, 1992, 67 min, 16 mm, b&w (CC)
Eight in Eight, 1995, video and mixed media installation
Out in South Africa, South Africa/USA, 1995, 54 min (WMM)
Tender Fictions, 1996, 58 min (WMM)
The Female Closet, 1998, 60 min, b&w (WMM)
History Lessons, 2000, 65 min, b&w
Devotion, Japan/USA, 2000, 82 min
My Babushka: Searching Ukrainian Identities, 2001, 53 min, v
Resisting Paradise, France/USA, 2003

Hubley, Faith (1924–2001)
Harlem Wednesday, 1958, 10 min
Of Stars and Men, Writer, 1961
Children of the Sun, 1961, 10 min
The Hat, 1965, 18 min
The Cruise, 1966, 8 min
The Year of the Horse, Writer, 1966
Windy Day, 1968, 8 min
Eggs, 1970, 9 min
Voyage to Next, 1974, 102 min
Cockaboody, 1974, 9 min
Everybody Rides the Carousel, Writer, 1975
WOW (Women of the World), 1975, 10 min
The Doonesbury Special, 1977, 9 min
Whither Weather, 1977, 11 min
Second Chance: Sea, 1977, 11 min
Step by Step, 1978, 11 min
Sky Dance, 1980, 11 min
Enter Life, 1981, 8 min
The Big Bang and Other Creation Myths, 1981, 11 min
Starlore, 1983, 8 min
Hello, 1984, 8 min
The Cosmic Eye, 1986, 71 min
Time of the Angels, 1987, 10 min
Who Am I?, 1989, 4 min
Yes We Can, 1989, 10 min
Amazonia, 1990, 10 min
Upside Down, 1991, 10 min
Tall Time Tales, 1992, 8 min
Seers and Clowns, 1994, 9 min
My Universe Inside Out, 1996, 25 min
"O Canada," director of episode, "The Cruise," 1997, 25 min
Rainbows of Hawai'i, 1998, 9 min
Cloudland, 1998, 9 min
Beyond the Shadow Place, 1998, 10 min
Africa, 1999, 10 min
Witch Madness, 2000, 9 min
Our Spirited Earth, 2000, 9 min
Northern Ice, Golden Sun, 2002

Jayamanne, Laleen (1947–present)
A Song of Ceylon, 1985, 51 min, 16 mm (WMM)

Keller, Marjorie (1950–94)

Backsection, n.d, 4 min, 16 mm (FCNY)

The History of Art, 3939, n.d., 2 min, 16 mm, silent (FCNY)

Part IV: Green Hill, n.d., 3 min, 16 mm (FCNY)

Turtle, n.d., 2 min, 16 mm, silent (FCNY)

She/Va, 1973, 3 min, 16 mm, silent (CC, FCNY)

The Outer Circle, 1973, 6 min, 16 mm (FCNY)

Objection, 1974, 18 min, 16 mm (CC, FCNY)

Superimposition (1), 1975, 15 min, 16 mm, silent (FCNY)

Film Notebook: Part 1, 1975, 12 min, 16 mm, silent (FCNY)

By 2's and 3's: Women, 1976, 14 min, 16 mm (CC, FCNY)

Film Notebook: Part 2, 1977, 27 min, 16 mm, silent (FCNY)

The Web, 1977, 10 min, 16 mm (CC, FCNY)

Some of Us in the Mechanical Age, 1977, 27 min, 16 mm, silent (FCNY)

Misconception, 1977, 43 min, 16 mm (CC, FCNY)

On the Verge of an Image of Christmas, 1978, 10 min, 16 mm, silent (FCNY)

Six Windows, 1979, 6 min, 16 mm (CC, FCNY)

Ancient Parts and Foreign Parts, 1979, 5 min, 16 mm, b&w (CC, FCNY)

Daughters of Chaos, 1980, 20 min, 16 mm (CC, FCNY)

The Fallen World, 1983, 10 min, 16 mm (CC, FCNY)

Lyrics, 1983, 5 min, 16 mm (CC, FCNY)

The Answering Furrow, 1985, 27 min, 16 mm (CC, FCNY)

Private Parts, 1988, 13 min, 16 mm, silent (FCNY)

Herein, 1991, 35 min, 16 mm (CC, FCNY)

Kipnis, Laura (1956–present)
(laurak@northwestern.edu; http://www.communication.northwestern.edu/rtf/faculty/
Laura_Kipnis/)

Your Money or Your Life, 1982, 46 min, v (EAI)

Ecstasy Unlimited: The Interpenetration of Sex and Capitol, 1985, 60 min, v (EAI)

A Man's Woman, made for TV, UK, 1988, 52 min, v (EAI, VDB)

Marx: The Video (A Politics of Revolting Bodies), 1990, 27 min, v (EAI, VDB)

Leaf, Caroline (1946–present)
(http://www.awn.com/leaf/)

Sand or Peter and the Wolf, Canada, 1969, 10 min, animation

Orfeo, 1972, 11 min, animation

How Beaver Stole Fire, 1972, 12 min, animation

The Owl Who Married a Goose, Canada, 1974, 8 min, animation

The Street, aka *La Rue,* Canada, 1976, 10 min, animation

The Metamorphosis of Mr. Samsa, Canada, 1977, 10 min, animation

Interview, Canada, 1979, 14 min, animation

Kate and Anna McGarrigle, 1981, 30 min

The Right to Refuse?, 1981, 13 min

An Equal Opportunity, Canada, 1982, 13 min
Pies, 1983, 12 min, animation
War Series, 1983, 1 min, animation
The Owl and the Pussycat, Canada, 1985, 4 min, animation
The Fox and the Tiger, 1986, 4 min, animation
A Dog's Tale: A Mexican Parable, Canada, 1986, 4 min, animation
Entre Deux Soeurs/Two Sisters, Canada, 1990, 10:26 min, animation
I Met a Man, Canada, 1991, :51 min, animation
Bell Partout, 1993, :27 min, animation
Feleay's Fauna Centre, 1994, :30 min, animation
Brain Battle, 1995, :30 min, animation
Radio Rock Détente, 1995, :30 min, animation
Drapeau Canada, 1996, :10 min, animation
Absolut Leaf, 1998, :10 min, animation
Odysseus and Olive, 2001, 1:15 min, animation

Lowder, Rose (?–present)

Roulement, rouerie, aubage, 1978, 15 min, 16 mm (CC, FCNY)
Rue des teinturiers, 1979, 32 min, 16 mm, silent (CC, FCNY)
Certaines observations, aka *Certain Observations,* 1979, 14 min, 16 mm, silent, b&w
   (CC)
Champ provençal, 1979, 9 min, 16 mm, silent (CC, FCNY)
Couleurs mécaniques, 1979, 16 min, 16 mm (CC, FCNY)
Parcelle, 1979, 3 min, 16 mm (CC, FCNY)
Retour d'un repere, 1979, 18 min, 16 mm, silent (FCNY)
Retour d'un repere: "Composed Recurrence," 1981, 60 min, 16 mm, silent (FCNY
Les tournesols and *Les tournesols colorés,* 1982–83, 6 min, 16 mm, silent (CC)
Les tournesols, 1982/1932, 3 min, 16 mm, silent (FCNY)
Scènes de la vie française: Paris, 1986, 26 min, 16 mm, silent (CC)
Scènes de la vie française: Avignon, 1986, 11 min, 16 mm, silent (CC)
Scènes de la vie française: La Ciotat, 1986, 31 min, 16 mm, silent (CC)
Impromptu, 1989, 8 min, 16 mm (CC, FCNY)
Quiproquo, 1992, 13 min, 16 mm (CC, FCNY)
Bouquets 1–10, 1994–95, 11 min, 16 mm, silent (CC)

Makhmalbaf, Samira (1980–present)
(http://www.makhmalbaf.com/)

Sokhout, aka *Le Silence,* aka *The Silence,* assistant director, 1998
Sib, aka *The Apple,* aka *La Pomme,* Iran/France, 1998, 86 min
Takhtè siah, aka *Blackboard,* aka *Lavagne,* Iran/Italy/Japan, 2000, 85 min
11'09"01—September 11, segment "God, Construction and Destruction," interna-
   tional, 2002, 11:09 min, 35 mm
Panj é asr, aka *À cinq heures de l'après-midi,* aka *At Five in the Afternoon,* Iran/
   France, 2003, 105 min

Menken, Marie (1909–70)

Visual Variations on Noguchi, 1945, 4 min, 16 mm, b&w (CC, FCNY)
Dwightiana, 1957, 3 min, 16 mm (CC, FCNY)
Glimpse of the Garden, 1957, 5 min, 16 mm (CC, FCNY)
Hurry! Hurry! 1957, 3 min, 16 mm (CC, FCNY)
Faucets, unfinished, 1960
Arabesque for Kenneth Anger, 1961, 4 min, 16 mm (FCNY)
Bagatelle for Willard Maas, 1961, 5 min, 16 mm (FCNY)
Eye Music in Red Major, 1961, 6 min, 16 mm, silent (FCNY)
Drips in Strips, 1961, 3 min, 16 mm, silent (FCNY)
Moonplay, 1962, 5 min, 16 mm, b&w (FCNY)
Notebook, 1962–63, 10 min, 16 mm, silent (CC, FCNY)
Go Go Go, 1962–64, 12 min, 16 mm, silent (CC, FCNY)
Mood Mondrian, 1963, 6 min, 16 mm, silent (FCNY)
Wrestling, 1964, 8 min, 16 mm, b&w&c (FCNY)
Lights, 1964–65, 7 min, 16 mm, silent, b&w (FCNY)
Andy Warhol, 1965, 22 min, 16 mm (FCNY)
Sidewalks, 1966, 7 min, 16 mm, b&w&c (FCNY)
Watts with Eggs, 1967, 3 min, 16 mm, silent (FCNY)
Excursion, 1968, 6 min, 16 mm (FCNY)
Zenscapes, unfinished
Here and There with My Octoscope, unfinished

Menkes, Nina (1963–present)
(ninamenkes@earthlink.net; www.ninamenkes.com)

A Soft Warrior, 1981, 11 min, Super 8
The Great Sadness of Zohara, Israel/Morocco, 1983, 40 min, 16 mm
Magdalena Viraga, 1986, 90 min, 16 mm
Queen of Diamonds, 1991, 77 min, 35 mm
The Bloody Child, UK, 1996, 86 min, 35 mm
The Crazy Bloody Female Center, 2000, 3 hours, CD-ROM
Massacre, 2003, 200 min, dv to 35 mm

Mikesch, Elfi (1940–present)

Ich denke oft an Hawaii, West Germany, 1978, 84 min, b&w
Execution: A Story of Mary, 1979
Was soll'n wir denn machen ohne den Tod, West Germany, made for TV, 1980, 101 min
Zechmeister with Angela Summereder, Austria, 1981, 79 min
Macumba, West Germany, 1982, 88 min
Das Frühstück der Hyäne, West Germany, 1983, 22 min, b&w
Die Blaue Distanz, West Germany, 1983, 25 min, b&w
Verführung: Die grausame Frau, aka *Seduction: The Cruel Woman,* made with Monika Treut, West Germany, 1985, 84 min

Marocain, West Germany, made for TV, 1989, 85 min
Soldaten Soldaten, West Germany, 1994, 14 min, b&w
Verrückt bleiben-verliebt bleiben, Germany, 1997, 89 min
Die Markus Family, aka *The Markus Family,* Germany, 2001, 80 min
Mon Paradis—Der Winterpalast, Germany/Russia, 2001, 48 min

Minh-ha, Trinh T. (1952–present)

San Francisco, 1980, 12 min, silent
Calligraphy, 1981, 10 min, silent
The Wedding, 1982, 15 min, silent
Reassemblage, 1982, 40 min, 16 mm (WMM)
Naked Spaces: Living Is Round, 1985, 135 min, 16 mm (WMM)
Surname Viet Given Name Nam, 1989, 108 min, 16 mm (WMM)
Shoot for the Contents, 1991, 101 min, 16 mm (WMM)
Framer Framed, 1992
A Tale of Love, made with Jean-Paul Bourdier, Germany, 1995, 108 min (WMM)
The Fourth Dimension, 2001, 87 min (WMM)

Moffatt, Tracey (1960–present)

Spread the Word, 1987, 9 min, 16 mm
Watch Out/Women 88, 1987, 5 min, 16 mm
Nice Coloured Girls, Australia, 1987, 16 min, 16 mm
A Change of Face, made for TV, Australia, 1988
Moodeitj Yorgas, Australia, 1988, 22 min, 16 mm
It's Up to You, Australia, 1989, 9 min
Night Cries: A Rural Tragedy, Australia, 1989, 19 min, 16 mm
The Messenger, 1993, v
Bedevil, Australia, 1993, 90 min
Let My Children Be, 1994, v
My Island Home, 1995, v
Heaven, Australia, 1997, 28 min, v
Artist, made with Gary Hilberg, 1999, 10 min, v
Lip, made with Gary Hilberg, 1999, 10 min, v

Mohabeer, Michelle (?–present)

Five Feminist Minutes, segment "Exposure," 1990
Coconut/Cane and Cutlass, 1994
Two/Doh, 1996
Child-Play, 1997

Negron-Muntaner, Frances (?–present)

AIDS in the Barrio, made with Peter Biella, 1989, 30 min
"Puerto Rican ID," segment of *PBS Signal to Noise,* 1994
Brincando El Charco: Portrait of a Puerto Rican, 1994, 57 min

Nelson, Gunvor (?–present)

Building Muir Beach House, made with Robert Nelson, 1961
Last Week at Oona's Bath, made with Robert Nelson, 1962
Schmeerguntz, made with Dorothy Wiley, 1966, 15 min, 16 mm, b&w (CC)
Fog Pumas, made with Dorothy Wiley, 1967, 25 min, 16 mm (CC)
Kirsa Nicholina, 1969, 16 min, 16 mm (CC)
My Name Is Oona, 1969, 10 min, 16 mm, b&w (CC)
Five Artists BillBobBillBillBob, made with Dorothy Wiley, 1971, 70 min, 16 mm (CC)
Take Off, 1972, 10 min, 16 mm, b&w (CC)
One and the Same, made with Freude, 1972, 4 min, 16 mm (CC)
Moon's Pool, 1973, 15 min, 16 mm (CC)
Trollstenen, 1973–76, 120 min, 16 mm (CC)
Before Need, made with Dorothy Wiley, 1979, 75 min, 16 mm (CC)
Frame Line, 1984, 22 min, 16 mm, b&w (CC)
Red Shift, 1984, 50 min, 16 mm, b&w (CC)
Light Years, 1987, 28 min, 16 mm (CC)
Light Years Expanding, 1987, 25 min, 16m (CC)
Field Study #2, 1988, 8 min, 16 mm (CC)
Natural Features, 1990, 30 min, 16 mm (CC)
Time Being, 1991, 8 min, 16 mm, silent, b&w (CC)
Kristina's Harbor, 1992, 50 min, 16 mm (CC)
Old Digs, 1992, 20 min, 16 mm (CC)
Before Need Redressed, made with Dorothy Wiley, 1993, 42 min, 16 mm (CC)
Tree-Line, 1998, 8 min, v (LUX)
Collected Evidence: 52 Weeks, 1998, installation (not distributed)
Snowdrift, 2001, 9 min, v (LUX)

Neshat, Shirin (1957–present)

Turbulent, Iran, 1998, b&w
Passage, 2002, 11 min
Logic of the Birds, Iran, 2002
Tooba, 2003, 12 min

Notari, Elvira (1875–1946)

Bufera d'anime, Italy, 1911, silent, b&w
Medea di Portamedina, Italy, 1919, silent, b&w
Gabriele il lampionaio del porto, Italy, 1919, silent, b&w
'A Legge, Italy, 1920, silent, b&w
È piccerella, Italy, 1922, 44 min, silent, b&w
A Santanotte, Italy, 1922 silent, b&w
'Nfama! Italy, 1924, silent, b&w
Fantasia e surdato, Italy, 1927, silent, b&w

Ottinger, Ulrike (1942–present)
(http://www.ulrikeottinger.com/)

Berlinfieber—Wolf Vostell, aka Berlin Fever, West Germany, 1973, 12 min

Laokoon and Söhne, aka Laocoon and Sons, West Germany, 1975, 48 min, b&w

Die Betörung der blauen Matrosen, made with Tabea Blumenschein, West Germany, 1975, 54 min

Madame X—Eine absolute Herrscherin, aka Madame X: An Absolute Ruler, West Germany, 1978

Bildnis einer Trinkerin, aka Aller jamais retour, aka Portrait of a Female Drunkard, aka Ticket of No Return, West Germany, 1979, 108 min

Freak Orlando, West Germany, 1981, 126 min

Dorian Gray im Spiegel der Boulevardpresse, aka The Image of Dorian Gray in the Yellow Press, West Germany, 1984, 150 min

China. Die Künste—der Alltag. Eine filmische Reisebeschreibung, West Germany, 1985, 270 min

Seven Women, Seven Sins, segment "Pride," USA/France/West Germany/Belgium/Austria, 1987, 120 min

Usinimage, West Germany, 1987, 11 min

Johanna D'Arc of Mongolia, aka Joan of Arc of Mongolia, West Germany/France, 1989, 165 min

Countdown, Germany, 1991, 188 min

Taiga, Germany, 1992, 501 min

Exil Shanghai, aka Exile Shanghai, Germany/Israel, 1997, 275 min

Blutgräfin, Die, aka The Bloodcountess, 2000

Sudostpassage, aka Southeast Passage, 2002, 360 min, dv, b&w&c

Twelve Chairs, 2004, in production

Parker, Claire (1906–81)

Une nuit sur le mont chauve, aka Night on Bald Mountain, made with Alexander Alexeieff, France, 1933, 8 min, b&w

Huilor, France, 1938

Les oranges de Jaffa, France, 1938

Parmar, Pratibha (?–present)

Emergence, UK, 1986, 20 min, v (WMM)

Sari Red, UK, 1988, 11 min (WMM)

Re-Framing AIDS, 1988

Memory Pictures, UK, 1989, 24 min

Bhangra Jig, 1990

Flesh and Paper, 1990, 26 min, 16 mm (WMM)

Khush, 1991, 24 min, 16 mm (WMM)

A Place of Rage, 1991, 52 min, 16 mm (WMM)

Double the Trouble, Twice the Fun, made for TV, UK, 1992, 24 min, v (WMM)

Warrior Marks, UK, 1993, 54 min, 16 mm (WMM)

Siren Spirits, segment "Memsahib Rita," UK, 1994, 20 min, 16 mm (WMM)
The Colour of Britain, UK, 1994, 50 min
Jodie: An Icon, made for TV, UK, 1996, 25 min, 16 mm (WMM)
Wavelengths, UK, 1997, 15 min, 16 mm (WMM)
The Righteous Babes, UK, 1998, 50 min, v (WMM)
Brimful of Asia, made for TV, UK, 1998, 24 min
Sita Gita, UK, 2000, 24 min

Portillo, Lourdes (?–present)
(portillo1@mindspring.com; www.lourdesportillo.com)
After the Earthquake, aka *Despues del Terremoto,* 1979, 27 min, 16 mm b&w
   (WMM)
Las Madres: The Mother of Plaza de Mayo, Argentina, 1986, 64 min, 16 mm
   (WMM)
Mütter, Dollars und ein Krieg—Der Kampf um El Salvador, made with Manfred
   Vosz, West Germany, 1986, 79 min
La Ofrenda, aka *The Days of the Dead,* Argentina, 1988, 50 min, 16 mm
Vida, 1990, 18 min, 16 mm
Columbus on Trial, 1992, 18 min, v (WMM, VDB)
Mirrors of the Heart, for PBS TV 1993, 60 min
The Devil Never Sleeps, aka *El Diablo Nunca Duerme,* Mexico/USA, 1994, 82 min,
   16 mm (WMM)
Sometimes My Feet Go Numb, 1994, 2 min, v
This Is Your Day, aka *Hoy es tu Dia,* 1998, video installation
Conversations with Intellectuals about Selena, 1999, 57 min
Corpus: A Home Movie for Selena, 1999 (VDB)
Senorita Extraviada, aka *Missing Young Woman,* Mexico, 2002, 74 min, (WMM)

Potter, Sally (1949–present)
Thriller, UK, 1979, 34 min, 16 mm, b&w (WMM)
London Story, UK, 1980, 15 min, 16 mm (WMM)
The Gold Diggers, UK, 1983, 87 min, b&w
Tears, Laughter, Fear and Rage: Rage, made for TV, UK, 1987, 60 min
Tears, Laughter, Fear and Rage: Tears, made for TV, UK, 1987, 60 min
I Am an Ox, I Am a Horse, I Am a Man, I Am a Woman, aka *Women Filmmakers in
   Russia,* UK, 1988, 60 min
Orlando, UK, 1992, 93 min
Tango-Fieber, aka *The Tango Lesson,* aka *Lección de tango,* aka *La Leçon de tango,*
   UK/France/Argentina/Germany/Netherlands, 1997, 100 min
The Man Who Cried, aka *Les larmes d'un homme,* UK/France, 2000, 10 min
Yes, UK, 2004

Rainer, Yvonne (1934–present)
Five Easy Pieces, 1966, 48 min, v (VDB)

Lives of Performers, 1972, 90 min, b&w
Film about a Woman Who . . . , 1974, 90 min, b&w
Kristina Talking Pictures, 1976
Trio A, 1978, 11 min, v (VDB)
Journeys from Berlin/1971, USA/UK, 1980, 125 min, b&w
The Man Who Envied Women, 1985, 125 min, b&w
Privilege, 1990, 100 min
MURDER *and murder,* 1996, 113 min
After Many a Summer Dies the Swan: Hybrid, 2002, 31 min, v (VDB)

Reiniger, Lotte (1899–1981)

Der Stern von Bethlehem, aka *The Star of Bethlehem,* Germany, 1921, silent, b&w
Das Ornament des verliebten Herzens, aka *The Ornament of a Loving Heart,* aka
    The Ornament of the Lovestruck Heart, Germany, 1919, silent, b&w
Sleeping Beauty, Germany, 1922, silent, b&w
Aschenputtel, aka *Cinderella,* Germany, 1922, 13 min, silent, b&w
Der Fliegende Koffer, aka *The Flying Coffer,* aka *The Flying Koffer,* Germany, 1922, 9
    min, silent, b&w
Das Geheimnis der Marquisin, Germany, 1922, 2 min, silent, b&w
Die Abenteuer des Prinzen Achmed, aka *The Adventures of Prince Achmed,* Ger-
    many, 1925, 65 min, silent, b&w
The Chinese Nightingale, Germany, 1927, silent, b&w
Dr. Dolittle und seine Tiere, aka *Dr. Dolittle and His Animals,* Germany, 1928, 25
    min, silent, b&w
Zehn Minuten Mozart, Germany, 1930, 10 min, silent, b&w
Harlekin, Germany, 1931, 23 min, b&w
Sissi, Germany, 1932, b&w
Carmen, Germany, 1933, 9 min, b&w
Das Gestohlene Herz, aka *The Stolen Heart,* Germany, 1934, 12 min, b&w
Galathea, Germany, 1935, 11 min, b&w
Kalif Storch, Germany, 1935, b&w
Papageno, Germany, 1935, 11 min, b&w
Silhouetten, Germany, 1936, b&w
Puss in Boots, aka *Der Gestiefelte Kater,* Germany, 1936, b&w
Daughter, UK, 1937, b&w
(Restlicher Stab—Filmographie)—Marseillaise, La, shadow puppets, 1938
Die Goldene Gans, aka *The Goose That Lays the Golden Eggs,* Germany, 1944, 10
    min, b&w
Mary's Birthday, UK, 1951, b&w
Aladdin, UK, 1953
The Magic Horse, UK, 1953
Caliph Storch, UK, 1954, 10 min, b&w
The Frog Prince, UK, 1954
The Gallant Little Tailor, UK, 1954, 10 min, b&w

The Grasshopper and the Ant, UK, 1954, 10 min, b&w
The Little Chimney Sweep, UK, 1954
The Sleeping Beauty, UK, 1954
Snow White and Rose Red, UK, 1954
The Three Wishes, UK, 1954, 10 min, b&w
Thumbelina, UK, 1954, 10 min, b&w
Hansel and Gretel, UK, 1955, 10 min, b&w
Jack and the Beanstalk, aka *Jack the Giant Killer,* UK, 1955, 10 min, b&w
Aucassin and Nicolette, aka *Aucassin et Nicolette,* Canada, 1975, 16 min

Ricci Lucchi, Angela (?–present)

Karagoez catalogo 9,5 made with Yervant Gianikian, Italy, 1981, 54 min, b&w
Dal polo all'equatore, aka *From Pole to Equator,* made with Yervant Gianikian,
    West Germany/Italy, 1987, 96 min, b&w
Uomini, anni, vita, made with Yervant Gianikian, 1990, 70 min
Prigionieri della Guerra, made with Yervant Gianikian, Italy, 1996, 64 min
Lo specchio di Diana, aka *Diana's Looking,* made with Yervant Gianikian, Italy,
    1996, 29 min
Nocturne, made with Yervant Gianikian, Italy, 1997, 18 min
Lo ricordo, made with Yervant Gianikian, Italy, 1997, 12 min
Passion, made with Yervant Gianikian, 1998, 7 min
Transparences, made with Yervant Gianikian, 1998, 6 min
Su tutte le vette e pace, aka *On the Heights All Is Peace,* made with Yervant Giani-
    kian, 1998, 71 min
Visioni del deserto, made with Yervant Gianikian, 2000, 16 min
Inventario balcanico, aka *Balkan Inventory,* made with Yervant Gianikian, Italy,
    2000, 63 min
Images d'Orient—"Tourisme vandale," aka *Images of the Orient—"Vandalic Tour-
    ism,"* made with Yervant Gianikian, Italy/France, 2001, 62 min
Frammenti Elettrici N° 1: ROM (Uomini), aka *Electric Fragments N° 1: ROM
    (MEN),* made with Yervant Gianikian, Italy, 2002, 14 min
Frammenti Elettrici N° 2: Viet Nam, made with Yervant Gianikian, Italy, 2001, 9
    min
Frammenti Elettrici N° 3: Corpi, made with Yervant Gianikian, Italy, 2003, 9 min 8
    mm

Robertson, Anne Charlotte (?–present)

Breakdown and *After the Mental Hospital,* Reel 23 of *Five Year Diary,* n.d.
Emily Died, Reel 80 of *Five Year Diary,* n.d.
Fall to Spring, Reel 76 of *Five Year Diary,* n.d.
Mourning Emily, Reel 81 of *Five Year Diary,* n.d.
On Probation, Reel 71 of *Five Year Diary,* n.d.
Niagara Falls, n.d. (FCNY)
Subways, 1976

Going to Work, 1981
Locomotion, 1981
Apologies, 1990
Suicide, 1990

Rose, Kathy (?–present)
(http://www.krose.com/)
Frances, 1970
Portraits, 1971
Pluto People, 1971
Movers, 1972
The Mysterians, 1973
The Arts Circus, 1974
Mirror People, 1974
The Moon Show, 1974
The Doodlers, 1975
Pencil Booklings, 1978
Strange Ditties, 1983
Primitive Movers, 1983
Syncopations, 1987
Oriental Interplay, 1991
Az-Tech, 1992
She, 1993
Ancient Mysteries, 1994
Kleopat'ra, 1999

Sander, Helke (1937–present)
(http://www.helke-sander.de/)
Subjektitüde, West Germany, 1967, b&w
Die Rote Fahne, West Germany, 1968, 12 min, silent
Eine Prämie für Irene, made for TV, West Germany, 1971, 50 min
Die Allseitig reduzierte Persönlichkeit—Redupers, aka *The All-Around Reduced Personality: Outtakes*, West Germany, 1978, 95 min, b&w
Der Subjektive Faktor, West Germany, 1981
Die Gedächtnislücke—Filmminiaturen über den alltäglichen Umgang mit Giften, West Germany, 1983, 62 min, b&w
Nr. 1—Aus Berichten der Wach- und Patrouillendienste, West Germany, 1984, 10 min
Der Beginn aller Schrecken ist Liebe, aka *Love Is the Beginning of All Terror*, West Germany, 1984, 117 min
Felix, West Germany, 1987, 82 min
Seven Women, Seven Sins, segment "Gluttony," West Germany, 1987, 120 min, 35 mm (WMM)
Die Deutschen und ihre Männer—Bericht aus Bonn, aka *The Germans and Their Men*, West Germany, 1989, 96 min, 1989 (WMM)

Befreier und Befreite, aka *Liberators Take Liberties,* Germany, 1992, 200 min, b&w
Dazlak, Germany, 1998
Das Dorf, made for TV, Germany, 2001, 90 min

Schneemann, Carolee (1939–present)
(http://www.caroleeschneemann.com/)
Meat Joy, 1964, 6 min, 16 mm (EAI)
Vietflakes, 1965, 7 min, 16 mm, toned b&w (CC, FCNY EAI)
Water Light/Water Needle (Lake Mah Wah), 1966, 10 min, 16 mm (EAI)
Water Light/Water Needle (St. Mark's Church in the Bowery), 1966, 4 min, 16 mm
  (EAI)
Body Collage, 1967, 3:30 min, 16 mm, silent, b&w (EAI)
Fuses, 1967, 18 min, 16 mm, silent (CC, FCNY EAI)
Snows, 1967, 17 min, 16 mm, silent, b&w (EAI)
Illinois Central Transposed, 1968, 4:30 min, 16 mm, silent (EAI)
Plumb Line, 1968–71, 18 min, Super 8 (CC, FCNY EAI)
Kitch's Last Meal, 1973–76, Super 8
Interior Scroll—The Cave, 1975, 4.5 min (EAI)
Up to and Including Her Limits, 1976, 29 min, (EAI, VDB)
Fresh Blood, 1983, 11 min (EAI)
Art Is Reactionary, 1987, 10 min (EAI)
Catscan, 1990, 13 min (EAI)
Ask the Goddess 1991, 7 min (EAI)
Four Recent Installations, 1993, 5 min (EAI)
Vulva's School, 1995, 7 min (EAI)

Solberg, Helena (?–present)
Carmen Miranda: Bananas Is My Business, UK/Brazil/USA, 1994, 91 min (WMM)
O Brilho das Coisas, Brazil, 2003

Strand, Chick (?–present)
Dementia Precox: Five Pieces, n.d., 25 min, 16 mm (FCNY)
Angel Blue Sweet Wings, 1966, 3 min, 16 mm (CC, FCNY)
Waterfall, 1967, 3 min, 16 mm (CC, FCNY)
Anselmo, 1967, 4 min 16 mm (CC, FCNY)
Mosori Monika, 1970, 21 min, 16 mm (CC, FCNY)
Cosas de Mi Vida, 1976, 25 min, 16 mm (CC, FCNY)
Elasticity, 1976, 22 min, 16 mm (CC, FCNY)
Guacamole, 1976, 11 min, 16 mm (CC, FCNY)
Mujer de Milfuegos, aka *Woman of a Thousand Fires,* 1976, 15 min, 16 mm (CC,
  FCNY)
Cartoon le Mousse, 1979, 12 min, 16 mm (CC, FCNY)
Fever Dream, 1979, 7 min, 16 mm, b&w (CC, FCNY)
Kristallnacht, 1979, 8 min, 16 mm, b&w (CC, FCNY)

Loose Ends, 1979, 25 min, 16 mm, b&w (CC, FCNY)
Soft Fiction, 1979, 55 min, 16 mm, b&w (CC, FCNY)
Anselmo and the Women, 1986, 35 min, 16 mm (CC, FCNY)
Artificial Paradise, 1986, 13 min, 16 mm (CC)
By the Lake, 1986, 10 min, 16 mm (CC)
Coming Up for Air, 1986, 27 min, 16 mm (CC, FCNY)
Fake Fruit, 1986, 22 min, 16 mm (CC, FCNY)

Tait, Margaret (1918–99)
(http://www.lux.org.uk/margarettait.html)
One Is One, UK, 1951
Three Portrait Sketches, UK, 1951
The Lion, the Griffin and the Kangaroo, UK, 1952
Happy Bees, UK, 1955
The Leaden Echo and the Golden Echo, UK, 1955
Orquil Burn, UK, 1955
A Portrait of Ga, UK, 1955
Calypso, UK, 1956
The Drift Back, 1956
Rose Street, UK, 1956
Hugh MacDiarmid: A Portrait, UK, 1964
Palindrome, UK, 1964
Where I Am Is Here, UK, 1964
The Big Sheep, UK, 1966
Splashing, UK, 1966
A Pleasant Place, UK, 1969
He's Back (The Return), UK, 1970
John MacFadyen (The Stripes in the Tartan), UK, 1970
Painted Eightsome, UK, 1970
Aerial, UK, 1974
Atmosphere, UK, 1974
Colour Poems, UK, 1974
On the Mountain, UK, 1974
These Walls, UK, 1974
Place of Work, UK, 1976
Tailpiece, UK, 1976
Aspects of Kirkwall: Shape of a Town, UK, 1977
Aspects of Kirkwall: Occasions, UK, 1977
Aspects of Kirkwall: The Ba, over the Years, UK, 1981
Aspects of Kirkwall: The Look of the Place, UK, 1981
Aspects of Kirkwall: Some Changes, UK, 1981
Landmakar, UK, 1981
Blue Black Permanent, UK, 1992
Garden Pieces, UK, 1998

Tajiri, Rea (1958–present)
(www.strawberryfieldsfilm.com)

Now I'm Turning to Face You, 1982, 6 min (EAI)

The Journal of Lennie Itoh One Year after the Death of Her Aunt Mako, 1986

The Hitchcock Trilogy (Vertigo, Psycho, Torn Curtain), 1987, 14 min, v (EAI, VDB)

Off Limits, 1988, 8 min, v (EAI, VDB)

History and Memory: For Akiko and Takeshige, 1991, 30 min, v, b&w&c (EAI, VDB, WMM)

Yuri Kochiyama: Passion for Justice, 1994, v (WMM)

Strawberry Fields, 1997, 90 min, 35 mm

Little Murders, 1998, 19 min, dv (VDB)

Aloha, 2000

Thornton, Leslie (1951–present)

All Right You Guys, 1976

Jennifer, Where Are You? 1981, 10 min, 16 mm (FCNY)

Adynata, 1983, 30 min, 16 mm (FCNY, EAI, WMM)

Oh China Oh, 1983, 3 min, 16 mm, b&w (FCNY)

She Had Her So He Do He to Her, 1987

Peggy and Fred in Hell: The Prologue, 1985, 20 min, v, b&w (FCNY, EAI, VDB, WMM)

Peggy and Fred in Kansas, 1987, 11 min, v, b&w (EAI, VDB, WMM)

Peggy and Fred and Pete, 1988, 23 min, v, sepia (EAI, VDB)

There Was an Unseen Cloud Moving, 1988, 58 min, v (VDB, WMM)

[Dung Smoke Enters the Palace], 1989, 16min, v, b&w (EAI, VDB)

Introduction to the So-Called Duck Factory, 1993, 7 min (EAI)

Strange Space, coproduced with Ron Vawter, 1993, 4 min, v (EAI, VDB)

The Last Time I Saw Ron, 1994, 12 min, v, b&w&c (EAI, VDB)

The Problem So Far, 1996, 7 min, b&w (EAI)

Old Worldy, 1996

Whirling, 1996, 22 min, b&w (EAI)

Or Lost, 1998, 7 min, 16 mm (FCNY)

Another Worldy, 1999, 22 min, b&w (EAI)

Bedtime, vol. 1, 2000, 4 min, v, b&w

Have a Nice Day Alone, 2001, 7 min, b&w (EAI)

The Splendor, 2001, 3 min, v, b&w

Bedtime, vol. 2, 2002, 7 min, v, b&w

Paradise Crushed, 2002, 12 min (EAI) ·

Troche, Rose (1964–present)

Gabriella on the Half Shell, 1994, 10 min, v

Go Fish, 1994, 84 min

Bedrooms and Hallways, UK, 1998, 96 min

The Safety of Objects, USA/UK, 2001, 121 min

Six Feet Under, episode "The Plan," made for TV, 2001
The L Word, made for TV, Canada/USA, 2004, 60 min
Touching Evil, episode "Memorial," made for TV, 2004

Weber, Lois (1881–1939)
　　The Martyr, made with Phillips Smalley, 1911, silent, b&w
　　A Breach of Faith, made with Phillips Smalley, 1911, silent, b&w
　　Fate, made with Phillips Smalley, 1911, silent, b&w
　　On the Brink, made with Phillips Smalley, 1911, silent, b&w
　　A Heroine of '76, made with Phillips Smalley, 1911, silent, b&w
　　The Heiress, made with Phillips Smalley, 1911, silent, b&w
　　The Realization, made with Phillips Smalley, 1911, silent, b&w
　　Faraway Fields, 1912, silent, b&w
　　A Japanese Idyll, 1912, silent, b&w
　　An Old Fashioned Girl, 1912, silent, b&w
　　The Troubadour's Triumph, 1912, silent, b&w
　　The Greater Love, 1912, silent, b&w
　　Power of Thought, 1912, silent, b&w
　　The Price of Peace, 1912, silent, b&w
　　The Greater Christian, made with Phillips Smalley, 1912, silent, b&w
　　Eyes That See Not, made with Phillips Smalley, 1912, silent, b&w
　　The Final Pardon, made with Phillips Smalley, 1912, silent, b&w
　　The Bargain, made with Phillips Smalley, 1912, silent, b&w
　　Fine Feathers, made with Phillips Smalley, 1912, silent, b&w
　　Angels Unaware, made with Phillips Smalley, 1912, silent, b&w
　　The Wife's Deceit, 1913, silent, b&w
　　The Jew's Christmas, made made with Phillips Smalley, 1913, silent, b&w
　　The Mask, 1913, silent, b&w
　　James Lee's Wife, made with Phillips Smalley, 1913, silent, b&w
　　The Blood Brotherhood, made with Phillips Smalley, 1913, silent, b&w
　　The Haunted Bride, made with Phillips Smalley, 1913, silent, b&w
　　Thieves and the Cross, 1913, silent, b&w
　　The Clue, 1913, silent, b&w
　　The Thumb Print, made with Phillips Smalley, 1913, silent, b&w
　　Memories, made with Phillips Smalley, 1913, silent, b&w
　　Shadows of Life, made with Phillips Smalley, 1913, silent, b&w
　　His Brand, 1913, silent, b&w
　　The Light Woman, 1913, silent, b&w
　　Just in Time, 1913, silent, b&w
　　Civilized and Savage, 1913, silent, b&w
　　The Fallen Angel, 1913, silent, b&w
　　Through Strife, made with Phillips Smalley, 1913, silent, b&w
　　How Men Propose, 1913, 6 min silent, b&w
　　The Pretender, 1913, silent, b&w

The King Can Do No Wrong, 1913, silent, b&w
The Cap of Destiny, made with Phillips Smalley, 1913, silent, b&w
The Rosary, made with Phillips Smalley, 1913, silent, b&w
The Dragon's Breath, 1913, silent, b&w
Until Death, made with Phillips Smalley, 1913, silent, b&w
Bobby's Baby, made with Phillips Smalley, 1913, silent, b&w
The Peacemaker, 1913, silent, b&w
An Empty Box, 1913, silent, b&w
Troubled Waters, 1913, silent, b&w
In the Blood, 1913, silent, b&w
Two Thieves, 1913, silent, b&w
His Sister, 1913, silent, b&w
The Merchant of Venice, made with Phillips Smalley, 1914, silent, b&w
The Traitor, made with Phillips Smalley, 1914, silent, b&w
Helping Mother, made with Phillips Smalley, 1914, silent, b&w
Daisies, made with Phillips Smalley, 1914, silent, b&w
Behind the Veil, made with Phillips Smalley, 1914, silent, b&w
Mary Plain, 1914, silent, b&w
Lost by a Hair, made with Phillips Smalley, 1914, silent, b&w
The Pursuit of Hate, 1914, silent, b&w
Closed Gates, made with Phillips Smalley, 1914, silent, b&w
The Stone in the Road, made with Phillips Smalley, 1914, silent, b&w
Avenged, 1914, silent, b&w
The Triumph of Mind, made with Phillips Smalley, 1914, silent, b&w
The Career of Waterloo Peterson, made with Phillips Smalley, 1914, silent, b&w
An Episode, made with Phillips Smalley, 1914, silent, b&w
On Suspicion, 1914, silent, b&w
The Man Who Slept, 1914, silent, b&w
The Babies' Doll, 1914, silent, b&w
In the Days of His Youth, 1914, silent, b&w
The Spider and Her Web, made with Phillips Smalley, 1914, silent, b&w
A Modern Fairy Tale, 1914, silent, b&w
The Weaker Sister, 1914, silent, b&w
Woman's Burden, 1914, silent, b&w
An Old Locke, made with Phillips Smalley, 1914, silent b&w
The Coward Hater, made with Phillips Smalley, 1914, silent, b&w
The Leper's Coat, made with Phillips Smalley 1914, silent, b&w
A Fool and His Money, made with Phillips Smalley, 1914, silent, b&w
The Female of the Species, made with Phillips Smalley, 1914, silent, b&w
Scandal 1915, aka *Scandal Mongers*, made with Phillips Smalley, 1918, silent, b&w
Betty in Search of a Thrill, aka *Madcap Betty*, made with Phillips Smalley, 1915, silent, b&w
Captain Courtesy, 1915, silent, b&w
Sunshine Molly, made with Phillips Smalley, 1915, silent, b&w

Hypocrites, 1915, silent, b&w
It's No Laughing Matter, 1915, silent, b&w
Jewel, made with Phillips Smalley 1915, silent, b&w
A Cigarette—That's All, made with Phillips Smalley, 1915, silent, b&w
Discontent, 1916, silent, b&w
The Rock of Riches, made with Phillips Smalley, 1916, silent, b&w
Idle Wives, made with Phillips Smalley, 1916, silent, b&w
Where Are My Children? made with Phillips Smalley, 1916, silent, b&w
The People vs. John Doe . . . , aka *God's Law,* 1916, silent, b&w
Wanted: A Home, made with Phillips Smalley, 1916, silent, b&w
Under the Spell, 1916, silent, b&w
Saving the Family Name, made with Phillips Smalley, 1916, silent, b&w
Shoes, 1916, silent, b&w
The Eye of God, made with Phillips Smalley, 1916, silent, b&w
John Needham's Double, 1916, silent, b&w
The Dumb Girl of Portici, made with Phillips Smalley, 1916, silent, b&w
There Is No Place Like Home, 1916, silent, b&w
The Flirt, made with Phillips Smalley, 1916, silent, b&w
Hop—The Devil's Brew, made with Phillips Smalley, 1916, silent, b&w
The Gilded Life, made with Phillips Smalley, 1916, silent, b&w
The Boyhood He Forgot, made with Phillips Smalley, 1917, silent, b&w
Even As You and I, 1917, silent, b&w
The Face Downstairs, 1917, silent, b&w
The Price of a Good Time, made with Phillips Smalley, 1917, silent, b&w
Hand That Rocks the Cradle, made with Phillips Smalley, 1917, silent, b&w
The Mysterious Mrs. Musslewhite, aka *The Mysterious Mrs. M.,* 1917, silent, b&w
Borrowed Clothes, aka *Orange Blossoms,* 1918, silent, b&w
For Husbands Only, made with Phillips Smalley, 1918, silent, b&w
The Doctor and the Woman, made with Phillips Smalley, 1918, silent, b&w
Forbidden, aka *The Forbidden Box,* made with Phillips Smalley, 1919, silent, b&w
Home, aka *There's No Place Like Home,* 1919, silent, b&w
Mary Regan, 1919, silent, b&w
A Midnight Romance, 1919, silent, b&w
When a Girl Loves, made with Phillips Smalley, 1919, silent, b&w
Life's Mirror, 1920, silent, b&w
Mum's the Word, 1920, silent, b&w
To Please One Woman, 1920, silent, b&w
The Blot, made with Phillips Smalley, 1921, 80 min, silent, b&w
Too Wise Wives, 1921, 80 min, silent, b&w
What's Worth While? 1921, silent, b&w
What Do Men Want? 1921, silent, b&w
A Chapter in Her Life, 1923, silent, b&w
The Marriage Clause, 1926, silent, b&w
Topsy and Eva, made with Del Lord and D. W. Griffith, 1927, silent, b&w

Sensation Seekers, 1927, silent, b&w
The Angel of Broadway, 1927, silent, b&w
White Heat, 1934, 62 min, silent, b&w

Wieland, Joyce (1931–98)

Barbara's Blindness, made with Betty Ferguson, 1965, 17 min, 16 mm (FCNY)
Patriotism, n.d., 4 min, 16 mm (FCNY)
1933, 1967, 4 min, 16 mm (CC, FCNY)
Hand Tinting, 1967, 6 min, 16 mm, (FCNY)
Water Sark, Canada, 1965, 14 min (FCNY)
Sailboat, 1967, 3 min, 16 mm (CC, FCNY)
Rat Life and Diet in North America, Canada, 1968, 14 min, 16 mm (FCNY)
Reason over Passion, aka *La raison avant la passion,* Canada, 1969, 80 min, 16 mm
   (CC, FCNY)
Cat Food, Canada, 1969, 13 min, 16 mm (FCNY)
Dripping Water, made with Michael Snow, Canada, 1969, 12 min, 16 mm, b&w
   (FCNY)
Pierre Vallieres, 1972, 33 min, 16 mm (CC, FCNY)
Solidarity, Canada, 1973, 11 min, 16 mm (CC)
The Far Shore, aka *The Art of Lust,* aka *L'autre rive,* Canada, 1976, 105 min
A and B in Ontario, Canada, 1984, 15 min (FCNY)
Birds at Sunrise, Canada, 1986, 10 min

Distributor Contact Information

Canyon Cinema (CC)
145 Ninth Street, Suite 260
San Francisco, CA 94103
415–626–2255
E-mail: films@canyoncinema.com
Web: www.canyoncinema.com

Electronic Arts Intermix (EAI)
535 W. 22nd Street, 5th floor
New York, NY 10011
212–337–6080
212–337–0679 (fax)
E-mail: info@eai.org
Web: www.eai.org

Facets Multimedia (FM)
1517 West Fullerton Avenue
Chicago, IL 60614
1–800–331–6197
Web: www.facets.org

Film-Makers' Cooperative (FCNY)
c/o The Clocktower Gallery
108 Leonard Street, 13 floor
New York, NY 10013
212–267–5665
212–267–5666 fax

E-mail: film6000@aol.com
Web: www.film-makerscoop.com

Gris-Gris Films (GGF)
818–881–8725
E-mail: grisfilm@ix.netcom.com
Web: www.grisgrisfilms.com
www.grisgrisfilms.com/filmmakers_
    cooperative.htm

LUX (LUX)
18 Shacklewell Lane
London E8 2EZ
United Kingdom
+44 (0)20 7503 3980
+44 (0)20 7503 1606 (fax)
E-mail: info@lux.org.uk
Web: www.lux.org.uk

Third World Newreel (TWN)
545 Eighth Avenue, 10th floor
New York, NY 10018
212–947–9277
212–594–6417 (fax)
E-mail: twn@twn.org
Web: www.twn.org

TLA Video (TLA)
1520 Locust Street, Suite 200
Philadelphia, PA 19102
1–800–333–8521
215–733–0637 (fax)
Web: www.tlavideo.com

Video Data Bank (VDB)
School of the Art Institute of Chicago
112 S. Michigan Avenue, 3rd floor
Chicago, IL 60603
312–345–3550
312–541–8073 (fax)
E-mail: info@vdb.org
Web: www.vdb.org

Women Make Movies (WMM)
462 Broadway, Suite 500
New York, NY 10013
212–925–0606
212–925–2052 (fax)
E-mail: orders@wmm.com
Web: www.wmm.com

Zeitgeist Films (ZF)
247 Centre Street
New York, NY 10013
212–274–1989, ask for non-theatrical
   booker
212–274–1644 fax
E-mail: mail@zeitgeistfilms.com
Web: www.zeitgeistfilms.com

Bibliography

Abramovic, Marina, Velimir Abramovic, and Kunstmuseum Bern. *Marina Abramovic: Artist Body: Performances 1969–1998*. Milan: Edizioni Charta, 1998.

Abrash, Barbara, and Catherine Egan. *Mediating History: The Map Guide to Independent Video by and about African American, Asian American, Latino, and Native American People*. New York: New York University Press, 1992.

Adorno, T. W. *Aesthetics of Theory*. Trans. C. Lenhardt. Ed. Gretel Adorno and Rolf Tiedmann. London: Routledge, 1970.

Andrade-Watkins, Claire. "A Mirage in the Desert? African Women Directors at FESPACO." In Martin, *Cinemas of the Black Diaspora*, 145–52.

Armatage, Kay. *Magdalena Viraga* in Toronto Festival of Festivals Program, 1986. *Magdalena Viraga* Press Kit.

Armstrong, Toni, Jr., and Dell Richards. "The Little Feminist Idea That Could: Women Make Movies." *Hot Wire*, May 1992, 22–24.

Arthur, Paul. "Lost and Found: American Avant-Garde Film in the Eighties." In *A Passage Illuminated: The American Avant-Garde, 1980–1990*. Ed. Nelly Voorhuis. Amsterdam: Mecano, 1991. 15–29.

———. "No More Causes? The International Experimental Film Congress." *Independent Film and Video Monthly* 12.8 (1989): 22–25.

Bakhtin, Mikhail. *The Bakhtin Reader*. Ed. Pam Morris. London and New York: E. Arnold, 1994.

Barker, Jennifer. "Bodily Irruptions: The Corporeal Assault on Ethnographic Narration." *Cinema Journal* 34.3 (1995): 57–77.

Barthes, Roland. *Camera Lucida: Reflections on Photography*. Trans. Richard Howard. New York: Hill and Wang, 1981.

———. *Essais critiques*. Paris: Éditions du Seuil, 1964.

———. *Image-Music-Text*. Trans. Stephen Heath. New York: Hill and Wang, 1977.

———. *Le plaisir du texte*. Paris: Éditions du Seuil, 1973.

Battcock, Gregory, ed. *Minimal Art: A Critical Anthology.* Berkeley: University of California Press, 1995.

Baudry, Jean-Louis. "The Apparatus: Metapsychological Approaches to the Impression of Reality in the Cinema." In Rosen, *Narrative, Apparatus, Ideology,* 299–318.

Bazin, André. *Qu'est-ce que le cinéma? Tome 1: Ontologie et langage.* Paris: Éditions du Cerf, 1958.

Beckett, Samuel. *Waiting for Godot.* New York: Evergreen, 1954.

Belton, Robert James. *The Beribboned Bomb: The Image of Woman in Male Surrealist Art.* Calgary, Alta.: University of Calgary Press, 1995.

Benjamin, Walter. *Illuminations.* Ed. Hannah Arendt. Trans. Harry Zohn. New York: Harcourt, Brace, 1968.

Berger, Maurice. *Minimal Politics: Performativity and Minimalism in Recent American Art.* Issues in Cultural Theory 1. Baltimore: Fine Arts Gallery, University of Maryland, 1997.

Bergson, Henri. *Matter and Memory.* New York: Zone Books, 1988.

Bergstrom, Janet, and Constance Penley. "The Avant-Garde: Histories and Theories." *Screen* 19.3 (1978): 113–27.

"The Bloody Child." *Film Threat* (July 1997): 51.

The Bloody Child: An Interior of Violence. Dir. Nina Menkes. Perf. Tinka Menkes. Menkesfilm, 1996.

Blumenthal, Lyn. "On Art and Artists: Yvonne Rainer." *Profile* 4.5 (1984): 2–44.

Bobo, Jacqueline. *Black Video and Filmmakers.* New York: Routledge, 1998.

Booker, Keith. *Techniques of Subversion in Modern Literature: Transgression, Abjection, and the Carnivalesque.* Gainesville: University of Florida Press, 1991.

Borden, Lizzie. "Trisha Brown, Sonnabend Gallery; Yvonne Rainer, Theater for the New City; Nancy Holt, Lo Giudice Gallery." *Artforum* 11.10 (1973): 79–82.

Bordwell, David, Janet Staiger, and Kristin Thompson. *The Classical Hollywood Cinema: Film Style and Mode of Production to 1960.* New York: Columbia University Press, 1985.

Bovenschen, Silvia. "Is There a Feminine Aesthetic?" *New German Critique* 10 (Winter 1977): 111–37.

Brakhage, Stan. *Film at Wit's End.* Kingston, N.Y.: Documentext/McPherson, 1989.

———. "On Marie Menken." In Haller, *Brakhage Scrapbook,* 91–93.

Brecht, Bertolt. *Brecht on Theater: The Development of an Aesthetic.* Ed. and Trans. John Willet. London: Methuen, 1990.

Brooks, Peter. *The Melodramatic Imagination: Balzac, Henry James, and the Mode of Excess.* New Haven: Yale University Press, 1976.

Bruno, Giuliana. *Streetwalking on a Ruined Map: Cultural Theory and the City Films of Elvira Notari.* Princeton: Princeton University Press, 1993.

Bruss, Elizabeth. "Eye for I: Making and Unmaking Autobiography in Film." In *Autobiography: Essays Theoretical and Critical.* Ed. James Olney. Princeton: Princeton University Press, 1980. 296–320.

Buck-Morss, Susan. *The Dialectics of Seeing: Walter Benjamin and the Arcades Project.* Cambridge, Mass.: MIT Press, 1989.

Burstow, Bonnie. *Radical Feminist Therapy: Working in the Context of Violence.* Newbury Park, Calif.: Sage, 1992.

Burton, Julianne. *Cinema and Social Change in Latin America: Conversations with Filmmakers.* Austin: University of Texas Press, 1986.

Butler, Judith. *Bodies That Matter.* New York: Routledge, 1993.

———. *Gender Trouble.* London: Routledge, 1990.

Cadbury, William, and Leland Pogue. *Film Criticism: A Counter-Theory.* Ames: Iowa State University Press, 1983.

Camper, Fred. "The End of Avant-Garde Film." *Millennium Film Journal* 16/17/18 (1986–87): 99–124.

Carroll, Noel. "Interview with a Woman Who . . ." *Millennium Film Journal* 7/8 (Fall 1980–Winter 1981): 37–68.

Carson, Diane, Linda Dittmar, and Janice Welsh, eds. *Multiple Voices in Feminist Film Criticism.* Minneapolis: University of Minnesota Press, 1994.

Carter, Angela. *The Sadeian Woman and the Ideology of Pornography.* New York: Pantheon Books, 1978.

Case, Sue-Ellen. *The Domain-Matrix: Performing Lesbian at the End of Print Culture.* Bloomington: Indiana University Press, 1997.

Castro, Donald S. *The Argentine Tango as Social History, 1880–1955.* Lewiston, N.Y.: Edwin Mellen Press, 1991.

Chadwick, Whitney. *Women Artists and the Surrealist Movement.* London: Thames and Hudson, 1985.

Cham, Mbye B., and Claire Andrade-Watkins, eds. *Blackframes: Critical Perspectives on Black Independent Cinema.* Cambridge, Mass.: MIT Press, 1988.

Chen, Nancy N. "'Speaking Nearby': A Conversation with Trinh T. Minh-ha." *Visual Anthropology Review* 8.1 (1990): 82–91.

Chénieux-Gendron, Jacqueline, and Timothy Mathews. *Violence, théorie, surréalisme.* Collection Pleine marge 3. Paris: Lachenal et Ritter, 1994.

Cheshire, Godfrey. "Sundance." *Variety* 26 (February 1996): 15.

Child, Abigail. *Retrospective: Film/Video Screenings* [program notes]. New York: Collective for Living Cinema, 1990.

Cixous, Hélène, and Catherine Clement. *The Newly Born Woman.* Trans. Betsy Wong. Minneapolis: University of Minnesota Press, 1986.

Clark, Vévé, Millicent Hodson, and Catrina Neiman. *The Legend of Maya Deren: A Documentary Biography and Collected Works,* vol. 1, pt. 1. New York: Anthology Film Archives and Film Culture, 1984.

Clifford, Gay. *The Transformations of Allegory.* London: Routledge, 1974.

Cook, Pam. "Duplicity in *Mildred Pierce.*" In *Women in Film Noir.* Ed. E. Ann Kaplan. London: British Film Institute, 1978. 68–82.

———. "The Point of Self-Expression in Avant-Garde Film." In *Theories of Authorship.* Ed. John Caughie. London: British Film Institute, 1981. 271–81.

Cook, Pam, and Philip Dodd, eds. *Women and Film: A Sight and Sound Reader.* Philadelphia: Temple University Press, 1993.

Cooper, Susan Fenimore. *Rural Hours.* 1850. Ed. Rochelle Johnson and Daniel Patterson. Athens: University of Georgia Press, 1998.

———. *Rural Hours.* 1887. Syracuse: Syracuse University Press, 1968.

Cornwell, Regina. "Maya Deren and Germaine Dulac: Activists of the Avant-Garde." *Film Library Quarterly* 5.1 (1971–72): 29–38.

Curtis, David. *Experimental Cinema.* New York: Delta, 1971.

DalMolin, Elaine. *Cutting the Body: Representing Women in Baudelaire's Poetry, Truffaut's Cinema, and Freud's Analysis.* Ann Arbor: University of Michigan Press, 2000.

Daly, Ann. "Dance History and Feminist Theory: Reconsidering Isadora Duncan and the Male Gaze." In *Gender and Performance.* Ed. Laurence Senelick. Hanover, N.H.: Tufts University Press, 1992. 239–59.

Dawes, Amy. "Nina Menkes's Trump Card." *Daily Variety,* August 1991, 23.

De Lauretis, Teresa. *Alice Doesn't: Feminism, Semiotics, Cinema.* Bloomington: Indiana University Press, 1984.

———. "Feminist Studies, Critical Studies: Issues, Terms, and Contexts." In *Feminist Studies, Critical Studies.* Ed. Teresa de Lauretis. Bloomington: Indiana University Press, 1986. 1–19.

———. "Film and the Visible." In *How Do I Look: Queer Film and Video.* Ed. Bad Object Choices. Seattle: Bay Press, 1991. 223–76.

———. "Strategies of Coherence: Narrative Cinema, Feminist Poetics, and Yvonne Rainer." In *Technologies of Gender: Essays on Theory, Film, and Fiction.* Bloomington: Indiana University Press, 1987. 107–26.

Deleuze, Gilles. *Cinema 2: The Time Image.* Trans. Hugh Tomlinson and Robert Galeta. Minneapolis: University of Minnesota Press, 1989.

De Man, Paul. *Allegories of Reading.* New Haven: Yale University Press, 1979.

Deren, Maya. *An Anagram of Ideas on Art, Form, and Film.* New York: Alicat Book Shop Press, 1946.

———. "Cinematography: The Creative Use of Reality." In Sitney, *The Avant-Garde Film,* 60–73.

Derrida, Jacques. *The Ear of the Other.* Ed. Christie McDonald. Trans. Peggy Kamuf. Lincoln: University of Nebraska Press, 1985.

Diawara, Manthia, ed. *Black American Cinema: Aesthetics and Spectatorship.* New York: Routledge, 1993.

Dittmar, Linda. "The Voice of the Other: Women in Third World and Experimental Film." In *Double Vision: Perspectives on Gender and the Visual Arts.* Ed. Natalie Harris Bluestone. Cranbury, N.J.: Associated University Presses, 1995. 125–37.

Doane, Mary Ann. *The Desire to Desire.* Bloomington: Indiana University Press, 1987.

———. "Film and the Masquerade: Theorizing the Female Spectator." In *Issues in Feminist Film Criticism.* Ed. Patricia Erens. Bloomington: Indiana University Press, 1990. 41–57.

———. "Woman's Stake: Filming the Female Body." In Kaplan, *Feminism and Film,* 86–99.

———. "Woman's Stake: Filming the Female Body." In Doane, *Femmes Fatales: Feminism, Film Theory, and Psychoanalysis.* New York: Routledge, 1991. 165–77.

Easterwood, Kurt, Susanne Fairfax, and Laura Poitras. "Yvonne Rainer: Declaring Stakes" (interview). San Francisco Cinematheque, 1990.

Ecker, Gisela, ed. *Feminist Aesthetics*. Boston: Beacon Press, 1986.

Egan, Jennifer. "The Thin Red Line." *New York Times Magazine*, July 27, 1997, 20–25, 34, 40, 43–44, 48.

Elder, Bruce. *A Body of Vision: Representations of the Body in Recent Film and Poetry*. Waterloo, Ont.: Wilfrid Laurier University Press, 1997.

Erens, Patricia, ed. *Sexual Stratagems: The World of Women in Film*. New York: Horizon, 1979.

Ernst, Max. *La semaine de bonté: A Surrealistic Novel in Collage*. Trans. Stanley Appelbaum. New York: Dover, 1976.

Eysteinsson, Astradur. *The Concept of Modernism*. Ithaca, N.Y.: Cornell University Press, 1990.

Farr, Judith. *The Gardens of Emily Dickinson*. Cambridge, Mass.: Harvard University Press, 2004.

Ferguson, Russell, et al., eds. *Discourses: Conversations in Postmodern Art and Culture*. Cambridge, Mass.: MIT Press, 1990. 44–64.

Fernandez, Sergio. "Nina Menkes' *Great Sadness of Zohara*." *Daily Bruin*, January 27, 1984, 12.

Film-Makers' Cooperative Catalogue No. 7. New York: Film-Makers' Cooperative, 1989.

Fineman, Joel. "The Structure of Allegorical Desire." In *Allegory and Representation*. Ed. Stephen Greenblatt. Baltimore: Johns Hopkins University Press, 1981. 26–60.

Fischer, Lucy. *Cinematernity: Film, Motherhood, Genre*. Princeton: Princeton University Press, 1996.

———. "'The Eye for Magic: Maya and Méliès." In Nichols, *Maya Deren and the American Avant-Garde*, 185–204.

———. "Shall We Dance? Feminist Cinema Remakes the Musical." *Film Criticism* 13.2 (1989): 7–17.

———. *Shot/Countershot: Film Tradition and Women's Cinema*. Princeton: Princeton University Press, 1989.

Fletcher, Angus. *Allegory: Theory of a Symbolic Mode*. Ithaca, N.Y.: Cornell, 1964.

Flitterman-Lewis, Sandy. "Montage/Discourse: Germaine Dulac's *The Smiling Madame Beudet*." *Wide Angle* 4.3 (1980): 54–59.

———. "Theorizing the 'Feminine': Woman as the Figure of Desire in *The Seashell and the Clergyman*." *Wide Angle* 6.3 (1984): 32–39.

———. *To Desire Differently: Feminism and the French Cinema*. Urbana: University of Illinois Press, 1990. Expanded, Morningside ed. with a new preface and epilogue. New York: Columbia University Press, 1996.

Fokkema, Douwe, and Elrud Ibsch. *Modernist Conjectures: A Mainstream in European Literature*. New York: St. Martin's, 1984.

Foster, Gwendolyn Audrey. *Women Filmmakers of the African and Asian Diaspora: Decolonizing the Gaze, Locating Subjectivity*. Carbondale: Southern Illinois University Press, 1997.

Foster, Patricia, ed. *Sister to Sister: Women Write about the Unbreakable Bond.* New York: Doubleday, 1995.

Foucault, Michel. *The History of Sexuality: An Introduction.* New York: Vintage, 1990.

Freedman, Eric. "The Return of the Repressed." *Filmmaker Magazine* (Fall 1996): 35.

Friedman, Ellen G., and Miriam Fuchs, eds. *Breaking the Sequence: Women's Experimental Fiction.* Princeton: Princeton University Press, 1989.

Fusco, Coco. "Fantasies of Oppositionality." *Screen* 29.4 (1988): 80–93.

Gentile, Mary C. *Film Feminisms: Theory and Practice.* Westport, Conn.: Greenwood, 1985.

Gever, Martha, Pratibha Parmar, and John Greyson, eds. *Queer Looks: Perspectives on Lesbian and Gay Film and Video.* London: Routledge, 1993.

Gidal, Peter. "Theory and Definition of Structuralist/Materialist Film." In *Structuralist Film Anthology.* Ed. Peter Gidal. London: British Film Institute, 1976. 1–21.

Gilbert, Sandra M., and Gubar, Susan. *The Madwoman in the Attic: The Woman Writer and the Nineteenth-Century Literary Imagination.* New Haven: Yale University Press, 1979.

Gledhill, Christine. "The Melodramatic Field: An Investigation." In *Home Is Where the Heart Is: Studies in Melodrama and the Woman's Film.* London: British Film Institute, 1987. 5–39.

———. "Rethinking Genre." In *Reinventing Film Studies.* Ed. Christine Gledhill and Linda Williams. London: Arnold and Oxford University Press, 2000. 221–43.

Goldberg, Rosalee. *Performance Art: From Futurism to the Present.* New York: Harry N. Abrams, 1996.

Goodeve, Thyrza Nichols. "Rainer Talking Pictures." *Art in America* (July 1997): 56–63.

The Great Sadness of Zohara. Dir. Nina Menkes. Perf. Tinka Menkes. Menkesfilm, 1983.

Grout, Donald Jay. *A History of Western Music.* New York: Norton, 1973.

Haller, Robert A., ed. *Brakhage Scrapbook.* New Paltz, N.Y.: Documentext, 1982.

———, ed. *First Light.* New York: Anthology Film Archives, 1988.

Halliwell, Leslie. *The Filmgoer's Companion.* 6th ed. New York: Avon, 1977.

Hames, Peter. *The Czechoslovak New Wave.* Berkeley: University of California Press, 1985.

Harmetz, Aljean. "Faith Hubley, Oscar Winner in Animation, Is Dead at 77." *New York Times,* December 10, 2001, A23.

Haskell, Molly. *From Reverence to Rape: The Treatment of Women in the Movies.* New York: Holt, Rinehart, Winston, 1974.

Haug, Kate. "Interview with Carolee Schneemann." *Wide Angle* 20.1 (1998): 20–49.

Heck-Rabi, Louise. *Women Filmmakers: A Critical Reception.* Metuchen, N.J.: Scarecrow Press, 1984.

Hewitt, Kim. *Mutilating the Body: Identity in Blood and Ink.* Bowling Green, Ohio: Bowling Green State University Popular Press, 1997.

Hirschorn, Michelle. "Body as Ready (to-be-re-)made." In *Generations and Geographies in the Visual Arts.* Ed. Griselda Pollock. London: Routledge, 1996. 110–34.

Hoberman, J. *Vulgar Modernism: Writing on Movies and Other Media.* Philadelphia: Temple University Press, 1991.

Holden, Stephen. "A Niece Rummages in a Rich and Enigmatic Uncle's Closet. *New York Times*, March 20, 1995, C12.

Holmlund, Chris. "Feminist Makeovers: The Celluloid Surgery of Valie Export and Su Friedrich." In *Play It Again, Sam: Retakes on Remakes.* Ed. Andrew Horton and Stuart Y. McDougal. Berkeley: University of California Press, 1998: 217–37.

———. "Fractured Fairytales and Experimental Identities: Looking for Lesbians in the Films of Su Friedrich." *Discourse: A Journal for Theoretical Studies in media and Culture* 17.1 (1994) 16–46.

———. "When Autobiography Meets Ethnography and Girl Meets Girl: 'The Dyke Docs' of Sadie Benning and Su Friedrich." In *Between the Sheets, In the Streets: Queer, Lesbian, and Gay Documentary.* Ed. Chris Holmlund and Cynthia Fuchs. Minneapolis: University of Minnesota Press, 1997. 127–43.

Honig, Edwin. *Dark Conceit: The Making of Allegory.* Evanston: Northwestern University Press, 1959.

hooks, bell. *Black Looks: Race and Representation.* Boston: South End Press, 1992.

Horak, Jan-Christopher, ed. *Lovers of Cinema: The First American Film Avant-Garde.* Madison: University of Wisconsin Press, 1995.

Howlett, Jana, and Rod Mengham. *The Violent Muse: Violence and the Artistic Imagination in Europe, 1910–1939.* New York: Manchester University Press, 1994.

Hunter, Lynette. *Modern Allegory and Fantasy: Rhetorical Stances of Contemporary Writing.* New York: St. Martin's, 1989.

Jablonko, Allison. "New Guinea in Italy: An Analysis of the Making of an Italian Television Series from Research Footage of the Maring People of Papua New Guinea." In *Anthropological Filmmaking.* Ed. J. Rollwagon. Chur, Switzerland: Harwood Academic Publishers, 1988. 169–96.

Jacoby, Roger. "Willard Maas and Marie Menken: The Last Years." *Film Culture* (1977): 119–24.

James, David E. *Allegories of Cinema: American Film in the Sixties.* Princeton: Princeton University Press, 1989.

———. "Film Diary/Diary Film: Practice and Product in *Walden*." In James, *To Free the Cinema,* 145–79.

———, ed. *To Free the Cinema: Jonas Mekas and the New York Underground.* Princeton: Princeton University Press, 1992.

———. "Yvonne Rainer: *Film about a Woman Who . . .*" In James, *Allegories of Cinema,* 326–35.

Jayamanne, Laleen, with Geeta Kapur and Yvonne Rainer. "Discussing Modernity, Third World and *The Man Who Envied Women*." *Art and Text* 23.4 (1987): 41–51.

Jezer, Marty. *The Dark Ages: Life in the United States, 1945–1960.* Boston: South End Press, 1982.

Johnston, Claire. "Women's Cinema as Counter Cinema." In *Movies and Methods: An Anthology.* Ed. Bill Nichols. Berkeley: University of California Press, 1976. 208–17.

Juhasz, Alexandra. *Women of Vision: Histories in Feminist Film and Video.* Minneapolis: University of Minnesota Press, 2001.

Kaplan, E. Ann. "The American Experimental Woman's Film: Yvonne Rainer's *Lives of Performers* and *Film about a Woman Who . . .*" In Kaplan, *Women and Film,* 113–24.

————, ed. *Feminism and Film.* New York: Oxford University Press, 2000.

————. "Feminism, Postmodernism, and MTV." In Kaplan, *Postmodernism and Its Discontents,* 30–44.

————, ed. *Postmodernism and Its Discontents.* London: Verso, 1988.

————. *Women and Film: Both Sides of the Camera.* New York: Methuen, 1983.

Katz, Ephraim. *The Film Encyclopedia.* 3rd ed. New York: HarperPerennial, 1998.

Kaye, Nick. *Postmodernism and Performance.* New York: St. Martin's, 1994.

Keller, Marjorie. "The Apron Strings of Jonas Mekas." In James, *To Free the Cinema,* 83–96.

————. *The Untutored Eye: Childhood in the Films of Cocteau, Cornell, and Brakhage.* Rutherford, N.J.: Fairleigh Dickinson University Press, 1986.

Klagsbrun, Francine. *Mixed Feelings: Love, Hate, Rivalry, and Reconciliation among Brothers and Sisters.* New York: Bantam, 1992.

Knight, Arthur. "Cine-dance." *Dance Perspectives* 30 (Summer 1967): 4–9.

Koch, Stephen. "Performance: A Conversation." *Artforum* 11.4 (1972): 53–58.

Kolodny, Annette. "Dancing through the Mine Field: Some Observations on the Theory, Practice, and Politics of a Feminist Criticism." *Feminist Studies* 6.1 (1980): 1–25.

————. *The Lay of the Land: Metaphor as Experience and History in American Life and Letters.* Chapel Hill: University of North Carolina Press, 1975.

Kotz, Liz. "Complicity: Women Artists Investigating Masculinity." In *Dirty Looks: Women, Pornography, Power.* Ed. Pamela Church Gibson and Roma Gibson. London: British Film Institute, 1993. 101–23.

————. "An Unrequited Desire for the Sublime: Looking at Lesbian Representation across the Works of Abigail Child, Cecilia Dougherty, and Su Friedrich." In Gever, Parmar, and Greyson, *Queer Looks,* 86–102.

Kramer, Lawrence. *After the Lovedeath: Sexual Violence and the Making of Culture.* Berkeley: University of California Press, 1997.

Kristeva, Julia. *Powers of Horror.* Trans. Leon S. Roudiez. New York: Columbia University Press, 1982.

Kubelka, Peter. "The Theory of Metrical Film." In Sitney, *The Avant-Garde Film,* 139–59.

Kuhn, Annette. "Textual Politics." In *Issues in Feminist Film Criticism.* Ed. Patricia Erens. Bloomington: Indiana University Press, 1990. 250–67.

————. *Women's Pictures: Feminism and Cinema.* London: Routledge and Kegan Paul, 1982.

Kuhn, Annette, and Susannah Radstone, eds. *Women in Film: An International Guide.* New York: Fawcett Columbine, 1990.

Laderman, David. "Interview with Yvonne Rainer." *Art Papers* 13.3 (1989): 18–24.

La Rochelle, Réal. "Ho-Hum! . . . Oui? . . . Votre mère . . ." *24 Images* 87 (Summer 1997): 50.

Lavin, Maud. *Cut with the Kitchen Knife: The Weimar Photomontages of Hannah Höch.* New Haven: Yale University Press, 1994.

LeGrice, Malcolm. *Abstract Film and Beyond.* Cambridge, Mass.: MIT Press, 1977.

Levenkron, Steven. *Cutting: Understanding And Overcoming Self-Mutilation.* New York: Norton, 1998.

Levitin, Jacquelin. "Mother of the New Wave: An Interview with Varda." *Women & Film* 1.5/6 (1974): 63–66.

Levy, Emanuel. *Cinema of Outsiders: The Rise of American Independent Film.* New York: New York University Press, 1999.

Lewis, C. S. *The Allegory of Love: A Study in Medieval Tradition.* London: Oxford University Press, 1936.

Lord, Catherine. "Looking Like a Lesbian: Yvonne Rainer's Theory of Probability." *Documents* 10 (Fall 1997): 31–42.

Lycos.com. "Sally Potter." http://entertainment.lycos.com/celebrities/celebrity-bio.asp?id=18352&pagetemplate=purple. Accessed February 3, 2005.

Lyotard, Jean-François. *La condition postmoderne.* Paris: Éditions de Minuit, 1979.

Maas, Willard. "The Gryphon Yaks." *Film Culture* 29 (1963): 45–53.

MacDonald, Scott. *Avant-Garde Film Motion Studies.* New York: Cambridge University Press, 1993.

———. "Avant Gardens." In MacDonald, *The Garden in the Machine: A Field Guide to Independent Films about Place.* Berkeley: University of California Press, 2001. 45–87.

———. *Cinema 16: Documents toward a History of the Film Society.* Philadelphia: Temple University Press, 2002.

———. *A Critical Cinema. Interviews with Independent Filmmakers.* Berkeley: University of California Press, 1988.

———. *A Critical Cinema 2: Interviews with Independent Filmmakers.* Berkeley: University of California Press, 1992.

———. *A Critical Cinema 3: Interviews with Independent Filmmakers.* Berkeley: University of California Press, 1998.

———. *A Critical Cinema 4: Interviews with Independent Filmmakers.* Berkeley: University of California Press, 2005.

———. "Interview with Sally Potter." *Camera Obscura* 35 (May 1995): 186–221.

———, ed. *Screen Writings: Scripts and Texts by Independent Filmmakers.* Berkeley: University of California Press, 1995.

MacDougall, David. "Films of Memory." In Taylor, *Visualizing Theory,* 260–70.

Madsen, Deborah. *Allegory in America: From Puritanism to Postmodernism.* New York: St. Martin's, 1996.

———. *Rereading Allegory: A Narrative Approach to Genre.* New York: St. Martin's, 1994.

Magdalena Viraga: Story of a Red Sea Crossing. Dir. Nina Menkes. Perf. Tinka Menkes. Menkesfilm, 1986.

Mandell, Leslie. "Interview with Marie Menken." *Wagner Literary Magazine* 4 (1963–64): 47–48.

Margulies, Ivone. *Nothing Happens: Chantal Akerman's Hyperrealist Everyday.* Durham, N.C.: Duke University Press, 1996.

Martin, Angela. "Four Filmmakers from West Africa." *Framework* 11 (1979): 16–21.

Martin, Michael, ed. *Cinemas of the Black Diaspora: Diversity, Dependency, and Oppositionality.* Detroit: Wayne State University Press, 1995.

———. *New Latin American Cinema. Vol. 1, Theory: Practices, and Transcontinental Articulations.* Detroit: Wayne State University Press, 1997.

———. *New Latin American Cinema. Vol. 2, Studies of National Cinemas.* Detroit: Wayne State University Press, 1997.

Maslin, Janet. "With Sizzling Tangos, Who Needs a Plot?" *New York Times,* February 12, 1999, E29.

Mayne, Judith. *The Woman at the Keyhole: Feminism and Women's Cinema.* Bloomington: Indiana University Press, 1990.

McGilligan, Pat. "Faith Hubley: An Interview." *Film Quarterly* 42 (Winter 1988–89): 2–18.

McHugh, Kathleen. *American Domesticity: From How-to Manual to Hollywood Melodrama.* New York: Oxford University Press, 1999.

McNaron, Toni A. H., ed. *The Sister Bond: A Feminist View of a Timeless Connection.* New York: Pergamon Press, 1985.

McRobbie, Angela. "Passionate Uncertainty." *Sight and Sound* 2.5 (1992): 28–29.

Mekas, Jonas. *Movie Journal: The Rise of the New American Cinema, 1959–1971.* New York: Collier Books, 1972.

Mellencamp, Patricia. "An Empirical Avant-Garde: Laleen Jayamanne and Tracey Moffat." In *Fugitive Images: From Photography to Video.* Ed. Patrice Petro. Bloomington: Indiana University Press, 1995. 173–95.

———. *Indiscretions: Avant-Garde Film, Video, and Feminism.* Bloomington: Indiana University Press, 1990.

Menkes, Nina. *The Bloody Child: An Interior of Violence.* Press kit. Available from Menkesfilm, 8996 Keith Avenue, West Hollywood, CA 90069.

———. *Great Sadness of Zohara.* Press Kit. Hollywood: Menkesfilm.

———. *Magdalena Viraga: Story of a Red Sea Crossing.* Press Kit. Hollywood: Menkesfilm.

———. *Queen of Diamonds: A Horseless Western.* Press Kit. Hollywood: Menkesfilm.

Metz, Christian. "Problems of Denotation in the Fiction Film." In Rosen, *Narrative, Apparatus, Ideology,* 35–65.

Michelson, Annette, and Giuliana Bruno. "Women in the Avant-Garde: An Interview with Annette Michelson." *Millennium Film Journal* 16/17/18 (Fall/Winter 1986–87): 141–48.

Minh-ha, Trinh T. *Framer Framed.* London: Routledge, 1992.

———. "If Upon Leaving . . . A Conversation Piece (with Leslie Thornton, Laleen Jayamanne." In *Discourses: Conversations in Postmodern Art and Culture.* Ed. Russell Ferguson et al. Cambridge, Mass.: MIT Press, 1990. 44–64.

———. *Woman, Native, Other.* Bloomington: Indiana University Press, 1989.

Misch, Georg. *A History of Autobiography in Antiquity.* Cambridge, Mass.: Harvard University Press, 1951.

Modleski, Tania. *Loving with a Vengeance: Mass Produced Fantasies for Women.* Hamden, Conn.: Archon Books, 1982.

Monk, Claire. "*The Tango Lesson.*" *Sight and Sound* (December 1997): 54–55.

Moran, James. "Wedding Video and Its Generation." In *Resolutions: Contemporary Video Practices.* Ed. Michael Renov and Erika Suderburg. Minneapolis: University of Minnesota Press, 1996. 360–81.

Mulvey, Laura. "Afterthoughts on 'Visual Pleasure and Narrative Cinema' Inspired by King Vidor's *Duel in the Sun* (1946)." In Mulvey, *Visual and Other Pleasures,* 29–38.

———. "Film, Feminism, and the Avant-Garde." In Mulvey, *Visual and Other Pleasures,* 111–26.

———. "Visual Pleasure and Narrative Cinema." In *Film Theory and Criticism: Introductory Readings.* 4th ed. Ed. Gerald Mast, Marshall Cohen, and Leo Braudy. New York: Oxford University Press, 1992. 746–57.

———. "Visual Pleasure and Narrative Cinema." In Mulvey, *Visual and Other Pleasures,* 14–26.

———, ed. *Visual and Other Pleasures.* Bloomington: Indiana University Press, 1989.

Naficy, Hamid. *An Accented Cinema: Exilic and Diasporic Filmmaking.* Princeton University Press, 2001.

———, ed. *Home, Exile, Homeland: Film, Media, and the Politics of Place.* New York: Routledge, 1999.

Neale, Steve. "Art Cinema as Institution." *Screen* 22.1 (1981): 11–39.

Nichols, Bill. "The Ethnographer's Tale." In Taylor, *Visualizing Theory,* 60–83.

———, ed. *Maya Deren and the American Avant-Garde.* Berkeley: University of California Press, 2001.

———. *Movies and Methods: An Anthology.* Berkeley: University of California Press, 1976.

Ong, Aihwa. "Colonialism and Modernity: Feminist Re-Presentations of Women in Non-Western Societies." In *Theorizing Feminisms: Parallel Trends in the Humanities and Social Sciences.* Ed. Anne C. Herrmann and Abigail Stewart. Boulder, Colo.: Westview, 1994. 372–81.

Parmar, Pratibha. "Black Feminism: The Politics of Articulation." In *Identity, Community, Culture, Difference.* Ed. Jonathan Rutherford. London: Lawrence and Wishart, 1990. 101–26.

Penley, Constance. *The Future of an Illusion: Film, Feminism, and Psychoanalysis.* Minneapolis: University of Minnesota Press, 1989.

Perreault, Jeanne. "Autography/Transformation/Asymmetry." In *Writing Selves: Contemporary Feminist Autography.* Minneapolis: University of Minnesota Press, 1995. 1–30.

Peters, Sally. "From Eroticism to Transcendence: Ballroom Dance and the Female Body." In *The Female Body: Figures, Style, Speculations.* Ed. Laurence Goldstein. Ann Arbor: University of Michigan Press, 1991. 145–58.

Petro, Patrice. *Aftershocks of the New: Feminism and Film History.* New Brunswick, N.J.: Rutgers University Press, 2002.

Phalen, Peggy. "Spatial Envy: Yvonne Rainer's *The Man Who Envied Women.*" In *Unmarked: The Politics of Performance.* New York: Routledge, 1993. 71–92.

Pines, Jim, and Paul Willeman, eds. *Questions of Third Cinema.* London: British Film Institute, 1989.

Polan, Dana. *The Political Language of Film and the Avant-Garde.* Ann Arbor: UMI Research Press, 1985.

Pramaggiore, Maria. "Performance and Persona in the U.S. Avant-Garde: The Case of Maya Deren." *Cinema Journal* 36.2 (1997): 17.

Puppi, Lionello. *Torment in Art: Pain, Violence, and Martyrdom.* New York: Rizzoli, 1991.

Quart, Barbara Koenig. *Women Directors: The Emergence of a New Cinema.* New York: Praeger, 1988.

Quilligan, Maureen. *The Language of Allegory: Defining the Genre.* Ithaca, N.Y.: Cornell University Press, 1979.

Rabinovitz, Lauren. *For the Love of Pleasure: Women, Movies, and Culture in Turn of the Century Chicago.* New Brunswick, N.J.: Rutgers University Press, 1998.

———. *Points of Resistance: Women, Power and Politics in the New York Avant-Garde Cinema, 1943–71.* Urbana: University of Illinois Press, 1991.

Rainer, Yvonne. "The Avant-Garde Humpty Dumpty." http://thecity.sfsu.edu/users/xfactor/participants/participants.html. Accessed 1996.

———, ed. *The Films of Yvonne Rainer.* Bloomington: Indiana University Press, 1989.

———. Letter to *Artforum* 12.16 (1973): 10.

———. "Looking Myself in the Mouth." *October* 17 (Summer 1981): 65–76.

———. *The Man Who Envied Women* (script). In Rainer, *The Films of Yvonne Rainer,* 173–218.

———. "More Kicking and Screaming from the Narrative Front/Backwater." In Rainer, *A Woman Who . . . ,* 207–13.

———. MURDER *and murder* (film script). In Rainer, *A Woman Who . . . ,* 352–423.

———. *Privilege* (film script). In MacDonald, *Screen Writings,* 270–331.

———."A Quasi Survey of Some 'Minimalist' Tendencies in the Quantitatively Minimal Dance Activity Midst the Plethora, or an Analysis of *Trio A.*" In *Minimal Art: A Critical Anthology.* Ed. Gregory Battcock. Berkeley: University of California Press, 1995. 263–73.

———. "Skirting." In Rainer, *A Woman Who . . . ,* 120–25.

———. "Some Ruminations around Cinematic Antidotes to the Oedipal Net(tles) while Playing with de Lauraedipus Mulvey, or He May Be Off-Screen, but . . ." In *Psychoanalysis and Cinema.* Ed. E. Ann Kaplan. New York: Routledge, 1990. 188–97.

———. "Thoughts on Women's Cinema: Eating Words, Voicing Struggles." In *Blasted Allegories: An Anthology of Writings by Contemporary Artists.* Ed. Brian Wallis. Cambridge, Mass.: MIT Press, 1987. 380–85.

———. *A Woman Who . . . : Essays, Interviews, Scripts.* Baltimore: Johns Hopkins University Press, 1999.

———. *Work, 1961–73.* New York: New York University Press, 1974.

———. "Working Round the L-Word." In Gever, Parmar, and Greyson, *Queer Looks,* 12–20.

Redding, Judith M., and Victoria A. Brownworth. *Film Fatales: Independent Women Directors.* Seattle: Seal Press, 1997.

Rees, A. L. *A History of Experimental Film and Video: From the Canonical Avant-Garde to Contemporary British Practice.* London: British Film Institute, 1999.

Reid, Mark A. "Dialogic Modes of Representing Africa(s): Womanist Film." In Martin, *Cinemas of the Black Diaspora,* 56–69.

Reynaud, Bérénice. "Impossible Projections." In Rainer, *The Films of Yvonne Rainer,* 24–35.

Rich, B. Ruby. *Chick Flicks: Theories and Memories of the Feminist Film Movement.* Durham, N.C.: Duke University Press, 1998.

———. "Yvonne Rainer: An Introduction." In Rainer, *The Films of Yvonne Rainer*, 1–23.

Ricoeur, Paul. *Oneself as Another.* Trans. Kathleen Blamey. Chicago: University of Chicago Press, 1992.

Riley, Denise. *Am I That Name: Feminism and the Category of "Women" in History.* Minneapolis: University of Minnesota, 1988.

Rooney, David. "The Tango Lesson." *Variety,* September 14, 1997, 78.

Rosemont, Penelope. *Surrealist Women: An International Anthology.* The Surrealist Revolution Series. Austin: University of Texas Press, 1998.

Rosen, Philip, ed. *Narrative, Apparatus, Ideology.* New York: Columbia University Press, 1986.

Rosenbaum, Jonathan. "Arresting Images." *Chicago Reader,* September 27, 1996, 40.

———. *Film: The Front Line, 1983.* Denver: Arden Press, 1983.

———. "Queen of Diamonds." *Chicago Reader,* October 22, 1991, sec. 2, p. 11.

Rosenbaum, Mitchell. "Interview with Yvonne Rainer." In Rainer, *The Films of Yvonne Rainer*, 36–45.

Rosenberg, Jan. *Women's Reflections: The Feminist Film Movement.* Ann Arbor: UMI Research Press, 1979.

Russell, Catherine. *Experimental Ethnography: The Work of Film in the Age of Video.* Durham, N.C.: Duke University Press, 1999.

Russo, Mary. "Female Grotesques: Carnival and Theory." In *Feminist Studies, Critical Studies.* Ed. Teresa de Lauretis. Bloomington: Indiana University Press, 1986. 213–29.

Savigliano, Marta E. *Tango and the Political Economy of Passion.* Boulder, Colo.: Westview, 1995.

Scholder, Amy. *Critical Condition: Women on the Edge of Violence.* San Francisco: City Lights Books, 1993.

Schwartz, David. "Magdalena Viraga: A Red Sea Crossing." *Newsletter for the American Museum of the Moving Image* (October 1992): 16.

Segal, Lynne. *Straight Sex: Rethinking the Politics of Pleasure.* Berkeley: University of California Press, 1994.

Seremetakis, C. Nadia. "The Memory of the Senses: Historical Perception, Commensal Exchange, and Modernity." In Taylor, *Visualizing Theory*, 214–29.

Shiri, Keith. *Directory of African Film-Makers and Films.* Westport, Conn.: Greenwood, 1992.

Silverman, Kaja. *The Acoustic Mirror: The Female Voice in Psychoanalysis and Cinema.* Bloomington: Indiana University Press, 1988.

———. "Dis-Embodying the Female Voice." In *Re-Vision: Essays in Feminist Film Criticism.* Ed. Mary Ann Doane, Patricia Mellencamp, and Linda Williams. Frederick, Md.: University Publications of America and the American Film Institute, 1984. 131–49.

Sitney, P. Adams. "Autobiography in the Avant-Garde Film." In Sitney, *The Avant-Garde Film*, 199–246.

———, ed. *The Avant-Garde Film: A Reader of Theory and Criticism.* New York: New York University Press, 1978.

———. "Marie Menken: Body and Light." In Haller, *First Light*, 48–53.

———. *Visionary Film: The American Avant-Garde Film, 1943–1978*. Oxford: Oxford University Press, 1974, 1979; 3rd ed., rev., 2002.

Slide, Anthony, ed. *The Memoirs of Alice Guy-Blaché*. Metuchen, N.J.: Scarecrow Press, 1986.

Smith, Paul. "The Will to Allegory in Postmodernism." *Dalhousie Review* 62.1 (1982): 105–22.

Smith, Sean. "Bewitched: Nina Menkes' Subterranean Voyages." *Los Angeles View*, April 26, 1996, 15–21.

Stacey, Jackie. *Star Gazing: Hollywood Cinema and Female Spectatorship*. London: Routledge, 1994.

Stallybrass, Peter, and Allon White. *The Politics and Poetics of Transgression*. Ithaca, N.Y.: Cornell University Press, 1995.

Starr, Cecile. "Maya: The Mother of the Avant-Garde Film." *New York Times*, May 2, 1976, sec. 2, p. 13.

Storr, Robert. "The Theoretical Come-on." *Art in America* 74.4 (1986): 159–65.

Strong, Marilee. *A Bright Red Scream: Self-Mutilation and the Language of Pain*. New York: Viking, 1998.

Tarantino, Michael. "The Moving Eye: Notes on the Films of Chantal Akerman." In *Bordering on Fiction: Chantal Akerman's "D'Est."* Ed. Bruce Jenkins and Kathy Halbreich. Minneapolis: Walker Art Center, 1995. 47–56.

Taussig, Michael. *Mimesis and Alterity: A Particular History of the Senses*. New York: Routledge, 1993.

Taylor, Julie. *Paper Tangos*. Durham, N.C.: Duke University Press, 1998.

Taylor, Lucien, ed. *Visualizing Theory*. New York: Routledge, 1994.

Thaxter, Celia. *An Island Garden*. Boston: Houghton Mifflin, 1894.

Thomas, Kevin. "*Child:* Haunting Meditation on Violence." *Los Angeles Times*, October 26, 1996, F6.

———. "Nina Menkes's Magdalena a Stunning Feature Debut." *Los Angeles Times*, August 9, 1991, F10.

Thompson, Andrew O. "The Birth of Nina Menkes' *Bloody Child*." *American Cinematographer* (October 1996): 16–18.

Thompson, Kristin. "The Concept of Cinematic Excess." In Rosen, *Narrative, Apparatus, Ideology*, 130–42.

Thornton, Leslie. "Leslie Thornton Interviewed." *Lightstruck* 7.2–3 (1991): 8–13.

———. "We Ground Things, Now, on a Moving Earth." *Motion Picture* 3.1–2 (1989–90): 13–15.

Tierney-Tello, Mary Beth. *Allegories of Transgression and Transformation: Experimental Fiction by Women Writing Under Dictatorship*. Albany: SUNY Press, 1996.

Turim, Maureen. "Childhood Memories and Household Events in the Feminist Avant-Garde." *Journal of Film and Video* 38 (1986): 86–92.

Tyler, Parker. *Underground Film: A Critical History*. New York: Grove Press, 1969.

Ukadike, N. Frank. "Reclaiming Images of Women in Films from Africa and the Black Diaspora." *Frontiers* 15.1 (1994): 102–86.

Vance, Carole S. *Pleasure and Danger: Exploring Female Sexuality.* Boston: Routledge and Kegan Paul, 1984.

Van Dyke, Carolynn. *The Fiction of Truth: Structures of Meaning in Narrative and Dramatic Allegory.* Ithaca, N.Y.: Cornell University Press, 1985.

Vogel, Amos. *Film as a Subversive Art.* New York: Random House, 1974.

Wallace, Michele. "Multiculturalism and Oppositionality" (review of *Privilege*). *Afterimage* 19.3 (1991): 6–9.

Wees, William C. *Recycled Images: The Art and Politics of Found Footage Films.* New York: Anthology Film Archives, 1993.

Weir, David. *Anarchy and Culture: The Aesthetics of Modernism.* Amherst: University of Massachusetts Press, 1997.

Willemen, Paul. *Looks and Frictions: Essays in Cultural Studies and Film Theory.* London: British Film Institute, 1994.

Williams, Linda. *Figures of Desire: A Theory and Analysis of Surrealist Film.* Urbana: University of Illinois Press, 1981.

———. "Melodrama Revisited." In *Refiguring American Film Genres: History and Theory.* Ed. Nick Browne. Berkeley: University of California Press, 1998. 42–88.

———. *Playing the Race Card: Melodramas of Black and White.* Princeton: Princeton University Press, 2001.

Willis, Holly. "An Interview with Nina Menkes." *Film Quarterly* 45.3 (1992): 7–12.

Wilmington, Michael. "Menkes' Hypnotic *Bloody Child* a Lyrical Nightmare." *Chicago Tribune,* September 26, 1996, sec. 7, p. 5.

Wollen, Peter. "The Two Avant-Gardes." *Readings and Writings: Semiotic Counter-Strategies.* London: Verso, 1982. 92–104.

Women Make Movies. *Film and Video Catalogue.* New York: Women Make Movies, 1996.

Wood, Robin. "The New Queer Cinema and Gay Culture: Notes from an Outsider." *CineAction* 35 (Spring 1994): 2–15.

Zalman, Jan. "Question Marks on the New Czechoslovak Cinema." *Film Quarterly* (Winter 1967): 18–27.

Zimmermann, Patricia R. *Reel Families: A Social History of Amateur Film.* Bloomington: Indiana University Press, 1995.

Contributors

LUCY FISCHER is a professor of film studies and English at the University of Pittsburgh, where she serves as director of the Film Studies Program. She is the author of seven books: *Jacques Tati; Shot/Countershot: Film Tradition and Women's Cinema; Imitation of Life; Cinematernity: Film, Motherhood, Genre; Sunrise; Designing Women: Art Deco, Cinema and the Female Form;* and *Stars: The Film Reader* (coedited with Marcia Landy). She has published extensively on issues of film history, theory, and criticism in such journals as *Screen, Sight and Sound, Camera Obscura, Wide Angle, Cinema Journal, Journal of Film and Video, Film Criticism, Women and Performance, Frauen und Film,* and *Film Quarterly.* Her essays have been anthologized twenty-seven times in volumes of film history, criticism and/or theory.

GWENDOLYN AUDREY FOSTER is a professor in the Department of English, University of Nebraska, Lincoln. Her books include *Performing Whiteness: Postmodern Re/constructions in the Cinema; Identity and Memory: The Films of Chantal Akerman; Captive Bodies; Women Filmmakers of the African and Asian Diaspora: Decolonizing the Gaze, Locating Subjectivity;* and *Experimental Cinema: The Film Reader.* Foster is editor-in-chief of *Quarterly Review of Film and Video.*

AMY LAWRENCE teaches in the Department of Film and Television Studies at Dartmouth College. She is the author of *The Films of Peter Greenaway* and *Echo and Narcissus: Women's Voices in Classical Hollywood Cinema.* She has also written on animation, television, and star issues.

PATRICIA LEVIN is a professor of art history and visual culture at Saddleback College in Mission Viejo, California. Her most recent essay, "The Camera Made Me Do It: Female Identity and Troubling Archives," appeared in *Mosaic* in the special issue on the photograph. She is also an independent curator working on projects in Canada and France.

SCOTT MacDONALD'S most recent books are *The Garden in the Machine: A Field Guide to Independent Films about Place; Cinema 16: Documents toward a History of the Film Society;* and the fifth volume of his *Critical Cinema* series of interviews with independent film/video makers. He teaches at Bard College and Hamilton College.

KATHLEEN McHUGH teaches in English and in Film and Television at the University of California, Los Angeles, where she is an associate professor of English. In *American Domesticity: From How-To Manual to Hollywood Melodrama* she reconsiders melodrama and the feminist commentary applied to it in relation to domestic labor and its representation in the United States. McHugh coedited the collection *South Korean Golden Age Melodrama: Gender, Genre and National Cinema.* She has published articles on domesticity, feminism, melodrama, the avant-garde, and autobiography in such journals as *Cultural Studies, Jump Cut, Screen, South Atlantic Quarterly,* and *Velvet Light Trap.* She is currently working on a book-length study of Jane Campion's films.

JEAN PETROLLE is professor of English at Columbia College Chicago. She has written about twentieth-century literature and painting, as well as film studies, in such venues as *Journal of Modern Greek Studies, Quarterly Review of Film and Video, Image: A Journal of Art and Religion,* and various anthologies.

MAUREEN TURIM is a University of Florida research professor of English and film studies. She is the author of *Abstraction in Avant-Garde Films; Flashbacks in Film: Memory and History;* and *The Films of Oshima Nagisa: Images of a Japanese Iconoclast.* She has also published over seventy essays in anthologies and journals on a wide range of theoretical, historical and aesthetic issues in cinema and video, art, cultural studies, feminist and psychoanalytic theory, and comparative literature. She has also written catalog essays for museum exhibitions.

WILLIAM C. WEES is an emeritus professor (McGill University) and the author of *Vorticism and the English Avant-Garde; Light Moving in Time: Studies in the Visual Aesthetics of Avant-Garde Film;* and *Recycled Images: The Art and Politics of Found Footage Films,* as well as many articles, chiefly on experimental/avant-garde film. He is also editor-in-chief of the *Canadian Journal of Film Studies/Revue canadienne d'études cinématographiques.*

VIRGINIA WRIGHT WEXMAN is professor of English and chair of the Program in Moving Image Arts at the University of Illinois at Chicago. Her books include *Creating the Couple: Love, Marriage, and Hollywood Performance* and *Film and Authorship.* She is past president of the Society for Cinema and Media Studies.

JERRY WHITE is assistant professor of film studies at the University of Alberta, editor of the *Canadian Journal of Irish Studies,* and a member of the education staff of the Telluride Film Festival. His writing on film has appeared in venues such as *Cinema Journal, Canadian Journal of Film Studies, CineAction, Éire-Ireland, Canadian Journal of Irish Studies,* and *S: European Journal for Semiotic Studies.* He is coeditor (with William Beard) of *North of Everything: English-Canadian Cinema since 1980.*

Index

The University of Illinois Press
is a founding member of the
Association of American University Presses.

Composed in 10.5/13 Adobe Minion
with Meta display
by Jim Proefrock
at the University of Illinois Press
Manufactured by Maple-Vail
Book Manufacturing Group

University of Illinois Press
1325 South Oak Street
Champaign, IL 61820-6903
www.press.uillinois.edu